NEVER GOING BACK:
A HISTORY OF QUEER ACTIVISM IN CANADA

Never Going Back: A History of Queer Activism in Canada is the first comprehensive history of its kind. Drawing on over one hundred interviews with leading gay and lesbian activists across the country and a rich array of archival material, Tom Warner chronicles and analyses the multiple – and often conflicting – objectives of a tumultuous grassroots struggle for sexual liberation, legislated equality, and fundamental social change.

Warner presents the history of lesbian and gay liberation in a Canadian context, in the process telling the story of a remarkable movement and the people who made it happen. The book encompasses efforts to attain legislated human rights for gays and lesbians, significant regional histories, autonomous lesbian organizing, and the histories of lesbians and gays of colour, two-spirited people, and those living outside the urban mainstream. It also examines the crises confronting the movement: the backlash against queer activism from social conservative 'family values' campaigns, state and police harassment, and the exigencies of responding to AIDS.

Moving beyond the discussions of equality-rights campaigns, *Never Going Back* delves inside the movement to look at dissent and debates over liberation and assimilation, sexual expression, race, the age of consent, pornography, censorship, community standards, and an identity forged from a common sexual orientation.

TOM WARNER is one of Canada's leading gay activists. During his thirty years of activism, he helped found the Coalition for Lesbian and Gay Rights in Ontario and several other organizations. He was a leader of the Coalition's campaigns to have sexual orientation included in the Ontario Human Rights Code and to secure the legal recognition of same-sex relationships.

NEVER GOING BACK

A History of Queer Activism
in Canada

TOM WARNER

UNIVERSITY OF TORONTO PRESS
Toronto Buffalo London

© University of Toronto Press Incorporated 2002
Toronto Buffalo London
Printed in Canada

ISBN 0-8020-3608-2 (cloth)
      0-8020-8460-5 (paper)

Printed on acid-free paper

National Library of Canada Cataloguing in Publication Data

Warner, Tom
    Never going back : a history of queer activism in Canada

    Includes bibliographical references and index.
    ISBN 0-8020-3608-2 (bound). – ISBN 0-8020-8460-5 (pbk.)

    1. Gay liberation movement – Canada – History. I. Title.

    HQ76.8.C3W37 2002   305.9'0664'0971   C2001-904187X

University of Toronto Press acknowledges the financial assistance to
its publishing program of the Canada Council for the Arts and the
Ontario Arts Council.

This book has been published with the help of a grant from the
Humanities and Social Sciences Federation of Canada, using funds
provided by the Social Sciences and Humanities Research Council of
Canada.

University of Toronto Press acknowledges the financial support for its
publishing activities of the Government of Canada through the Book
Publishing Industry Development Program (BPIDP).

For Ivan Dorsey

lover, partner, and friend

Contents

Illustrations follow page 192

Preface

Writing a comprehensive history of gay, lesbian, and bisexual activism and organizing that covers a period of some thirty years has been a daunting and thrilling experience. The topic is vast, the issues many and complex. The sheer number of organizations and individuals involved dooms to failure the desire to be encyclopaedic and inclusive. Hard decisions had to be made. For example, I decided to focus much of my research on events and activities outside Toronto. Consequently, many worthy individuals and significant happenings in that city have been excluded. Similarly, while interviews with over one hundred leading activists from every province and one territory helped immeasurably to provide context and sequencing, texturizing and filling in gaps in my knowledge, great amounts of this taped material could not be included if the manuscript were to be kept to a manageable length. The tapes will be given to the Canadian Lesbian and Gay Archives for future researchers to access. I also have had to resist a recurring urge to name every name, cite every group, salute every achievement, and tell every story.

Never Going Back proceeds chronologically, its three parts reflecting three distinct historical periods. Part One covers a huge swath, from ancient times to 1975. I trace the historical roots of the oppression of lesbians and gays in Canada, especially in the period following the Second World War. Moving on from there, I examine the growing consciousness of gays and lesbians at mid-century, and the social transformation occurring in the 1960s, immediately prior to Stonewall and the Criminal Code amendments that decriminalized homosexual acts in certain circumstances. I further chronicle and analyse the emergence of both a social movement of lesbians and gay men and the genesis of a visible, identifiable community and culture.

Part Two covers the tumultuous period from 1975 to 1984, which saw backlash, dissent, and crises, but also great progress, as evidenced by the rapid expansion of visible gay and lesbian communities in many parts of Canada. A dominant theme here is the emergence of the social conservative movement, characterized by counter-offensives, under the guise of protecting 'family values,' and renewed state repression in the form of police raids, a war on obscenity and gay sexuality, and the trials of *The Body Politic*, then Canada's national gay liberation journal. I also explore the enormous difficulties faced by activists pursuing inclusion of sexual orientation in human rights laws while fighting against discrimination in a climate of fear mongering, homophobia, and political resistance. Delving inside the movement, Part Two also looks at dissent and the raging debates over issues of sexuality – especially whether the promotion of sexual liberation was nothing more than the sexual libertarianism of gay men enjoyed at the expense of women and others. I further examine the wisdom of pursuing human rights activism, the turbulent history of the National Gay Rights Coalition, the first organizing for custody rights for lesbian mothers, and the advent and early impact of AIDS. In addition to those problematic issues, Part Two also shows that the period from 1975 to 1984 witnessed great growth and progress for lesbian, gay, and bisexual communities, including the autonomous organizing of lesbians, the expansion of the movement into smaller and rural communities, and the emergence of the first organizations for lesbians and gays of colour.

A major theme in Part Three, covering 1985 to 1999, is the impact of the Charter of Rights and Freedoms on the lesbian and gay movement, and the change in tactics that resulted. The chapters in this section show how the movement of gays, lesbians, and bisexuals, more demonstrably than in the earlier periods, branched into two distinct tracks, equality-seeking assimilationism and liberation activism, with the latter being marginalized but not vanquished. I spend considerable time examining the ultimate victory of the campaigns that used the Charter to challenge and to amend federal and provincial human rights laws to include sexual orientation. The efforts to forge a fragile consensus on the legal recognition of same-sex relationships, and the gulf that emerged between assimilationists and liberationists because of that issue, are also discussed, as is the gradual progress made in achieving legislative amendments to recognize same-sex relationships.

Part Three demonstrates that, even in the 1990s, there was more to the movement of lesbians, gays, and bisexuals than the mere pursuit of equality-seeking assimilationism. I tell how liberation consciousness influenced organizing in response to AIDS, fighting renewed state repression of obscenity and pornography, and reacting to police campaigns that targeted gay men and gay sexuality. I trace the continuing endurance and manifestation of lesbian and gay liberation consciousness in contexts – outside the largest cities of Canada, and among gays and lesbians of colour and two-spirited people – that, while seemingly new, are remarkably reminiscent of the early 1970s. Also explored are new campaigns by activists across the country to confront homophobia and heterosexism in the education system, and in the provision of health and social services – efforts that have more in common with early lesbian and gay liberation activism than with the pursuit of equality rights. Part Three ends with an update on the development and evolution of queer communities, and with an examination of the phenomenon of lesbian and gay pride as the most visible manifestation, even in the 1990s, of the messages that gay is good and that coming out everywhere is essential to achieving sexual and social freedom.

Throughout each of the book's parts, I have examined some common themes: the outlaw status of same-sex sexuality and how gays, lesbians, and bisexuals have habitually pushed the envelope to force social and legal change; and police harassment and state repression or regulation, and the community's responses to it. I address the forces of religion and religion-based social movements, especially the more recent manifestations of the religious right and social conservatism. Woven throughout are explorations of the identity, community, and culture forged around a common sexual orientation and how these have been fostered by lesbian and gay liberation.

I would like to acknowledge several people and organizations for their assistance and support. Christine Donald, David Rayside, and Michael Riordon offered me early support, ongoing encouragement, and wise advice. I am also indebted to those who gave me names of key individuals to interview: David Myers in Vancouver; Bob Read in Ottawa; Robin Metcalfe in Halifax; Jeremy Buckner in Winnipeg; Liz Massiah in Edmonton; Stephen Lock in Calgary; Ross Higgins in Montreal. David Rayside and Line Chamberland generously provided me with copies of papers they had written. The Canadian Lesbian and Gay Archives proved once more to be an invaluable repository of precious queer history. Siobhan McMenemy at the University of Toronto Press supported this project from the outset of the long process leading to publication. Others I would like to thank are Naomi Black, Gary Kinsman, copy editor Ward McBurney, editor Frances Mundy, and the two anonymous readers who provided valuable suggestions for improving the manuscript. The Canada Council, through the Explorations Program, provided a grant to help defray costs incurred for travelling the country to conduct interviews.

Abbreviations

AAN	AIDS Action Now! (Toronto)
ACT UP	AIDS Coalition to Unleash Power
ADGQ	Association pour les droits des gais du Québec
ALOT	Asian Lesbians of Toronto
APPLE	Atlantic Provinces Political Lesbians for Equality
ASAP	Alliance for South Asian AIDS Prevention
ASIA	Asian Society for the Intervention of AIDS (Toronto)
ASK	Association for Social Knowledge (Vancouver)
BAN	Black AIDS Network (Vancouver)
BCFW	British Columbia Federation of Women
Black CAP	Black Coalition for AIDS Prevention (Toronto)
CALGM	Canadian Association of Lesbians and Gay Men
CAS	Canadian AIDS Society
CEF	Campaign for Equal Families
CFV	Coalition for Family Values (Ontario)
CGRO	Coalition for Gay Rights in Ontario
CHAL	Centre humanitaire d'aide et de libération (Quebec City)
CHAN	Canadian Homophile Association of Newfoundland
CHAT	Community Homophile Association of Toronto
CHE	Campaign for Human Equality (Saskatchewan)
CHRA	Canadian Human Rights Act
CLGRC	Canadian Lesbian and Gay Rights Coalition
CLGRO	Coalition for Lesbian and Gay Rights in Ontario
COR	Confederation of Regions Party (New Brunswick)
C-SAM	Comité SIDA Aide de Montréal
CURE	Citizens United for Responsible Education

DARC	Differently Abled Rainbow Club (Winnipeg)
DAWN	DisAbled Women's Network
DOB	Daughters of Bilitis
DSM	*Diagnostic and Statistical Manual of Mental Disorders*
EGALE	Equality for Gays and Lesbians Everywhere
ERA	Equal Rights Amendment (U.S.)
FLA	Family Law Act
FLH	Front de libération homosexuel (Montreal)
GAA	Gay Activist Alliance (New York City)
GAAP	Gay Asians AIDS Project (Toronto)
GAE	Gay Alliance for Equality (Halifax)
GAIN	Gay Association in Newfoundland
GALA	Gay and Lesbian Alliance (Edmonton, Halifax)
GALT	Gays and Lesbians Together (St John's)
GAT	Gay Asians of Toronto
GATE	Gay Alliance Toward Equality
GAU	Gay Academic Union
GFE	Gays for Equality (Winnipeg)
GLF	Gay Liberation Front
GLHS	Gay and Lesbian Health Services (Saskatoon)
GNG	Gai.es Nor Gay (Bathurst, NB)
GO	Gays of Ottawa
HALO	Homophile Association of London Ontario
IRPA	Individual Rights Protection Act (Alberta)
LAR	Lesbians Against the Right
LASS	Lesbian Association of Southern Saskatchewan
LEAF	Women's Legal Education and Action Fund
LEGIT	Lesbian and Gay Immigration Task Force (Vancouver)
LGBT	Lesbian, Gay, Bisexual and Transgendered Health Association (BC)
LGRNS	Lesbian and Gay Rights Nova Scotia
LISO	Lobby for Inclusion of Sexual Orientation (Manitoba)
LOC	Lesbians of Colour (Toronto)
LOON	Lesbians of Ottawa Now
LOOT	Lesbian Organization of Toronto
MOTHER	Movement Opposed to Homosexual Extra Rights (Yukon)
NAMBLA	North American Man-Boy Love Association
NGEC	National Gay Election Coalition

NGRC	National Gay Rights Coalition
NOW	National Organization for Women (U.S.)
PLWA	People Living with AIDS
RTPC	Right to Privacy Committee (Ontario)
SAGA	Sudbury All Gay Alliance
SEARCH	Society for Education, Action, Research and Counselling on Homosexuality
TBP	*The Body Politic*
TGA	Toronto Gay Action
TNF	Toronto New Feminists
TNTMen	Totally Naked Toronto Men Enjoying Nudity
TPFN	Two-Spirited People of the First Nations
TWLM	Toronto Women's Liberation Movement
UTHA	University of Toronto Homophile Association

NEVER GOING BACK:
A HISTORY OF QUEER ACTIVISM IN CANADA

Coming to Terms

The last three decades of the twentieth century were, for queer communities, truly remarkable and historically unprecedented. Lesbian and gay liberation emerged and matured, asserting a revolutionary new consciousness and launching a movement that profoundly changed the lives of gays, lesbians, and bisexuals. Pioneering advocacy and community building proceeded from the premise that progress towards liberation necessarily required confronting and rejecting the many anti-homosexual and anti-lesbian prejudices intricately woven into the fabric of Canadian society. More and more lesbians, gays, bisexuals, and transgendered people came out of the closet, made demands on the rest of society, and organized themselves into visible and viable communities. They worked to change laws that permitted discrimination and repression and to create a safer, more diverse society in which they could lead their lives openly, without reprisal and fear. They did so by militantly rejecting the quasi-human role in which gays, lesbians, and bisexuals had been cast throughout history, a role that forced them to hide their sexual orientation, to disguise themselves, and to lead double lives filled with fear, isolation, and self-loathing. Until the advent of lesbian and gay liberation, the bravest and most tenacious – those who refused to succumb to such social oppression – were branded as miscreants, condemned as criminal, sinful, deviant, malevolent, or predatory. They were harassed and discriminated against in many ways, were imprisoned or feared being imprisoned, were subjected to psychiatric treatment, were victimized by acts of violence, and were subjected to cruel social ridicule and ostracism. Integral to the movement of gays, lesbians, and bisexuals that erupted in the late twentieth century, therefore, was a radical change in consciousness about themselves and their place in society that took hold of them, igniting their anger and committing them to action.

Lesbian and Gay Liberation

Throughout this book, I use the phrase *lesbian and gay liberation* rather than the more common *gay liberation*. The choice is deliberate. Gay liberation is a dated term, historically correct only for the first few years of the movement. A term appropriate for one rather brief historical period, I submit, is inappropriate for all of the following periods. Lesbians have always been part of the queer struggle to liberate same-sex sexuality. Over the first half of the 1970s, *lesbian* became promoted and gradually accepted as the preferred term, over *gay women*, which had been widely used until then. Lesbian asserted identity, visibility, and advocacy agendas separate from those of both gay men and heterosexual women, although an autonomous lesbian movement has not yet taken root in Canada. Most lesbians committed to liberation stayed within mixed groups with gay men or in women's organizations with straight feminists. Advocacy groups that had called themselves gay added lesbian to their names to encourage the presence of lesbians in them and to affirm the need to address lesbian concerns. Separate lesbian organizations remained few and sporadic.

I also reject the notion that lesbian and gay liberation died out as a phenomenon a couple of decades ago. Rather, I present it as an ideology or ethos situated within, and which continues to exert varying degrees of influence on, a broad and still manifest movement for social and sexual change having many dimensions even today. In presenting my exposition, I have not wanted to repeat a habitual shortcoming of other too narrowly focused examinations of what has been commonly called the lesbian and gay rights movement. As *Never Going Back* will demonstrate, rights attainment has been only one, albeit dominant, thrust of a movement of gays, lesbians, and bisexuals that now spans some thirty years. Much has been done in the pursuit of liberation over that period. *Never Going Back* thus differs from other recent books on the subject of lesbian and gay advocacy. Reading them leaves the impression that gay liberation is either dead or near death, that the totality of the lesbian and gay rights movement in recent years has been exclusively devoted to achieving equality rights and launching legal challenges. Liberationist issues such as sexuality, censorship, and police harassment would appear, from such other works, to have dropped off the advocacy agenda. *Never Going Back* argues that *lesbian and gay* liberation is the continuation of the gay liberation born in earlier times and is still an important presence within a broad movement of gays and lesbians.

Lamentably, apart from Gary Kinsman's book, *The Regulation of Desire: Homo and Hetero Sexualities* (second edition, 1996), and two books addressing pornography and censorship, the liberation dimensions of lesbian and gay activism after the early 1980s have been largely undocumented. Kinsman's book covers a broad sweep of Canadian history, devoting only the last three chapters to providing what is essentially an overview of lesbian and gay liberation in Canada. *Restricted Entry: Censorship on Trial* by Janine Fuller and Stuart Blackely (1995) and *Bad Attitude/s on Trial: Pornography, Feminism, and the Butler Decision*, by Brenda Cossman, Shannon Bell, Lise Gotell, and Becki L. Ross (1997) explore the laws and attitudes of the courts towards pornography and censorship. As valuable and insightful as these books are, they do not present a comprehensive history of lesbian and gay liberation as a grass-roots social movement.

The first book to leave the impression that gay liberation was abandoned in the early 1980s for the pursuit of equality rights was Didi Herman's *Rights of Passage: Struggles for Lesbian and Gay Legal Equality* (1994). An essentially superficial exploration of human rights advocacy, Herman's book evidences little understanding of the strategy adopted by liberationists – that using such advocacy in the short term would advance gay liberation in the long term, a strategy which I examine in Part One. After conducting a cursory exploration of the liberation activist view that campaigning for human rights politicizes and mobilizes members of lesbian and gay communities, thus enabling pursuit of liberation, Herman then dismisses and marginalizes such campaigns, asserting that they have become instead merely the politics of liberal equality. Problematically, Herman's analysis is that of an academic, not an activist, and she expresses the belief that 'I do not view politicization as an inherently progressive process.' She further dismisses as 'lesbian and gay liberalism' the efforts to secure the inclusion of sexual orientation in Ontario's Human Rights Code. Then, without conducting any significant examination of the liberationist view of human rights advocacy as a necessary stepping stone on the road to liberation – a view espoused by the Coalition for Gay Rights in Ontario (CGRO) in its organizing on the issue – Herman leaves the misimpression that the amendment of laws was CGRO's only objective.[1]

Barry D. Adam's *The Rise of a Gay and Lesbian Movement* (revised edition, 1995) situates gay liberation as a historical phenomenon of the 1970s and early 1980s, suggesting it is now largely a spent force. Similarly, Becki L. Ross, in *The House That Jill Built: Lesbian Nation in Formation* (1995), chronicles and assesses liberation in the context of lesbian feminism and the Lesbian Organization of Toronto, ending her study in the early 1980s. More recently, Miriam Smith, in *Lesbian and Gay Rights in Canada: Social Movements and Equality-Seeking, 1971–1995* (1999), focuses on the impact of the Charter of Rights and Freedoms and court challenges on lesbian and gay activism. While Smith acknowledges that her intention is not to have her book 'read as a story of how the gay liberation movement was eventually compromised by engagement with litigation and the Charter,' it nonetheless leaves the reader with that impression.[2] Moreover, Smith's book explores the 'lesbian and gay rights movement' only in the context of rights activism, omitting any analysis of liberation advocacy in the other areas. David Rayside's *On the Fringe: Gays and Lesbians in Politics* (1998) is devoted, in his own words, to 'an assessment of the relevance of legislative politics for achieving gay and lesbian equality.'[3] Rayside doesn't attempt to discuss lesbian and gay liberation. Neither does Kathleen Lahey, in *Are We 'Persons' Yet? Law and Sexuality in Canada* (1999), or Bruce MacDougall in his *Queer Judgments: Homosexuality, Expression and the Courts in Canada* (2000).

Because the preponderance of scholarly publication has, thus far, concentrated on the human rights and equality-seeking dimensions of the lesbian and gay movement, the notion that gay liberation is dead is pervasive. It is true that deconstructing and analysing equality rights campaigns have correctly shown how liberation activism, which gave impetus to the pursuit of human rights objectives, was gradually surpassed in public consciousness by more conservative, assimilationist advocacy. Yet, seeking human rights protections and legal recognition of same-sex relationships, for example, has never been the whole lesbian and gay movement. While I agree that assimilationist equality seeking now dominates, I contend that lesbian and gay liberation is alive and well, and continues as a force. I argue that it has been excitingly manifest in campaigns against repression and censorship of same-sex sexual imagery, in challenges to community standards concerning sexuality, and in resisting the efforts of the state to moralistically interpret and enforce archaic sex laws. Liberationists also have exerted pressure on, and critiqued, the equality-rights agenda, urging rights activists to curtail the rush to respectability and assimilation. Unlike other books, *Never Going Back* traces the history of a capacious movement of lesbians, gays, and bisexuals in which the promotion of liberation, along with many other dimensions, is an important element. It takes an expansive view of *activism* and *organizing*, going beyond the constraints imposed by examining only the lesbian and gay rights movement. I assert that, fundamentally, gay liberation – today more appropriately termed lesbian and gay liberation – is a presence still, and is needed as much now as it was thirty years ago.

Defining Lesbian and Gay Liberation

The lesbian and gay movement and the ideology of lesbian and gay liberation are the products of anger and outrage channelled into collective action. Their history is one of resistance and astonishing perseverance, textured with the exuberance of outlaw sexuality. History abounds with testimonies to the power of small bands of committed individuals who succeeded against the most daunting odds. In keeping with this, virtually all progress made over the last three decades for gays, lesbians, and bisexuals has resulted directly from their boldness and militancy. Fed up, they decided to take control of their own destinies despite many obstacles. They dared to confront attitudes and deeds that had led to marginalization and social oppression. Individually and as organized communities, they fought back, coming out of the closet, noisily and defiantly, demanding to be both seen and heard, and revelling in their new visibility. They attacked systemic and institutional prejudice, and combated hatred directed towards them, by demanding that an end be put to centuries of lies, ignorance, prejudice, and fear. By rising up to confront some of Canada's most powerful beliefs and institutions, lesbian, gay, and bisexual activists launched a movement that has changed their world forever. As the movement took root and grew, activists realized they would necessarily need to battle the forces of social conservatism, to prevent these forces from turning back the clock, from erasing even the smallest steps towards change, from returning laws and social conditions to darker, more repressive times. The vast heterosexual majority, in the process, has been forced to deal with lesbians, gays, and bisexuals, even as it has generally resisted their struggle.

What is lesbian and gay liberation? Defining it is, admittedly, daunting. Complex and multifaceted, it is an ideology that resists reduction to a simple sentence or two. Fundamentally, lesbian and gay liberation has been about changing self-image. Like all victimized groups, bisexuals, lesbians, and gays have had to tackle how they see themselves in order, in turn, to change how others see them. They have had to come to terms with their sexual orientation, not only accepting it as healthy and normal, but also celebrating it as special and liberating. Lesbian and gay liberation has militantly rejected notions of gays and lesbians as sick, sinful, criminal, abnormal, deviant, strange, or pathetic. It has condemned the pathologizing of homosexuality and the social oppression of gays and lesbians. Liberationists unapologetically articulate the naturalness of homosexuality as an alternative – but in no way inferior or disordered – sexual orientation and identity. They see gays and lesbians as an oppressed people struggling for sexual and social liberation who, by so doing, advance the liberation of others as well.

Changing a few laws and achieving tolerance are necessary, but insufficient in themselves to achieve fundamental social change. Lesbian and gay liberation means coming to a positive consciousness of oneself and of other gays and lesbians. It requires a personal transformation based on an understanding that gays and lesbians are taught by our society in various ways, both subtle and blatant, to hate and thereby oppress themselves. It means recognizing and fighting against the cultural conventions that reinforce and perpetuate inequities of power. Lesbian and gay liberation requires opposing the repression of sexuality and combating sexual stereotyping, sexism, heterosexual supremacy, violence, hatred, bigotry, and hypocrisy. It is based on an analysis of how and why gays and lesbians, individually and as a group, are oppressed. An important element of this analysis is a realization that sexism and rigid gender-role socialization contribute significantly to that oppression. It further sees the traditional or nuclear family as a key agent of social control, embodying sexism that oppresses women and gays. Other powerful influences contributing to such socialization, and bolstering its effects, have been the state's regulation of sexuality and non-conforming behaviour, the churches' teachings about sin and morality, and the medical models of deviance, abnormality, and perversion. Lesbian and gay liberation means rocking the boat, by confronting harassment, discrimination, and paternalism, so that attitudes, laws, and social institutions are changed. It is predicated on visibility, both in the daily lives of individual gays, lesbians, and bisexuals and in society as a whole; it maintains a public presence on the streets and in the media. Lesbian and gay liberation acknowledges that being impelled to remain invisible by passing as heterosexual is one of the most insidious ways in which gays, lesbians, and bisexuals have been oppressed. Individuals who are unable to pass (e.g., men deemed to be effeminate or women deemed to be masculine), or those who refuse or otherwise fail to do so, face harassment and social censure. As Gary Kinsman, deploying the term *queer*, which gained currency during the last decade, wrote in 1998, 'Queer liberation requires that people achieve control over our bodies and sexualities and an end to institutionalized heterosexuality.'[4]

Lesbian and gay liberation also means that sex does not have to await a monogamous relationship, that it can be engaged in without guilt or shame, solely as a form of recreation. It can be enjoyed anonymously, with several partners or in groups, and in multiple ways involving acts that are not to be judged by others, provided the participants are capable of giving informed consent and do so. Lesbian and gay liberation acknowledges and celebrates the diversity and complexity of human sexuality. It holds that the body in all of its forms, sizes, and shapes is beautiful and erogenous; that fantasy, voluntary role playing, and dressing up can add excitement and fulfilment to sex acts. Liberationists do not see genitalia as gross and unclean. They reject the notion that sexual acts are inherently dirty, and only appropriately performed in private, with two people behind closed doors. Lesbian and gay liberationists are thus as much in conflict with the tyrannical views of dominant heterosexual society today as they were in the early 1970s. This is because the regimented social order resulting inevitably from heterosexism is maintained by, and benefits, a consortium of powerful interests with vast resources. Belonging to this consortium are the churches, state institutions, conservative organizations and movements, the medical establishment (including psychiatry), the social sciences, the media, the entertainment industries, the educational system, and corporate elites.

Homophobia and Heterosexism

In an attempt to define the many negative beliefs and perceptions about their sexual orientation, gay, lesbian, and bisexual activists have created or championed terms such as *homophobia* and *heterosexism*. The former term had its roots in a 1967 book by Wainwright Churchill, which described the pervasive cultural fear of same-sex erotic or sexual contact as *homoerotophobia*.[5] In 1971, an American psychologist broke new ground by using the term homophobia in a study of the personality profile of individuals having negative or fearful reactions to homosexuality.[6] At about the same time, a growing number of social scientists became less concerned about the 'causes' of homosexuality, and devoted their efforts instead to researching 'attitudes towards homosexuals, methods of assessing attitudes, characteristics of those holding negative attitudes towards homosexuals, and methods for changing attitudes.'[7] Their research represented a significant departure from examining the 'homosexual problem' and the beginning of a change in focus to one of studying attitudinal biases against homosexuals. In 1972, George Weinberg published his pioneering book, *Society and the Healthy Homosexual*,[8] popularizing the term homophobia, which Weinberg defined as a pervasive, irrational fear of homosexuality.

Throughout the 1970s, homophobia was adopted as the preferred term to describe the cause of the oppression of and discrimination against homosexuals. In Canada, the organization Gays of Ottawa published a leaflet in 1975, *Understanding Homophobia*, that talked about the pervasiveness of homophobia as follows:

> Homophobia like other kinds of prejudice – racism, sexism – manifests itself in many ways. Historically the routing out and murder of homosexuals during the Inquisition and in Nazi Germany have been among the most extreme forms of anti-homosexual oppression. Today there is a whole gamut of homophobic reactions – outright queer-bashing, psychiatry's attempts to 'cure' the homosexual, discriminatory laws and employment practices, inability on the part of social service agencies to deal with the homosexual, the media's demeaning and stereotypical images of the homosexual, pseudo-liberalism's tolerance of the homosexual so long as she or he remains invisible – all reactions from a combination of ignorance and fear.[9]

Homophobia as the cause of oppression rested on the assumption that the oppression was attributable to the combined effects of fear and loathing of homosexuality, and to sexism. This analysis was problematic, however, as most people cannot be said to have a phobia about, or fear of, homosexuality. Nor would the elimination of sexism by itself elevate homosexuality to equal status with heterosexuality as a form of sexual orientation. Sexism and homophobia do not adequately define the cultural supremacy of heterosexuality.

Consequently, a discourse emerged that sought answers in a different kind of analysis. One of the Canadian contributions was an undated document written by Ken Popert and Brian Mossop in the late 1970s called 'Why Are Gay People Oppressed?' It argued that anti-homosexual ideologies (Judeo-Christianity, psychoanalysis, machismo, and homophobia, for example) are only parts of the whole that make up that oppression, often providing the rationalization, rather than the reason, for it. They noted that all human societies have divided labour between the sexes. In modern industrialized societies, men earned the family income in the labour market while women tended to the household and raised children. Marriage is the legal contract that expresses such division, and men and women are socialized from birth to assume the role in marriage to which their gender has been assigned. The result is an economic unit, the family, which is also oppressive because it is not based on an equal pairing.[10] Adding that women traditionally have not had the same access as men to the labour market, and therefore to economic independence, Popert and Mossop argued that so long as the family is an economic unit support-ing the division of labour among the sexes, gays and lesbians will have no place in the family and, therefore, will suffer oppression. According to this analysis, 'a non-sexist culture [cannot be estab-lished] as long as the division of labour exists, for the behavioural and personality division between men and women is rooted in that eco-nomic division.'[11] For Mossop and Popert, the increasing visibility of homosexuality and the advent of gay liberation were signs that the family system was in trouble because the division of labour along gender lines was outdated.

Another person who saw the nuclear family as the problem was lesbian activist Chris Bearchell. She wrote in 1983, 'Gay liberation, like feminism, is a danger, not to children, but to the family. It breaks individual young people away from the process of adjustment and conformity to the next heterosexual family-centred generation.'[12] Other contributors to the debate were the Americans Charlotte Bunch (1978) and Adrienne Rich (1980). They were among the first to develop an analysis of oppression that went beyond a focus on homophobic atti-tudes, on the one hand, and biology and socialization, on the other. Bunch pointed the finger at 'the institutional and ideological domina-tion of heterosexuality, as a fundamental part of male supremacy.' Rich attributed the oppression of lesbians, and all women, to 'compulsory heterosexuality.'[13]

The notion that heterosexuality is obligatory and has supremacy eventually led to the coining of the term *heterosexism*. American lesbian and Black activist Audre Lorde defined heterosexism in her ground-breaking 1984 book, *Sister Outsider*, as 'the belief in the inherent superi-ority of one pattern of loving and thereby its right to dominance.'[14] Heterosexism attempts to give a better definition to the cultural and institutional prejudices that form the basis of anti-gay and anti-lesbian attitudes. Borrowing from feminist analysis, heterosexism encompasses sexism, sexual stereotyping, and socializing individuals to avoid the perceived social ill of gender role confusion, but remains distinct from the fear of homosexuality. Heterosexism also entrenches and enforces rigid gender roles and sanctifies marriage. Mariana Valverde, a lesbian activist and academic in Toronto, noted in her 1985 book, *Sex, Power and Pleasure* that, as the twentieth century progressed, women became 'increasingly defined and evaluated according to their heterosexual market value.' Marriage was increasingly 'viewed neither as an eco-nomic partnership nor a parenting project but as a glorious romance.' Thus 'the stage was set for the social institution known as "compulsory heterosexuality."' Valverde then perceptively commented, 'Compul-sory heterosexuality refers to the ideology and social practice that pushes properly gendered women and men into couples and makes them believe this is a free choice. It must be emphasized that compulsory heterosexuality need not rely on extreme bigotry against homosexual-ity in order to achieve its goal of instituting the heterosexual couple as the *sine qua non* of personal success and social stability.'[15] Valverde added that 'heterosexism oppresses not only homosexuals but anyone who is either celibate or is in a casual relationship' and can even oppress coupled heterosexuals – despite their enjoyment of many of its privileges – by creating enormous social expectations that they may not be able to meet. It is particularly oppressive for women, she observed, by pressuring them in various ways into believing they have to 'find a man' or keep one if they have found him, and must engage in behav-iour and adopt dress and appearance that achieve that objective.

Heterosexism – the social supremacy of compulsory heterosexuality acceptably manifested in only certain prescribed ways – is thus sys-temic. Its supremacy is predicated on rigid gender roles (that is, sex-ism), the division of labour based on gender, the apportioning of social and economic benefits according to sex and marital status, and the exclusivity of privatized, monogamous, heterosexual sexuality. All people are indoctrinated with heterosexism from birth, which fosters, socially, a formidable totalitarianism. Little room exists for freedom of choice or alternative forms of relationships, or for opting out. Those who conform are rewarded. Those who do not are ostracized and punished. The further one deviates, the greater the social disapproval and punishment. The heterosexual paradigm validates, promotes, and accepts those things which 'prove' heterosexual superiority. Anything challenging or not fitting the paradigm is denigrated, dismissed, or rejected. Like all paradigms, heterosexual superiority acts as a filter on information used for judgment, behaviour, and beliefs. A sense of superiority leads heterosexuals to feel justified in repressing homosexuality. As one American academic, Joseph H. Neisen, has stated, 'Heterosexism is the continued promotion by the major institutions of society of a heterosexist lifestyle while simultaneously subordinating any other lifestyles (i.e. gay/lesbian/bisexual). Heterosexism is based on unfounded prejudices. When our institutions knowingly or unknowingly perpetuate these prejudices and intentionally or unintentionally act on them, heterosexism is at work.'[16]

Heterosexism is, therefore, a manifestation not only of prejudice and fear, but also of the power wielded by the state and by social and commercial institutions that systematically promote, tolerate, or sanction prejudice. At its most basic level, heterosexism is the belief that heterosexual sexuality and rules of sexual and gender interaction are inherently superior or right. In its most insidious form, it demands and ruthlessly enforces compulsory heterosexuality. In order to keep sex a private privilege of heterosexual marriage, the champions of heterosexism attack, under the banner of family values, not only homosexuality, but such things as abortion, birth control, erotica and pornography, prostitution, sex education in the schools, premarital sex, and common-law relationships. Sexual preferences or activities incompatible with procreative sex within marriage are characterized as dirty, disgusting, or immoral. For that reason, gays and lesbians are characterized as perverted, deviant, and repugnant.

At the risk of oversimplification, lesbian and gay liberation may be summed up as a revolutionary struggle that seeks the eradication of heterosexism and the overthrow of the dictatorship of compulsory heterosexuality. This struggle is manifested most directly by fighting the danger to freedom of sexual and social expression posed by the imposition and enforcement of laws proscribing consensual sex, and by the religious right, family values advocates, and their many supporters. But it also requires challenging liberal notions of tolerance and compassion, which are promoted within a set of beliefs dismissing homosexuality as pathological or immoral.

Never Going Back, Making No Apologies

The lesbian and gay movement, and lesbian and gay liberation in particular, is the defiant response to pervasive, systemic homophobia and heterosexism. Through activism and organizing over the last three decades, lesbians, gays, and bisexuals have sent out a simple, clear message: We're out, we're proud, and we're never going back. It is a message this book is happy to deliver. It does not seek to strike a balance between differing points of view on the lesbian and gay movement as a social phenomenon. It presents the history of activism and organizing by lesbians, gays, and bisexuals as told by an activist who was and is still part of that movement. Readers looking for a more 'balanced' view will not find it here. For that, I make no apologies.

PART ONE

From Oppression to Liberation:
Gays, Lesbians, and Bisexuals in
Canada Prior to 1975

ONE

The Roots of Oppression

Homophobia and heterosexism have always been with us, although in earlier times they weren't given names or serious consideration. Instead, lesbians, gays, and bisexuals endured them, finding ways to mitigate their impact on their lives. They developed networks and managed to exist, largely in secret and always with vulnerability, on the edges of society, where they remained ostracized and vilified as immoral and socially dangerous. For gays, lesbians, and bisexuals, Canadian laws, institutions, and social structures, historically, imposed a system of social oppression. Homosexuals generally were seen and treated as criminal, sinful, sick, degenerate, furtive – members of an undesirable, almost subhuman, group against which acts of bigotry, discrimination, injustice, and violence were tolerated or even encouraged. Understanding this historical context and examining how gays, lesbians, and bisexuals survived on the fringe of society are essential to gaining an understanding of lesbian and gay liberation.

Religion and State Regulation

For centuries, the church and the state labelled homosexuality as a sin or a crime and sought to curtail or punish it. They were concerned with particular 'immoral' sexual acts thought to be dangerous to society. The proscription dated back to the Mosaic law of the ancient Hebrews.[1] Many Hebrew laws and beliefs were adopted by Christianity, which became the official religion of the Roman Empire. In AD 527, Emperor Justinian introduced the first civil law against homosexuality, and that proscription gradually became enforced throughout Europe, as Christianity became the dominant religion. The amalgamation of Christian morality with earlier Roman civil law was an easy fit. As Kathleen A. Lahey notes in her exhaustive book, *Are We 'Persons' Yet?*, Roman civil law, even before the rise of Christianity, reflected the social hierarchy of the times, in which the legal capacity, or personhood, of women, children, slaves, and others of inferior social status was subsumed into that of the husband/father/owner. In 18 BC, for example, punitive laws and taxation were introduced 'to promote heterosexual marriage, monogamy within marriage, and biological reproduction of the ruling classes.'[2]

The fall of the Roman Empire curtailed centralized law and administration, and the evolution towards feudalism tended to further encourage the development of local customs and laws in Europe. Nonetheless, after the Norman conquest of England, selective elements of the old Roman civil law became reflected in what would become English common law. The result, as Lahey observes, was a culture 'that extended feudal hierarchies to new lengths and within which was embedded a deeply patriarchal system of legal rights and property ownership.' Married women became, in law, legal minors whose legal capacities were absorbed by their husbands.[3] By the time of papal supremacy, the laws of the church and state concerning sexual matters became almost indistinguishable, and remained that way for centuries. Not only did homosexuality become criminal, but at times the Roman Catholic Church associated it with heresy. Acts of terror and murder were perpetrated against homosexuals; gays and lesbians were among the victims of the Inquisition.[4] In later times, particularly in Protestant countries, homosexuals, like women suspected of being witches, were tortured and executed. Most of the focus was on male homosexuality, but lesbians were also persecuted. The first European law against lesbian acts dates from AD 1270, in France. Later, similar condemnations of lesbian sexual activities were to be found elsewhere throughout Europe. Many of the women executed had been caught cross-dressing or assuming the identities of men.[5]

Britain adopted the church's stance against homosexual acts, but it was not until the sixteenth century that the condemnation was formalized as a statute prescribing death as the penalty for 'the Abominable Act of Buggery.' The penalty was effectively abandoned in 1836, and was formally abolished only in 1861, when it was replaced with imprisonment for a period of ten years to life.[6] British laws governing sexual practices were eventually incorporated into the Criminal Code of Canada. The Consolidated Statutes of Canada, 1859 included buggery as an offence punishable by death. In 1892, it was reclassified as one of the 'Offences Against Morality,' and remained an offence even for consenting adults until 1969.[7] As the language of the law indicates, Canada's Criminal Code, like the statutes in Britain on which it was modelled, largely ignored lesbians. This omission reflected the prevailing male belief that lesbian sexuality was either non-existent or should not be encouraged by being mentioned.[8] Patriarchal society viewed women as without sexual interest or passion; they were to engage in sexual activity only in response to a dominant male to whom they were married, and for the purpose of procreation. Accordingly, until the 1950s the Criminal Code contained no specific reference to same-sex acts involving women. The focus on male same-sex acts was further demonstrated in 1886, when *indecent assault* was redefined to apply only to a male assaulting another male. In 1890, a new offence, *gross indecency*, was introduced to apply to 'every male person who, in public or in private, commits any act of gross indecency with another male person.' *Public, private,* and *indecency* were not defined, thus leaving courts to determine their meaning. Although gross indecency was amended in 1953 to apply to heterosexuals and lesbians, police continued to employ it almost exclusively against gay men.

A 1948 amendment to the Criminal Code also was used predominantly against gay men. The charge of *criminal sexual psychopath* was applied to sexual misconduct in which a lack of power to control the sexual impulses was evidenced to such a degree that the individual would be 'likely to attack or otherwise inflict injury, loss, pain or other evil on any person.' If the court established, in relation to certain sexual offences such as indecent assault, that the accused was a criminal sexual psychopath, he could be sentenced to an indefinite period of imprisonment.[9] A horrendous new twist was added in 1961, when Parliament replaced criminal sexual psychopath with *dangerous sexual offender.* The definition of such an offender included anyone 'who is likely to commit another sexual offence.' Men who engaged in consensual sexual activity with other men were nonetheless convicted of buggery or gross indecency, offences that could result in the accused being designated as a dangerous sexual offender; only a celibate homosexual could be assured of avoiding being branded a dangerous sexual offender.

The Movement for Social Purity

Traditional Christian moral values and the social and economic demands of burgeoning industrialization and capitalism converged, in the nineteenth century, to give even greater impetus for control through 'social purity.' Mariana Valverde has traced the rise and influence of that movement in the years from 1885 to 1925 in her book, *The Age of Light, Soap, and Water* (1991). She examines how religion, certain social science theories, and myriad prejudices combined to forge a movement of moral and social reform. Religious and secular reformers united and succeeded in enlisting the power of the state to wage war on both prostitution and racial and sexual impurity. Urban centres, particularly the slums within them, were seen as presenting a host of moral problems, and the religious beliefs of the reformers saturated approaches to charitable involvement, welfare policies, social work, the law, and the regulation of morality. The social purity movement responded to the perceived fragmentation of society caused by the industrial revolution and migrations, both of which led to increasing urbanization. Poverty, crime, alcoholism, and other perceived threats to social order were blamed on these developments.

The desire to ensure social purity was manifested in a highly organized movement that, by the early twentieth century, contributed even further to prescribing sexual morality and enforcing the containment of sexual activity within marriage. The movement's leaders feared unrestricted sexuality would weaken the family, which they held as the foundation of a stable and moral society. Thus, social purists sought to strengthen marriage and the family by vigorously condemning pre- and extra-marital heterosexual copulation, as well as masturbation, prostitution, and 'sexual perversion' such as same-gender sexuality. Laws were enacted to deter and punish rampant sexuality and other forms of social behaviour deemed unacceptable, such as nudity, vagrancy, or gambling.[10]

As an added deterrent, businesses catering to the sex trade, as well as the 'criminal' or 'immoral' persons engaged in it, were punished. New offences, including operating or frequenting 'a common bawdy house' were added to the Criminal Code. The bawdy house law was first introduced in 1892, primarily to deal with houses of prostitution. But it was amended in 1917 to apply to a place that is kept or occupied, or resorted to by one or more persons, for the purpose of prostitution or the practice of acts of indecency. *Place* was defined widely; it meant any place, whether or not it is covered or enclosed, it is used temporarily or permanently, or any person has an exclusive user right with respect to it. This odious law overrode the right to privacy, and did not define *acts of indecency*. It has been used for decades to harass and prosecute prostitutes, and persons engaging in consensual sex, such as two adults of the same sex, group sex, and sadomasochism.

By the mid-nineteenth century, pornography also became identified by the state and social purity advocates as an evil that had to be sternly addressed. Criminal law was used to stem its production and circulation, including its importation from other countries. Whereas in earlier times the charge of obscenity was applied to materials that were politically or religiously subversive, it was now associated primarily with sex. The change came about first in Britain, in the 1850s, with the introduction of customs and criminal laws to curtail obscenity, including that of a sexual nature. These laws, and the rulings of British courts as to what constituted obscenity, were later adopted in Canada. For most of the post-Confederation period, Canadian courts determined obscenity with reference to an 1868 case in Britain, *R. v. Hicklin*. The case established the *Hicklin* test, under which material was considered obscene if it tended to deprave and corrupt the minds of those who are 'open to such immoral influences.' In *Bad Attitude/s on Trial*, a book on pornography and censorship in Canada, Brenda Cossman and Shannon Bell note that 'Underlying the *Hicklin* test was the nineteenth-century concern with obscene materials: that these materials might fall into the hands of those who were particularly vulnerable to bad influences – namely, the young, the female (often one and the same), and the uneducated, the working class male ... The *Hicklin* test was intended to protect the morals of the lower classes and other vulnerable groups, and thereby promote public morality that was based on the Victorian discourse of sexuality as a dangerous force to be controlled and repressed.'[11] Two post-Confederation statutes, the Postal Service Act (1875) and the Customs Act (1879), explicitly prohibited importing obscene materials or using the mail to distribute them. Canada's first criminal law addressing obscenity was adopted in 1892. It outlawed the public sale or display of any obscene book or print materials. The first significant revision of this law occurred only in 1959 when obscenity was redefined to apply to material which depicts the 'undue exploitation of sex, or of sex and any one or more of ... crime, horror, cruelty, and violence.'[12]

Cossman and Bell note that the introduction of the laws against obscenity and the periodic use of them during the twentieth century corresponded to the ebb and flow of social purity activism. At its zenith between 1892 and 1920, this movement successfully pressured state authorities to act against pornography as part of 'the more general agenda of policing sexual morality and controlling excessive sexuality.'[13] The waning of that movement in the 1920s resulted, for several years, in a lessening of state campaigns against pornography. Following the Second World War, however, a new drive to counter the increasing availability of pornography was launched, as a renewed social purity movement took root. Pulp novels and adult magazines became sources of public concern in the 1940s and 1950s, creating a climate that led to the 1959 amendment. This renewed movement was, according to Cossman and Bell, a return to the efforts of the century's first decades to shore up the family as 'the most basic and sacred of social units' against 'all that was outside it, all that condoned and portrayed sex outside its borders – pornography, prostitution, and homosexuality.'[14]

Deviance and Abnormality

As the nineteenth century ended, another dimension was added to the social mixture that oppressed same-sex sexuality: medical models of sickness, deviance, and abnormality. Gays, lesbians, and bisexuals became the subjects of myriad studies of 'cause' and 'cure.' A school of thought emerged that associated so-called perverted sexual acts between members of the same sex with a certain type of identifiable pathology. This trend marked the rise of psychiatry and the social sciences, which took up the battle to suppress homosexual acts and to define them in clinical terms. In fact, it was at this time that the word 'homosexuality' was actually coined. For most of history, sexual relations between members of the same sex did not have a name associated with a particular group of people or with a sexual orientation. Homosexuality appeared in print for the first time only in 1869, in the writings of Hungarian physician K.M. Benkart, who described it as a congenital condition.[15] Even after the term was invented, its use was limited primarily to medical discourse. It did not become part of most ordinary people's vocabulary until nearly a century later.

Homosexuality as a medical condition emerged in scholarly publications during the 1890s. Richard von Krafft-Ebing's 1896 book, *Psychopathia Sexualis*, was particularly influential in this respect. It referred to homosexuality as a 'physiologically based psychiatric pathology' attributable to congenital weakness of the nervous system. Homosexuals were thought to be 'inverts' – men who for congenital reasons adopted the behaviours and characteristics of women. A man acquiring such characteristics was thought, in the vernacular, to be a 'pervert.' Prominent among those who joined the debates at the end of the nineteenth century and during the first decades of the twentieth was Sigmund Freud, generally seen as the founder of modern psychiatric practice. Freud held that heterosexuality represented a more advanced level of development than homosexuality. He described homosexuality as a form of 'arrested sexual development.'

The new experts were preoccupied with the notion of sexuality, and thereby homosexuality, as primarily male. The relative lack of interest in lesbians stemmed from the views of the men dominating the medical and scientific professions at that time. As Madiha Didi Khayatt notes in *Lesbian Teachers*, these men viewed women as 'passionless, incapable of sexual feelings, submitting to male aggressive desire only for the purpose of procreation.' It was thought to be inconceivable that a woman could sexually arouse another woman.[16] To the extent that lesbian sexuality was acknowledged, it was placed within the emerging theories of sexual inversion and perversion applied to male homosexuals. The views expressed about lesbians were imbued with stereotypical notions of female homosexuality as immature and irresponsible, as a disgusting or degrading form of female sexuality. Women, it was contended, had to take on the characteristics and behaviours of men in order to express such sexuality. Nonetheless, it was because of the views promoted by the new science of sexology that lesbians and lesbianism were finally given an identity, even if they could not be approved of socially or spoken about in polite society. Mariana Valverde, in *Sex, Power, and Pleasure*, comments that the new identity was 'a mixed blessing': lesbians could name and recognize themselves, but the price was 'being marked as abnormal personality types, as "masculine" women' who had 'rejected femininity.'[17]

As the twentieth century progressed, homosexuality and lesbianism were firmly cast in the public consciousness as medical conditions, with the 'afflicted' individuals labelled 'homosexuals' and 'lesbians.' They were thought to be abnormal, perverse, deviant, dysfunctional, neurotic, and so on. These views soon rivalled those of the church and state in influencing the attitudes of society. By about 1950, in fact, the psychiatric profession officially labelled homosexuality as a mental disorder caused by environmental and psychological conditions, characterizing it as a deviation from the heterosexual norm. Psychoanalysis, drugs, electroshock treatments, aversion therapy, and even lobotomies were used to 'cure' gays and lesbians. In addition, lesbians were forced to endure hysterectomies and estrogen injections. Before long, the deviance/disorder theories of homosexuality found their way into public policy. The Ontario government, for example, appointed a committee in the 1950s to examine delinquents in provincial reform institutions. One focus was on 'sex deviates' who threatened decency and morality. Homosexuals were among those studied, and the committee considered whether such individuals were sick and could be cured. It expressed alarm at the degree to which homosexuality was found in society and at the fact that institutions segregating the sexes only helped to facilitate its spread.[18]

The deviance/disorder theory of homosexuality was codified in the *Diagnostic and Statistical Manual of Mental Disorders* (DSM), the first edition of which was published in 1952. Since then, it has been the authoritative source used by psychiatrists and other therapists. The first *DSM* labelled homosexuality as a 'sexual deviation' under the heading of 'Sociopathic Personality Disturbances.' Within a short period, the *DSM* was translated into several languages. It quickly became, in the words of two Canadian academics, 'the bible of psychiatric diagnosis, an encyclopedic compendium of mental illnesses, personality disorders and aberrant behaviour.' Sitting on desks and on bookshelves around the world, the *DSM* became 'a powerful social weapon that determines who is and who isn't mentally ill.' It shaped, in no small way, the views of healthcare and social service professionals in the postwar era.[19] Another scathing critic of the *DSM* and its influence has been clinical psychologist Paula J. Caplan. In her book *They Say You're Crazy*, she contends, 'Every category of mental disorder in the *DSM* is a construct, just as "normality" and "mental disorder" are constructs.' She cited its treatment of homosexuality as 'one of the most glaring illustrations of this fact.'[20] Caplan also accused the *DSM* of being replete with sexism and of reflecting the values and beliefs of a relatively small number of mainly male psychiatrists. Nonetheless, the postwar period's increasingly negative portrayal of homosexuality, as validated by the *DSM*, became the subject of writings by psychiatrists, which in turn influenced mainstream opinion. A host of books on the subject were widely read, including Edmund Bergler's *Homosexuality: Disease or Way of Life* (1957), Irving Bieber's *Homosexuality: A Psychoanalytic Study* (1962), and Albert Ellis's *Homosexuality: Its Causes and Cure* (1964). The authors of these books were clear in their views. Bergler declared there was no such thing as a healthy homosexual. Bieber described homosexuality as a pathological deviation from the heterosexual norm.

Even liberal psychiatrists of this period believed homosexuals were deviant, although increasing numbers came to conclude they could not be cured and, therefore, should be treated with compassion and tolerance. One of these was D.J. West. His book, *Homosexuality*, became a classic of the period. First published in Britain in 1955, it used the term *sexual deviants* frequently as an alternative to homosexuals. West believed that homosexuals could be cured of their deviance only under certain circumstances. He argued that the prospect of successful cure increased if the person was still 'young and compliant in outlook,' if there was an absence of 'strong cross-sex identification,' and if there was, 'above all, a history of some heterosexual interest or experience.' He also subscribed to the view that lesbians had better prospects for cure than homosexuals did because 'they can attempt heterosexual relations, without fear of impotence.'[21]

West continued: 'Psychiatrists can often give more relief by attending to secondary symptoms than by tackling sexual orientation. Many sexual deviants suffer from neurotic guilt feelings, and to alleviate this source of distress is a desirable end in itself, and a task much easier to accomplish than a conversion to heterosexuality.'[22] He viewed homosexuality as a neurosis and perversion that could not be eradicated from society, and argued for greater tolerance and the removal of criminal penalties. Yet, clearly there was a strongly judgmental element to his liberal views, reinforced at the end of his book: 'But tolerance towards homosexuals is not the same as encouragement. No doctor should advise a young person to rest content with a homosexual orientation without first giving a grave warning about the frustration and tragedy that so often attend this mode of life.'[23] The acceptance of homosexuality as a deviant and tragic form of sexuality, and the drawing of a clear distinction between tolerating and encouraging it, gradually gained widespread acceptance throughout the 1950s and 1960s. This represented a liberalization of mainstream attitudes, but still relegated homosexuals to a secondary status in society. They were to be treated with compassion and pity, but such attitudes continued to perpetuate their underclass existence.

Public consciousness about homosexuals was heightened shortly after the Second World War by the release of two studies of human sexuality published by American researcher Dr Alfred Kinsey. *Sexual Behavior in the Human Male* (1948) and *Sexual Behavior in the Human Female* (1953) challenged the belief that discrete populations of heterosexuals and homosexuals existed. Kinsey claimed his research proved the existence of a heterosexual-homosexual continuum that applied to all people. Kinsey's first study found that 4 per cent of men were exclusively homosexual, 6 per cent were primarily homosexual, and 37 per cent had at least some overt same-sex experience causing orgasm. His second study reported that 2 per cent of women were exclusively lesbian and 15 per cent were bisexual. The findings sent shock waves through North America, unleashing a torrent of publicity and discussion in the mainstream American press, scholarly journals, and tabloids.

According to Canada's pioneer gay activist, Jim Egan – who as early as 1949 began writing articles and sending letters to politicians calling for law reform – no other findings up to that time 'caused such outraged clamour, such scandalized condemnation, such scornful denunciation' as Kinsey's studies. Kinsey's conclusions, Egan wrote in 1954, contradicted 'all our tired, old, out-moded moral myths,' and exposed that the 'the nation was living the kind of sex-life that could, were the laws enforced, place 95% of the population in prison as sex-offenders.'[24] Following publication of Kinsey's reports, Egan observed, North Americans were subjected to 'a veritable flood of magazine articles, all of a highly sensationalized and inaccurate nature, that were instrumental in not only bringing the existence of homosexuals to the public's attention, but at the same time completely and thoroughly blackened and misrepresented homosexuals until the readers were left with no alternative except to believe that the country was swarming with sex-mad degenerates who constituted a "problem" of some vague kind or other, but, in lieu of anything else, closely connected with the "youth of the land."'[25] Still, Egan maintained that the overblown reaction to Kinsey would have eventually subsided had it not been for developments emanating from the hysteria generated by Cold War politics in the United States.

Threats to National Security

The Cold War mentality that gripped Western countries cast gays and lesbians as potential traitors and subversives and, accordingly, threats to national security. Governments charged that their furtive lifestyle, filled with shame and guilt, caused social ostracism, risked blackmail, and created susceptibility to coercion by Communist regimes. One result was amendment of Canada's Immigration Act in 1953 to declare homosexuals a prohibited class – that is, one to whom entry into the country could be denied. Another was a witch-hunt against homosexuals, launched first in February 1950 in the United States, that began when ninety-one U.S. federal government employees were dismissed from their jobs because they were homosexuals. A special U.S. Senate subcommittee was struck to investigate homosexuals in government, with several hundred more gays eventually being uncovered and fired. These events generated a round of sensational news reports with screaming headlines. For the first time, the word 'homosexual' appeared on the front pages of many 'respectable' newspapers. Such news reports created the impression that U.S. government agencies were infiltrated by sexual degenerates providing state secrets to foreign governments in order to protect themselves from disclosure. The image of the homosexual as a threat to national security thus became firmly implanted in the public consciousness, and was used by politicians to whip up hysteria and paranoia.[26]

The Canadian government, in the early 1950s, followed the U.S. lead, prohibiting homosexuals from all positions deemed 'sensitive.' The policy was enforced with special rigour for foreign affairs positions, the military, and the Royal Canadian Mounted Police. As Gary Kinsman has chronicled in *The Regulation of Desire*, a concerted campaign of surveillance and harassment was launched, directed towards gays and lesbians employed by the federal government, who were spied on and exposed. They lived in fear of being dismissed or refused promotion. Indeed, until the early 1960s, External Affairs summarily dismissed homosexual employees of any rank. The situation worsened following a 1955 federal cabinet directive on 'defects of character,' including homosexuality, which set off a protracted period of surveillance, harassment, and purges. At first, such actions were limited to federal civil servants, but before long RCMP surveillance was extended to the civilian population.[27]

The Canadian government justified its actions by claiming the Soviet Union was recruiting homosexuals who 'could get linked up with somebody in the federal government who was also homosexual.'[28] Files were opened as government informants watched bars, public parks, and other gathering spots, reporting the names of those found in them. One indication of the absurd lengths to which the RCMP went to ferret out gays was the infamous 'Fruit Machine' project. Although they were ultimately unsuccessful, the RCMP spent considerable time and effort in the 1950s trying to develop a machine that would identify gay men by recording changes in the pupils of a subject's eyes when he was shown erotic pictures.[29] Although scores of people were investigated and dismissed from their positions, there were no known instances of national security having been put at risk. Most of those exposed as homosexuals were loyal and dedicated public servants. Yet, the concern was that they might be risks because of blackmail, despite the fact that almost all of those who were questioned freely acknowledged their sexual orientation.

Gays, Lesbians, and Human Rights Laws

Given the 'sin, sickness, and crime' attitudes towards homosexuality that dominated most of Canada's history, it is not surprising that the first human rights laws, such as they were, completely omitted any reference to discrimination on the basis of sexuality. Canada does not have a long history as a guardian of human rights. Bigotry and prejudice have been more noteworthy for most of its history. Religious and language intolerance featured prominently in most of the post-Confederation decades. Canadian women were not declared 'persons' under the Constitution Act until the late 1920s, and then only because the British Judicial Committee of the Privy Council – not the Canadian government – ruled it so. First Nations peoples have been treated reprehensibly both during and after the colonization of the country. Many First Nations peoples and Blacks were slaves of European colonials in Canada. Slave ownership continued even after the slave trade was outlawed in 1797. Racial segregation of Blacks and Aboriginals existed until the 1960s. Racism characterized Canadian immigration laws and attitudes towards non-white immigrants for most of our history, as evidenced by campaigns against the 'yellow peril' and imposition of a head tax on Asian newcomers. Chinese allowed into the country often endured appalling conditions as railroad construction workers or led lonely, isolated lives running stores and restaurants. Early Eastern European immigrants who helped to settle Western Canada were confronted with bigotry and prejudice. Canadian immigration policy prior to the Second World War did not extend to accepting Jews trying to escape Nazi Germany. The internments of residents of German, Italian, Japanese, and other ancestries during that conflict were national dis-

graces. Until quite recently, people with disabilities were institutionalized because of a belief that it was more compassionate (and economi-
cal) to warehouse them in this fashion than to ensure their access to
education, the workforce, and the community as a whole. For decades,
their rates of unemployment and dependence on social assistance far
exceeded – and still do – those of the rest of the population.

As this sampling makes clear, legislated human rights are relatively
recent developments in Canada, gaining widespread support only after
the Second World War. The impetus to adopt such laws was prompted
largely by the United Nations International Declaration of Human
Rights, to which Canada was a signatory, in 1948.[30] Astonishingly, no
constitutional human rights existed in Canada until 1982. Until then,
the constitution consisted of an act of the British Parliament, the British
North America Act (BNA Act) of 1867, British common law, and judicial
principles and rulings. The BNA Act merely referenced 'a constitution
similar in principle to that of the United Kingdom.' As historian Edgar
McInnis noted, the British constitution was a 'vast and somewhat indefinite agglomeration of prerogatives and conventions, of customs and
statutes and judicial decisions, which underlie the British system of government.'[31] In addition, certain imperial powers were retained with the
British Parliament, among them the right to amend the fundamental
principles of Canada's constitution. These judicial and legal ties to the
imperial government remained strong well into the twentieth century.

The BNA Act reflected the British common law tradition, founded
upon a citizenry composed of loyal and obedient subjects of the sover-
eign. Unlike their counterparts in the United States, Canada's founders
did not see any need for a constitution that set out individual rights or,
following from such a principle, that constrained the state's ability to
restrict those rights. *Civil rights* in the Canadian context were thus
largely undefined, and such references as did exist were limited to the
protection of language and religion. Much was left to be determined
through judicial review. In addition, the BNA Act granted the provinces
exclusive authority over matters 'of a merely local or private nature in
the province.' One of these was control over property and civil rights.
Between 1867 and 1949, a substantial body of constitutional decisions
by the courts, most notably the Judicial Committee of the Privy Council in Britain (then the court of final appeal for Canada), strengthened
the rights of the provinces. Provincial control over property and civil
rights thus gradually took supremacy over the federal responsibility
for peace, order, and good government. It is not surprising, then, that

the first human rights legislation in Canada originated with provincial governments.

Ontario was first, adopting human rights legislation in 1944, in the form of the Racial Discrimination Act. It prohibited the publication or display of signs, symbols, or representations expressing religious or racial discrimination. In 1947, Saskatchewan became the first province to introduce antidiscrimination legislation in the areas of employment, the sale of land, accommodation, and public services. Otherwise, until the 1950s, few statutory remedies existed against racial or other discrimination in Canada. Cases generally had to be dealt with in the criminal justice system; an offence had to be proven beyond a reasonable doubt and the accused had the right to remain silent. Accordingly, enforcement was virtually impossible.[32] Progress towards a more effective system of human rights protections was made during the 1950s and 1960s as provincial governments established fair employment and accommodation practices: persons found to be in breach of these laws could be fined. In 1962, Ontario became the first province to consolidate its antidiscrimination laws into a comprehensive Human Rights Code with a human rights commission to investigate complaints. Other provinces followed suit over the next decade or so. However, the protection of gays, lesbians, and bisexuals from discrimination was omitted from such legislation.

In 1960, the government of John Diefenbaker attempted unsuccessfully to establish legislated civil rights for all Canadians with the adoption of the Canadian Bill of Rights. It was intended to ensure that laws, unless expressly exempted, were subject to its provisions and could not 'abrogate, abridge or infringe' any of the fundamental rights it purported to guarantee. Those rights included equality before the law and protection of the law; freedom of the press, religion, speech, assembly, and association; and the right of the individual to life, liberty, security of the person, and enjoyment of property. The Bill of Rights did not have constitutional status, since it was only an act of the Canadian Parliament and was inconsistent with the provisions of the BNA Act. Judges, in addition, were reluctant to enforce its provisions. Consequently, it had little practical effect in protecting individual rights.

Even if it had been effective in that broad objective, the Bill of Rights would likely have been useless in ensuring that gays and lesbians had legal recourse in the face of discrimination. A statement in the preamble affirmed 'that the Canadian Nation is founded upon principles that acknowledge the supremacy of God, ... [and] the position of the family in a society of free men and free institutions.' The Bill of Rights then went on to state that 'men and institutions remain free only when freedom is founded upon respect for moral and spiritual values and the rule of law.' The problem with the Bill of Rights was ominously evidenced in a 1981 court case involving a challenge of indecent assault charges laid against a gay man. His lawyer argued that the particular Criminal Code section contravened the Bill of Rights. The trial judge agreed, but the Manitoba Court of Appeal overturned the decision. The appeal court held that the section addressed 'a kind of activity which, according to age-old traditions of Judaeo-Christian morality, was always viewed with greater repugnance, and consequently it was not inconsistent with the Bill of Rights that homosexual activity be visited with greater punishment than illicit heterosexual activity.'[33]

The Canadian Family Structure

Social attitudes for much of the twentieth century were strongly influenced by the domination of the nuclear family model of male breadwinner and stay-at-home wife and mother, especially in the era immediately following the Second World War. Such a model differed in significant ways from the form families had taken throughout history. Until the mid-nineteenth century, trapping, agriculture, logging, fishing, and other forms of staples production provided subsistence in many parts of Canada, and required multifunctional family groupings. But regardless of what form they took, family entities generally were given some form of social recognition different from other kinds of relationships. To achieve the objectives of social order and group preservation, societies through the ages determine acceptable behaviour and taboos. Regulating sexuality and imposing controls on, and subordinating, sexual gratification were some of the ways of ensuring conformity.[34]

The advent of the industrial revolution significantly altered the nature of the family. The male's role as patriarch was entrenched in new ways. The division of labour by gender became more rigid: men were increasingly separated from women to take up waged work outside of the home, such as in factories. At the same time, women's work was relegated to the home, and was much less valued than men's. Males in the industrial workforce benefited from a complex system of privileges afforded to them. Attitudes towards sex and relationships also changed. By the early twentieth century, the ideal of romantic love became the predominant basis for spousal relationships in Western societies.[35] Children of the middle class did not have to work to supplement their families' incomes, as they often did in poorer households. Working-class wives often undertook paid domestic chores (taking in laundry, or cooking and cleaning for a boarder), sometimes supported by their children. The relatively few married women who worked outside of the home held low paying 'female' jobs that were extensions of domestic work, such as maids, waitresses, secretaries, school teachers, or nurses.

The twentieth-century family unit became smaller, more uniform, and more socially and legally regulated. Through the efforts of the social purity movement, the development of mass advertising, and the images portrayed in literature, theatre, movies, radio and, much later, television, this version of the family became idealized. John F. Conway writes that, by the 1940s and 1950s, the 'traditional industrial nuclear family reached its apotheosis.' The result was an 'era of glorification of *the* family – dad at work and mom at home with the kids – imposed as the norm on the general society.'[36] The middle-class family living serenely in a bungalow in the suburbs, with a picket fence, car, garage, and a host of mass-produced products, and mother staying at home while father provided the economic well-being, thus became a mid-twentieth-century icon.

Important to understanding the nature of the new notion of family is the recognition that it was based on the inequality of women and the rejection of sexual or lifestyle diversity. The inequality of women was in fact woven into Canada's laws and social fabric. Canadian women did not get even the limited right to vote in federal elections until the First World War, and were legally the chattels of their husbands until 1928. Until very recently, jurisprudence held that a wife could not say no to sexual intercourse with her husband; thus, a husband could not be convicted of raping his wife. Taxation policy, family law, and social benefits were predicated on a dependent female spouse. Within this dominant social structure, gays, lesbians, and bisexuals had no place. They were the sexual deviants, the social miscreants that threatened the stability of the family and the social fabric of which it was the central thread. Thus the family, always a significant source of social conditioning for heterosexual conformity and of the repression of same-sex orientation, became an increasing agent of oppression in the years following 1945.

Aboriginal or Two-Spirited People

Of course, while European cultures and Judaeo-Christian beliefs have dominated Canadian society for nearly four hundred years, they do not represent the mores and spiritualities of the First Nations from which the country was expropriated. In addition, as Albert McLeod of the Manitoba Aboriginal AIDS Task Force has stressed, many Aboriginal people did not significantly interact with whites until the 1940s.[37] Nonetheless, white beliefs and values permeated their lives. One dimension of the colonization of Aboriginal peoples, and the suppression of their cultures, was that members of the First Nations having a same-sex attraction have been virtually invisible within the larger gay and lesbian communities. Sadly, little is known about the traditional beliefs and practices of North America's Aboriginal peoples concerning what today is called homosexuality. The European conquest was achieved in no small way through the efforts of missionaries who lived among the Native peoples, converting them to Christianity and steering them away from their 'savage' customs. Through 'immersion courses,' a process described by Harold Cardinal in his book *The Unjust Society: The Tragedy of Canada's Indians*, traditional beliefs and practices were ridiculed and obliterated: 'As the missionary gradually pushed his only rival, the medicine man, out of the teepees and lodges, he began to introduce his own European value system. The missionary and the trappers and settlers who followed him laughed at the Indian version of religion, scoffed at the all-important visions and dreams, defied the ancient taboos without visible harm.'[38]

Over time, Cardinal added, 'The old religion of the Indian's forefathers slowly was twisted into moral positions that had little relevance to his environment, twisted to fit seemingly senseless white concepts of good and bad.' Among the practices that horrified the missionaries was the dispensing of birth control methods by medicine men. Christian views about sexuality, including homosexuality, became pervasive. Additionally, as colonization progressed, various levels of European government exercised financial control over and custodial responsibilities for Aboriginal people. During the last hundred years or so, this has been accomplished based on treaty rights, the Indian Act, and policy decisions. Residential schools, run by Christians, particularly Anglican, Roman Catholic, and United Church clergy, dominated the lives of Native people in Canada until the 1960s.[39]

This colonization has made reclaiming the history and identity of gays and lesbians in the First Nations extremely difficult; moreover, prior to colonization, there appears not to have been a single view of homosexuality across First Nations. Written historical records are rare, and current attitudes are influenced by Christian teachings. Evan Adams, a gay Native activist on the West Coast, believes the most Christianized

Native communities have been the most likely to be homophobic.[40] At the same time, he and Albert McLeod emphasize, the treatment of gays and lesbians in Aboriginal communities, as related through the passing on of knowledge, has been influenced by the views of heterosexuals, and by the adoption of European beliefs.

Obviously, gay and lesbian are terms of European origin that originally had no meaning in the First Nations. It is known, however, that some North American Native societies had a place of honour for homosexual men, giving them different names from society to society, including *winkte*, *alyha*, or *mexagò*. Some were later given the common French term of *berdache*, men who were androgynous and played many roles, including that of mediator between humans and spirits, and in tribal disputes. In some tribes, they were medicine men, oracles, or figures of religious or ceremonial importance.[41] In other First Nations, *two-spirited people* were recognized as special because they maintained balance and harmony by containing both the male and the female spirits.[42] Even less known today are the attitudes towards, and roles of, women who were attracted to other women, although historical records of some American tribes do make specific reference to such individuals. Among these were American Lakota known as 'manly-hearted women.' The Cherokee called them 'beloved women.'[43]

Until quite recently, finding an identity as gay or lesbian, and connecting with an identifiable community of other such individuals, was extremely difficult for Aboriginal gays and lesbians. Fighting against the racism of the dominant white society added to their sense of vulnerability and isolation. Amanda White, a Native lesbian profiled in *Forbidden Love*, a 1992 documentary exploring lives of lesbians in the 1950s and 1960s, noted that the racist violence she experienced as a school teacher in a white community on Vancouver Island drove her to seek refuge in the skid row area of Vancouver, where other Native people congregated. It was there in the late 1950s that she discovered that lesbians gathered at the Vanport Hotel. However, she felt more comfortable going to a straight club for Black people, in which street people, Natives, Blacks, and Asians were among the clientele.[44] White's choice indicated that the racism present within both the broader Canadian society and the underground gay and lesbian networks dominated the lives and shaped the identity of the few Native women and men courageous enough to assert a same-sex orientation during this period. Like most white gays and lesbians, they could hide their sexual orientation, but they could not hide their race. Understandably, they sought out social environments where they would be comfortable. Ultimately, they preferred the presence of other Natives and people of colour, even if straight, to being lonely and marginalized, and running the very real risk of experiencing racism, in establishments frequented by white gays and lesbians.

Other Cultural and Racial Minorities

Prior to and immediately after the Second World War, Canada did not see itself as a multicultural and multiracial country. Reflecting this, there was little racial or cultural diversity within the lesbian, gay, and bisexual communities. The few non-white individuals with a same-sex orientation who sought out the networks, bars, and clubs available to them were marginalized and isolated. They also had to confront issues of identity, religious beliefs, and disclosure of sexual orientation within their cultural communities, while combating racism and stereotyping within the predominantly white gay and lesbian communities. No single characterization accurately describes the identities and experiences of non-European members of racial, cultural, and religious communities having a same-sex orientation during this era: there was tremendous diversity among them in terms of religion, social organization, family structures, and customs. At the same time, Christian attitudes to homosexuality, following from European colonialism, had already affected the cultures of many peoples in Asia, Africa, South America, and the Caribbean, long before they came to Canada.

Definitions of what North Americans and Europeans call homosexuality, and the attitudes towards it, have differed historically and from culture to culture. Some cultures did not (and do not) define a concept that Western societies call homosexuality. For many, the whole notion of being homosexual, gay, lesbian, or bisexual was and is a Western ritual – identity based on sexual orientation is foreign to them.[45] Differing concepts of family, and the roles they play in encouraging or hindering same-sex activity, are also important distinguishing factors. In some African cultures, for example, there has been no word for homosexuality. In others, the only terms have been derogatory. One gay man of African descent who immigrated to Canada has stated that in his country of origin 'homosexuality is a white man's disease.' A black man who was 'that way' was 'a sick child molester, and he was better off dead.'[46]

As Madiha Didi Khayatt has noted, Arab languages historically have not had neutral, descriptive words for homosexuality. The only comparable word is 'pervert.'[47] An Asian lesbian recently commented, 'There is no word in [the Tagalog language] for "lesbian."' One of the conclusions of a workshop at a 1988 conference for gay and lesbian Asians was that 'Language is a problem since homosexuality is not translated in Asian tongues.'[48] For gays, lesbians, and bisexuals from Asian, African, and Middle Eastern cultures, the dominant role of the family, as much as explicit religious condemnations of homosexuality, have historically been barriers to publicly disclosing a same-sex orientation. Negative reactions stemmed from the traditional belief that 'individuals are expected to get married, parent children and continue the religious and ancestral traditions. These are parental, family and community expectations rather than religious requirements.' In such cultures, gays and lesbians worry about bringing shame on the family by being known publicly as other than heterosexual.[49] Added to all of this, lesbian, gay, and bisexual members of racial, ethnic, and cultural minorities, like Aboriginal people, have had to deal with racism and discrimination. The difference for them has been that, while they could usually receive support from their families or communities against racism, admitting publicly to a same-sex orientation could jeopardize that support.[50]

The Mainstream Media and Entertainment Industries

For most of the immediate postwar period, the mainstream press in Canada paid virtually no attention to homosexuality or homosexuals. In fact, some mainstream newspapers, such as the *Toronto Star*, did not begin compiling news stories on homosexuality until the 1960s.[51] Such stories as did appear were usually reports on murders or sexual offences, or dealt with deviancy, quoting the opinions of psychiatrists. There was virtually no mention of homosexuality in a positive light. Rare exceptions included letters to the editor, often by courageous crusaders like Canada's first gay activist, Jim Egan, which occasionally appeared in dailies and magazines such as *Saturday Night*. In them, Egan called for reform of the Criminal Code, an end to discrimination, and greater understanding and tolerance. Egan once wrote a letter to the editor of *Time* magazine protesting its use of the word 'pervert' to describe homosexuals.[52]

A turning point in the publication of articles on homosexuality by the mainstream press occurred in 1964. The *Toronto Telegram* ran a three-part series on the gay underground that quoted police and psychiatrists. Typical of the attitudes of the time, in one of the articles a Toronto police officer said, 'The butch lesbian can be dangerous,' and that 'Some boss two or three prostitutes.' Another article was headlined 'The Sick Life.'[53] Also in 1964, the *Vancouver Sun* ran a story on a public forum held by Canada's first gay organization, the Association for Social Knowledge. In 1965, it published an appeal by an Anglican priest for law reform using the model then being proposed in the United Kingdom.[54] *Maclean's* magazine broke new ground that same year with a two-part article for which Jim Egan assisted the author. Egan was extensively quoted, as were the chief of police and psychiatrists. The articles referred to the 'homosexual problem' and to homosexuals as 'inverts.' The first major Canadian television documentary on homosexuals, produced by the Canadian Broadcasting Corporation in the same year, similarly presented a relatively tolerant view.[55]

At this time, gays and lesbians were portrayed in movies only as tragic, pitiful, stereotyped, or villainous – if they appeared at all. One researcher of Hollywood movies has found that during the 1950s

> the image of the homosexual changed almost overnight, from court jester to vague menace, as if the threats to social order posed by an alternative form of affective life were genuine and imminent.
>
> Between 1959 and 1961, a flurry of films appeared that redefined the image of the homosexual around two extremes – that of the frightening and that of the pathetic – extremes that, under pressure, tend to merge into a single confused, conflicted muddle.[56]

Television was even more of a wasteland. The 1950s was the era in which even married heterosexual couples could not be seen sharing the same bed. Portrayals of homosexuality were strictly forbidden, even in news reports and documentaries. At best, foppish, effeminate characters would appear in comedies, but would never be identified as gay and there would be absolutely no suggestion of any kind of sexuality.

Attitudes of the Police and Courts

Consistent with the law casting homosexuality, historically, as criminal and a threat to public morality, the police viewed gays and lesbians as an undesirable underclass, as either criminals or degenerates who attracted criminals. Police harassment was a common occurrence, and attitudes such as those expressed in one of the 1964 *Toronto Telegram* articles caused little concern or outrage. In it, a morality squad officer stated, 'I have nothing against homosexuals if you put them on an island – say about 5,000 miles square.'[57] The same officer opined a few months earlier in the *Globe and Mail*, that 'These perverts are no longer ashamed to admit what they are: in fact, they're even proud of it.' He went on to say that the police successfully prosecuted a night club to prevent it from holding drag shows. Such actions were justified, the officer maintained, as growing tolerance towards homosexuals was 'permitting the spread of a vicious social cancer.' The article's headline referred to gays as 'degenerates.'[58]

Toronto police had a long history of harassing gays and lesbians. During the 1940s and 1950s, they systematically rounded up lesbians, took them to a secluded spot at Cherry Beach, beat them up, and then left them to fend for themselves.[59] The Maison de Lys, a Toronto gay club opened in 1961, became the focus of police attention because it was the first place gays and lesbians could go for same-sex dancing. As protection from arrest, when the police arrived, someone would give a signal, and people would change partners so that men and women would be dancing with each other as the cops entered.[60] Even private parties were not safe. One gay party in the 1950s was raided by Toronto police demanding to know the names, addresses, and places of employment of all those in attendance. At other times, police raiding private parties assaulted and harassed the partiers and, whenever possible, laid charges.[61]

Similar tactics were used frequently by police in Montreal, who become notorious for anti-gay and anti-lesbian activities. They periodically raided gay and lesbian meeting places, with a particularly concerted series of raids taking place in the 1960s. Charlie Hill, one of Canada's first gay activists, recalls that his gay friends were terrified about coming out in the city during this period, because, in the spring of every year, police raided gay bars in preparation for tourist season. During the 1966 campaign, Hill and a friend were dancing in a downtown gay club when the police raided it. The two were charged with committing an 'indecent act in a public place' for dancing and allegedly groping each other's genitals. Fortunately, they were found not guilty after the arresting officer conceded in court that there had not been any groping. Nonetheless, the laying of charges in such cases served the purpose of intimidation, whether or not convictions were obtained.[62] For years, police threatened lesbians entering and leaving Montreal bars with breach of the peace or loitering, or subjected them to derogatory remarks of a sexual nature.[63] Similarly in Vancouver, one police officer at this time was notorious for harassing lesbians on the street outside the Vanport Hotel bar by hassling them, demanding their names, and then writing them down in his notebook.[64]

None of this should come as a surprise, since the police forces and courts of the country were deeply homophobic during this era. The Canadian Association of Chiefs of Police opposed the 1969 Criminal Code amendments that decriminalized homosexual acts. As Kinsman has reported, they believed it was necessary to take 'a firm stand against easing the law regarding homosexuality on the grounds that it leads to depravity, blackmail, robbery, and murder.'[65] The courts were often just as negative. In 1961, a Winnipeg magistrate, after finding five men guilty of gross indecency, imposed small fines rather than suspended sentences or probation. He did this, he said, because 'all admitted to being confirmed homosexualists [sic] and it would appear that none has any thought of mending his ways.' He referred to homosexuality as a 'disease' and a 'revolting and sickening offence.'[66] In 1963, a Toronto magistrate found two adult men guilty of a homosexual act committed in a private home. During sentencing, he commented that sending the men to reformatory 'would be like putting two rats into a food storage plant.'[67]

Activist and criminal lawyer Doug Sanders recalls being in court one day in the 1960s when a case came up involving a charge of gross indecency laid against two men parked in a car in Vancouver's English Bay. Sanders thought the evidence seemed to be rather flimsy, consisting entirely of the testimony of a police officer who saw the head of one of the men rise up, suggesting that a sex act had taken place. It was, however, enough to convince the judge.[68] Sanders also published a 1967 article in the *Criminal Law Quarterly* on the sentencing of gay men found guilty of gross indecency. He found that most of the arrests were made in public washrooms, parked cars, or public parks. Reflecting the dominance of the psychiatric theories about homosexuality at that time, many of the sentences included the requirement to undergo treatment at a mental health clinic.[69]

Even in the early 1970s, police continued to view gays and lesbians as criminal elements. Police harassment remained a common occurrence. Toronto's chief of police, for example, derisively told gay and lesbian community members during a 1970 meeting that homosexuals were all 'incipient criminals.'[70] Diane McMahon, active in Edmonton's gay and

lesbian community at this time, remembers how police would frequently show up at parties. Using the pretext of a noise complaint, they
would force everyone to show identification documents and then shut
down the gathering. After moving to Calgary, McMahon, along with
other members of that city's lesbian and gay community, endured
many nights at Club Carousel when the police would descend and
intimidate those present. As she recalls, 'they'd line you up ... I could
feel their hands grabbing me ... people were taken downtown, and
people suffered, you know, I mean women were raped. And I can
remember the rule of so many articles of women's clothing, you know,
down to the underwear and stuff. And the guys and women were
stripped. And you come out of that, and you say, "This is bullshit."'[71]

The most famous of the incidents of police harassment in the early
1970s involved four lesbians at the Brunswick House pub, a popular
drinking spot in Toronto. After singing their own composition, 'I Enjoy
Being a Dyke,' as part of the bar's amateur night on 5 January 1974,
Adrienne Potts, Pat Murphy, Sue Wells, and Heather (Beyer) Elizabeth
were ordered out of the bar by the manager. When they refused to
leave, he called the police. The women, later known as the Brunswick
Four, were taken to a police station by eight uniformed police officers
after being dragged from the bar and loaded into a paddy wagon. Two
of the women were injured in the trip to the police station. They later
stated they were subjected to harassing comments by police. Ultimately
not charged, but having been denied the right to phone a lawyer, they
refused to leave the police station when finally ordered to do so. Police
then forcibly evicted them from the station, punching Potts and throwing her to the ground. Upon returning to the Brunswick House to get
witness statements about what had happened, the four women were
again ordered to leave by the manager, a bouncer, and two uniformed
police officers. They were physically ejected, and three of them, Potts,
Murphy, and Elizabeth, were taken back to the police station. During
the next five hours, police verbally harassed them, and charged them
with creating a disturbance. Elizabeth faced an additional charge of
obstructing police.[72] Anger and concern by community members grew
as word of the incidents spread. A public meeting was called at which
the HASP Defence Fund was launched (the acronym consisted of the
initials of the women's first names). At trial, Potts was convicted of
causing a disturbance, but Elizabeth and Murphy were not. The charge
of obstruction of justice against Potts was dropped.[73] Nonetheless, the
community response to the police action and charges against the Bruns-

wick Four indicated a radical change in the consciousness of gays, lesbians, and bisexuals, and of a hardening resolve to fight back. By the early 1970s, gay and lesbian communities in the larger cities were angrily and actively resisting police homophobia and harassment, as a new, more militant consciousness took root, and the impact of what became known as the gay liberation movement became felt.

TWO

Decriminalization and Early Gay and Lesbian Organizing

By the late 1960s, a considerable social and political consensus had developed favouring the decriminalization of homosexual acts, although the prevailing social attitudes towards homosexuality remained negative and condemnatory. At the same time, there was great upheaval in North America. Social and sexual attitudes were rapidly changing. New movements, particularly feminism, the youth counterculture, and, in the United States, the drive for Black civil rights, emerged to exert tremendous pressure for change in the laws and within state and social institutions. Aware of the historic repression of same-sex sexuality and those who expressed it, and conscious of other forces for change swirling around them, lesbians and gays began to form a new consciousness, and their first organizations, along with a sense of community from which they could draw strength.

Consensus for Decriminalization

Although the prevailing North American perception of gays, lesbians, and bisexuals after the Second World War was profoundly negative, the 1950s saw the beginnings of a debate about whether same-sex activity should be considered criminal. This debate reflected a shifting of opinion, mainly by civil libertarians and liberal lawyers, clergy, social scientists, and academics, towards viewing homosexuality as a sexual deviation or psychiatric disorder to be treated with compassion, rather than criminal sanction. The more liberal view held that homosexuality was morally wrong, deviant, and disgusting, but could be dealt with through psychoanalysis or medical treatment. In Canada, the discourse was influenced significantly by the publicity generated from a high profile 1954 trial in Britain involving Lord Montague, Peter Wildeblood, and a third man. The Montague–Wildeblood trial, as it became known, received massive media coverage around the world, inflamed by the prosecution's exaggerated and sensationalized description of a small party attended by the defendants as an orgy. The men involved were portrayed as stereotypes, 'decadent, corrupt, effete, and effeminate.' All three were found guilty and imprisoned.[1]

The trial polarized British public opinion, creating a growing sentiment for liberalization of the law, which in turn influenced opinion in Canada. In response, the British government appointed Sir John Wolfenden to review the laws on homosexuality and prostitution. The result was the famous *Wolfenden Report*, released in 1957, which argued that homosexuality should not result in criminal charges unless the sexual acts were in public or involved youth. Wolfenden's report generated a great debate on both sides of the Atlantic, leading, in 1967, to Britain's decriminalization of homosexual acts between consenting adults. The leading participants in that debate were H.L.A. Hart, who supported Wolfenden, and Lord Patrick Devlin, who opposed him, claiming there could not be a distinction between public and private morality, and that the law must be based on Christian morals.[2] In Canada, a Royal Commission studying the *criminal sexual psychopath* law, which heard conflicting views on homosexuality, engaged itself in the debate. Public events like the *Toronto Star*'s 1956 Citizens Forum on Sex Deviates joined in. A number of scholarly articles appeared in the *Canadian Medical Association Journal* arguing various views on the sexual deviation, mental illness, and sickness approaches to homosexuality. A prominent law professor, Alan Mewett, supported the Wolfenden recommendations in a 1959 *Criminal Law Quarterly* article in which he argued for the decriminalization of homosexual acts, using an age of consent of 21.[3]

The pace for reform picked up dramatically in the mid-1960s. By then, North American society was in a transformational ferment. The civil rights movement in the United States attained more visibility and militancy. Civil rights marches, acts of civil disobedience, and riots by impoverished Blacks in large American cities changed the consciousness of social activists. The mobilization of youth in protest against the Vietnam War and the threat of nuclear holocaust politicized university campuses. At the same time, youth challenged traditional morality and sexual relationships, adopted radically different music and fashions, and experimented with drugs. They explored alternative lifestyles, rejecting the values of their parents and grandparents. By end of the 1960s, a youth counterculture of hippies and flower children swept across the continent. A new wave of feminism gave articulation to the oppression of women by sexism, misogyny, and patriarchy. Feminist discourse was politicizing legions of young women – and some men. Campaigns were launched to secure access to birth control and abortion. Women's centres emerged and laws entrenching the second-class status of women came under challenge. Many of the organizers of these other movements were lesbian or gay. They saw what could be accomplished through public action to promote political and social objectives. At the same time, they encountered within these other movements anti-gay prejudice and a refusal to either understand or deal with the oppression of gays and lesbians. Using the theories and strategies of these other groups, many of them, mostly young and well educated, first in the United States and then in Canada, would, by the end of the 1960s and the early 1970s, gravitate to lesbian and gay liberation as their preferred movement for social change.

In politics, Canadians were enthralled with the charisma and modern thinking of their new justice minister and future prime minister, Pierre Trudeau. 'Trudeaumania' – the mass media – produced adulation for this younger, more 'with it' bilingual politician with a non-conformist aura and a suave, sexual appeal – was about to sweep the country. Contributing to Trudeau's cachet as a new and exciting figure was his introduction in December 1967 of amendments to the Criminal Code. The reforms were expected, having been under review by the justice department for several years. By stating in a media interview after the legislation's introduction that 'The state has no place in the bedrooms of the nation,' however, Trudeau became associated in the public consciousness with liberalization and reform. The provisions dealing with divorce were to be relaxed, as was the criminal penalty for sexual acts by two consenting adults in private, if over the age of twenty-one. Although his bedrooms of the nation comment simply repeated a position put forward a few days earlier in a *Globe and Mail* editorial, Trudeau had, through his various public pronouncements, 'expressed a widely felt need to bring Canada up to date in a way that everybody could understand. Here was a man who was willing to declare himself in opposition to the established order, a man who was saying that Canada did not have to be a Victorian backwater, a museum of outmoded ideas.'[4]

By the time Trudeau made his famous declaration, social attitudes had evolved to the point of significant support for decriminalizing homosexual acts. A number of churches adopted a position of enlightened paternalism, allowing them to support *consenting adults* reform. They argued homosexuality was, at best, a sin, to be treated in the same way as other forms of immorality, such as adultery. While they could never condone homosexuality, they expressed the need for a tolerant society to show 'compassion' for those who could not break free from its shackles to live moral, decent lives. One of the first organizations to support legal change was formed on 8 February 1965 in Ottawa. Known initially as the Committee of Social Hygiene, it held discussions about how to help 'homosexuals with their spiritual problems.' Soon renamed the Canadian Council on Religion and the Homosexual, it comprised gay male federal civil servants and supportive heterosexual doctors, psychiatrists, and clergy dedicated to conducting public education on homosexuality and 'the plight of the homosexual in society.'[5] Active until 1967, the council urged Wolfenden-type reforms in Canada. Similarly, an Anglican priest who was head of religious studies at the University of British Columbia published a newspaper article in 1965 condemning the laws against homosexual acts as 'unjust and barbaric.'[6] The Canadian Council of Churches stated in a 1969 report that the appropriate Christian response was 'to dispel all popular misconceptions and grotesque views of homosexual characteristics and behaviour, to alter criminal legislation having to do with this matter, and in general to create a social climate where homosexual men and women can experience some measure of acceptance.'[7]

Liberal psychiatrists and even the courts were sounding similar notes. Renowned psychiatrist Alex K. Gigeroff argued for decriminalization in his influential 1968 book, *Sexual Deviation in the Criminal Law*. He cited research findings to support the position that adult homosexual acts should be the subject of psychiatrists and other medical practitioners and not the judicial system. The Canadian Bar Association joined the campaign, proposing an age of consent of sixteen years. As Kinsman noted in *The Regulation of Desire*, another important factor in decriminalization was that the 'Wolfenden and law-reform frameworks were beginning to enter into courtroom discussions, trials, and sentencing hearings in Canada by the mid-1960s.' The courts exerted pressure for clarification of the law, and imposed relatively light sentences for convictions involving consensual same-sex acts.[8] Criminal Code reform also was being pushed by Doug Sanders, a member of Canada's first gay advocacy group, the Association for Social Knowledge, who proposed Wolfenden-type Criminal Code reform in a paper to the Criminal Law Subsection of the British Columbia Division of the Canadian Bar Association.[9]

The federal government was ultimately driven to act after an embarrassing Supreme Court of Canada decision involving George Everett Klippert, charged with four counts of gross indecency after disclosing to the RCMP that he had engaged in consensual sexual acts in private with males. Klippert pleaded guilty and was sentenced to three years' imprisonment. Shortly thereafter, he was visited in prison by psychiatrists retained by the Crown, resulting, in March 1966, in his being deemed a dangerous sexual offender and given a period of indefinite detention. The Supreme Court, in a shocking 1967 decision, denied his appeal, agreeing with the psychiatrists' assessment.[10] Adopting a literal interpretation of the Criminal Code section on dangerous sexual offenders, the court's majority decision meant that individuals convicted of consensual gross indecency or buggery could be determined dangerous if they were unable to control their behaviour and/or were likely to commit a further sexual offence. This decision raised the chilling prospect that any gay man could be imprisoned for life unless he could prove he was unlikely to recommit a same-sex act. It produced a public outcry, and the liberal press denounced it, speeding up the pace for law reform. In November 1967, New Democratic Party leader Tommy Douglas raised the Klippert case in Parliament, calling for the establishment of a government commission similar to that of the Wolfenden committee.

Following the 1968 federal election, Justice Minister John Turner reintroduced Trudeau's reforms. Defending the provisions relating to buggery and gross indecency, Turner drew upon many of the Wolfenden arguments. Almost all MPs who were supportive took the view that homosexuality was repugnant and homosexuals were sick deviants who required psychiatric help, but who should not be subjected to criminal prosecution for engaging in sexual activity in private with another adult. Opponents claimed that the reforms amounted to condoning homosexual activity and would lead to the undermining of social values and family life.[11] The bill ultimately was passed on 14 May 1969, with its provisions taking effect in August of that year.

Resistance from Political and Social Conservatives

The 1960s liberalization spawned a renewed movement of social conservatives, principally fundamentalist and other conservative Christian forces, aided and abetted to a large degree by so-called liberal denominations. Social conservative ascendancy surged as the memberships of evangelical churches soared. Many churchgoers rebelled against the movement towards relevance and secularism in liberal denominations. They preferred a more rigid set of beliefs and structures in response to a world which they saw as too permissive, where social change was frighteningly rapid and destructive, and the old truths less widely held. Evangelical or fundamentalist Christian churches began to thrive, and some took extreme positions on social and moral issues. One example was a 1966 article published in the *People's Magazine,* issued by the People's Church in Toronto, that called for the execution of homosexuals. It was only following a public outcry that the church's pastor, preaching on the 'The Sin of Sodom,' called instead for the abolition of the law prohibiting same-sex acts between consulting adults, while still condemning homosexuality as a sin. In another instance, the Fellowship of Evangelical Baptists, in August 1968, called on the federal government to halt its proposed legislation to decriminalize homosexual acts between consenting adults. At the same time, it was clear even the changing views of more mainstream churches would be able to go only so far. A 1965 article published in the *United Church Observer,* for example, caused alarm among clergy by stating that homosexuals should be warmly welcomed by the church and that some same-sex relationships should be given church blessing. Speaking at the second North American Conference on Church and Family Life in 1966, a divinity professor from McGill University declared that the Christian church could never approve or condone homosexuality, that it would always be impossible for a practising homosexual to also be a practising Christian. A Presbyterian cleric lecturing to university students in January 1966 declared that Toronto had become the Canadian centre for homosexuals. Homosexuality, he stated, was a sin and not a 'biological problem.'[12]

But it was fundamentalism that led the charge, and, as its influence grew it fuelled a backlash of bigotry and resentment that took root socially. Traditionalists saw many threats to social stability: the Black civil rights movement, feminism, opposition to the war in Vietnam, the anti-nuclear movement, recreational drug use, a perceived increase in violent crimes, sexualized and 'unwholesome' music, the widespread acceptance of abortion as a matter of choice, a rising divorce rate, the loosening of sexual mores among youth, the increase in single mothers, and the diminishment of the stigma associated with having children out of wedlock. Such phenomena alarmed political conservatives, who easily embraced social conservative issues, using the rhetoric of protecting Christian society and the family, long before the term 'family values' came into vogue. A new convergence of social conservative opinion and political opportunity, dramatically evidenced by the 1969 Parliamentary debates, harkened back to the earlier social purity movements. Previously, social conservatism, as an electoral movement, had been manifested principally in the Social Credit Party, founded by a Christian fundamentalist preacher, William 'Bible Bill' Aberhart, in Alberta in the 1930s. Outside of western Canada, it remained an essentially fringe phenomenon, a form of right wing populism rooted in Christian evangelism and a bizarre economic philosophy that blamed the problems of capitalism and the Great Depression on the exploitation of the international banking and credit system which, it was claimed, was controlled by a Jewish conspiracy. Social Credit formed the government of Alberta in 1935, holding office until the early 1970s. Aberhart's successor as premier, a preacher named Ernest Manning, was renowned for his radio program *The National Bible Hour*; he pursued a curious mixture of populism and religious fervour, combining explicitly right wing economic policies with a belief in 'Christian democracy.' Social Credit maintained that one role of government was to preserve the ability of the citizen to find salvation in God.[13] During the 1950s, Social Credit also took power in British Columbia, under W.A.C. Bennett. During the 1960s, Social Credit members were elected to the House of Commons, where they played a leading role in opposing the 1969 Criminal Code amendments.

Social Credit was not taken seriously by the traditional political elites or the media, especially in central and eastern Canada. Mainstream conservatives, while espousing many of the beliefs held by right wing populists, had managed, for the most part, to be seen as more acceptable politically. Still, the 1969 Parliamentary debates on the Criminal Code amendments gave witness to how readily both mainstream and social conservatives found common ground on matters such as homosexuality. Most Progressive Conservative members of Parliament, including former Prime Minister John Diefenbaker, joined with Social Credit, and its Quebec splinter group, the Créditistes, in opposing decriminalization. In doing so, they cited moral, religious, or other reasons, decrying the decline of society and decency that would ensue.[14] One Social Credit MP warned that the amendments dealing with divorce and homosexuality were 'pernicious' and would 'lead the nation to its own destruction.'[15] In a refrain that would be heard from family values advocates many times in later years, arguments against liberalizing the law were based on homophobia and heterosexism. Homosexuality was linked with bestiality and paedophilia. For example, Marial Asselin, Conservative MP for Charlevoix, charged that 'Homosexuals are mostly inclined to pervert youngsters and the Minister [John Turner] opens the door wider.' Police, he lamented, would no longer 'be very much interested in chasing homosexuals after the passage of this legislation.' Instead, he claimed, Parliament should be 'voting legislation to help homosexuals cure themselves, since they are really sick.'[16] Erik Nielsen, a Conservative MP for the Yukon, lashed out at permissiveness, stating, 'We must not legislate to permit activities which are repugnant, morally degenerative or socially destructive.'[17] Walter Dinsdale, Conservative MP for Brandon-Souris, thundered that by adopting the amendments, 'We are reversing completely values and traditions which have been the foundation stone upon which our western Christian civilization has been established.' Eldon Wooliams, a Conservative member from Calgary North, stating Parliament 'governs a Christian nation,' claimed the consenting adults amendment would lead to sex between people and animals.[18]

As the events leading to the 1969 amendments were unfolding, the groundwork was being laid for a confrontation between the aspirations of gays, lesbians, and bisexuals, which would be given political expression in later decades, and the objectives of Christian evangelical–dominated political parties, which would so vigorously oppose them. Preston Manning, the son of Alberta's premier, began formulating the political doctrine that would lead to the establishment of the Reform Party and its evolution into the Canadian Alliance. In the late 1960s Preston Manning began to urge the blending of conservative economic and social beliefs into a new political movement. Influenced by the evangelical Christian denomination to which they belonged, Preston Manning and his father advocated establishing a new right wing party having a philosophy they called 'social conservatism.'[19] Adamant, often extreme, opposition to rights for gays and lesbians, articulated as the defence of family values, became one of the issues with which the resulting party became identified.

The Development of Community

Although they did not have a concept of community as we know it today, gays, bisexuals, or lesbians living in what we now call the pre–gay liberation era recall that distinctive, though underground, subcultures thrived in many urban centres. They had social and sexual networks, often couched in secrecy, and rules of conduct and deceptions characterized by elaborate codes. The networks and customs of the subcultures offered protection from a hostile world and secured existence on the margins of society, sometimes in creative ways, but also with vulnerability and fear. These subcultures provided the foundation for a community with a common sexual orientation; it was born, and given political meaning, in the 1970s. As Mary Axten, who was active in Toronto's lesbian subculture for over forty years, recalled in 1988,

> Forty years ago in Toronto ... the term homosexual, if it was heard at all, was heard to be whispered. We had no place to go and beyond the dubious distinction of being characterized as sick in psychiatric journals and some kind of abomination in religious teachings, we had hardly any identity. And life for homosexuals was quite simply total contempt. Nevertheless we did exist and in no small numbers. Despite the places available to us to meet being so few, somehow we found each other. We made friends, we had parties, we formed relationships and most importantly, we built networks. We existed as a subculture with a life and lifestyle of our own. Two lives in other words.[20]

Despite hostility and repression during this era, many gays and lesbians lived their lives with great ingenuity and tenacity. Men seeking to meet or have sex with other men often could do so, in larger cities, by cruising public parks and street corners late at night, or in washrooms in bus stations, department stores, and other public buildings. Some cities had bathhouses, porno movie theatres, and a small number of gay bars, often hard to find. In smaller cities, gay men brave enough to cruise public parks, bus depots, or public washrooms made sexual contacts with other men. Of course, the risk of arrest and public humiliation from any resulting publicity made such activity dangerous and furtive.[21] Similarly, living invisibly, with deception, was the key to survival in rural areas. Gay activist Doug Wilson, while doing rural outreach in Saskatchewan during the 1970s, encountered the situation of a gay man whose amazing story illustrates the lengths to which rural lesbians and gays were forced to go to form relationships. The man came to Canada from Belgium after the Second World War. En route, he met an older man with whom he formed a relationship. They became homesteaders together in Saskatchewan, pretending to be father and son. The younger man eventually married, but the older man stayed in the household as the 'grandfather' and eventually outlived the wife. After the death of his lover, the younger man took a series of other men as lovers.[22]

There were also social networks and house parties, for those fortunate enough to gain an entrée to them. John Grube, a chronicler of early Canadian gay history, has noted that, prior to 1969, homosexuals 'had a historic culture, whether "underworld" or not, with points of entry, established territories, initiation procedures, annual festivities, and "circles" with leaders ("queens").'[23] An important feature of that culture, Grube observed, 'was its ideology about patterns of adaptation in which members of the subculture might resolve the tensions between their stigmatized status and the world at large. These patterns varied from becoming a "flaming queen" or "flaunting" homosexual to leading a double life in which one's public status was entirely heterosexual (married, with children), while one's private sexual outlet was known only to a few.'[24] While some gays were open, they tended to be artists, interior decorators, or hairdressers, or they worked in low-status jobs. Often, access to a network or social circle was gained through a mentor. Mentors were typically older men, sometimes queens, who took younger men under their wings – sometimes, but not always, in exchange for sex.[25]

Generally, bars and pubs became known meeting places for gays in Canada's larger cities only after the Second World War. Those that did exist, with few exceptions, were on the margins of society, sometimes in skid row or other disreputable parts of town, and were frequented by various other subcultures: prostitutes, transvestites, and street people. Toronto and Montreal had a small number of upscale cocktail lounges, but they had rigid dress codes and women generally had to be escorted by men. Almost all of the establishments were owned by heterosexuals, who merely tolerated their queer clientele, often imposing on them requirements of discretion and conduct that would not identify the establishment publicly as a gay place. Class distinctions were prevalent, with working-class and street people relegated to the least respectable places.[26] In addition, the gays who frequented the bars and pubs were predominantly, if not exclusively, white. Few, if any, people of colour or Aboriginal people were part of these networks. Vancouver had more limited options. The New Fountain Hotel, in what is now fashionable Gastown, became a gay bar about 1964. At that time, it was located in a seedy and disreputable part of the city; the vicinity of the bar was called Blood Alley. A gay man who frequented it has described the bar as a war zone: 'The New Fountain was a place where everyone and anyone went. [I saw] fights break out in there. [I saw] people come back into the New Fountain with blood gushing from their stomachs and fall over dead. It was that kind of place. It was a place where the waiters wore hardhats to deal with bottles, chairs.'[27]

Lesbians generally had even fewer options. Because they were women, they could not safely be in public places, especially to seek sexual contacts. Few had jobs that allowed them to live independently, or that enabled them to afford to go to bars. Lesbian social networks did exist, of course, but were harder to find than those of gay men. Often, two lesbians fortunate to find each other and become lovers would live quietly by themselves, without contact with others. If lucky, they might, over time, discover others who were like them, and forge discreet social circles. Lesbians who lived in a larger city had one or two rundown, rough-hewn taverns where women could go unescorted – if they could find out about them. Montreal had the most lesbian bars and lesbian sections of other bars where men were not allowed. These were often rough places where class or economic status was important. Maureen Irwin, a frequenter of Montreal bars while in the Air Force in the 1950s, has memories that are less than fond: 'it was butchy and it was tough ... there was fights, I mean, there was a lot of fights and a lot of drinking.'[28] The earliest lesbian bars, like those for gay men, were located in the Main area, known for prostitution, strip clubs, vices, and criminality. Poolrooms on or near St Lawrence Street (rue St-Laurent) were also popular. The customers included lesbians, single men, prostitutes, petty criminals, transvestites, and transsexuals.[29] In Toronto, a hotel tavern called the Continental opened as a lesbian bar in 1947, located in Chinatown, an area seen by the mainstream at the time to be crime-ridden.[30] Lesbians in Vancouver during this period could go to the Vanport Hotel tavern, located in skid row. It was described as filthy and full of cockroaches, with table clothes that were never changed and a sticky floor. Others who hung out there were hookers, drug addicts, and drug dealers.[31]

By the late 1960s, gays and lesbians in Montreal, Toronto, and Vancouver had staked out tiny territories where they lived and socialized. These areas were the precursors of the visible communities that would spring up a few years later with the advent of lesbian and gay liberation, downtown neighbourhoods demarcated by high-rise apartment buildings and a small number of taverns, bars, and clubs where gays and lesbians were tolerated. Montreal was famous for the variety of hot spots, generally concentrated in the English part of the city, near the intersections of Ste Catharine and Stanley streets. Toronto bars in the late 1960s were concentrated on a stretch of Yonge Street, between College and Bloor, near a neighbourhood of high-rise apartments into which many gay men had moved. Vancouver's West End, especially the English Bay area, also increasingly experienced a concentration of gays and lesbians. However, restaurants and other businesses where gays and lesbians could go, be comfortable and be themselves, generally did not exist, even in these more advanced cities. Walking down the street wearing something that signified a gay or lesbian identity, let alone expressing openly gay or lesbian behaviour, was dangerous and rarely done. There was genuine and well-grounded fear of being seen entering or leaving a queer bar, and thereby losing a job or experiencing harassment. Most bars catering to a gay or lesbian crowd did not publicize the nature of their clientele and had backdoor entrances away from bright lights and passing traffic.

For gay men and lesbians who lived outside Canada's three largest cities, life was often more circumscribed. Well into the 1970s, private parties and other social functions, such as dinners and potlucks, were the main social activities for homosexuals in cities like Edmonton and Calgary. In smaller cities that had them – and many did not – the known gay drinking spots were a contrast between skid row beverage parlours and fancier, more class-conscious cocktail lounges – the latter found in cities like London, Hamilton, Calgary, Saskatoon, or Regina. In Ottawa, the Coral Reef, a lounge where gays could dance, opened by the late 1960s. Typical of the period was the Chez Henri across the river from Ottawa, in Hull. There the clientele was a mixture of skid row types, older people, prostitutes, and gays. A Hamilton bar, the Night Life, was, according to one gay man who went to it, 'a sleazy after-hours club frequented by drag queens.' The gay scene in Sudbury centred on the Nickel Range hotel, frequented by gays, transvestites, bikers, and drug dealers.[32]

Harold B. Desmarais, a Windsor resident during this period, recalls there wasn't much in the way of a social scene in that city. There were cruising parks for gay men and two bars that tolerated gays and lesbians as long as they weren't too obvious. One, the Ritz, was used mainly by gay men; the other, the West Side, was frequented by lesbians. The West Side was a beer parlor owned by a lesbian who did not appreciate people being open about their sexuality. The climate in Windsor's bars, Desmarais remembers, was oppressive: 'You had to watch your behavior very closely ... While they allowed you in there, excessively flamboyant or outrageously or openly gay behavior was definitely discouraged. I mean, you could get barred, and some people did.'[33] Finding out about the bars was also challenging – information was strictly by word of mouth. Outside the bars, gay men in Windsor formed cliques, as opposed to social networks. If gay men didn't belong to certain groups or social strata, they had difficulty finding a group in which they felt welcome. In contrast, Desmarais remembers, such social divisions did not exist among lesbians: few were upwardly mobile at the time, so little emphasis was placed on one's social standing.

It was not until the early 1960s that the first openly lesbian and gay themes were presented in film, theatre, art, and literature, especially in Quebec. The first Canadian films dealing with gay subjects were *A tout prendre*, produced by Claude Jutras in 1963, and an English-language film, *Winter Kept Us Warm*, in 1965.[34] Theatre productions featuring openly gay characters also premiered in the 1960s. In Montreal, gays were achieving prominence in mainstream theatre and were able to do gay productions. Michel Tremblay, in particular, was well on his way to becoming a giant of Quebec theatre, with some of his plays featuring gay characters.[35] Montreal was alive with emerging gay and lesbian authors publishing plays, fiction, and poetry with gay content. In 1964, Paul Chamberland published two books of poetry, followed by another in 1967. Jean Paul Pinsonneault published a novel, *Les terres sèches*, in 1964. Also in that year, a collection of essays by Paul Toupin appeared.[36] Toupin published his first memoir, *Mon mal vient de plus loin*, in 1969.[37] One of Quebec's most renowned lesbian authors, Marie Claire Blais, published *Une saison dans la vie d'Emmanuel* (1965), *David Sterne* (1967), and *Manuscrits de Pauline Archange* (1968). In contrast, gays and lesbians in English Canada were not as prolific, but were starting to make progress. Toronto's Global Village Theatre produced avant-garde drama, including John Herbert's internationally acclaimed play, *Fortune and Men's Eyes*, about homosexuality in prison. General Idea, an artistic collective in Toronto formed in 1967, introduced satiric and humorous gay sensibility to art, and continued to do so until it disbanded in 1994. Elsewhere, Jane Rule published her first novel, *The Desert of the Heart*, in 1964 and followed it with a succession of others. Scott Symons's gay novel, *Combat Journal for Place d'Armes*, appeared in 1967. Toronto poet Ian Young published two books of gay poetry in 1969, *White Garland: 9 Poems for Richard* and *Year of the Quiet Sun*.[38] With these developments, the first seeds of a distinctive queer artistic culture were sewn, and would blossom over the next two decades.

Early Gay and Lesbian Consciousness

Until well after the Second World War, using the word 'homosexual' to refer to same-sex attraction was generally limited to medical or criminal reports. Men who had an orientation towards members of the same sex did not generally use that word to identify themselves. 'Queer' was more commonly heard in the wider society until the 1960s, but gays and lesbians often simply referred to themselves as being 'that way.' Jim Egan, who grew up in Toronto during the 1930s, recalled in an interview that even though he began 'sexual fooling around' with other males at puberty, he had never heard the words 'homosexual' or 'gay.' George Hislop, born in 1927, also remembers, 'The word "faggot" didn't exist. We were "queers."'[39] Similarly, Charlie Hill, born in 1945, recalls not knowing anyone who described himself as gay during sexual encounters he began having with other males at age twelve.[40] Doug Sanders has described his experiences as a young man growing up in Alberta in the 1960s as equally deprived of identity: 'homosexuality was something I had never encountered before. We didn't have them in Alberta when I grew up.'[41]

The first use of 'lesbian' in popular discourse is thought to have been by Radclyffe Hall's famous 1928 book, *The Well of Loneliness*. But, unlike 'homosexual,' 'lesbian' does have a historical association with same-sex love. It derives from Lesbos, a Greek island which was home to a poet named Sappho (612 to 558 BC), who wrote love poems and songs to other women. As Madiha Didi Khayatt points out in *Lesbian Teachers*, 'Sapphic love' was the prevalent term to describe the erotic and affectionate attraction of a woman for another woman at the beginning of the twentieth century. By the 1930s, 'lesbian' became associated with woman-to-woman eroticism.[42] The little public awareness about homosexuality concerned males almost completely; practically nothing was known or said about lesbians. As a group, lesbians were even more invisible than gay men, their networks and meeting places fewer and harder to find. 'Lesbian,' when used at all, was derogatory. For that reason, most women who loved other women shunned the term. Mary Meigs was one such woman, recalling years later, about living with another woman during this era, 'Strangely enough, I did not come into contact with other lesbians. The word "lesbian" was taboo. I did not have any sense of other lesbians and was absolutely terrified of the word and the whole world of lesbians.' Rather, the consciousness was one of simply knowing that 'A lot of us were that way, women my age.'

Meigs internalized the negative things that she had heard, and held those views for many years: '[Being lesbian] was not only not talked about, it was perceived with horror by most people, including me ... When [an acquaintance] said to me you're really sort of a lesbian, I almost, I felt sick with a kind of terror – being given a name, a label. I almost sort of denied it, I guess. That was in the 1960s.'[43]

Other women of that same generation were even more unaware and reticent. A Regina woman, when asked to talk about being a lesbian in the early 1950s and 1960s, stressed how careful people had to be: 'there were certainly women with those feelings but they were just not able to exercise them. It just wasn't done. You just didn't question anything.' Ascribing 'those feelings' to being a lesbian, for her, was unimaginable. 'I can identify the feelings now. At the time, I just couldn't identify the feelings, beyond, "Isn't she neat." Coming from a small town, you just didn't hear about those things, nobody talked about it. In those days, they called those people "fruits." There was never a kind word in those days.'[44] Maureen Irwin found herself among many 'women who loved other women' after joining the armed forces in 1953. They did not describe themselves as lesbians, but some would refer to themselves as 'dykes.' But they were aware they would be kicked out of the armed forces if their attractions became known.[45] A woman profiled in the 1992 film, *Forbidden Love*, tells of having given in to pressure to get married only to subsequently meet another woman, who began giving her pulp novels with lesbian themes. The other woman eventually said, 'I think I'm that way' and suggested that the first woman might be too. Although the first woman adds, 'Whatever *that* meant,' they nevertheless formed a relationship.

Women who did self-identify as lesbians often did so in a very negative way. In 1951, a sensationalistic Toronto tabloid contained one of the rare articles on lesbians published during that period. Identified only as 'Sapho,' the author parroted the prevailing views: 'Lesbians fall into three groups: those who are homosexual because of a glandular deficiency; those who, while normal at birth, become homosexual as a result of a psychic shock in childhood, and those who, in maturity, turn voluntarily to Lesbianism as a release from the vulgarity and bestiality of men.' Then, in a self-hating manner common for that period, she declared with resignation, 'The Lesbian who is really fortunate is the one who discovers her abnormality early in life, who studies the whole problem and reconciles herself to what life may bring her.'[46]

Although the first gay groups did not appear in Canada until the 1960s, individuals, as early as the 1950s, nonetheless began developing analyses that rejected the era's anti-homosexual attitudes. George Hislop recounts that politics would often be discussed at the house parties that were an important element of the social scene during this period: 'I remember that, even then, the thing that bothered us most was the world's perception of us as compared to *our* perception of ourselves. We knew that we had to focus our energy collectively, that we had to have some sort of organization.'[47] But the only person to speak out publicly at this time was Jim Egan. Beginning as early as 1950, he submitted articles and letters to 'scandal sheets' such as *True News Times* and *Justice Weekly*, presenting legal aspects of homosexuality and challenging the attitudes and beliefs that caused hostility and animosity. Egan called for the repeal of the anti-homosexual laws, calling them 'unjust and cruel' and 'utterly incapable of being enforced.'[48] In 1954, he called on a parliamentary committee to repeal the Criminal Code's gross indecency offence. He also urged a consenting-adults amendment similar to those that had been introduced in some European countries. Egan further maintained contact with the first gay groups formed around this time in U.S. cities, and attended a gay conference in Los Angeles.[49] Seeking to influence the community, he became a mentor, sharing with Hislop and others the gay publications to which he subscribed. Organized activities evidencing a new consciousness did not appear, however, until the mid-1960s, when discussions held in the Music Room, a popular Toronto gay club, drew as many as seventy-five people. Through these events, the club's owners, particularly popular lesbian singer and community figure Sara Ellen Dunlop, did heroic groundwork. They invited psychiatrists to talk about homosexuality, and Egan urged the community to organize itself, to not be pushed around.[50]

Homophile Organizing

While gay visibility at this time was limited to lonely voices such as that of Egan, advocacy groups began forming in the United States. In 1950, North America's first gay rights organization, the Los Angeles Mattachine Society, was formed. The group had adopted the name of the secretive, all-male societies formed in the fifteenth century in Europe, which traced their origins to ancient Roman festivals of revelry and sexuality. The Mattachines – flamboyant masked and costumed jesters who satirized persons holding positions of power and ridiculed social pretenses – were also social activists working on behalf of the oppressed peoples of their time. Ancient Mattachine Societies were seen by Harry Hay and other early American queer activists as a powerful symbol for modern homosexuals living in disguise but working to remove the oppression they experienced. Mattachine championed the proposition, put forward as early as 1948, that homosexuals were a minority with a common language and culture who warranted protection under civil rights laws. Mattachine recognized how crucial was the need for a more positive gay self-identity and rejected use of 'homosexual,' which by this time had such clinical and pathological connotations. Instead, the society coined another word, *homophile*, derived from the Latin *philia*, meaning friendship, and the Greek, *philos*, meaning loving. Mattachine called for unifying homosexuals, giving them a sense of belonging, and educating them and the public at large about homosexuality. Its members asserted homosexuals could 'lead well-adjusted, wholesome and socially productive lives once ignorance and prejudice against them are successfully combated, and once homosexuals themselves feel they have a dignified and useful role to play in society.'[51] Chapters, or 'guilds,' of Mattachine sprang up in other U.S. cities over the next few years, helping to foster the founding, in 1952, of *ONE Magazine: The Homosexual Viewpoint*, the first widely distributed gay magazine in the United States. It became a source of news about police entrapment, harassment of bars, and other acts of oppression.

The first lesbian organization was formed in 1955, when four lesbian couples got together in San Francisco and, under the leadership of Del Martin and Phyllis Lyon, launched the Daughters of Bilitis (DOB). The name chosen by the new group derived from a fictional character named Bilitis – heroine of the late-nineteenth-century *Songs of Bilitis* – who had lesbian relationships and was a contemporary of Sappho. Chapters soon formed throughout the United States, dedicated to educating lesbians and the public about 'female homosexuals,' providing social alternatives to lesbian bars, and educating other lesbians about the law and what to say in court if arrested for being in a bar.[52] DOB also published *The Ladder*, which was passed from hand to hand and mailed from one person to another. As one DOB member recalled, its impact on the lives of lesbians was remarkable: '*The Ladder* was bringing to the surface years of pain, opening a door on an intensely private experience, giving voice to an "obscene" population in a decade of McCarthy witch hunts.'[53] Just as Mattachine attempted to change the perception that gay men had about themselves, the DOB tried to instil in lesbians a more positive consciousness. One of its early members recalls, 'Our goal in helping our people fit in was to allow them to live within whatever societal guidelines and frameworks and limitations they had to contend with and to come out of it as whole and healthy and sane as possible. You have to remember how dangerous the world was then.'[54]

Inspired by the establishment of the homophile groups in the United States, Canada's first gay community organizations formed. The first and most successful group was the Association for Social Knowledge (ASK), founded in Vancouver in April 1964.[55] Modelling itself on Mattachine in San Francisco, ASK committed to 'seriously confront Canadian society with the fact of it's [sic] homosexual minority and challenge Canadians to treat homosexuals with justice and respect and to work for reform of criminal laws on sexual activity.'[56] ASK organized social activities and dances, published a newsletter, held public forums featuring clergy and psychiatrists as speakers, and undertook some pioneering advocacy. Most noteworthy of its advocacy efforts were a brief that ASK member Doug Sanders presented to the Royal Commission on Security and papers he wrote on law reform calling for decriminalization of homosexual acts. Unfortunately, faced with the financial and resourcing strains of operating a community centre, ASK died in the spring of 1969.[57]

In Toronto, the first gay and lesbian group emerged in the fall of 1969, when Jearld Moldenhauer placed an advertisement in the *Varsity*, the student newspaper at the University of Toronto, asking others to join in setting up an organization. Moldenhauer, Charlie Hill, and Ian Young established contact and, on 24 October 1969, held the first public meeting of the University of Toronto Homophile Association (UTHA).[58] Its constitution stated it was 'dedicated to educating the community about homosexuality, working to combat discrimination against homosexuality, and bringing about social and personal acceptance of homosexuality.'[59] UTHA began holding meetings, discussions, and set up information tables on campus. Growing out of these developments was the Community Homophile Association of Toronto (CHAT), which focused on providing social services for the growing gay and lesbian community beyond the university campus. Born in December 1970, CHAT addressed the concerns of some UTHA members, including George Hislop, about how to establish social service programs for gays and lesbians, assist gay men arrested for consensual sexual activities, and provide information and assistance to doctors and lawyers about the lesbian and gay community.[60] In early 1971, CHAT moved into an office, started a telephone distress line, began holding public forums and dances, and conducted educational activities. Later that year, the group scored a political breakthrough when it received a federal government grant of $9,000 to hire six summer students to contact social service agencies and develop projects dealing with street youth. Receipt of a second federal government grant of $14,602 a year later embroiled CHAT in controversy after outraged media and politicians claimed tax money was being squandered on a gay group through 'kookie grants.'[61] Other homophile groups later cropped up in London and Guelph (1971), Kingston and Regina (1973), and St John's (1974).

But CHAT, like most of the other Canadian homophile groups of the early 1970s, was ultimately short-lived, and for all practical purposes died in 1977, although it remained in existence on paper for another couple of years. It never succeeded in capturing the enthusiastic or sustained support of a generation of activists emerging in the early 1970s who asserted a much more radical politics. The homophile movement, progressive and groundbreaking in the 1950s and 1960s, was by the early 1970s, outdated and conservative. A revolution called gay liberation was sweeping many parts of the world, fostering a radical new consciousness and unleashing a militancy not previously seen. The irony of CHAT and the other Canadian homophile groups formed in the early 1970s – based as they were on organizational models developed in the 1950s – is that they were seen from the outset as backward and embarrassing by the legions of young activists bursting onto the scene, influenced by developments in the United States. The gay liberation era had arrived. Homophilism no longer had relevance or value, and few mourned its passing.

THREE

Lesbian and Gay Liberation

As the 1970s began, there was a sense among activists and intellectuals that individuals working in mass movements could make a difference, that through such means the world could be made a better place. Amid this ferment, lesbian and gay liberation burst onto the scene. It rode the momentum created by a riot against police repression at the Stonewall Inn in New York City. Gays and lesbians everywhere, especially those in their early twenties (often university students), became politicized about their sexuality and the identity that derived from it. In the short period between 1970 and 1974, the new ideology blossomed on several fronts: breaking through isolation and loneliness; rejecting the notions of sin, sickness, and criminality that previously defined homosexuality; fighting against oppression, discrimination, and harassment; asserting pride in same-sex sexuality as good and natural; engaging in aggressive public advocacy for social and legislative reform; and building both a community and a culture based on a commonly shared sexuality. Visibility and organizing became the objectives through which liberation would be attained. 'Out of the Closets and into the Streets,' 'Gay is Just as Good as Straight,' and 'Better Blatant than Latent' were among the rallying cries. It was an amazing time of exuberance, optimism, astonishing innovation, and sometimes breath-taking courage – characterized by impatience and a willingness to confront all oppressors. Even gays, lesbians, and bisexuals of a less political bent were unavoidably affected, and began to move, if somewhat tentatively, from out of the darkness of earlier times, becoming more visible and assertive. Gay and lesbian groups sprang up across Canada like flowers in spring, promoting a radical new agenda and confronting mainstream mores and values. Identifiable communities formed in Canada's largest cities, centred on bars and clubs. In smaller centres, gays, lesbians, and bisexuals decided to take matters into their own hands, forming social clubs and phone lines, holding dances, and creating safe spaces for themselves. The first initiatives were launched at establishing and defining what could be called a gay and lesbian culture.

Setting a More Militant Course

Lesbian and gay organizations in the United States at this time were much more advanced than their fledgling counterparts in Canada. By 1969, they had acquired nearly twenty years of experience, and were confronted with the opportunity to strike out on a more militant course. More and more of them began holding public demonstrations protesting anti-homosexual criminal laws and discrimination based on sexual orientation. Mattachine made history in 1965 by holding the first gay demonstration at the White House. San Francisco's Committee for Homosexual Freedom, thought to be the first of the new gay liberation groups, was formed by young counterculture radicals in the spring of 1969 to protest the firing of a gay man from his job. The group represented a significant departure from its forerunners by using both 'homosexual' and 'freedom' in its name.[1] But it was on the East Coast that the lesbian and gay liberation movement was propelled into existence and into the consciousness of gays and lesbians around the world. A police raid on the Stonewall Inn, a gay bar in New York City, on the night of 27–28 June 1969 so angered the bar's patrons that they rioted, marking the first time the city's gays had fought back against police harassment. Within a few days, young, militant members of Mattachine organized community meetings. The result was the formation of a new group, the Gay Liberation Front (GLF), which, using a radical new rhetoric, stated one of its objectives as being to 'examine how we [gays] are oppressed and how we oppress ourselves.'[2] GLF's use of 'front,' a word borrowed from the National Liberation Front, the Vietcong group within Vietnam engaged in a war against the United States, was deliberate. Some of the founders of GLF also had close ties, or at least affinity, with the militant Black Panther Party, which worked for the liberation of oppressed and impoverished black Americans, and the left wing, antiwar group, Students for a Democratic Society. They saw themselves as a revolutionary front that would free gays, lesbians, and all oppressed peoples.

As Donn Teal relates in *The Gay Militants: How Gay Liberation Began in America, 1969–1971*, the early meetings of the New York GLF 'literally shook the walls,' were 'mind-bending,' raucous, and chaotic. Teal quotes one participant as saying, 'There was no agreement about methods or philosophy.' The group's members were deeply divided about whether it should be devoted to 'self-enlightenment' or 'integration immediately with other revolutionary or militant movements.' In Teal's words, 'The combination of the ingredients radicalism *and* homosexuality in GLF created problems unique to the organization.'[3] Splits and schisms resulted. While many GLF members were left-leaning or even revolutionaries, others were more moderate. The leftists generally had been involved in other radical movements for social change and wanted to cast GLF in that mould, believing it should ally itself with those other movements – the women's movement, the peace movement, and the Black civil rights movement in particular. Many of them saw gay liberation as a means of achieving political revolution. Others felt that GLF had to restrict itself to the particular needs and concerns of gays and lesbians. They put priority on ending discrimination and self-hatred, and on building a community and culture for gays and lesbians. Thus a debate was engaged that raged over subsequent decades, spreading to other groups and communities throughout the world. It consumes lesbian and gay activism even today: whether the movement should be concerned with addressing the oppression of all peoples (gays and lesbians, women, people of colour, the poor, and so on) or only the issues that affect gays, lesbians, and bisexuals, and whether the tactics deployed should be more in line with achieving liberation or equality.

Nonetheless, the events in New York City in 1969 had changed forever the nature of lesbian and gay aspirations and advocacy. Despite conflicts over the direction their new movement should take, the broad coalition that formed GLF, notes Teal, was unified on one level: 'The call of a liberation movement appealed, in summer 1969 as it still does, to a variety of young or young-minded American homosexuals whose sole common denominator was impatience. They had shed, or were shedding, all vestiges of homosexual shame, wanted to live in the light. They were ready for a confrontation with anybody who might challenge or even delay their right to do so.'[4] The power of their message was such that, throughout 1969 and 1970, Gay Liberation Front groups spread to several cities across the United States, articulating a sexual-identity radicalism not seen before. Unfortunately, these groups also proved to be unstructured, generally without direction and, as a result, short-lived. Most lasted little more than a year or two but left as their legacy a liberation analysis that helped to change the politics and consciousness of gays and lesbians throughout North America. This analysis held that homosexuality is a natural and normal alternative sexuality that must be liberated from oppression imposed by the church, state, and medical institutions, rigid gender-role socialization, and the supremacy of the nuclear family. It further held that the means to achieve liberation were militant public action, the rejection of shame and guilt, the assertion of visibility, and the espousal of sexual freedom. A flurry of American leaflets, position papers, articles, and manifestos attempted to give voice and definition to the new movement. Circulated widely on campuses and within urban neighbourhoods having significant numbers of gays, lesbians, and bisexuals, many were later published in a seminal 1972 anthology, *Out of the Closets: Voices of Gay Liberation*, edited by Karla Jay and Allen Young.

A number of the articles and polemics published in *Out of the Closets* rang with the radicalism of the times, and serve today as a remarkable record of the analyses of oppression and liberation that were the hallmarks of the new ideology. One such article, by the New York GLF's Martha Shelley, entitled 'Gay Is Good,' boldly celebrated the new militancy as 'springing up like warts all over the bland face of Amerika, causing shudders of indigestion in the delicately balanced bowels of the movement.'[5] Speaking to straight liberals, Shelley warned that gays wanted 'something more than the tolerance you never gave us.' As to the causes of gay oppression, Shelley proclaimed, 'We are the women and men who, from the time of our earliest memories, have been in revolt against the sex-role structure and nuclear family structure. The roles we have played among ourselves, the self-deceit, the compromises and the subterfuges – these never have totally obscured the fact we exist outside the traditional structure – and our existence threatens it.'[6]

In another article, 'Out of the Closets, Into the Streets,' Allen Young described gay liberation as a struggle against sexism. He asserted that because of sexism, anti-homosexualism permeates society, leading to the oppression of gays by the 'overtly male-supremacist, anti-homosexual institutions of our society: the legal system and the police, the church, the nuclear family, the mass media and the psychiatric establishment.'[7] Similarly, a caucus within GLF, the Gay Liberation Front Women, viewed gay liberation as revolutionary, proudly declaring in 'Lesbians and the Ultimate Liberation of Women' that 'Gay Liberation is a movement and a state of mind challenging history's basic legal and social assumptions about homosexuality. Openly proclaiming ourselves lesbians is a revolutionary act and a threat to the prevailing society, which excludes people who live outside the norm. We work for a common understanding among all people that lesbianism is the most complete and fulfilling relationship with another woman and a valid lifestyle.'[8]

Overcoming sexism and gender conditioning were essential, according to the 'The Woman-Identified Woman,' issued by New York City's Radicalesbians in 1970. Radicalesbians was one of the first groups to stress the importance of lesbians organizing themselves separately from both straight feminists and gay men. They asserted lesbian identity and consciousness that were militant responses to the marginalization and invisibility imposed on lesbians by both of these other groups. Speaking with the anger of the oppressed, Radicalesbians stated, 'A lesbian is the rage of all women condensed to the point of explosion.'[9] Noting that lesbianism plays a different role in social oppression than does male homosexuality, in that the accusation of lesbianism is used to oppress all women, Radicalesbians contended, 'Lesbian is the word, the label, the condition that holds women in line. When a woman hears this word tossed her way, she knows she is stepping out of line.'[10] Radicalesbians also articulated the view that by adopting the identity given to them by men, lesbians and all women engage in self-hatred and lack a sense of their real selves. They asserted that 'being "feminine" and being a whole person are irreconcilable,' that only women can give each other a new sense of self that is not developed in relation to men and arises out of a consciousness that is a 'revolutionary force.'[11] Radicalesbians made 'lesbian' into both a political statement and a sexual identity, by reclaiming a word that had acquired derogatory connotations. They believed doing so gave lesbians a visibility and a separateness that had not been theirs previously, in an empowering way that had enormous resonance, and which continues to resonate even today.

Allen Young and another gay liberation polemicist, Carl Wittman, championed sexual and social liberation as integral parts of gay liberation. Young concluded 'Out of the Closets and Into the Streets,' as follows: 'For gay people, the essential point is to see limited sexuality as an end result of male supremacy and sex roles. Gay, in its most far-reaching sense, means not homosexual, but sexually free. This includes a long-ranged vision of sensuality as a basis for sexual relationships. This sexual freedom is not some kind of groovy life style with lots of sex, doing what feels good irrespective of others. It is sexual freedom premised upon the notion of pleasure through equality, no pleasure where there is inequality.'[12]

Wittman addressed same-sex oppression in 'A Gay Manifesto,' lamenting the fact that gays lived in ghettos – areas of large cities with high concentrations of gay residents and bars. Gays, he argued, were 'refugees from Amerika' imprisoned in 'refugee camps' that bred self-hatred. Wittman emphasized the importance of understanding the different facets of gay oppression: physical attacks; police harassment; psychological warfare from a 'barrage of straight propaganda'; self-oppression, including the 'don't rock the boat' and 'things are OK as they are' attitudes of ghettoized gays; denial by gays that they are oppressed; institutional oppression; and acts of discrimination.[13] The pursuit of sexual freedom and the necessity of liberating gays and lesbians from oppression have remained important features of the lesbian and gay liberation ideology for more than three decades.

Gay Liberation Groups in Canada

Small numbers of Canadian lesbians, gays, and bisexuals, not too long after these developments in the United States, adopted the analysis and social-movement objectives of gay liberation. But for them, the Stonewall riot was something they learned about only after the fact, by reading U.S. books and periodicals. Its significance was not so much the event itself, as the movement and the literature it generated, and what it quickly came to symbolize. Such impact was seen first in Montreal, when *Mainmise*, an alternative publication that served as a forum for Quebec's counterculture movement, called in October 1970 for the establishment of a gay liberation group. A month later, Montreal's Front de libération homosexuel (FLH) was formed in response to police raids on and closure of gay bars after the Trudeau government invoked the War Measures Act. That act suspended civil liberties and gave police and the military broad powers normally exercised only in times of war. It was a brutal reaction to the kidnappings of a Quebec provincial cabinet minister and a British diplomat by the Front de libération du Québec (FLQ), a group that sought Quebec's independence from Canada. Montreal police, with a long history of harassment against gays and lesbians, used these conditions to carry out yet one more campaign against bars and clubs in that city. FLH functioned for about two years, its demise being precipitated in June 1972, after it opened a community centre and celebrated the occasion by holding a dance without obtaining a liquor permit. Forty people were charged in a police raid and, although the charges were later dropped, the centre and FLH folded within a few months.

GLF-style activism soon also appeared briefly in Vancouver and Toronto. The Vancouver Gay Liberation Front (GLF) resulted from weekly meetings at the Pink Cheeks commune, a left wing, counter-culture group, in the spring of 1971. Within weeks, GLF opened a drop-in centre and published at least one issue of a newsletter, *Brite Lite*.[14] Barry Adam, then a freshman at Simon Fraser University, attended some GLF meetings and vividly recalls that attempting to form a group like GLF during this era was 'a pretty scary thing.' Meetings took place behind drawn curtains with an expectation that the police would invade at any moment. GLFers were people who considered themselves on the edge, mainly radical students and hippies. But, notes Adam, 'It was very anarchic, really, as many GLFs I think were. It was more of an encounter group than it was a social movement. It was, I think, in a kind of a constant state of surprise and panic over its very existence much less entering out into the larger world. The most it got as far as visibility, I think, was through the *Georgia Straight*, which was the left alternative media of the day.'[15]

In Toronto, the University of Toronto Homophile Association (UTHA), influenced by the radicalism of groups in the United States, began shedding its homophile orientation, producing a leaflet, *GAY IS GOOD!*, that exhorted gays to take to the streets to fight against bigotry. The leaflet unapologetically asserted that 'same-sex relationships are a natural and important part of human sexuality, and ... should be accepted and affirmed rather than slandered through ignorance and rejected through fear.'[16] Other signs of the growing influence of gay liberation was the publication, in July 1971, of Wittman's 'A Gay Manifesto' in two issues of a Toronto counterculture magazine and the founding at about the same time of a new group, Toronto Gay Action (TGA). This group, which lasted until about the fall of 1972, demanded 'complete acceptance of our life style,' and identified the 'hierarchical, white-dominated, materialistic, violence oriented' social system as the reason that such acceptance would not be achieved unless there was fundamental social change. Among the changes it sought were rejection of the nuclear family, removal of 'restrictions on the sexual experimentation of young people,' and a de-emphasizing of 'role playing in social interaction.'[17]

The Rights Way to Liberation

Shortly after the birth of lesbian and gay liberation, it became clear that establishing organizations capable of galvanizing individuals into action under that banner would be extremely difficult. Consequently, following the demise of the GLF groups, a new model for organizing emerged and spread across North America. It focused on pursuing solely gay-issue activism, primarily advocacy for legislated civil rights, and was first advanced by the Gay Activist Alliance (GAA), started in New York City in December 1969. GAA described itself as a 'militant (though non-violent) homosexual civil rights organization.'[18] It claimed to be 'exclusively devoted to the liberation of homosexuals and avoids involvement in any program of action not obviously relevant to homosexuals.' A hybrid, GAA staked out the middle ground between the more conservative homophile groups and the revolutionary liberation fronts. It combined the liberation analysis and rhetoric of oppression with a strategy of attaining civil rights and an end to discrimination by the use of high-visibility tactics such as demonstrations, pickets and press conferences, as well as more traditional forms of lobbying.

GAA, and the groups that grew up throughout North America that were modelled on it, abandoned the commitment many GLFers had made to fighting all forms of oppression as a necessary element of attaining liberation for gays and lesbians. The new GAA-type groups did not actively seek alliances with other movements and did not give top priority to fighting sexism, racism, and other forms of oppression. Indeed, the new groups, focused as they were on gaining rights for gays and lesbians, argued the overriding need to fight homophobia and sexual orientation discrimination exclusively, because no others would do it. They also believed that the members of the other movements, in any event, frequently held and expressed the homophobic attitudes of the broader society. This positioning was particularly problematic, however, in not clearly recognizing the need to fight against the oppression experienced by many gays and lesbians because of race, gender, class, and culture, as well as because of their sexual orientation. These groups, like their predecessors in the 1960s, also were predominantly male and almost exclusively white. Lesbians, if present at all, were a distinct, although often influential, minority. Similarly, there were typically no aboriginal people or gays and lesbians of colour active in them.

Within a short time, GAA-like groups formed in a half-dozen Canadian cities. By the end of the seventies, they had transformed gay and lesbian advocacy, radicalizing it and, in the process, launching lesbian and gay liberation on a new and highly successful path. The new groups were invariably small and lacking the resources normally deployed by those seeking social and legislative change. Instead, they were propelled by the ideology, dedication, and innovation, as well as the impatience and anger, of their members. The first of these groups, Vancouver's Gay Alliance Toward Equality (GATE), was formed in May 1971. GATE's early members believed a liberation organization should encourage all gays and lesbians to become a part of the fight. They contended that the most effective tactic was to work out a set of demands for gay civil rights, and then engage in public actions to achieve them. *The Body Politic (TBP)*, established in Toronto in November 1971 as Canada's national gay liberation journal, took a similar approach, arguing in an early editorial that 'the most important tactic is building well organized and well publicized actions such as demonstrations, public meetings and debates, conferences, pickets at anti-gay media establishments, etc. etc. These actions will carry a clear message to our brothers and sisters in the closet – you are not alone, gay is good, gay is proud! – and which are aimed at social institutions which not only reflect the prevailing anti-homosexual attitudes of society at large, but also have the power to physically oppress us and perpetuate these attitudes.'[19]

For *TBP*, the success of lesbian and gay liberation also required winning the support of gays and lesbians as whole: 'As the gay liberation movement and organizations grow, the newly recruited activists, like ourselves, must maintain the perspective of eventually winning the support of the overwhelming majority of our fellow gays. We can have every confidence that they will eventually follow our path from the closet to the streets.'[20] Recognizing the need to involve the lesbian and gay community in the struggle, Nancy Walker, in the same issue of *TBP*, wrote: 'No one is going to hand us the gift of freedom on a plate. We have to work for it. When progress is made, it is because a large number of us have done what is necessary to achieve our ends. If you want to live a freer, more natural, more socially mobile life, you have to participate, you have to be politically aware and politically active. It must be the concern of every gay person to attain civil rights for all.'[21]

The early activists were acutely aware of the obstacles presented by the disparate networks of gays and lesbians that could not yet be described as a community. They themselves were few in numbers and socially isolated because of their visibility and beliefs. They had to fight against the hostility of other lesbians and gays while at the same time struggling against homophobia and heterosexism. Accustomed to living in the closet and surviving on the margins of society, most gay women and men shunned those who wanted to 'rock the boat' or 'attract attention to themselves.' Visibility and militancy, the majority feared, would generate a backlash that could threaten them and the few meeting places that they had been able to establish. Nonetheless, the handfuls of activists who formed groups across the country persevered. They believed there was sufficient understanding of human and civil rights among enough lesbians and gays to provide a basis for developing an agenda and organizing around it. Civil rights were simple to understand, even for those lesbians and gays having no use for demonstrations or other public actions. Heterosexual civil libertarians and progressive politicians also could appreciate the need to protect lesbians and gay men from discrimination, even if they did not approve of homosexuality.

These pioneering activists realized that, in Canada, the existence of provincial human rights legislation provided political and legal frameworks within which an agenda for social change could be promoted. Advocating that sexual orientation become a prohibited ground of discrimination in such laws was a strategy that could be embraced by gays and lesbians in large urban centres and in smaller communities alike. Consensus and coalitions could be built around the issue. Equally important, human rights advocacy was a focused strategy, but one that could be supported by both conservatives and militants. Conservatives (that is to say, assimilationists) tended to view the obtaining of legal rights as the primary objective. Militant liberationists viewed human rights campaigns as short-term, necessary in the longer-term struggle for liberation from the oppression of homophobia, but not the ultimate objective. The Gay Alliance Toward Equality (GATE) of Toronto articulated the militant, liberationist position in a leaflet circulated during this era. Asserting that 'Gay civil rights must be an immediate concern in the struggle for gay liberation,' GATE placed the pursuit of such rights in a broader context: 'Neither the abolition of antihomosexual laws nor the enactment of civil rights are ends in themselves. These are focal points around which gay people can build a movement which will eliminate sexual oppression and thereby contribute to the creation of a society free of all oppression.'[22]

While their differences in perspectives would later produce divisions and disagreements on many occasions, the liberationists asserted the leadership role in the new movement, and managed to forge a shaky alliance with conservatives that, in the years ahead, proved to be remarkably successful. The human rights strategy was attractive because it allowed the use of a variety of actions. Demonstrations, rallies, and press conferences could generate media coverage and increase visibility in a positive context. At the same time, more traditional efforts such as writing briefs, organizing letter-writing campaigns, and lobbying elected officials could be undertaken. Cases of discrimination could be publicized to present a human dimension and aid public education and consciousness-raising. The support of straight community groups, religious organizations, trade unions, and political parties could be enlisted. But perhaps most important of all, the human rights strategy was proactive. Lesbian and gay activists could set the agenda and carry it out, in contrast to reacting to the police, the state, the church, or other institutions.

Toronto Gay Action member Brian Waite, one of the first to articulate the need to pursue a human rights strategy as a means of moving toward liberation, argued in 1972 that 'Winning this demand [sexual orientation in the human rights code], in itself, will not end our oppression, but in the process of fighting for it many gay men and women will develop a higher level of pride and consciousness. With a victory, thousands more will find it easier to come out and begin the task of educating their fellow workers, neighbours, families and friends about the nature of homosexuality, without fear of losing a job or apartment, being harassed at school, or facing discrimination in innumerable other ways because we have no rights guaranteed by law.'[23]

'Homosexuality is a human right' was the slogan Waite developed to symbolize the strategy to be pursued. He was convinced human rights advocacy would politicize gays and lesbians, whether on the left or the right of the political spectrum, since 'having got someone involved at that level, the basic level of human rights, the whole experience of putting up posters, of discussing, of organizing demonstrations, is a tremendous and wonderful politicizing experience where people grow and change politically and become radical ... And also once you have a large demonstration, the feeling of power and strength and optimism certainly grows.'[24] Similarly, Denis LeBlanc, active in Gays of Ottawa throughout the seventies and beyond, has offered this explanation of the human rights strategy: 'The big thing was we wanted to get the word out. We wanted to get the word "gay" out there. We wanted people to see the word gay out there. It wasn't so much the issue that was important, it was the strategy. It was a strategy of getting visible, of letting our brothers and sisters know they were not alone.'[25]

Another important consideration was the belief that fighting for the inclusion of sexual orientation in human rights laws could promote long-term political unity among lesbians and gays. Unlike many other issues, developing the legal means to counteract discrimination was not focused entirely on the concerns or interests of gay men. While lesbians were active in promoting this strategy and worked on efforts to amend human rights and others laws, many others were sceptical of the benefits that would be derived merely from obtaining legal rights. Lesbians who had worked for women's organizations, in particular, knew from their experience in fighting for women's rights that amending laws had not achieved social or economic equality for women, and they doubted that much would change for lesbians and gays by similar achievements.

It was within the context of working for the attainment of human and civil rights in pursuance of liberation that activist groups, between 1970 and 1974, mounted the first campaigns to amend provincial laws. In doing so, they set out on a course of action that, over the next twenty-five years, ultimately saw all provincial human rights codes amended to prohibit discrimination on the basis of sexual orientation. But in the early 1970s, the suggestion that human rights laws should be amended to protect gays and lesbians from discrimination was a radical and controversial notion not popular with politicians or the media. Activists were repeatedly rebuffed, and outright rejection of the issue as unimportant was common. Gay and lesbian claims about widespread and systemic discrimination were dismissed or trivialized. Homophobic and heterosexist comments, uttered freely and publicly, justified continuing discrimination. The media generally ignored the question and most Canadians were unaware of it. The only effective tactics, therefore, were visibility, confrontation, and constant education.

It was within this social and political environment that Ontario activists began what would prove to be a fifteen-year campaign when, during the 1971 provincial election, they produced a leaflet urging lesbians and gays to vote for candidates supporting sexual equality legislation. They also generated publicity on the issue for the first time after two UTHA members questioned the Progressive Conservative attorney general Allen Lawrence at a public meeting about whether he would support a sexual orientation amendment. In a contemptuous response, he stated: 'A homosexual is a pervert and this perversion should not be legally recognized in any shape or form.'[26] Re-elected, the Conservatives introduced Human Rights Code amendments adding sex, age, and marital status to the prohibited grounds of discrimination. CHAT, TGA, and other groups responded with a letter-writing campaign and a brief to members of the legislature urging that sexual orientation also be included. In June 1972, about twenty-five lesbians and gay men demonstrated outside the legislature to protest the bill's omission of such an amendment.[27] After the demise of TGA, the strategy of maintaining high visibility, including frequent pickets and demonstrations, was continued with the formation of Toronto's Gay Alliance Toward Equality in 1973. GATE made the attainment of legislated human rights a strategic priority and the following year secured Toronto City Council's passage of a policy prohibiting sexual orientation discrimination in municipal employment, marking the first time that a legislative body in Canada had done so.[28]

Vancouver GATE also became a leader in human rights activism using a liberation analysis, following an influx of activists determined to give the group a more militant edge. GATE vigorously promoted the strategy of achieving liberation through attainment of human rights, proclaiming that gay people 'have the right to self-determination and control over their own lives.' Linking the struggle for human rights with gay liberation, GATE contended, 'Whenever equality is denied, Gay Liberation *can not go forward!*'[29] GATE became one of Canada's leading gay rights groups, staking out a position that influenced the movement nationally, which included abolition of the age of consent laws, self-determination for Quebec, choice on abortion, opposition to the Vietnam war and rejection of gay liaison with the police. It used pickets and other public actions and published a newspaper, *Gay Tide*, from 1973 to 1976, to get out its message.

During the 1972 provincial election in British Columbia, Vancouver GATE sent a questionnaire to all candidates on changes to a range of provincial legislation. Some support for amending the Human Rights Act was expressed by New Democratic Party candidates, but the right wing Social Credit party, then in power, was blatantly homophobic. One of that party's candidates, in response to a question at an all-candidates meeting, stated crudely, 'One day society will castrate the whole works of you [gays] to keep you from reproducing your own kind.'[30] Following the surprise election of the NDP, a more effective Human Rights Act was introduced, in which GATE lobbied vigorously for the inclusion of sexual orientation, without success. The labour minister stated omitting that term would avoid giving homosexuality 'legal sanction.' Instead, he argued that the *reasonable cause* provision, a unique feature of the act, would ensure that 'gays ought not to be discriminated against in any way.' Under that provision, discrimination against any person or class or class of persons without reasonable cause would be prohibited.[31] GATE took up the challenge by filing a human rights complaint in the fall of 1974, citing the reasonable cause provision after the *Vancouver Sun* refused a classified advertisement promoting GATE's newspaper, *Gay Tide*. The *Sun* claimed the ad was unacceptable because it might offend some of their readers. GATE's complaint became the basis for what would eventually become the first gay rights case to make it to the Supreme Court of Canada (see chapter 7).[32]

Lesbian and gay liberation activism was also taking root in other cities across the country. In Edmonton, a group led by Michael Roberts launched their Gay Alliance Toward Equality in the summer of 1971. Despite an extremely negative climate for gays and lesbians in Alberta, where the right wing Social Credit government had been replaced with a slightly more moderate Progressive Conservative one, Edmonton GATE conducted the first pioneering lobbying for human rights protection for gays and lesbians. In an October 1972 brief, Roberts called on the legislature to add sexual orientation to the provincial Bill of Rights and the Individual Rights Protection Act.[33] Saskatoon Gay Action, also formed in 1971, embarked, in February 1973, on securing human rights protection for gays and lesbians, when Doug (Gens) Hellquist and Bruce Garman met with the Saskatchewan Human Rights Commission, calling for an amendment to that province's Bill of Rights. Shortly thereafter, the commission became the first in Canada to call for the inclusion of sexual orientation in human rights legislation. SGA followed up with a brief to all members of the legislature in February 1974.[34]

Similarly, the Campus Gay Club at Winnipeg's University of Manitoba, born in February 1972 and renamed in 1973 as Gays For Equality (GFE), was particularly active on political issues.[35] GFE immediately launched a human rights act amendment campaign directed at the NDP government led by Premier Edward Schreyer. The government was publicly negative towards lesbian and gay rights and, in 1973, had refused to grant non-profit charitable status to a gay social club in Winnipeg. The attorney general defended the decision by saying, 'Such groups ought not to be clothed with the same rights and respectability as other groups.'[36] Nonetheless, GFE, in September 1974, presented the government with a brief calling for inclusion of sexual orientation in the Human Rights Act, and for research and educational programs to alleviate discriminatory practices. The government flatly rejected taking such action, arguing the public was not ready for gay rights legislation.[37] The following year, GFE held its first demonstration, in the town of Steinbach, after a printing house refused to print an educational booklet on homosexuality, which attracted national media coverage and a front page photograph in the *Winnipeg Free Press*.[38] In Ottawa, human rights and gay liberation activism were promoted by Gays of Ottawa (GO), founded in the fall of 1971.[39] It organized effectively against police harassment, held pickets to protest anti-gay immigration policies, and engaged in extensive lobbying to have sexual orientation included in the federal and provincial human rights codes.

On the East Coast, the Gay Alliance for Equality (GAE) in Halifax emerged as the sole focus for liberationist activism for most of the 1970s. Founded in 1972, GAE engaged in political activism and a range of other activities: a telephone counselling and information service, meetings and drop-ins, and a newsletter called *Gaezette*, which later grew into an important regional newspaper. In March 1973, GAE presented the first brief to the Nova Scotia legislature calling for the amendment of the human rights act to include sexual orientation. This initiative was followed later in the month by a meeting with the provincial human rights commission, which decided not to support GAE's amendment call, claiming there were not enough cases of discrimination against gays to warrant such action.[40] In the 1974 provincial election, GAE polled candidates on introducing an amendment and on homosexuality as a topic to be covered in sex education classes in the public schools.[41] After the election, GAE presented a second brief to the human rights commission, but little political headway was made on the subject for well over a decade. Briefly joining GAE as an activist group in Atlantic Canada was the short-lived Canadian Homophile Association of Newfoundland (CHAN), based in St John's. Formed in 1974, CHAN prepared a brief to the government urging a sexual orientation amendment, but because of the homophobic climate in Newfoundland at the time had it presented on their behalf by a supportive heterosexual.[42]

Organizing Nationally

The rapid emergence of activist groups in several cities meant that, by 1971, gays and lesbians across Canada began working to establish national organizations and strategies. The immediate result was the first lesbian and gay rights demonstration on Parliament Hill, on 28 August 1971. Under the name of the August 28th Gay Day Committee, twelve gay and lesbian groups across Canada set out a list of demands that formed their basic advocacy agenda for many years.[43] The committee presented a brief to Parliament calling for reform of the sexual offences sections of the Criminal Code, an end to housing and private-sector job discrimination, and the right of gays and lesbians to be employed and be eligible for promotion at all levels within the federal public sector. Among the latter demands were abolishing the bans on gays in the Royal Canadian Mounted Police and the Armed Forces.

Later, two National Gay Election Coalitions (NGEC) were formed, for the 1972 and 1974 federal elections, at the suggestion of Maurice Flood of Vancouver GATE. The first consisted of sixteen organizations in five provinces, and was co-ordinated by Toronto Gay Action.[44] It concentrated on raising issues with candidates for all political parties through a questionnaire and interventions at meetings and rallies. These interventions elicited a statement from Prime Minister Pierre Trudeau that further legal initiatives would have to await changes in public opinion. Conservative Leader Robert Stanfield rejected the entreaties outright: 'I just have to tell you frankly, very bluntly, that I want to leave the laws where they are.'[45] Another blunt response came from a Liberal candidate, later a senior cabinet minister, who told Saskatoon Gay Action at a public meeting he did not support removing the ban on gay and lesbian immigrants because most Canadians didn't want any more homosexuals, drug addicts, or prostitutes in the country.[46]

Nonetheless, encouraged by their success in raising the profile of lesbian and gay rights, activists reconstituted NGEC at a 1973 'quasi-national' conference. They accepted Toronto GATE's proposal for publishing a booklet detailing the relevant issues and distributing it to candidates in the next election. Tom Warner of GATE became the national coordinator.[47] The second NGEC, in the 1974 election, consisted of twenty groups. Two thousand copies of its booklet and questionnaire, in English and French, were distributed to candidates nationally. But getting candidates to take gay rights issues seriously proved daunting, and raising these issues at public meetings generated animosity. At one election meeting, a GATE Toronto member was thrown to the floor by a Liberal party functionary. A question on gay rights at another all-candidates meeting generated jeers from the audience and statements such as 'Get the queers out of here': anti-gay statements by candidates drew hearty cheers. In another incident, members of the University of Guelph Homophile Association, including activists Heather Ramsay, Jim Dougan, and Paul Shepherd, were met with hissing, jeering, and other forms of verbal abuse after picketing a Trudeau rally. One member of the audience, in reaction to a question on gay rights, shouted, 'Put them in jail.'[48]

Such reactions convinced NGEC activists of the need to continue their aggressive stance, otherwise their issues would be completely ignored. Accordingly, the national gay rights conference held in Winnipeg following the election agreed to launch a permanent national group dedicated to the public struggle for gay civil rights.[49] The other major event of 1974 that lead to national cooperation occurred after Canadian immigration officials turned away American gay activist John Kyper at the border because he had in his possession two U.S. gay rights publications.[50] Deported, Kyper immediately contacted Toronto GATE. It successfully brought Kyper across the border for interviews with Canadian media and called for a public statement by the immigration minister to repeal the Immigration Act's ban on gays. Groups in Edmonton, Saskatoon, and Ottawa added their support, issuing press releases and organizing letter-writing campaigns. Gays of Ottawa demonstrated at the offices of the Department of Immigration. In response, the government announced that a review of the act then underway would include a recommendation to remove the prohibition.[51] The new militancy had scored its is first significant victory.

Lesbian Visibility and the Rise of Separatism

In the late 1960s and early 1970s, as women developed analyses of their oppression and strategies for liberating themselves from it, the second wave of feminism emerged. In the United States, the first new feminist group, the National Organization for Women (NOW), founded in 1966, presented political lesbians with both a challenge and a dilemma. Many lesbians did not feel they needed to be involved in a movement of straight women seeking to free themselves from the oppression of heterosexuality. Other lesbians were attracted by the emphasis NOW and other women's groups placed on the wide range of opportunities and lifestyles that should be available to women. One of the groups captivated by the feminist movement was the Daughters of Bilitis, which proclaimed in its newsletter, *The Ladder*, in 1967, that lesbians had more in common with heterosexual women than gay men. Yet, the role and visibility of lesbians in the new women's organizations generated much debate and controversy. NOW, for one, did not want the involvement of open lesbians, viewing them as deviants and undesirables. Group leaders considered lesbians to be the 'lavender menace.' From 1969 to 1971, NOW staged a series of purges to drive lesbians out of the organization.[52]

Similarly, Canadian lesbians in the early 1970s generally struggled for a voice and visibility within feminist organizations. The first skirmishes took place in the Toronto Women's Liberation Movement (TWLM) and the Toronto New Feminists (TNF). In October 1970, TWLM sponsored the Indochinese Women's Liberation Conference, in respect of which planned lesbian workshops were cancelled at the last minute. The action embroiled the group in a divisive debate about 'the lesbian question.' The TNF leadership viewed lesbians as a negative influence and eventually asked them to leave, in response to their criticism that the group had anti-lesbian attitudes. On the West Coast, lesbians in the Vancouver Women's Caucus ran into traumatic conflict with heterosexual women when they began to openly identify.[53] Yet, despite such experiences, lesbians in the women's movement defiantly asserted their presence. A significant milestone occurred at the 1971 Indochinese Women's Conference, organized by Voice of Women activists in Vancouver and women from the United States. Among the five hundred women in attendance was a group of very visible, radical lesbians declaring that 'lesbianism is revolution.'[54] Gradually, as more and more lesbians came out of the closet, several women's collectives and organizations became places for them to meet and coalesce. In 1972, a gay women's drop-in was started at the Vancouver Women's Centre, and a lesbian resource centre began operating out of that city's A Woman's Place, carrying lesbian feminist materials and becoming a lesbian meeting place. Members of Edmonton Lesbian Feminists were instrumental in the same year in founding the Women's Centre, at which lesbian drop-ins became regular activities. Montreal Gay Women helped to found that city's Women's Centre in 1973.[55] Another turning point was the 1974 founding of a lesbian caucus in the British Columbia Federation of Women (BCFW). Impetus for the caucus emerged following a challenge made by a delegate at the BCFW's inaugural conference about why there was no policy on lesbians. A week later, about thirty lesbians formally launched the caucus and sought recognition from the BCFW, later becoming the influential Lesbian Rights Subcommittee.[56] Early feminist publications also provided space for expressing the burgeoning lesbian consciousness. *Velvet Fist*, the Toronto Women's Caucus newspaper, broke new ground between 1970 and 1972 by including lesbian content. *The Other Woman*, published in Toronto from May 1972 to January 1977, regularly contained articles on lesbian issues, and had a number of lesbians, such as Adrienne Potts and Pat Leslie, involved with its production. Subsequently, other feminist journals, like *Pedestal, Broadside, Fireweed, Kinesis,* and *Upstream* were all widely read by lesbians and devoted considerable coverage to lesbian concerns.[57]

Despite such positive developments, however, women's centres and organizations were frequently unhappy places for lesbians. Years later, many lesbian activists remained bitter, angry, and saddened by their experiences in such places. 'My most painful memories are from the women's centre in Ottawa,' Marie Robertson has recalled. Political lesbians stopped becoming involved in the centre because of the homophobia and heterosexism they encountered. Years later, she lamented, 'We weren't warmly welcomed at all ... When we were going to organize a women's march ... there I'd be saying, "OK, we need to have a banner saying, Custody Rights for Lesbian Mothers. We need to have a banner saying, Include Sexual Orientation in the Ontario Human Rights Code." And we'd get into these big debates with the straight women, saying, and with some lesbians, I might add, *sadly*, saying, "Oh, we can't do that. We can't do that because we'll turn off the housewives."'[58]

When Maureen Cullingham first started going to the Ottawa Women's Centre in the early 1970s she thought it was a lesbian centre, because of all of the lesbians she met there. Yet, the centre tried to project an image that de-emphasized their presence. An important contributor to the situation were media portrayals of how 'dykey' it was. To accommodate the concerns of straight women, lesbians tried not to put up too many lesbian posters, and 'acted heterosexual.'[59] Another lesbian having sorrowful memories is Erin Shoemaker, an out lesbian in Saskatoon's feminist movement during the early 1970s. As she has stated, 'Almost immediately, as soon as I started identifying as a lesbian the shit hit the fan. We started seeing all of the red baiting and the reactions on the part of the feminists for the lesbians and I just started floating away from those organizations, it was just too painful ... It's still often seen as a divisive thing to have lesbians be really public in feminist organizations and groups because it tars everybody, right?'[60] Ottawa lesbian activist Bea Baker also became involved in women's organizations, only to discover that 'a dyke in the [women's] movement worked secretly and carefully because lesbians weren't always welcome.'[61] Echoing these sentiments, Lynn Murphy, active in Halifax's Rape Relief at this time, has recalled how lesbians formed the core of most feminist groups. But as more and more of them began to come out of the closet, straight women became resentful, putting out the mixed message that 'lesbians were welcome but why did they have to be so pushy about it, you know. Why did they have to be so open about it?'[62]

Similarly, gay organizations – in which men were often predominant – were hostile or unwelcoming. Confrontations erupted between lesbians and gay men about power and organizational process. Lesbians became angry at the sexism and misogyny of gay men, and the reluctance of these men to deal with them. They encountered a profound disinterest on the part of gay men to take up issues important to lesbians, a preponderance of male sexuality and imagery, and organizational structures that kept them powerless. Many men persistently declined to develop an analysis of gender roles in society and the resultant power and privilege, or lack of them, that go with these roles. They adamantly refused to conduct self-education, to introduce nonhierarchic organizational structures, and to commit to feminist concerns. One of the most well-documented organizational conflicts between gay men and lesbians happened in late 1971, within CHAT. The relationship between CHAT men and women had been uneasy from the outset, but the culminating event was the adoption of the constitution. At the first of two meetings to approve one, Chris Fox read a statement on behalf of a group of women, called the Cunts, proposing an amendment that would have established equal representation for women and men at all decision-making levels in the organization. 'Sexism, not the amendment, is the issue,' proclaimed the amendment. It then went on to boldly assert,

The members of CHAT do not realize that understanding and smashing sexism are the means of destroying the oppression of 'queers.' Most people in CHAT dismiss sexism as a 'Woman's Problem.' This is sexism.

As lesbians we are oppressed both as cunts and as dykes. Until the gays of CHAT see the necessity of struggling against sexism, until the structure of

CHAT is revolutionized, then CHAT will reflect the status quo through legalization and acceptance. That is shuffling.[63]

After lengthy debates, described as 'acrimonious and vituperative,' the amendment was defeated, and many of the women walked out of CHAT in protest.[64] Sadly, similar incidents were repeated in mixed organizations around the country, with predictable outcomes. As Becki Ross has commented in *The House That Jill Built*, the CHAT constitutional episode, and other stories told by lesbians about the sexism they encountered in gay organizations, 'picked up steam and momentum as they reverberated across the country and resonated with the anger shared by increasing numbers of gay women and lesbian feminists.'[65]

Not surprisingly, negative experiences in both women's and gay organizations, plus a new politicization of lesbians and the emergence of lesbian feminist analysis, led to the rise of *lesbian separatism*. This was a school of lesbian feminist thought based on the idea of radical lesbianism first articulated in Radicalesbians' manifesto, 'The Woman-Identified Woman.' The concept gained momentum, particularly after American lesbian feminist writer and activist Rita Mae Brown fostered the need for an autonomous lesbian-feminist movement in a series of articles published in *The Furies* in 1972.[66] Radical lesbians argued the primary oppression is of women by men and it is this from which flows all other forms of oppression. By rejecting men and living independently, lesbians, they maintained, were in the vanguard of the social revolution that is women's liberation: lesbians are models for other women to emulate. They heralded themselves as 'proud Amazons,' challenging other women to come out of the closet and thereby free themselves from oppression. Lesbian separatism contemplated severing, or at least limiting to the unavoidable, contact and involvement with straight women and all men, including straight feminists and gay liberationists. They became proponents of the *lesbian nation* (a term popularized by Jill Johnston's 1973 book of the same title) in which, according to Ross, there was 'shared language, ideology, cultural capital (including symbols and aesthetics), and collective identity.' Lesbian feminists envisaged 'non-violent militancy, feminist utopia, and the power of women-only collective agency.'[67] In Canada, separatism remained, for the most part, a small, but very vocal, minority view among lesbians. It never really took root here, being dismissed by other lesbian activists and writers as being impractical and divisive, with the real prospect of alienating lesbians from their allies in the gay and women's movements. While there were proponents of separatism in Canada, the majority of lesbian activists argued for some form of collaboration with straight feminists and to a lesser extent with lesbian and gay liberationists.[68]

Autonomous Lesbian Organizing

But if lesbian separatism did not really take hold in Canada, lesbian autonomy did. Lesbian autonomy proceeded from recognizing the importance of building separate lesbian groups and spaces, but accepted the necessity of working with both straight feminists and gay men when the need arose. It was more in keeping with this outlook that the first lesbian organizations formed in the early 1970s, one of which was Edmonton's Cybelline House, a lesbian co-op with a separatist bent, that existed between 1969 and 1972. It had a resource centre and a phone line and was a place for potlucks and other events.[69] Vancouver's first exclusively lesbian organization, Gay Sisters, functioned briefly in 1971. Later, a collective on the west side became the precursor of organizations called Lavender Hill and Ringwood that were started by lesbian feminists and briefly existed in that city.[70] Also short-lived was the Winnipeg Lesbian Society, formed in the early 1970s, that lasted for only for a couple of years. After that, women's groups were founded that were in reality lesbian organizations that did not use that word in their names. The first of these was a lesbian resource centre operated by A Woman's Place, in conjunction with Winnipeg Women's Liberation, starting in 1973.[71] The objective of establishing separate spaces for lesbians and an agenda for lesbian action motivated lesbians in the Toronto Women's Liberation Movement to hold 'lesbian rap groups' in early 1971.[72] In 1972, The Woman's Place began holding weekly lesbian drop-ins, featuring music and supportive discussions, for about a year. One outcome of this work was Canada's first lesbian conference, held at the Toronto YWCA in 1973. Then, in 1974, a group composed predominantly of lesbians set up a collective, the Amazon Workshop, which, in turn, helped spawn Women's Self-Defense, Amazon Press, and what would later become the Toronto Women's Bookstore.

Lesbians in Montreal's Gay McGill began meeting separately in the homes of members during the early months of 1973. They progressed to holding social events to attract women not involved with Gay McGill. Within a short time, the meetings were moved to A Woman's Place, which had been opened in downtown Montreal by lesbians and heterosexual feminists. Eventually, the group split from Gay McGill, calling itself Montreal Gay Women.[73] Tensions between gay and straight women in A Women's Place led Montreal Gay Women, in March 1974, to find meeting space elsewhere. A couple of months later, they moved into office space operated by the Gay Montreal Association. They used the space for popular lesbian social evenings. A newsletter and bulletins were published in both English and French, and some attempts at providing translation at meetings were undertaken, in response to the increased number of francophones becoming involved with the group. By the end of the year, Montreal Gay Women had changed its name to Labyris. A few months after its founding, some members of Montreal Gay Women began publishing *Long Time Coming*, the first regularly produced publication exclusively for lesbians in Canada. *Long Time Coming* found a receptive readership that stretched across North America. But, in testament to the times, none of the women involved allowed her real name to be published. In all, *Long Time Coming* produced approximately twenty issues from June 1973 until it folded in 1976.[74]

It is striking, to say the least, to note the dramatic differences in the objectives of these first autonomous lesbian groups from those of groups that were exclusively or predominantly made up of gay men. The lesbian groups gave little or no priority to organizing for legislative changes, such as the amendment of human rights laws. The emergence of these autonomous groups was a reaction to overcoming the much greater difficulties that lesbians faced in coming out of the closet. They took a proactive approach to either creating meeting places where none had existed up to that point, or providing safe, comfortable alternatives to the few venues for lesbians that did exist, where they could safely and comfortably be themselves. The priority for the new lesbian groups was on creating spaces free of the sexism and preoccupations of men, and the homophobia of straight women.

Child Custody and Lesbian Parenting

Child custody rights for lesbian mothers and gay fathers first began to emerge as both a political and legal issue in the early 1970s. Coming out publicly as gay or lesbian and then contesting the custody of children in those circumstances was an extremely risky and traumatic experience. The social climate was hostile to parents who were homosexuals; they were seen as subjecting children to a perverted and unnatural lifestyle.

There was also fear that the children might be damaged or be influenced into becoming gays or lesbians themselves. Writing in 1974, on the subject of statements from feminist women that she was denying her daughter free choice and was 'indoctrinating her into a Lesbian lifestyle,' a lesbian mother named Jeanne said, 'Look at the world around you. How many ads, stories, TV shows do you see that acknowledge the existence of Lesbianism? My kid lives in that world too. The only place in her life that she sees anything to do with Lesbianism, with women loving women, is in her home.'[75] Seeking legal custody of children was equally difficult. In 1972 the first known Canadian case occurred in which a lesbian's sexual orientation was used against her successfully in a divorce proceeding.[76]

The first reported case of an openly lesbian mother attempting to gain custody of her children, *Case v. Case*, was determined in Saskatoon in 1974. Following the divorce from her husband, Darlene Case was initially granted custody of the children but the father went to court to obtain custody on the basis that, being a lesbian, she was an unfit mother. The father then illegally seized the two oldest children and was allowed to keep them pending the outcome of the court case. Darlene Case fought back – supported by Saskatoon Gay Action, which set up a defence fund for her – arguing that being lesbian was irrelevant. Unfortunately, the judge's decision was contradictory in its opinion about the effects of the mother's sexual orientation on the children. While he stated that homosexuality was not a bar to custody, he concluded 'I greatly fear that if these children are raised by the mother they will be too much in contact with people of abnormal tastes and proclivities.'[77] He negatively cited the mother's overt homosexuality, her same-sex lover, her attendance at homosexual clubs and participation in the gay movement, and the fact she invited homosexuals to her home. Lamentably, the reasoning of the judge, that homosexuality was acceptable only if it was kept in the closet and out of sight of the children, would be repeated in other custody cases over the next two decades.

Celebrating Pride, Building Visible Communities

Pride in same-sex sexuality, a fundamental tenet of lesbian and gay liberation, predicated on the assertion that gay is good, and should be celebrated, was first promoted in the early 1970s, as a visible and militant way of rejecting the dominant social attitudes. Pride events originated in large U.S. cities at the end of June each year to commemorate Stonewall. By the mid-1970s, they were attracting tens of thousands of people. In Canada, however, the establishment of lesbian and gay pride events was more modest. The celebrations also were originally held in August, to mark the anniversaries of both the 1969 Criminal Code amendments and the first gay demonstration on Parliament Hill in 1971, later changing to the virtually universal commemoration of the Stonewall anniversary. Canada's first gay pride celebration, held in Toronto from 19–28 August 1972, featured community events and a picnic at the gay section of Hanlan's Point on the Toronto Island. By the next year, gay pride celebrations had spread to seven other cities across the country, with Vancouver and Toronto coordinating their gay pride marches to occur at the same time. Winnipeg's events focused on a symposium on homosexuality held in October.[78]

With the new consciousness and the celebration of pride in same-sex orientation came prolific community building. From the early 1970s onwards, the lesbian and gay communities across Canada witnessed incredible growth, especially outside the largest cities of Montreal, Toronto, and Vancouver. Gay membership clubs and community service organizations formed in several cities, providing dances or bars and social activities. Other groups offered phone lines to assist with coming out of the closet, published newsletters, conducted public education, and engaged in political advocacy. Starting such groups required great courage and perseverance. It was, after all, very risky, especially in smaller communities, to be known publicly as gay or lesbian. In most cities, identifiable communities simply did not exist beyond one or two sleazy bars or a cocktail lounge where gays and lesbians might discreetly gather. Typically, one or two, or at most a very small cluster of people, often politicized by lesbian and gay liberation and determined to fight against homophobia and heterosexism, used ingenuity and few resources to make significant strides forward. Among the innovative approaches seen in Canadian cities were the first registered, not-for-profit organizations with exclusively gay and lesbian members – a progressive idea for the times. The first two, Carousel Club in Calgary and Club 70 in Edmonton, both founded in 1970, achieved great success and popularity.[79] The pattern of community development in other cities was very similar. Atropos in Regina, founded in January 1972, undertook similar activities. It ran weekly dances as the Odyssey Club and a phone line. The homophobic climate of the time meant, however, that Atropos had to maintain the pretext of using the house in which the club was located as a dwelling, and entrance into the functions was by an unmarked backdoor.[80] A not-for-profit social club, Happenings, was founded in 1971 by the Mutual Friendship Society in Winnipeg to run dances and other activities in response to the lack of commercial establishments where gays and lesbians could feel welcome. It has functioned ever since, providing a location for a bar and dancing.[81]

The legacy of the social clubs was significant. They remained, for several years, the sole tangible evidence of the arrival of lesbian and gay liberation, and the resultant breaking down of isolation, fear, and guilt. Run initially by volunteers, they often reached the point of hiring staff for their events. Typically the only gay-operated social spaces in their cities, their clienteles reflected the diversity of the queer communities: youth, drag queens, the leather crowd, butch dykes, older gays and lesbians, couples, working class people, and professionals. However, lesbians and gays of colour, and Two-Spirited peoples generally were either not present in any significant numbers or completely absent. In time, the ongoing existence of the clubs became more precarious, with frequent financial crises and shortages of volunteer labour. Sadly, some collapsed under the strain of operating on a volunteer, not-for-profit basis in the face of increasingly stiff competition from other ventures. Ironically, they became victims of their own success in creating a viable social environment that could be tapped for commercial benefit. By providing evidence of a gay and lesbian market, they laid the bases for the rise of a gay business sector, even as they struggled to provide music, decor, or ambience that could not compete with the new, for-profit places they helped to spawn.

More politically inclined organizations also attempted to provide social services and social events, endeavouring to delicately balance those activities with political advocacy. Many of their efforts created public awareness and visibility for the first time, bringing gay and lesbian concerns to the media, legislators, police forces, and mainstream community health and social service agencies. They provided news and information for gays, lesbians, and bisexuals, helped with the coming-out process, and created alternative meeting places. They were critical to the development of a sense of positive identity that nurtured the growth of the more visible gay and lesbian communities that we see today. For a few amazing years, they cropped up everywhere, trying to do everything to meet the urgent needs of their communities. In Edmonton, GATE operated a phone line, held dances and drop-ins, ran a library, and hosted other events. Calgary's People's Liberation started out in 1973 on the campus of the University of Calgary, at the initiative of a small band of volunteers. By securing an office in the YMCA building and holding drop-ins, it established a safe meeting environment. It also ran a phone line and offered peer counselling.[82] About the same time, Saskatoon Gay Liberation put together a nucleus of people to form a broadly based community group, the Zodiac Friendship Society, founded in January 1972. A month later, the society held the first gay dance in Saskatoon, attended by fifty men and women. A year later, it opened a community centre offering counselling, a phone line, drop-ins, dances, and political action meetings.[83] Erin Shoemaker, active in the Saskatoon Community Centre, as it later became known, remembers it as a safe, positive meeting place, the biggest success of which was simply bringing people together: 'When you have been hiding out in small towns and so on believing that you are the only one in the world, just simply discovering other people, in spite of the differences, is the unifying factor.'[84]

The establishment of community groups with broad mandates similarly improved the social climates in several other cities. In London, the University of Western Ontario Homophile Association, founded in early 1971, began holding dances at university locations, creating a positive environment for local people to attend gay events away from the downtown area of the city. The group was reconstituted in 1974 as a broadly based community organization, and incorporated as the Homophile Association of London Ontario. In Ottawa, Gays of Ottawa, founded in September 1971, was a broad, multipurpose, community-based group. Initially operating out of a church basement, it moved, in the fall of 1972, to office space in Pestalozzi College, an alternative postsecondary institution functioning as a co-operative that was a product of the 1960s' counterculture. Shortly afterwards, GO held Ottawa's first gay dance, starting a community institution that would continue for over two decades. Other activities included a phone line, counselling, public education, outreach to social agencies, and a newsletter that soon became a respected newspaper, *GO Info*.[85] University campuses provided the organizing grounds for several other communites at this time, including Kitchener-Waterloo, Guelph, Hamilton, Kingston, and Windsor. In nearly all cases, the impetus was the need to create meeting places and social events, with other activities such as phone lines, newsletters, and occasional advocacy being added on. The University of Waterloo, in particular, was an important focal point for the emerging lesbian and gay rights movement. Left wing student politics were dominant, creating an environment that brought people together to work for social change. From such ferment sprang the Waterloo Universities' Gay Liberation Movement in February 1971. It drew members from both the University of Waterloo and Waterloo Lutheran University (later Wilfrid Laurier University). Activities included publishing a newsletter and holding public forums, pub nights, discussion groups, film nights, and private parties. Later, it organized regular dances to provide a social climate in the Kitchener, Waterloo, and Cambridge areas.[86] The University of Guelph Homophile Association was started in February 1971, after about fifty people attended the first meeting.[87] Another campus group, the Hamilton-McMaster Gay Liberation Movement, started up in January 1973 and was active until 1977. Within weeks, it was holding dances, conducting advertising, organizing lectures, establishing a library, and publishing a newsletter. A grant from the university student union enabled it to launch Gay Line in 1974 as a lifeline for information and coming out.[88] Similarly, Queen's University began the critical role for the gay and lesbian communities in Kingston that it has played for nearly three decades. The university's first group, Queen's Homophile Association, formed there in October 1973. It provided a meeting place for gays beyond the 'sleazy semi-gay bar and the local park.' It immediately organized meetings, parties, and dances and set up an information phone line.[89]

Activists at a left wing labour centre started the University of Windsor Homophile Association in 1971. Shortly thereafter, the group was renamed Windsor Gay Unity, and began to attract members from the broader gay community to drop-ins, meetings, dances, and social gatherings, and through its phone line. Fragile from the beginning, Gay Unity held dances for awhile that, although they often did not make much money, helped to foster a sense of community. Harold B. Desmarais, who helped organize the dances, remembers they were 'wonderful' and 'safe':

> Several people did come up to me and tell me that they had a wonderful time and they didn't think they could ever, ever feel as safe – I think safety was the prime thing – that they were very concerned, that they had gone around the block a dozen times before they decided to come in, they were afraid people were going to break into the dance and beat up everyone. The level of fear back then was quite tangible. I mean you could almost cut it with a knife, and they were times when you certainly couldn't say people were paranoid because fag bashing was quite a sport. And, the danger was very real. But it was surprising that we had very few confrontations in our public manifestations of community.[90]

Gay Unity died and was revived several times before it collapsed for good in 1982. Equally sporadic were the efforts at community organizing in other smaller cities at this time, as groups were more tenuous in taking root. The first group in British Columbia to crop up outside Vancouver appeared in 1974, in Victoria. It began when Randy Notte distributed a leaflet addressing the difficulty of living in that city because of the loneliness and isolation caused by having no gay bars or clubs. Notte's efforts led to the establishment, briefly, of the Gay People's Alliance. Unfortunately, the group collapsed shortly after Notte moved to Toronto.[91] In Northern Ontario, in 1972 or 1973, the Gay Alliance of Sudbury appeared through the efforts of a small group of gay men who knew each other socially. Located above a confectionery, the group's venue was open on Friday and Saturday nights as a private membership club. Unfortunately, it never caught on with the local community, especially lesbians and younger gays, and died out after a short time.[92] Thunder Bay's first group, Lakehead Gay Liberation, started in 1974. A core group of about a half-dozen, including coordinator David Belrose, attempted to keep the group going but it died out after six months. It was replaced with the Backstreet Athletic Club, a private-member social group.[93] The only Quebec group outside of the Montreal area at this time was the Centre humanitaire d'aide et de libération (CHAL). Initially proposed in 1972 as a social service centre for gays, it eventually opened its doors in May 1973. Gradually, however, CHAL became less and less identified as a gay and lesbian organization. By early 1974, it established the Service d'accueil, d'information et de référence du CHAL Inc. to provide counselling and referrals, an organization that became independent of CHAL a year later.[94]

In New Brunswick, Gay Friends of Fredericton formed in 1974. Primarily intended as a way for gays in the city to meet one another, it also waged letter-writing campaigns on lesbian and gay rights issues and distributed educational information. By early 1975, however, it had only three active members and by August of that year had vanished.[95] In Moncton, the University of Moncton fostered a climate in which young francophone gays and lesbians could be open about their sexual orientation. According to Noella Richard, who came out as a lesbian in 1972 or 1973 while a student there, the campus had an identifiable gay and lesbian community whose members hung out together and 'were on the radical fringe on campus.'[96] Gays and lesbians were out and active in University of Moncton student associations and councils. One year, in fact, the entire student council in the arts faculty was gay men and lesbians. They also occupied about one-third of the campus pub – a situation that was understood and accepted by the heterosexual students, who wanted to attend gay and lesbian parties 'because it was cool.' Still, this liberal environment did not lead to the formation of a gay and lesbian group, and living an out life off-campus was risky.[97] Meanwhile, St John's first gay group, the Canadian Homophile Association of Newfoundland (CHAN), undertook both political and social activities. John Cashin, who first heard about CHAN shortly after coming out in 1974, recollects that by then it was quite active, with about forty people attending weekly meetings. There was no gay bar in St John's at the time, so the group provided a much-needed social milieu. CHAN had a regular newsletter and ran a phone line from a spare room in the house in which Cashin lived.[98]

Community building also took place in larger cities, although a variety of commercial establishments serving gays and lesbians could be found in them as well. Activists promoting a lesbian and gay liberation perspective believed such places essentially contributed to the oppression of queers. The emerging communities, they argued, should offer alternatives that were more positive. Bars and other establishments in these cities, and their environs, became, in the vernacular of lesbian and gay liberation, 'ghettos.' Carl Wittman summed up activist sentiments in his 'Gay Manifesto,' when he stated such ghettos breed exploitation and self-hatred. In the ghettos, he wrote, gays 'stagnate' by 'accepting the status quo,' and 'the status quo is rotten.'[99] The anti-ghetto theme also was taken up in the pages of *The Body Politic*. Its first issue reprinted an article highly critical of Vancouver's bars and clubs, accusing them of ripping off and exploiting their gay patrons. Writing about 'seven gay ghetto centres' that existed in the city at the time, John Forbes commented that their owners were 'vultures who get pig fattened from the money of people who believe there is no alternative.' The second issue condemned Toronto businesses that 'surround us with cheap and tacky furniture, cheap and tacky wallpaper, in other words, a cheap and tacky environment,' while getting rich from it and asserting, 'You're lucky you have someplace to go.'[100]

Efforts to create a liberated alternative to these ghettos came to fruition, for a short time in 1972, when CHAT was offered free use of an old building by land developers, turning it into Toronto's first gay community centre. The dream, according to George Hislop, was for it to be 'a place run by gay people for gay people ... where gay community is a reality.' It initially housed a library, a bookshop, and an office for *The Body Politic*, until the latter two moved to separate quarters.[101] CHAT operated its centre out of various locations over the next five years before shutting down in 1977. Even more clearly political groups like Toronto GATE ran community dances as ghetto-alternatives for several years. Similarly in Montreal, the desire for these alternatives led Gay Montreal to organize dances, which quickly grew to over two thousand people, almost all men, on a regular basis.

Other liberation-focused initiatives at this time helped to create what would later become important community institutions or moved gay liberation consciousness into new social frontiers. The first gay-owned stores selling books and periodicals positively asserting gay and lesbian sexuality appeared, refuting the old notions of sin, sickness, and criminality, and celebrating lesbian and gay liberation as a movement for social change. Jearld Moldenhauer began in 1971 to sell gay liberation books at community events, giving birth to Glad Day Bookshop. By 1972, he had opened his first store. Androgyny Books in Montreal established itself the following year at the initiative of members of Gay McGill, most notably Will Atkin, Bruce Garside, and John Southin.[102] The first attempts at opening the doors of academia to out-of-the-closet gay and lesbian professors and students, and at establishing gay studies programs, also were made in the early 1970s. In November 1974, a Canada-wide chapter of the U.S.-based Gay Academic Union (GAU) was formed by faculty in Toronto and Halifax. GAU Toronto was started a year later by a small group of professors wanting to maintain a visible gay presence in the university community, including by offering gay studies programs and improving the collections of gay materials in libraries. Other GAU groups were started in Saskatoon and Calgary by the mid-1970s.[103]

The formation of sports and recreation groups for gays and lesbians, and those providing safe, affirming environments for liberated lifestyles, added to the increasingly more numerous options available in larger cities. Toronto's Judy Garland Memorial Bowling League was founded in 1972, joined shortly afterwards by the Toronto Historical Bowling League. Toronto's Spearhead, a leather and denim club for gay men, was launched in 1970. A second Toronto group, Lanyards, formed in 1974. Two leather/denim clubs, Border Riders and Zodiac M.C. (Motor Club) appeared in Vancouver in 1971, and Iron Cross M.C. was constituted in Montreal in 1972.[104] Toronto's new, more upscale nightclubs provided venues for showcasing drag performers. One of Canada's most famous female impersonators, Craig Russell, started performing in Toronto gay clubs in 1970, eventually gaining a huge following in that city and across North America. A drag troupe, the Great Impostors, starring Rusty Ryan, was founded in 1972.[105]

Outside of the bars, a system or network of drag 'courts' began to spread across North America. Starting originally in San Francisco, the court system was exported to other cities. The courts began holding spectacular drag balls, each of which elected an 'Emperor' and an 'Empress,' regularly raising large amounts of money for community and charitable causes. The first Canadian drag court had its origins with a huge drag ball in 1971. This eventually led to the establishment of Vancouver's Dogwood Monarchist Society and Imperial Dogwood Court. The Dogwood Monarchist Society, unlike most other groups at this time, was additionally noteworthy because it had Aboriginal men in it. Drag queens, while controversial, were among the first to break down racial and other barriers within gay male communities. In the 1970s, Black drag queens were practically the only Black men to be seen in Toronto's gay bars.[106]

Lesbian and gay Christians were another large segment of the community that began organizing in separate groups and communities at this time. The first was Toronto's Unitarian Universalist Gays, founded in 1971. Then, two years later, the Metropolitan Community Church was launched in Montreal and Toronto, spreading out soon thereafter to Ottawa, Winnipeg, Calgary, Edmonton, and Vancouver. Born in Los Angeles under the leadership of Troy Perry, the Metropolitan Community Church, while not describing itself as a gay church, had clergy and members who were gay or lesbian.[107] At about the same time, Dignity, a group for gay Catholics, and Integrity, for gay Anglicans, formed, first in Toronto and then other cities. Gay and lesbian Jewish groups also began to form in the early the 1970s, marked by the formation of a gay synagogue in Montreal in 1974.

Lesbian and gay liberation consciousness also significantly influenced the development of lesbian and gay arts and culture in the years between 1970 and 1974. Catalyst Press was now at its peak, publishing Graham Jackson's book of short fiction, *The Apothecary Jar*, in 1972, and Ian Young's *Lions in the Stream* and *Some Green Moths* in 1971 and 1972, respectively. In 1973, Young gained international recognition with the publication of *The Male Muse: A Gay Anthology*. It was the first contemporary anthology of English language poetry having gay male themes.[108] Vancouver's Talonbooks published David Watmough's *Ashes For Easter and Other Monodramas* in 1973 and Scott Watson's book of short fiction, *Stories*, in 1974. In Montreal, Nicole Brossard, a francophone lesbian who has since published many novels, had her first, *Un Livre*, printed in 1970, followed by *French Kiss* in 1974.[109]

Books dealing with the emerging lesbian and gay community and the movement for lesbian and gay rights also began to appear. The first was *A Not So Gay World: Homosexuality in Canada* (1971), by Marion Foster and Kent Murray – both pseudonyms. It was the first non-fiction, non-medical book on the subject of gays and lesbians in this country. Criticized by liberation activists of the day as being closeted and out of date, the book, which was based on interviews across the country, has since become a valuable history of the way things were in most of the country in the late 1960s and early 1970s. The first Canadian book indicating a gay liberation perspective, Jean Le Derff's *Homosexuel? Et pourquoi pas!* was published in 1973. A year later, his theoretical analysis of gay liberation, *Homolibre*, was released.[110]

In theatre, Toronto's Global Village was the location of a 1974 performance of *Tubstrip*, a play set in a gay bathhouse. It also was the site of a performance, in English, of Michel Tremblay's *Hosanna*. The play had premiered in Montreal in May 1973, and was a milestone in the history of gay theatre. By exploring the relationship of a drag queen hairdresser and his biker lover-husband, *Hosanna* was embraced as the first Canadian drama dealing in any significant way with a same-sex spousal relationship.[111] But less progress was made in other cultural pursuits. Ottawa area artist Evergon was practically the only visual artist dealing with gay themes in the early 1970s. He used photography to produce erotic or sexual imagery of men in a manner one reviewer described as provoking 'thought about the politics of sexuality, and of the treatment of sexuality in art.'[112]

A Movement Firmly Launched

Lesbian and gay liberation did not emerge from a vacuum. It evolved from a history of oppression, characterized by the church's religious and moral teachings, and from the state and society criminalizing, pathologizing and ostracizing gays, lesbians, and bisexuals. In many instances, the roots of the oppression, and the seeds of the movement for liberation from it, were planted centuries ago; in others, the seeds of liberation were sown more recently, having been nurtured only within the last few decades. The recent concepts of identity and community based on a common sexuality, and of an advocacy agenda for broad social and legislative change, are rooted in the experiences of the past:

discrimination, harassment, marginalization, isolation. These concepts built upon the tentative, but nonetheless identifiable, consciousness of gays, lesbians, and bisexuals that began to emerge following the Second World War, and on the networks, often underground and secretive, that predate today's more visible communities.

By 1969, the ground was prepared for the rise of a revolution called lesbian and gay liberation – and for the emergence of the counter-revolution of socially conservative, family values advocacy. Sexual acts between members of the same sex, in certain circumstances, were no longer illegal, and attitudes towards sexuality in general were changing. Identifiable queer communities and a culture associated with them were starting to establish themselves, even while heterosexism and homophobia remained as pervasive as ever. The five short years from 1970 to 1974, in particular, stand out as a golden age of activism. The first concerted organizing in the liberationist mode, as well as the initial attempts at forging national networks, marked these years. Visibility, the creation of social infrastructures, and the promotion of an advocacy agenda were firmly established. Breaking down the isolation and vulnerability of individuals, creating safe spaces, assisting in the process of coming out, and reaching out to gays and lesbians everywhere became entrenched as organizing imperatives, manifested through phone lines, drop-ins, dances, public actions, and the first publications with a liberationist outlook.

By the end of 1974, the foundation for political and social activism was firmly laid, enabling the efforts of the next several years to concentrate on discrimination in employment and housing, breaking down loneliness and isolation, and dispelling notions of sin, sickness, and deviance. An analytical context for organizing around these issues in a systematic manner had been developed. All was new and untested, especially the infant strategy of pursuing liberation by obtaining, in the short term, civil and human rights. There was great optimism regarding what small groups of committed lesbian and gay liberationists scattered about the country would be able to do to create broad social change – a revolution in which liberated sexuality would play a leading role. Activists took encouragement from the federal government's response to the public actions that challenged the Immigration Act's ban on gays and lesbians. They celebrated the visibility achieved by their interventions in federal and provincial elections, raising, for the first time, public awareness about the need for greater law reform.

The forces of bigotry and backlash had not yet risen to become vocal agents of counter-revolution. The agents of the state, while remaining largely hostile, or at best indifferent, were not particularly prepared to take repressive action. Within the lesbian and gay liberation movement, hopes for unified, coordinated action were high. Unforeseen were the trials and tribulations, the settling in of backlash, the advent of intensified state repression, and the devastation of an unprecedented health crisis that lay ahead – phenomena which would, in short order, consume the efforts of activists everywhere. Also not significant at this time were division and dissent over the focus of the new movement, and the tactics it should use to achieve its goals – indeed, over what the goals should be: liberation or equality, revolution or integration.

PART TWO

Progress amid Backlash, Dissent, and Crises, 1975–1984

FOUR

Police Repression and Judicial Homophobia

The advent of lesbian and gay liberation, as we have seen, had an enormous impact on queer communities and consciousness by the mid-1970s. But progress towards changing the dominant social attitudes was slow. The police and the judicial system remained deeply homophobic, and the courts were replete with heterosexism. A decade after the amendments to the Criminal Code, the attitudes of the judiciary and the police had changed little from those of earlier decades. One legislative change by itself could not have been expected to magically alter centuries of ingrained opinion and prejudice. Accordingly, renewed police repression, beginning in the late 1970s, presented lesbian and gay liberation activists with threats to which they needed to respond, massively and militantly.

Unabated Homophobia in the Judiciary and the Police

Police and judges, like all of us, grow up in and are socialized by a homophobic society. Charged with the duty to serve and protect that society, they have embraced and upheld its dominant, conservative social values. Judges, in addition, hold a privileged position, forming part of the elite. For the most part – certainly well after 1969 – they seldom if ever came into contact with homosexuals other than through adjudication of criminal cases. As Bruce MacDougall states in his exhaustive study of over eight hundred court cases between 1960 and 1997, *Queer Judgements: Homosexuality, Expression and the Courts in Canada*, 'there has been a remarkable persistence of general judicial attitudes toward homosexuality' over that period. 'In the judicial context,' he notes, 'the persistence of prejudice plays out in part as a judicial distancing of itself from homosexuality. Homosexuality is "other" and something that has always been judged.'[1] In addition, the judiciary historically has displayed irrational fears about homosexuals and homosexuality, and, MacDougall argues, 'the concern about the spread of homosexuality is particularly strong in cases where the homosexual person could expose children to homosexuality.' Amplifying on that view in the context of the 'censoriousness and censorship' of homosexuality, of gays, lesbians, and bisexuals, and of expression by and about them, MacDougall expounds, 'Despite their frequent assumption that homosexuality is unnatural and perverse, the courts at times also assume that it is contagious and must be controlled for that reason. It is seductive while still being aberrant, and, like a contagious disease, imperils the health of society. The courts act as the guardians of civilization in this respect, in inhibiting the undue spread of homosexuality ... [S]ome people are thought to be peculiarly susceptible to conversion to homosexual "lifestyles," to socialization in "rings," to a perverse opting-out of a heterosexual union. Many refuse treatment.'[2]

Particularly in the years immediately following the 1969 Criminal Code amendments, the judiciary held tenaciously to the view that the decriminalization of consenting sexual acts between two adults in private achieved by that amendment did not mean that homosexuality should be condoned or encouraged. As we shall see in the subsequent discussion of prominent cases occurring between 1975 and 1984, the courts continued much as they always had in viewing homosexuality as a menacing 'other' and meting out punishments for homosexual conduct – a conduct that presiding judges considered destructive, immoral, or corrupting.

Nowhere were such attitudes more evident than in cases involving lesbian mothers and gay fathers seeking custody of their children from heterosexual relationships. It was the one issue during this period that stood out as being of primary importance to lesbians and, while identified by mixed groups like Toronto Gay Alliance Toward Equality (GATE) and the National Gay Rights Coalition (NGRC) as important, was never given the priority awarded to the amendment of human rights codes. NGRC's initial platform, crafted in 1975, addressed the issue by demanding 'that homosexual parents not be denied custody of their children on grounds of their sexual orientation; and furthermore that parents not be denied custody of children on the grounds of homosexual unions.'[3] The Coalition for Gay Rights in Ontario, also founded in 1975, included in its initial list of demands 'that homosexuality, not be considered a factor in cases of child adoption and custody.'[4]

Using the precedent set in the 1974 decision in *Case v. Case*, family court judges consistently ruled that being openly gay or lesbian, and especially being active in the community or promoting 'militant' views about homosexuality, was sufficient to establish unsuitability for custody of children. This homophobic and heterosexist reasoning was apparent in a 1975 case involving an Alberta lesbian mother who succeeded in winning custody of her children. The judge in *K. v. K*, finding the woman was a good mother, stable and capable of providing for the physical and emotional needs of her children, nonetheless was swayed by the fact the mother was not overt in her homosexuality and was not apt to flaunt it or become militant.[5] Similarly, in 1977, the High Court of Justice in Ontario, in *Wine v. Wine*, involving a woman who left the matrimonial home and took with her the three children, aged eleven, nine, and seven, granted interim custody to the woman. But the court noted that if the husband's allegations that the woman 'espouses bisexuality' were true, 'then obviously it could have a detrimental effect upon the children and quite possibly the mother should not have custody.'[6]

That the courts relied on a distinction between being gay or lesbian and being open about it was made plain in two other notable custody cases during this era, in Ottawa and Kingston. The 1978 Ottawa case was the first known instance of custody being granted to an openly gay father. A judge granted the man custody of two sons aged eight and thirteen because the wife had both psychiatric problems and a strained relationship with the children. Although the father was in a stable same-sex relationship, the judge attached significance to his being a discreet bisexual. It was critical to the judge that the father had 'not indulged in unusual exhibitionistic behaviour in the presence of children ... his sexual orientation is not known outside his immediate circle ... [and he] has never exhibited any inclination towards militancy in this difficult area of homosexual behaviour.'[7] In the second case, in Kingston in 1980, a judge rejected claims by the father's lawyer that the child's lesbian mother might 'proselytize' and that the child, who was ten, might become homosexual. Echoing earlier decisions, the judge noted that the mother was not militant, did not flaunt her homosexuality, and did not engage in overt sexual contact with her same-sex partner.[8]

A small step towards liberalizing the courts' views about bisexual, gay, and lesbian parents occurred following a decision of the Ontario Court of Appeal, in 1980, in the case of *Bezaire v. Bezaire*.[9] A year earlier, Gayle Bezaire had initially gained conditional custody of her children after a judge was persuaded that homosexuality was not a determining factor in a parent's ability to raise a child. Nonetheless, he imposed stringent conditions, prohibiting Bezaire from engaging in homosexual acts, from living with another homosexual without the court's consent, and from being overt or militant about her homosexuality.[10] Not surprisingly, Bezaire eventually lost custody of the children for contravening the terms of the order. She appealed, but the Ontario Court of Appeal refused to interfere with the prior decision, even though the appeal court's judgement disagreed with the original judge: 'Homosexuality, either as a tendency, proclivity or a practised way of life is not in itself alone a ground for refusing custody to the parent ... The question is and must always be what effect upon the welfare of the children that aspect of the parent's lifestyle has, and it will therefore be a question of evidence in that very case as to whether what has been shown to exist has or may tend to have effects averse to the welfare of the children ... It would be wrong to lay down a general rule as to the weight to be given evidence of homosexuality on the part of one of the parents.'[11]

Going further than the two male justices, Bertha Wilson, who would later be the first woman appointed to the Supreme Court of Canada, wrote, 'In my view, homosexuality is neutral and not a negative factor as far as parenting skills are concerned. To the extent that the learned trial judge proceeded on a different view, I would respectfully disagree with him.'[12] But while this minority opinion represented a significant step towards modernizing the courts' view of homosexuality in custody cases, there would continue to be mixed outcomes in later cases on the determination of whether the homosexuality of a parent was a neutral or negative factor. In *Droit de la Famille – 31*, a Quebec Superior Court justice denied custody to a lesbian mother, but did permit her to have access to her two daughters. Being a lesbian was seen as a negative factor, even if the mother was to be discreet. Noting that the family lived in a small town, the judge felt the children would be adversely affected by public views about homosexuality. The mother was thus victimized because of the homophobia and heterosexism of the straight community. As if that were not enough, the judge expressed the belief that the father would be able to prevent the daughters from attempting to imitate the mother's 'proclivity.'[13]

An important contribution to the fight to secure custody rights for lesbian mothers during this dark era was the work of the Lesbian Mothers Defence Fund. It offered financial and moral support for many women. Writing in 1983, the fund's Francie Wyland noted that, after four years, the organization had 'helped almost two dozen women keep or win custody, usually through out-of-court settlements.' Wyland added that, 'It's an uphill battle every time, and we haven't always been successful, but ten years ago the idea that a woman could be a lesbian and a mother was inconceivable to most people. Judges routinely dismissed women as "unfit" mothers if they were gay.'[14]

If the courts, historically, passed harsh judgment on homosexual acts and expressions, the role of the police has been, as MacDougall contends, 'to find homosexuals engaging in sordid sexual practices as much as possible ... to go to elaborate lengths to find homosexual activity to prosecute,' even when that has required setting up the circumstances, through the use of entrapment, in which homosexual acts may take place.[15] Nothing more vividly exposed the homophobic attitudes of the police rank and file, even a decade after the adoption of the consenting adults legislation, than an article appearing in the March 1979 issue of the Metropolitan Toronto Police Association's newsletter. In it, a staff sergeant asserted, 'This sickness or aberration [homosexuality] should never become a right.' Calling gays such names as 'fags,' 'fruits,' 'weirdos,' and 'misfits,' he described them as 'prancing and wiggling, and sometimes dressing in effeminate garb; smelling like polecats.'[16] Two years later, a study of police attitudes, commissioned by Toronto's mayor after pressure from the gay and lesbian community, quoted a senior police officer as saying 'wherever they [gays] go, crime does occur.' The study found that 'verbal horseplay' among officers routinely involved calling each other such names as 'nigger,' 'wop,' 'queer,' and 'faggot.' Newspaper clippings and notices dealing with the gay community and posted on police station bulletin boards elicited derogatory comments.[17] Nor did Toronto's police want any gays and lesbians in their ranks. As the report noted, 'the majority of [police union] members were strongly opposed to the hiring of homosexual policemen.' A long list of stereotypes and prejudices was then cited, including that gay police would be 'prone to engage in overt sex acts with each other in inappropriate places,' and would 'attempt to seduce heterosexual policemen – particularly young ones – and could not be trusted with duty that involved children.'[18]

Homophobic police, often in collusion with the media, contributed throughout the 1970s and early 1980s to a climate of backlash and bigotry. One notorious incident occurred in Ottawa in 1975, when police announced a 'Homosexual Vice Ring' with great media fanfare. The owner and sixteen clients of the Unique Male Modelling Agency were arrested during an operation police described as 'the most sordid crime we've investigated for some time.' Media coverage, based on police information, used terms such as 'white slavery ring' and claimed that over one hundred boys, some only eleven years old, were involved. In fact, it was later established that all of the escorts charged were between sixteen and twenty-one years of age.[19] To maximize publicity, Ottawa police, over a three-week period, released to the media the names and addresses of all of those who had been charged in the 'ring.' The media reported the names, with devastating consequences. Eight men required psychiatric care and were deluged with hate letters and phone calls. Nine were fired from their jobs, or were suspended or transferred. One was identified in the press by his place of employment and position title. And thirty-four-year-old Warren Zufelt committed suicide after his first court appearance by jumping from the thirteenth floor of his apartment building.[20]

Similar cooperation between police and the media followed a 1978 raid on a Toronto bathhouse called the Barracks. Police disclosed in press releases that items used for sadomasochism, bondage, and other sexual practices had been seized, generating sensational media reports. Following raids on four gay bathhouses in 1981, a Toronto police press release linked those charges with the separate, and unrelated, arrest of a gay man who had been found with 'implements of torture' and 'kiddie porn.' They also alleged links between the bathhouses and organized crime activity, and claimed that drug deals and prostitution were occurring in those businesses. Yet no evidence of such activities was ever produced and no charges relating to them were ever laid.[21] In a reprehensible and retributive action, a police officer reported the names of three teachers arrested in the raids to school board officials.

Police-initiated publicity, including giving the media the names of men arrested in bathhouses, parks, and public washrooms had, by this time, become a common occurrence. The publicity caused humiliation, social censure for those arrested, and created the impression the police were protecting the public – particularly children – from the evils of homosexuality. Arrests typically followed acts of entrapment – plainclothes officers enticed other men into making sexual advances or gestures and then charged them with criminal offences. Another tactic involved videotaping public washrooms to record those engaging in sexual acts. In one notorious police operation in a public washroom during 1983, thirty-one men in Orillia, Ontario were charged with sexual offences after having been videotaped by hidden cameras. Assisted by the police, local newspapers reported their names. Extensive media coverage of the first court appearances featured TV camera crews rushing to get pictures of the accused. The men endured insults and catcalls from twenty-five people gathered outside the courthouse in a modern day version of the stocks-and-pillories treatment meted out to offenders in earlier centuries.[22] Three arrested men who were teachers were subsequently fired by their board of education for 'immoral criminal conduct.' One man tried to commit suicide.[23]

Negative police attitudes towards gays and lesbians also were expressed in other ways, through condoning, remaining indifferent towards, or refusing to effectively respond to acts of violence inflicted by homophobic assailants. The most infamous example was a well known tradition in Toronto for many years. Each Halloween, a vicious mob of onlookers gathered on Yonge Street, in front of the St Charles Tavern, within which a Halloween drag show was held. As drag queens or others thought to be gay were spotted on the side streets or entered the bar, they were subjected to jeers, taunts, and a barrage of eggs, tomatoes, and other objects. Some were gay-bashed. This annual spectacle was tolerated by police and civic officials and was prominently reported in the media with photos and commentary as part of the city's Halloween festivities. Few outside the gay and lesbian community saw the event as an outpouring of hate and prejudice; the terror inflicted on that community was rarely reported or was downplayed. In fact, the spectacle was often presented in the news as a kind of good-natured carnival, with no reports of violence.

Toronto activists repeatedly called on the police during the 1970s to either disperse the mob or stop it from forming. Police officials contended there was little they could do, and made only a small number of arrests for throwing eggs, generally charging the perpetrators with breach of the peace. In 1978, Toronto's police chief actually told Toronto GATE that police had no power to stop people from gathering and that, to avoid acts of violence, gays should stay clear of the area surrounding the St Charles.[24] Activists persisted nonetheless, holding pre-Halloween meetings with the police and municipal politicians each year. In 1979, pressure from GATE and the Metropolitan Community Church, aided by the support of progressive politicians, resulted in an increased police presence on Yonge Street. Gay community volunteers also provided their own security network, escorting bar patrons and reporting incidents of violence and harassment to the police. But it was not until 1980, under pressure from activists, gay-owned businesses, Mayor John Sewell, and city councillors that the police finally erected barricades to narrow the sidewalk and did not permit people to stop in front of the St Charles. By 1981, as a result, this particular Halloween tradition was only an ugly memory.[25]

Because of such police actions and attitudes, groups like Gays of Ottawa, GATE in Vancouver and Toronto, and, later, both the Comité homosexuel anti-repression in Montreal and the Right to Privacy Committee in Toronto, focused advocacy efforts on ending police harassment and repression. Activists in larger communities across Canada also attempted to establish police liaison mechanisms in the hope that greater education and awareness would lead to better policing. But their efforts were largely unsuccessful due to distrust of the police, homophobia on the part of the cops themselves, and continued harassment. As *The Body Politic* noted in a 1978 editorial, distrust of the police was widespread, 'so we don't co-operate – even in the solving of murders within our own community.' Sceptical of police attitudes and intentions – 'The police are not neutral' – *TBP* acknowledged that 'some kind of co-operation, then, may be necessary. We need to understand what kind it is, and when it should happen.' Still, cooperation did not mean, for *TBP*, 'joining them [police] in the backrooms as quasi-informers, letting them in on where the "troublesome" cans and parks are.' It meant ensuring '*they* co-operate with *us* – calling them into the streets to do their job, for instance, when a gay demonstration has to be protected from straight thugs.'[26]

Vancouver's police liaison efforts were led by SEARCH, the Society for Education, Action, Research and Counselling on Homosexuality, founded in 1974 as a response to 'a crisis in gay bottle clubs' following police raids. Together with other groups, a gay businessman, and a city councillor, SEARCH later formed the Gay-Police Committee to formally communicate with the police and discuss 'approaches to better education on minority issues.'[27] For several years, Vancouver GATE organized strong responses to police harassment, such as a 1977 community forum at which 350 people confronted police over a campaign to 'clean up' the downtown area that featured selective law enforcement. Some at the meeting complained about being harassed by the police for kissing and holding hands on the street.[28] Two years later, three hundred people attended a GATE forum to protest police inaction to increasing violence against gays and lesbians. A few weeks after that, four hundred people rallied in front of the courthouse.[29] In Calgary, the first police liaison initiative started in 1983 to deal with complaints of harassment by people going to gay bars and by men cruising in a city park. The initiative eventually broke down, however, as a result of distrust of the police, and suspicions that information obtained by them at the liaison meetings was being used to increase harassment and arrests of gay men.[30]

Police Raids and Repression of Gay Sexuality

From 1975 to 1984, a series of police raids and other actions by the state to repress same-sex sexuality convinced activists that a campaign was underway to recriminalize and demonize gays, and turn public opinion against legislating equality within human rights laws. The police campaign began in March 1975 with the arrests of the clients of the Unique Modelling Agency in Ottawa, and intensified in August 1975 with a raid on Sauna Aquarius, a Montreal gay bathhouse, that resulted in a number of men being charged with bawdy house offences. The raid took place during a period of increased police presence at gay and lesbian bars, and greater entrapment of men in washrooms. These actions were part of a clean-up of Montreal in preparation for the 1976 Olympic games. A police source in a Montreal community paper, *Gay Times*, noted that the campaign was 'designed to frighten gays from frequenting public places where Olympic tourists are likely to be, particularly downtown Montreal.'[31]

Further confirmation of a clean-up campaign occurred when six Montreal gay and lesbian bars were raided in October 1975, with the presence of gun-toting police sending terror through the lesbian and gay communities.[32] Subsequent raids on the Club Baths and the Neptune Sauna in January and May 1976 resulted in more bawdy house charges.[33] Suspicions that the Olympic clean-up had spread to Ottawa, where some events were to be held, arose following a police raid, and the laying of bawdy house and gross indecency charges, at that city's Club Baths in May 1976, a few days after the Montreal police actions.[34] Angered at the dramatic increase in police repression, Montreal activists formed the Comité homosexuel anti-repression/Gay Coalition Against Repression. On 19 June 1976, the Comité held what was to that date the largest gay demonstration in Canada, when some three hundred people protested the raids. Gays of Ottawa (GO) responded with a press conference decrying the Club Baths raid and requesting a meeting with the mayor, which took place a few days later. They also contacted the arrested men, to refer them to sympathetic lawyers, and picketed the Ottawa police headquarters, drawing fifty protesters.

An even more momentous police raid was executed on 22 October 1977 at Truxx, a Montreal gay bar, carried out by fifty officers wearing bulletproof vests and armed with machine guns. One hundred and forty-six men were charged as found-ins and the owner was charged as a keeper of a common bawdy house. Eight charges of gross indecency and two for drug trafficking were also laid. Bar patrons were loaded into police vans, held for eight hours in overcrowded cells without being allowed to call lawyers, and forced to take compulsory venereal disease tests. Some accused the police of verbal and physical abuse.[35] In response, the Comité, now transformed into l'Association pour les droits des gais du Québec (ADGQ), held a demonstration the next night during which two thousand people blocked a downtown intersection. A melee ensued when police attempted to disperse the crowd by riding their motorcycles through it while officers on foot began clubbing them. Protesters fought back, throwing beer bottles and glasses, creating shocking images for a national media coverage that embarrassed the police and the Quebec government. A few days later, three hundred people attended an ADGQ public forum at which a defence committee was set up for the found-ins.[36]

Despite the mass response to the Truxx actions, over the next few years Montreal police continued their raids on bars and bathhouses. They charged twenty-two men at the Dominion Square Tavern with bawdy house offences in October 1978.[37] In April 1980, sixty-one men were arrested as found-ins and six as keepers at the Sauna David; fifteen charges of gross indecency were also laid. Some men claimed they were charged as found-ins while they were outside the sauna walking towards it.[38] And in June 1984, ADGQ once more galvanized community anger with a large demonstration the night after a raid on Bud's, a popular gay bar, during which seventy-five police laid 122 found-in charges, eight keeper charges and thirty-three gross indecency charges. Reprehensibly, police photographs of bar patrons found their way into a weekly crime tabloid.[39] ADGQ demanded a public inquiry, accusing police of arresting the patrons indiscriminately, holding them overnight to sleep on floors and benches, and not informing them of their rights.

Similarly, in Toronto, on 30 December 1977, a police raid on *The Body*

Politic sent shock waves through the gay and lesbian community, generating outrage and anger. The pretext for the action was an article by Gerald Hannon, 'Men Loving Boys Loving Men' that a *Toronto Sun* columnist claimed promoted paedophilia. *TBP* held a press conference denouncing the raid as an attack on freedom of the press. The Body Politic Free the Press Fund formed soon afterwards to cover the legal fees of *TBP's* officers Ed Jackson, Gerald Hannon, and Ken Popert, who were charged under the Criminal Code with using the mail to distribute 'immoral, indecent, and scurrilous' material.[40] The raid immediately became a focus of concern for activists nationally. GATE Vancouver held a demonstration protesting it, on 1 January 1978, marking the first of many such events held over the subsequent years. On 14 January, one thousand people marched down Toronto's Yonge Street to protest the visit of Anita Bryant – an American evangelical Christian then leading a high-profile campaign against gay rights legislation – and to 'defend the Body Politic.'[41]

In 1978 and 1979, two bathhouse raids by Toronto officers prompted more denunciations of police homophobia and repression. On 9 December 1978, twenty officers descended on the Barracks, which drew a leather and SM clientele, and charged twenty-eight men. Infuriated community activists immediately formed the December 9th Defense Fund to organize legal defences and coordinate community responses. (A few months later, the fund's name was changed to the Right to Privacy Committee.)[42] Following the raid, four hundred people demonstrated in protest and activists held a press conference, at which they accused the police of attacking the entire gay community and attempted to counter the lurid press coverage of SM activities at the Barracks.[43] More protest occurred in October 1979, after police raided the Hot Tubs Club and laid forty bawdy house charges. During a separate but related action, the owners of the bathhouse were charged with producing pornographic films.[44]

A particularly outrageous and vindictive police action, also in 1979, transpired when Toronto police charged a gay man, Don Franco, with keeping a bawdy house in his home after a plainclothes officer responded to a classified advertisement Franco placed in *The Body Politic* seeking sexual contacts. The police and the Crown alleged that because Franco publicly advertised for sexual contacts, the sex acts with the men who responded were committed in a public place. They also alleged that the paraphernalia for SM sex found in Franco's residence was offensive to community standards of tolerance. Fortunately, Franco was acquitted two years later. The trial judge actually criticized the use of a plainclothes officer to entice Franco, and ruled that the 1969 consenting adults legislation included the types of acts in question.[45]

But the biggest and most terrifying of all the raids took place on the night of 5 February 1981 during a well-orchestrated, militaristic campaign. Toronto police carried out simultaneous raids on four bathhouses, arresting 304 men as found-ins and twenty others as keepers. The police told the media the raids were the culmination of six months of investigation, and that 'acts of prostitution and indecent acts' were taking place in the bathhouses.[46] The press later revealed that police caused $35,000 in damages to the bathhouses by using hammers, crowbars, and shears to smash doors, shatter mirrors, rip open mattresses, and wrench doors off lockers. Some officers kicked huge holes in the walls. In addition, several of the men arrested were physically and verbally abused. One man arrested at the Barracks told of having been 'pushed hard into the wall. My nose was lacerated and bloodied. The cop kept punching me in the lower back and pulling my hair and saying, "You're disgusting, faggot. Look at this dirty place."' A police officer was quoted saying, 'Too bad the place doesn't catch fire, we'd have to catch them escaping custody.' Another was reported as stating, 'Too bad the showers aren't hooked up to gas.'[47]

Word of the raids reached members of *TBP*'s collective and Jim Monk, the chairperson of the Coalition for Gay Rights in Ontario (CGRO), who went to the police station at about eleven p.m. to talk to the people who had been arrested.[48] The next day they and a network of activists sprang into action, holding a meeting that organized a demonstration for the evening of February 6. Initially, three hundred people gathered at the corner of Yonge and Wellesley Streets, but their ranks swelled quickly to more than fifteen hundred. Enraged, they headed to police Division 52, shouting 'Fuck you 52' as their rallying cry, blocking traffic and seizing control of Yonge Street.[49] The demonstration grew to over three thousand as it surged along, becoming more frenzied the closer it came to 52 Division. CGRO activist Christine Donald, who helped organize the response to the raids, recalls, 'I was actually quite frightened on that demo. The anger was enormous, just enormous.'[50] The anger was also fuelled by clumsy police attempts to curtail the demonstration. They blockaded the intersection of Yonge and Dundas with cruise cars, further incensing the demonstrators, who rocked the cars, smashing windshields and headlights. A paddy wagon had its side dented. Two demonstrators urinated on one cop car and a window was smashed on a streetcar caught in the altercation.[51]

Pressing on along Dundas Street, the crowd faced more danger as about thirty counter-demonstrators gathered on the sidewalk, chanting 'Fuck the queers!'[52] Then, as the protestors arrived at 52 Division, they encountered a wall of about two hundred police standing shoulder-to-shoulder, batons held behind their backs, out of sight. Fearing the police were poised to start cracking open heads, a small group of activists huddled to find a way to keep a riot from erupting. They decided to divert the demonstrators away from 52 Division, so CGRO's Tom Warner exhorted them to proceed to the nearby provincial legislature to protest the government's refusal to add sexual orientation to the Ontario Human Rights Code.[53] The change of venue prevented a violent confrontation with the police at 52 Division but did not defuse the anger. Demonstration marshals had trouble controlling the crowd as it approached the legislature. Hordes of protesters charged onto the front lawn, bolting towards the legislature's main entrance, repeatedly heaving themselves against the doors and nearly breaking them down before the police appeared and beat them back. A violent confrontation between police and demonstrators broke out, with much punching, kicking, and shoving. Finally, at the urging of organizers, the crowd dispersed. However, skirmishes between police and protesters continued for some time afterwards in the streets nearby.

Relations between the community and Toronto police worsened dramatically following revelations published in a community newspaper that, during the bathhouse raid protests, plainclothes officers acted as *agents provocateurs*, inciting demonstrators to acts of violence and then arresting them.[54] Outraged by the raids and these events, Brent Hawkes, pastor of the Metropolitan Community Church, began a hunger strike on 17 February. He pledged to continue it until Mayor Arthur Eggleton established an independent inquiry into relations between the police and the gay community. On 12 March, supported unanimously by City Council, Eggleton appointed lawyer and former journalist Arnold Bruner to prepare a report, at which point Hawkes ended his strike.[55] Two months after the raids, however, more fodder was provided for community fury, as charges of conspiracy – including conspiracy to obtain proceeds obtained by crime – were laid against the shareholders and officers of the Club Baths. Two of those charged, Peter Maloney and George Hislop, had been vocal police critics, which fuelled activist suspicions that the charges were a form of reprisal designed to discredit them. Consequently, thirty-four gay organizations held a press conference condemning the attempt 'to characterize our leaders, and by implication the gay community, as criminal.'[56] But such protestations proved futile, as police, undeterred, raided two more bathhouses later in 1981, laying a number of bawdy house charges.[57] What would turn out to be the last bathhouse raid for many years occurred on 20 April 1983, when police laid bawdy house charges against nine customers, the owner, and three employees of the Back Door Gym.[58]

Police action against bathhouses spread westward on 20 May 1981, when forty Edmonton police, six RCMP officers, and two crown attorneys raided the Pisces Spa. Doors to private cubicles were smashed, and men found on the premises were videotaped and photographed. In all, sixty men were arrested, four as keepers and fifty-six as found-ins. The membership list of over two thousand names was seized.[59] Within hours, the arrested men were fingerprinted, issued summonses, and loaded into a police paddy wagon. They were then taken to a provincial court where two judges, court clerks, and crown attorneys awaited. The men were questioned about sexual activity they saw or had engaged in at the Pisces. Told that what they said could not be used against them in court, they were not advised that what they said could be used as evidence against others who had been accused, and that what others said could be used against them. They felt intimidated into testifying without benefit of counsel. Later, some said they had asked to speak to a lawyer but had been refused. Michael Phair, one of the men arrested on what he called a 'harrowing' night, recalled, 'I certainly felt extremely powerless because I didn't know anything ... which was very disconcerting to me.'[60]

Phair felt the ordeal was over upon being released, until he later heard a radio newscast featuring the raid as the top story. It was then that he began 'realizing that this wasn't over and it wasn't just going to go away, and it wasn't just a kind of nightmare kind of thing.'[61] Phair immediately called Edmonton GATE, which, along with members of Dignity (the group for gay Catholics) and the Metropolitan Community Church, swung into action. Within twenty-four hours, GATE had a leaflet circulating in the city's gay bars containing information about what had happened and announcing plans for a community response. Counselling and advice was offered to found-ins. A demonstration of one hundred people to protest the raid was held by straight civil libertarians, labour leaders, and supportive churches. A few days later, a public meeting of the gay and lesbian community set up the Privacy Defense Committee to support the found-ins.[62]

Back in Toronto, in April and May 1982, police targeted Glad Day Bookshop, then Toronto's only gay bookstore and, once more, *The Body Politic*. Kevin Orr, manager of Glad Day, was charged with 'possession of obscene material for the purpose of sale' after two morality squad officers visited the store and seized two gay male magazines containing sexually explicit material. Shortly afterwards, nine members of *TBP*'s editorial collective and the officers of Pink Triangle Press were charged with publishing obscene material after they ran an article, 'Lust with a Very Proper Stranger' in the paper's April 1982 issue. The Toronto Gay Community Council, an umbrella group of community organizations, responded by holding a press conference to denounce the Glad Day and *TBP* charges, describing them as 'yet another example of selective enforcement of the law designed to discredit and harass our community.' Spokesperson Harvey Hamburg commented that the charges 'lead us to the conclusion that there is, indeed, a concerted police effort against us.' A few days later, a demonstration of seven hundred people protested the charges. During the demo, Eve Zaremba, a writer and member of the editorial board for *Broadside*, a feminist paper, declared, 'This harassment of *The Body Politic*, using obscenity as an excuse, is aimed at destroying one of the few voices open to us.'[63]

The community organizing in response to various raids between 1975 and 1984 in Ottawa, Montreal, Toronto, and Edmonton had powerful symbolic significance and an energizing impact on gay and lesbian communities across the country. Indeed, the empowerment achieved from spontaneous, mass uprising in the face of police harassment is the raids' most significant legacy. As sociologist and activist Gary Kinsman stresses, the community response to the 1981 Toronto bathhouse raids closed off certain options for the police and probably prevented some even bigger acts of state repression. The police could no longer conduct mass raids, and the balance of power shifted a little in favour of the gay and lesbian community: 'The mobilization cannot be under-estimated. And I think part of that also is that the police actually have been, historically, quite a central regulator of gay men's lives, so I think that the resistance to it had this kind of popular character to it that could really go quite far.'[64] Although the mobilization gradually dissipated, it is clear the lesbian and gay community in Toronto was forever changed by, and became more visible from, the militancy of its response and what that response came to symbolize.

CGRO's Jim Monk, a resident of Windsor, holds similar views, and notes in addition that the massive Toronto community response was important for gays and lesbians in smaller communities. They feared that if the police in Toronto could get away with brutal acts of repression despite the existence of a well-organized activist community in that city, then more vulnerable and less organized gays and lesbians in smaller places had reason to dread what might happen to them. As Monk saw things, nearly twenty years afterwards, 'We had a victory there over the police that really made a lot of people think things were possible. Always in the '70s, I think we thought we were in this for the long haul and getting the human rights code amended or getting public acceptance of homosexuality was way, way in the future. After the horror of the bath raids had subsided, and people started to fight back, and the determination that they had, I think that what came out of that was a sense of, hey, we can win. We can actually, maybe not right away, we will win.'[65]

As had been the case in Toronto, the period following the bathhouse raid in Edmonton saw increased visibility for the gay and lesbian community there. Phair notes that 'it did unleash probably one of the most active periods for the gay and lesbian community here and a real blossoming of the diversity, and stuff ... The whole bath raids woke up the community. I mean, I remember people saying to me that they never thought it could happen here, that this [city] was just too quiet and laid back and no one cared and that jarred, took that out from under people's feet, you couldn't argue that, couldn't think that way any more. It really pushed people to have to re-think.'[66] Edmonton's gay pride events, the Gay and Lesbian Alliance, lesbian groups, sports groups, and religious groups began to blossom from 1981 to about 1984. Like Toronto, Edmonton's community was forever changed by the raid.

The Trials

Despite the obvious success of community mobilizing, however, the courts were far less susceptible to accepting the notion of homophobic police harassing gays and lesbians. In the trial arising from the first of the bar and bathhouse raids, the Sauna Aquarius manager was convicted of being a bawdy house keeper. He appealed, but in 1976, a Quebec Court of Appeal judge found that it was inconceivable the manager was unaware of sexual activity occurring on the premises. He ruled the sauna was 'a rendezvous where homosexuals could find partners for the performance of indecent acts, and facilities for such acts.'[67] The Truxx and Sauna David cases demonstrated that courts would accept uncorroborated police testimony as sufficient evidence to convict. On 2 April 1980, the owner of Truxx was found guilty of being a keeper when the presiding judge dismissed the testimony of twenty-seven bar patrons that they did not see any sexual acts taking place. Instead, he accepted police testimony that men were hugging, kissing, and sometimes feeling each others' bodies or genitals, that acts of masturbation were committed at urinals, and that two men were observed engaging in sexual activity in a washroom cubicle. One undercover officer stated that he had been groped and grabbed in the bar, and another claimed to have been propositioned for oral sex. A third testified to being invited to engage in sex in the washroom.[68]

The owner of Truxx was sentenced to ten days in jail, to be served on weekends, and fined $5,000. On appeal, the Quebec Court of Appeal upheld his conviction, but reduced the fine and removed the jail term. More positively, on 14 December 1982, a judge dismissed the charges against 120 Truxx patrons upon being advised by the Crown attorney that he would not be proceeding – after five years! – because it would cost 'too much money.'[69] The trial of Sauna David's owner also ended with a finding of guilty. The trial judge, when passing sentence, commented, 'This so-called sauna bath was in fact a place where men gathered with the precise, chosen and unconcealed goal of having sexual relations with other persons of the male sex.'[70] The 1984 trials of the men arrested during the raid on Bud's resulted in a mixture of not guilty and guilty verdicts.[71]

The trials of the keepers and found-ins arrested during the 1978 raid on the Barracks and at the Hot Tubs Club also produced mixed results. During the Barracks keepers trial, the Crown attorney produced more than eighty sex toys and aids, and a police officer testified he witnessed sex acts in the bathhouse during an undercover visit. At the conclusion of the trial, the judge ruled gay sex acts themselves are not indecent, but when performed so that others may see them are not within community standards of tolerance. He ruled, however, that the Crown had not proven the owners' active participation in respect of acts of indecency committed on the premises, but he found two employees guilty, granting them conditional discharges.[72] All but one of the Barracks found-ins were convicted. On the other hand, some of the Hot Tub Club found-ins and keepers pled guilty while others had their charges dismissed or were found not guilty.[73]

Convictions on the charges laid against bathhouse customers in the February 1981 raids were not as common. In fact, only one of the 304 found-ins was given a criminal record. Nineteen pled guilty and were fined, and thirty-six others were given conditional or absolute discharges. All of the others were either found not guilty or had their charges withdrawn.[74] The Crown's success rate for the various 1981 keepers was much better. An employee of one bathhouse pled guilty, receiving an absolute discharge, in a plea bargain arrangement that allowed the charges against the other keepers to be dropped. Similarly, owners of another bathhouse pled guilty in exchange for dropping the charges against their employees. Owners of two other bathhouses were found guilty, and a third owner was convicted of possessing obscene materials.[75] The owner of the Back Door Gym was found guilty of keeping a common bawdy house and fined $3,000, while two co-accused were given conditional discharges, with a requirement of one year's probation. Three years later, guilty verdicts were reached on the keeper's charge arising from the second Back Door Gym raid, following plea bargaining which resulted in charges against the found-ins being dropped.[76]

As the Pisces trials got underway in Edmonton during mid-1981, it became clear that the courts and media would administer harsh punishment. At one point, a television station sent a film crew to the court, and then ran news footage showing the docket bearing the names of the accused. The trials also featured expressions of disgust over overt homosexuality, with one Crown attorney using sensational police testimony about group sex activity in a darkened room that he described as 'rutting like animals.'[77] The climate of intimidation and humiliation prompted nineteen men to plead guilty. The remaining thirty-four decided to plead not guilty but were all convicted. Five of them appealed, four successfully. The Pisces' owners were convicted.[78]

If the overall outcome of the gay bar and bathhouse trials was mixed, The Body Politic and Glad Day Bookshop trials resulted ultimately in acquittals – although they did not come quickly or easily. The cases played out against a backdrop of fear and hysteria as the media, politicians, and social conservative forces played to homophobia, revulsion towards paedophilia, and the association of gay men with child molesting. In the first TBP case, the Crown persisted through two trials in Ontario Provincial Court (Criminal Division), three separate but related court actions, six appeals, and two trips to the Supreme Court of Canada. During these protracted prosecutions, Ontario Attorney General Roy McMurtry held that the law needed to be clarified. At the same time, the case served as a convenient rallying cry for those opposed to lesbian and gay rights. As sociologist Thelma McCormack of York University has commented, 'In *The Body Politic* trial, [the Attorney General] had the perfect instrument, because what mother, however liberal she might be about homosexuality, was going to defend men loving boys loving men? It was an ideal case for his purposes.'[79]

The charges against *TBP* were heard initially in Ontario Provincial Court (Criminal Division) over six days, beginning on 2 January 1979. It was a major news story nationally, especially after Mayor John Sewell spoke at a rally in support of *TBP*.[80] On 14 February, Judge Sidney Harris found Pink Triangle's officers not guilty, stating that he found *TBP* to be 'a serious journal of news and opinion.' His judgment also spoke to the fact that *immoral* in the Criminal Code was undefined, and it was therefore impossible to determine in law what is or is not moral. He concluded that the Crown had not established beyond a reasonable doubt that the article was obscene, and that neither the terms indecent nor scurrilous applied to it.[81] Three weeks later, McMurtry appealed, claiming Judge Harris had erred in acquitting the defendants. A year later, a county court judge set aside the acquittal and ordered a new trial. *TBP* unsuccessfully appealed to the Ontario Court of Appeal. That disappointment was followed by the paper's application for leave to appeal to the Supreme Court of Canada. Unfortunately, in October 1981, the Supreme Court stated it would not hear the case.[82] The new *TBP* trial resulted in a second acquittal on 15 June 1982, with the court concluding that although 'Men Loving Boys Loving Men' advocated paedophilia, such advocacy did not make it immoral or indecent. Again McMurtry appealed, arguing that the article exceeded Canadian community standards of tolerance. Finally, on 10 September 1983, a county court judge ruled that the trial judge had not erred in granting the second acquittal. Accepting the inevitable, McMurtry allowed the appeal period to expire. Similarly, when the second case against *TBP* arising from the 'Lust with a proper stranger' article, heard in November 1982, ended with an acquittal, McMurtry announced he would not appeal.[83]

In the Glad Day Bookshop obscenity trial, store manager Kevin Orr was found guilty at the lower court level. The judge in the case concluded the magazines in question went well beyond community standards of tolerance, describing them as 'lewd and disgusting.' He opined that they included 'disgusting sexual acts, sodomy in the presence of a third party, the actual ejaculation of semen and other unspeakably filthy subjects.' Orr received a conditional discharge with two years' probation, which he successfully appealed. Although a new trial was ordered, the Crown ultimately did not appeal further or proceed to a new trial.[84]

The trials of Glad Day Bookshop, *The Body Politic*, and the hundreds of individuals charged in various bathhouse and bar raids in this era were vivid reminders that the state and police still relegated gays and lesbians to criminal status. The difficulties experienced by lesbian and gay parents to win custody of their children drove home the message that queers were, at best, seen as poor role models and, at worst, vilified as deviants, perverts, and corrupters of children. The censorship and repression of sexually expressive materials produced by and for gays and lesbians dramatically illustrated that, notwithstanding the Criminal Code amendments of a decade earlier, the state felt the need to harshly curtail same-sex sexuality, and to keep it out of public view. Queers continued to be cast as immoral and menacing, as threats to public morals and social order. Not surprisingly, lesbian and gay liberation activists became alarmed by what they saw as concerted, and highly organized, attempts to repress their still fledging movement. They were convinced the instruments of the state sought to turn public opinion against the demand for legislated human rights and to drive gays, lesbians, and bisexuals back into the closet, back underground. Pursuing the path to liberation required that they fight back massively, in the streets and the courts. That they largely succeeded, despite the most formidable odds, was a testament to their resourcefulness and tenacity. In the end, there were both hard-won victories and bitter defeats. But the mere fact of resisting with such militancy marked a critical turning point in the history of queer activism in Canada.

FIVE

Raging Debates, Elusive Consensus

Advocating liberated sexuality, protesting police harassment, and overcoming judicial homophobia were contentious issues. This was true not just for the heterosexual mainstream, but within activist circles and the broader lesbian and gay communities. Political unity was impossible to maintain. Angry, divisive debates raged over the agenda of sexual liberation, especially with regard to issues principally driven by gay men: abolition of the age of consent; support for pornography and opposition to censorship; promotion of consensual sex in places the law considered to be public. Particularly problematic were radically differing views of sexuality expressed by some elements of gay and lesbian liberation on the one hand and many feminist lesbians on the other, causing a deep rift that seemed unbridgeable. The results, by the late 1970s, were raging debate and bitter dissent that rent the movement, consuming precious energies at a time when external threats were increasing in intensity and number.

Age of Consent

The trials of *The Body Politic*, and the defence of men engaging in sex in public places, even if they were bathhouses, caused controversy and volatile debates. Many questioned whether the agenda being promoted, principally by male activists with the support of some lesbians, was nothing more than sexual libertarianism presented in the guise of liberation. The issues comprising that agenda often were seen, and condemned, as gay men seeking to expand their options for sexual expression at the expense of women and others. But also present in the debates on such issues was a growing dissonance between liberationist and assimilationist voices still ostensibly speaking for a single movement. On no issue was such incipient discord expressed more vehemently than the call by liberation activists to abolish the age of consent, the focal point for which became the *TBP* trials arising from the 'Men Loving Boys Loving Men' article. Abolitionists advocated for the right of children and youth to express their sexuality, arguing there were already many provisions within the Criminal Code that protected them from coercive and non-consensual sex. Many gay men in particular noted that, as children or youths, they had initiated sexual contacts with adults that were pleasant and non-exploitative. Those opposed to abolishing the age of consent laws generally supported a uniform age of consent for both heterosexual and homosexual activity. They feared the impact that calling for abolition would have on the pursuit of equality rights and on efforts to gain mainstream acceptance.

Many influential gay liberationists argued that abolition was fundamental to the pursuit of liberating sexuality from the constraints of the church and the state. The Gay Alliance Toward Equality (GATE) Toronto called for 'doing away with the age-of-consent laws which make homosexual love illegal between young people.'[1] Maurice Flood of Vancouver GATE commented in 1973, 'At the centre of the Gay Liberation Movement is the whole critical issue, which we cannot ignore, of sexual rights for gay youth and youth in general. That simple right – to freely express one's sexual being unfettered by family, church, school, and government – cannot be easily granted or achieved in the context of repressive social relations that limit and stunt us at every point.'[2] Ken Popert, in a *TBP* report on the founding conference of the National Gay Rights Coalition, noted, 'Militant gay organizations ... maintain that the gay movement must demand the abolition of the age-of-consent laws. They point out that such laws attempt to deprive younger gays of the sexual use of their own bodies, in much the same way as the law, before being reformed in 1969, negated the right of homosexuals and lesbians to enjoy sexual activities. The militants argue that the gay movement must uphold the rights of all gay people, not just the rights of those above a certain age determined by lawmakers.'[3]

Popert then went on to chastise movement conservatives and those guilty of political expediency in a manner, typical of the times, that succeeded more in polarizing and than attempting to reach consensus:

Conservatives in the movement ... have argued that gays should demand a uniform age of consent, that is, a single age of consent, enshrined in law, which would govern all sexual activity, whether heterosexual or homosexual. Relying on the unscientific assertion that sexual activity of any kind is harmful to people below a certain age, some supporters of a uniform age of consent maintain that such a law is both legitimate and necessary. Others express support in principle for the abolition of all age of consent laws, but argue that to make such a demand at the present time would simply cater to the stereotyping of gays as child molesters. These people support the demand for a uniform age of consent out of political expediency.[4]

Thus was drawn a line of demarcation between conservatives and militants, between liberationists, and assimilationists, that characterized the invariably bitter debates of the 1970s and early 1980s. The for or against positioning, in conjunction with a belief that support for abolition was the litmus test for radical activism, allowed little room for finding common ground. For some activists caught up in the ideological whirlwind, such as Terry Phillips of GATE Vancouver (and later GATE Toronto), abolition was an intellectual or theoretical position put forward solely on that basis.[5] This critical flaw reduced a highly complex and emotive issue, with its many nuances and sensitivities, to a simplistic position or slogan that fit compactly onto placards and in leaflets – which then raised more questions than it answered. As three members of the *TBP* editorial collective wrote in the wake of fending off criminal charges for publishing 'Men Loving Boys Loving Men,' 'It should be apparent by now that this topic is too complex to be dealt with as a debate "for" or "against" sexual relationships between adults and people under the [then legal] age of twenty-one. We should be beyond that point. We should be trying to find out more about those relationships themselves, trying to discover ways in which power operates within them, and for whose benefit.' Chris Bearchell, Rick Bébout, and Alex Wilson observed, 'Much valuable criticism of "Men loving boys loving men" came from feminists who reacted not against the subject matter per se, but against a treatment of it which they felt left too many important areas unexplored.'[6] Many lesbians were opposed to abolition of age of consent laws because of their awareness of sexual molestation or assault of children by, primarily, heterosexual men. They saw gay men's demand for no age of consent as representing nothing more than expanding their realm of potential sexual partners. Even lesbians active with gay men in advocacy organizations criticized the *TBP* article for putting forward the views of the men involved with sex with boys while insufficiently addressing those boys' circumstances: 'The inequality inherent in most adult-child relationships is not adequately dealt with,' noted the Atlantic Provinces Political Lesbians for Example.[7]

Abolitionists attempted to respond to such concerns by emphasizing that younger males often did *not* feel exploited, and in some instances even exerted power or control over the older men. Problems arose only later when parents, clergy, or counsellors induced guilt or coerced them into laying charges. The abolitionists did not, however, develop an analysis about how to address this situation, other than to condemn such reactions as homophobic and anti-sexual. There also was no significant discussion of what would constitute informed consent and only cursory consideration of whether there is an age below which informed consent could not be considered to have been given. Abolitionists also largely failed to address the concerns of women about widespread sexual abuse and exploitation of children, especially female children by adult males. Opponents, including lesbians approaching the issue from a feminist perspective, were suspicious of the claim that sexual contact between adults and youth could be characterized in many circumstances as consensual or without harm. Becki L. Ross, in her book, *The House That Jill Built*, has incisively captured those views. Feminist critics, she noted, 'were not encouraged by the stories that some gay men, as teenagers, delighted in the sexual education they sought and received from older gay men, or that virtually all boys, as males, are taught to view themselves as sexual subjects. That intergenerational sex among males often entailed a positive and genuinely different experience from intergenerational heterosex was not a tradition with which women, lesbian or straight, identified.'[8]

At the street level, lesbians otherwise supportive of demands such as ending police harassment or adding sexual orientation to human rights laws were leery of groups lobbying for such reforms while at the same time proposing the abolition of the age of consent laws. They felt conflicted and angry. Ottawa lesbian Maureen Cullingham, speaking nearly two decades after the *TBP* controversies, has recalled,

> I didn't like this idea, you know, of things being seized, people being busted. I was at a demonstration and there was a fellow walking around

with a sign ... [and] the thing on the sign was 'No Age of Consent.' And I really remember that because that had been ... a position Gays of Ottawa at one point took in terms of, you know, their kind of platform. And I remember really being outraged and just sort of sickened by how male that was and how, you know, there were no women involved in Gays of Ottawa and obviously they weren't thinking of women. [The] women's movement, and feminists and women in their own life experiences would have been able to tell anybody that 'no age of consent' was a very bad idea, you know, girls were being molested.[9]

One lesbian who joined the debate on the issue was author Jane Rule. Writing in *TBP* in June 1979, she said, 'As a society we are so fearful of sexual initiation we pretend that by ignoring it, it will not take place. What we really want is not to know when or how it does.' She added that 'embarrassed liberality' on the subject of child sexuality does not extend to consenting acts between adults and children, noting that,

> There are adults who do sexually exploit, damage and kill children. It makes no more sense to deal with the question by taking them as the norm than it would to take rapists as the norm for heterosexual relationships between adults. To say any sexual activity between adults and children is exploitative because of the superior size and power of the adult is really to acknowledge that, overall, relationships between adults and children are unequal. Why we feel more concerned over children's sexual dependence than over their physical, emotional, and intellectual dependence says more about us as sexual incompetents than as responsible adults.[10]

Certainly intergenerational sex is not limited to gay men, although they have carried the issue and borne the consequences of advocating and practising it. Lesbians, too, have fantasies and real experiences, as indicated by discussions that took place at the first lesbian sexuality conference held in Toronto in 1984. Noted one conference participant, 'There were a lot of stories about being young and being seduced by an older woman. And then of the dire consequences; there weren't very many happy endings. Dire consequences like not being able to see their beloved any more, or being kicked out of home or school.'[11] But lesbians having such experiences generally were not heard, in favour of those who condemned intergenerational sex as a form of child abuse.

An activist who supported abolition was Jim Monk. Looking back on the debates twenty years later, he stressed the necessity of seeing them in the context of the times. There was a significant disparity in the 1970s between the age of consent for gay and straight sex. In addition, he noted, 'Like many other things it sort of got taken to an extreme where there's a group of people who just cannot recognize the existence of consensual sex, and then there are others who, you know, are in denial about the existence of abuse.'[12] Monk, like others, struggled with arriving at a position that acknowledged the polarities while seeing the strategic value of demanding abolition. 'I came to a position where I thought the age of consent laws did more harm than good,' he concluded. 'I also felt if they were abolished, the next day we would have a horrendous situation of massive abuse going on at the same time. I never expected them to be abolished, but I thought a call for their abolition was useful. And I think it was in the late 70s. By the end of the 80s, it wasn't a useful discussion at all. And plus we'd had [in the 1980s] a major change in Canadian law, where we had an age of consent set at 14, far below what we had expected.'[13]

The complexities, divergent opinions, strong feelings, and public association of gay men with paedophiles also made abolition of the age of consent an extremely difficult position to present to politicians. Activists advocating for it faced a tough time, to say the least. Ron Dayman, active in NGRC in the 1970s, explained years later in an interview that the abolitionist position 'was a nightmare' to defend before legislators. He added, 'Now, personally, I have no problem with it still, even today, the abolition of the age of consent. But it's been very hard to defend and sort of took attention away from our more serious demands, frequently, because, let's face it, the average straight person really cannot conceive or understand that and even the average gay, for that matter – let's say, it's not an issue that they are going to support.'[14] These tensions, conflicted views, and disputes over the position the gay and lesbian movement should take on the age of consent issue, featured prominently in activist circles until well into the 1980s. After that, however, it gradually receded from the frontlines of advocacy, especially as groups seeking legislated equality rights gained ascendancy and the liberationist groups of the 1970s went into decline. It remained at best an explosive issue that most felt should be left alone.

The Crusade against Pornography

The mid-to-late 1970s also witnessed an inflammatory debate over pornography and censorship in which gay liberationists and feminists, among others, became embroiled. The agendas of an assemblage of social and political conservatives, law enforcement officials, and some feminist organizations converged to seek greater state regulation of pornography and obscenity. Considerable organizing by women's groups against pornography in which women were humiliated, degraded, or victims of violence – including 'snuff' movies in which women were killed to stimulate male sexual gratification – was securing both political and mainstream support. Demonstrations in front of porno theatres were held by groups such as Toronto's Women Against Violence Against Women, in which many lesbians were active. This vigorous anti-pornography crusade pressured the federal government to strengthen the laws by, among other things, expanding the definition of obscene material to address depictions of violence and degradation that are not primarily sexual in nature. Canada Customs readily complied by adopting a policy of extraordinary vigilance under which books and periodicals destined for sale in Canada were placed on a banned list maintained under the Customs Tariffs. As we shall explore in more detail later, materials dealing with gay and lesbian subjects, in particular, were targeted.[15]

The censorship campaign picked up steam in 1976 after the Roman Catholic Archbishop of Toronto, Philip Pocock, launched a public assault on pornography. A *Pastoral Letter of Concern*, read in Toronto-area churches and printed in church newspapers, led to meetings with politicians and community organizations. An alliance was forged with these interests and with other churches. Ontario's attorney general responded with a number of public statements decrying the proliferation of 'depraved filth' and the harmful effects it would have on children exposed to it. A joint task force of the Ontario Provincial Police and Metropolitan Toronto Police was established to coordinate a war on pornography that later became a permanent unit named Project P.[16] Federally, MPs united to fight 'the rising flood of filth,' supported by a police officer from the Toronto Morality Squad, the Canadian Council of Churches, and five religious denominations. In March 1978, a parliamentary committee recommended the significant tightening of the prohibition on pornography by extending its definition to include exploitation of crime, horror, cruelty, violence, or the undue degradation of the human person.[17]

For many feminists, pornography presented a major social problem because it degraded and dehumanized women, reflected hostility towards them, and portrayed them as merely objects for the sexual gratification of men. One prominent feminist, Andrea Dworkin, character- ized pornography in a 1978 lecture as a 'woman-hating plague.' For her, the war against pornography required the introduction and enforce- ment of strong laws. Declaring pornography to be a form of terrorism against women, she asserted, 'Pornography is the propaganda of sexual fascism. Pornography is the propaganda of sexual terrorism. Images of women bound, bruised, and maimed on virtually every street corner, on every magazine rack, in every drug store, in movie house after movie house, on billboards, on posters pasted on walls, are death threats to a female population in rebellion.'[18] Anti-pornography femi- nists succeeded impressively in obtaining political support for their calls for tougher laws. There was, in fact, a political advantage for otherwise conservative politicians to embrace this feminist analysis of pornography. They re-packaged in progressive feminist wrapping the traditional morality that formed the foundation of criminal sanctions against pornography and used it to implement a campaign of repres- sion. In the process, they created social cleavages by 'placating the women and bashing the gays,' as Thelma McCormack noted.[19] Con- servatives found that the feminist critique was infinitely more palatable than their old proscriptions rooted in religious and anti-sexual beliefs.

But for large numbers of gay men and, increasingly, lesbians, pornog- raphy was seen as a vital component of a liberated sexuality. Gay and lesbian pornography celebrated sexuality, they argued, and in particu- lar affirmed same-sex sexuality as good. Liberationists thus responded with alarm to the call for stronger laws. Writing in *TBP* in April 1978, Gerald Hannon declared, 'Obscenity laws are laws without content. Like vagrancy laws, they exist to be used for political purposes only, to harass unpopular groups and censor divergent opinion.' Referring to the presentation of the National Advisory Council on the Status of Women to a parliamentary committee during which it supported stronger obscenity laws, Hannon said they 'were thoughtful, intelli- gent, articulate, impassioned – and wrong.' He ended his essay by calling for the abolition of all laws that would restrict the use or distri- bution of pornography.[20]

The rift between lesbian and gay liberation activists and feminist advocates arising from conflicting views of pornography quickly be- came a prominent feature of social movement politics. Calls for the repeal of obscenity laws were greeted with outraged opposition by feminists such as Susan Cole and Eve Zaremba. While they acknowl- edged there was risk that censorship guidelines could be used against gay and lesbian art or politics, running that risk, and condemning the censor when necessary, was preferable to settling back and watching 'the ongoing brutalization of women for profit, content with the fact that we are being victimized in a "free" society.' 'Gay liberation is male,' they claimed, 'regardless of the number of lesbians – never very many – who are in its ranks. This is reflected in its political stance and in its priorities. And *this is as it should be.*' Cole and Zaremba went on to reflect that, 'Specifically in the case of censorship, [feminism and gay liberation] are not wrong when we disagree; our interests are legitimately different.'[21] Other anti-pornography feminists tried to find middle ground, drawing a distinction between erotica and pornography, acknowledging that sex is not inherently dirty and not all representations of it should be banned. They attempted, in the words of Thelma McCormack, to 'construct an alternative notion of eroticism based on mutuality and equality.'[22] Some conceded that pornography involving gays and lesbians, where one participant does not hold power over another, should be viewed differently than heterosexual pornography.

Unfortunately, the lesbian and gay liberation and feminist movements proved unable to close the ideological gap between their positions on pornography. The two movements pursued their separate agendas with vigour over the ensuing years. Lesbian and gay liberationists in particular continued to voice grave concerns about feminist calls for more censorship, fearing that anti-pornography laws would be used disproportionately against representations of same-sex sexuality without being effective against violent and degrading representations involving women produced for the gratification of heterosexual men. A resolution passed at the 1978 conference of the Canadian Lesbian and Gay Rights Coalition reflected this view, opposing new obscenity laws on the basis that the 'suppression of erotic material does nothing to attack the roots of the oppression of women.'[23] Lesbian and gay liberationists also argued that the law is simply too blunt an instrument to make subtle distinctions between erotica and pornography, or gay and straight porn, and that the police and the courts cannot be trusted to enforce the laws with such sensitivity. As Mariana Valverde, reporting on a 1979 debate on pornography in the U.S. publication *off our backs*, observed: 'Whatever the solution to pornography as violence against women may be, it's not hard to imagine the way that the same laws we might now wish to see strengthened could, some day, be used against us. All too often our goals run contrary to those of many a law enforcement agency.'[24] Similarly, Chris Bearchell, basing her views on the belief that 'gay liberation sees lesbians as an erotic minority,' wrote in 1983 that it is 'unpopular minority tastes, violent or not, that are the first to be hit with the full force of the law.' She warned that 'the hotter lesbian pornography becomes the more vulnerable it will be to the whims of the guardians of public morality.'[25] As we shall see in Part Three, these predictions came true, when obscenity charges were laid in the early 1990s against a lesbian pornography magazine, *Bad Attitude*.

Promiscuity and Sex in Public Places

The promiscuity of gay men, their engaging in sexual acts in places the state deems public, and their celebration of such activity have long been features of gay male culture. This results from the ability of men, whether heterosexual or homosexual, to move about with relative freedom even late at night, and of the historic, underground nature of gay sexuality. Sex in parks, public washrooms, parking lots, or dark alleyways provides anonymity for closeted gays who fear being seen going into a gay bar or club; moreover, they are the only options in places where there are no bars or clubs. But many gays also enjoy the thrill of quick, anonymous sex in public places or outdoors, as a form of sexual freedom and adventure. For liberationists the issues surrounding these activities become political. What are public and private spaces, who makes that distinction, and who decides when it is, and is not, acceptable or criminal to engage in sex in either of them? Liberationists reject the notion that sexuality is a purely private matter reserved for private spaces and note that heterosexuals generally seem freer to violate such a notion with an impunity not extended to queers. They see ample evidence that same-sex activity is more severely regulated using the privacy pretext than is heterosexual sexuality and that lesbian and gay offenders generally are more severely punished for violations. Heterosexual couples having sex on beaches, in parked cars at lovers' lanes, at rock concerts and, yes, even in washrooms or public parks late at night rarely are charged with offences. Heterosexuals need not fear entrapment or police surveillance. In respect of same-sex sexual activity, there is the added factor that heterosexuals don't want to encounter it, and especially don't want children to observe it. A common argument used to condemn gay sex in public places is that unsuspecting passers by, particularly children, will be traumatized should they see it.

Politically, sex in public places has been another of the issues that has divided gay men from many lesbians, and from feminists and liberal heterosexuals, as well as putting queers into conflict with the police and the state. Writing in 1977, Andrew Hodges noted that criticism of gay male sexual liberation by feminists and heterosexual liberals incorrectly assumes that 'if uncommitted heterosexual sex is a sexist exploitation of women by men, then uncommitted gay sex must be an exploitation of men by men.' Yet, if it were not for sexism, he concluded, heterosexuality also would not be exploitative. According to Hodges, 'Essentially gay males, by being males, have had the privilege of an environment in which a sex-positive attitude can work out well. They would like to see this extended to all – women and men, heterosexual and homosexual. Women have not had this privilege, and justifiably are apt to regard sexual liberation as simply an extension of male privileges.'[26] Similarly, Ken Popert maintained in a 1982 essay that the social fabric of the gay male community is knitted together by promiscuity, with public sex being central to the lives of gay men. To make 'analogies with heterosexual institutions and practices' does not lead to understanding gay sex. Popert claimed public sexuality 'can be afforded a legitimate social space.' He also observed that 'the question of so-called public sex is one which threatens to divide gays from supportive straights, gay men from lesbians and gay men from gay men. To place this issue in its proper political setting, we have to grasp a significant but little discussed aspect of gay male promiscuity: I mean its tendency to create a collective consciousness.'[27]

As with pornography, however, gay men's engagement in and promotion of public sex presented challenges and problems for lesbians, both inside and outside the lesbian and gay liberation movement. Christine Donald, responding to gay male defences of sex in public during a discussion held at a 1983 conference, noted that 'it's an issue of consent. Male sexuality is already inescapable without women being forced into the role of voyeur in the service of men's sexual pleasure. And of course it would mean more freedom for men only, since this is a world in which women can't do anything in public with any degree of safety.'[28] Becki Ross, in *The House That Jill Built*, addressed the abhorrence felt by members of the Lesbian Organization of Toronto (LOOT) and lesbian feminists generally in the 1970s, about gay male sexuality. They used words like 'sexist,' 'exploitative,' 'predatory,' and 'objectifying' to describe it. Gay male liberation was, as one LOOT member lamented, essentially 'centred around their right to fuck ... the right to fuck whoever they want, whenever they want, as many as they want.'[29] A lesbian active in the Canadian Lesbian and Gay Rights Coalition cited male sexuality as an impediment to be becoming involved politically with gay men: 'I'm expected to march in support of your "right" to romp in public toilets, but my right to walk safely at night is over-looked. You raise thousands of dollars to support the defense of bath owners, but the travel equalization fund [to assist lesbians in attending the annual conference] is empty.'[30]

Other lesbian activists were more in step with gay male liberationists, although they were a minority within the broader lesbian and gay movement. One of them was Chris Bearchell who, while acknowledg-ing that men have had greater freedom to engage in sex acts, argued that a goal of gay liberation is to expand the opportunities for women who 'can't have sex on the streets, in parks, in steambaths,' but should be able to. This is because 'female sexuality has been tailored to hetero-sexual male reproductive and property needs, backed up by violence or the threat of violence.' Yet, despite popular notions, Bearchell stated that lesbians, too, push the envelope on matters of sexuality. 'Many dykes, including those who call ourselves feminists, are compulsive rule-breakers. We take women to beaches, or find them there, and head for the dunes. Or take barroom tricks to the bathroom cubicles for quickies.' It was untrue, Bearchell maintained, that public sex, pornog-raphy, SM, or child-adult sex are not lesbian issues. Rather, the extent to which they are not taken up by lesbians as issues, she declared, 'is a reflection of the extent to which women have been denied sexual choices.'[31]

Indeed, the lack of sexual choices for lesbians (and women generally) and the exploration of issues such as promiscuity, SM, and intergener-ational sex, formed some of the discussions at a groundbreaking les-bian sex conference in 1984. It was a difficult experience for some. As one conference participant commented afterwards, 'we feel vulnerable talking about our sexual experiences – admitting we have sexual expe-riences we enjoy.' Another observed there was reticence on the part of many women at the conference to describe as SM sexual activity they enjoyed and which involved 'power and passion.' A discussion about casual sex among lesbians, it was recalled, became 'polarized into a debate over monogamy versus non-monogamy.'[32] Reporting on the conference's keynote speech given by Susan Cole, Lee Waldorf criti-cized the 'lesbians and victims' perspective that formed the basis of Cole's position. Waldorf noted that Cole expounded on the fear of violent attack from men as being critical to lesbians' sexuality. Even more controversial was her assertion that misogyny has so strongly influenced attitudes towards sex that even lesbians reinforce abuse of women through sexual arousal. Lesbians, Waldorf reported Cole as suggesting, should be suspicious of sex.[33]

The widely divergent views on sexuality among activists at this time help to explain the huge gulf existing between many gay men and lesbians over the role that sexuality issues should play in the promotion of an agenda for social change. They also demonstrate the enormous difficulties that confronted liberationist activists in attempting to forge a political alliance between themselves and feminists, whether lesbian or heterosexual. By the early 1980s, it seemed that more divided the lesbian and gay liberation and feminist movements than united them. Lesbians who sought to work with gay men were caught in the middle – and in the crossfire. Similarly, liberationist militancy on sexuality issues grated on assimilationist, equality-seeking advocates, who saw them as impediments to securing legislative reform.

SIX

Backlash and Social Conservative Insurgency

As the 1970s ended, lesbian and gay liberation, like feminism, became the target of religious fundamentalists and social conservatives. These forces, in allegiance with economic and political conservatism, created a climate of backlash, mean-spiritedness, and outright hatred. Same-sex sexuality, and the liberation movement itself, came under attack, as part of a broad constellation of issues identified as undermining social stability, historic rights, and traditional values. Fighting against bigotry and backlash, consequently, became an urgent organizing objective for the still nascent lesbian and gay liberation movement, although those active in it had scarce resources and, initially, little mainstream support for doing so.

Born-Again Bigotry and the Rise of Social Conservatism

By the late 1970s, economic and social conservatives began to coalesce into a formidable social and political movement. They believed that spendthrift, interventionist governments were ruining the economy, destroying the free enterprise system, and undermining individual rights by catering to minorities. Other issues included supporting a strong military, espousing vociferous anti-Communism, and championing law and order initiatives. In the United States, right wing politicians and social conservative activists opposed bussing to force racial integration of schools, the Equal Rights Amendment (ERA) to give women constitutional equality, gun control, and the banning of school prayers. In Canada, the foot soldiers of this movement opposed bilingualism, multiculturalism, metrification, constitutional human rights,

BACKLASH AND SOCIAL CONSERVATIVE INSURGENCY 133

gun control, and liberal immigration laws. In both countries, Christian evangelicals mounted public campaigns to oppose abortion, birth control, sex education in the schools, liberalizing the laws dealing with homosexuality, and legislating human rights for gays and lesbians. Social conservatives held that women and men are not equal in all respects. They asserted inherent differences between men and women attributable to biology and other factors, which should be acknowledged and celebrated. They argued that traditional gender roles and the 'traditional family' are not only necessary, but must be preserved at all cost by strong supports and rewards from the state and social institutions.

From out of this reactionary ferment emerged groups opposing rights for lesbians and gays in order to advance a strategy based on homophobia, stereotypes, myths, misinformation, and distortion. These groups spread hatred and bigotry through conjuring images of children being molested by demonic, predatory, proselytizing homosexuals who recruited and seduced them into depraved sexuality. They warned against permitting gays and lesbians to be teachers or child-care workers, and characterized them as unsuitable role models for impressionable young people. For social conservatives, lesbian and gay liberation was an evil undermining the social order, moral values, and the traditional family. They quoted the Bible, cited selectively or inaccurately from scientific studies, and promoted the dubious or discredited works of certain social science professionals. Homosexuality, they asserted, is not a morally neutral or an acceptable lifestyle. They portrayed it as primarily genital, trivialized it as a chosen lifestyle, and denied it was a fundamental and immutable human characteristic. They viewed it as psychologically damaging and sexually dysfunctional. Homosexuals, they alleged, could be changed through criminal and social prohibitions, prayer, therapy, or sexual abstinence.

One of the first organizations to mix conservative politics with religious fundamentalism formed in Pasadena, California, in the mid-1970s under the name Christian Voice. Headed by an evangelical minister, its preferred strategy was to generate public hysteria by raising the spectre of school children being taught by 'a practising homosexual.'[1] Other evangelicals soon joining the fray included Jerry Falwell, who founded the Moral Majority, and Pat Robertson, who used his 700 Club TV show to promote strong social conservative views. Another group, Focus on the Family, founded in 1977 by a pediatrician, Dr James Dobson, billed itself as a 'non-denominational Christian organization.'

It was a product of 'growing concern that the traditional family, founded on Judeo-Christian moral values, is coming under increasing pressure in modern society.'[2] Particularly vitriolic were television evangelists like Jimmy Swaggart, renowned for hate-mongering commentary, such as the following, which appeared in the Canadian edition of his magazine, *The Evangelist*, in May 1983: 'The terrible sin of homosexuality is an evil sin against nature. In other words, it is an attempt by Satan to twist and pervert the way man was made in the beginning ... Homosexuality is his supreme effort.' Swaggart also warned, 'The only way the homosexual community can perpetuate itself is by recruiting through enticement.' He accused homosexuals of using every 'effort to beguile and allure (recruit) these naïve individuals [those of a tender age] in the homosexual lifestyle.'[3]

Other prominent U.S. social conservative leaders emerging at this time were anti-feminist women. They claimed not to want equality with men if that meant abandoning the privileges or preferential treatment married women historically received. They saw the social status of wife and mother as something to which all women should aspire: once having been attained, it should be preserved and cherished.[4] In the United States, Phyllis Schlafly organized the Eagle Forum and Stop-ERA, aligning her organization with Christian fundamentalists and conservative Republicans. Anita Bryant, an anti-feminist woman motivated by religious fervour, launched her famous anti-gay rights campaign in Dade County, Florida, in 1977 under the name of Save Our Children. Bryant sought to overturn an ordinance prohibiting discrimination against gays and lesbians. Her campaign activated hundreds of conservative women who believed the ERA and gay rights were threats to the traditional family and the way of life represented by it. Demanding traditional role models for children in the schools, Bryant and her supporters opposed the hiring of lesbian and gay teachers. Bryant soon launched a crusade that took her across the United States and catapulted her into the pages of newspapers and magazines and onto TV news broadcasts. She succeeded in having gay rights ordinances repealed in five communities. Only one of her initiatives failed – Proposition 6, a 1977 Orange County, California, initiative that sought a prohibition on the employment of gays and lesbians in public schools. Bryant was also one of the first to launch so-called Christian counselling organizations to cure gays and lesbians.[5]

These religious-right groups quickly became adept at using the media to promote their message, and at raising the enormous amounts of money necessary for their campaigns. They swiftly branched out into Canada to assert a leadership role in the family values movement in this country. Following groups led by Schlafly and Bryant, anti-feminist women in Canada created REAL Women (Realistic, Equal, Active for Life) in 1983. It believes the 'family is the most important unit in Canadian society,' the fragmentation of which 'is one of the major causes of disorder in society today.' Among REAL Women's stated objectives have been support for 'legislation which upholds the Judeo-Christian values of marriage and family life' and for the 'right to life of all innocent individuals from conception to natural death.' It has, from its founding, vigorously opposed lesbian and gay rights, dismissing the argument that gays and lesbians are an oppressed minority who should be protected from discrimination. In their view, what gays and lesbians have sought is 'special rights which recognize in law their lifestyle and behaviour. Homosexuality is a lifestyle and behaviour which one may chose to act out or not to act out. It is NOT an unchangeable, morally neutral characteristic or status.'[6]

While the emerging social conservative groups were popularly dismissed as radical fringe elements not respected by the mainstream, the fact is their message resonated with political conservatives because they espoused traditional beliefs and values that conservatives of all stripes cherished. Social conservatives, moreover, formed a critical voting block that political conservatives needed to placate in their pursuit of elected office. Thus, a cataclysmic convergence of the agendas of the religious right and social and political conservatives rocked lesbian and gay liberation and queer communities in the late 1970s and early 1980s. A concerted campaign was mounted with the objective of snuffing out the still nascent lesbian and gay movement, to turn public opinion against efforts to amend human rights codes, and to ensure that greater social tolerance would not occur.

In Toronto, anti-gay sentiment was stirred up following a series of events seized upon by social and political conservatives, supported by a homophobic media, beginning in July 1977. The catalyst was the release of the Ontario Human Rights Code Review Committee's report, *Life Together*, which recommended inclusion of sexual orientation in the Human Rights Code as a prohibited ground of discrimination. This recommendation unleashed a furore of homophobia. It was followed within a few days by mass vilification of homosexuals, occasioned by the sexual assault and savage murder of a twelve-year-old shoeshine boy, Emanuel Jaques, by three gay men. The media fulminated about a 'homosexual murder' committed during a 'homosexual orgy,' creating a climate of guilt by association in which all gays were connected in some sinister way with the boy's death. One newspaper columnist laid the blame at the feet of 'depraved' homosexuals who 'seem anxious to gain recruits, create a new "morality," and who thirst for political power.'[7] Such a vicious backlash was unleashed that Tom Warner of the Coalition for Gay Rights in Ontario and George Hislop of the Community Homophile Association of Toronto called a media conference at which they denounced the sensationalistic and homophobic coverage.[8]

But the period of backlash against rights for gays and lesbians is generally marked by Anita Bryant's tour of Canadian cities in 1977 and 1978 at the invitation of Renaissance International, founded by Ken Campbell, a Christian minister from Milton, Ontario. Bryant and Campbell crusaded against legislated human rights for lesbians and gays, using fears of children being recruited to homosexuality and the Christian family being undermined. Canadian gay and lesbian activists had anticipated that Bryant's popularity in the United States would lead ultimately to her campaign being imported to this country. To prepare for that eventuality, the Coalition to Stop Anita Bryant was formed in Toronto in early 1977. It soon thereafter began holding demonstrations, and in the fall of 1977 accelerated its organizing after the People's Church announced Bryant would be appearing at one of their services.[9] As threatening to gays and lesbians as the Bryant crusade was, it also provided unprecedented opportunity. In order to report on her story and speculate about Bryant's anticipated arrival in Canada, the media, which up to this time had largely ignored or trivialized gay and lesbian liberation, needed another point of view to balance their coverage. That meant seeking out lesbian and gay activists for their views, thus affording them media exposure that had until then been elusive. When Bryant's Canadian visits finally occurred, front-page headlines and lead-story billing on television, along with sympathetic opinion columns and feature interviews, made them a huge news story. Seizing the opportunity, the Coalition to Stop Anita Bryant, on the evening before her first Toronto appearance, held a lively rally after which eight hundred people marched up Yonge Street – Canada's largest gay and lesbian rights demonstration up until that time. A second demonstration was held the next day, in front of the church at which Bryant was speaking.[10]

Bryant returned to Canada three months later to lead crusades in Peterborough, Edmonton, Winnipeg, Moose Jaw, and London. Her presence galvanized the lesbian and gay communities in these cities. A demonstration in Peterborough to protest her visit in April was the first for gays and lesbians in that city. A crowd of one hundred and fifty people wound their way through residential neighbourhoods to picket outside the hockey arena where Bryant spoke, the ranks of the Trent University Homophile Association being bolstered by activists bussed in from Toronto. Local residents stood on the sidewalks gawking at the spectacle. Some jeered the demonstrators and others pelted them with eggs.[11] Bryant's descent on Edmonton similarly produced that city's first gay-organized demonstration, with over three hundred people rallying at the provincial legislature. Motorists honked their car horns and onlookers waved from the windows of their buildings to express support as the march proceeded through Edmonton streets. In Winnipeg, more than 350 people attended an anti-Bryant rally at the Manitoba legislature. Later in 1978, activists from Regina and Saskatoon travelled to Moose Jaw to protest Bryant's visit to that city. And in London, about one hundred lesbians and gays protested outside the hockey arena where Bryant spoke.[12]

Shortly after these events, Bryant's Save Our Children collapsed, but her allies in Canada remained active, basking in the attention her visits generated and forming themselves into various groups and 'crusades' aimed at generating a public backlash against lesbian and gay rights. One of the crusaders, the Reverend Hudson Hilsden of the Scarborough Gospel Temple, circulated widely a 1 December 1977 letter calling on the 'morally respectable people of Ontario' to organize against the 'satanic' gay rights movement. Condemning the threat of gay teachers and gay speakers in the schools, Hilsden exhorted the righteous to send letters to provincial politicians urging that lesbians and gays not be protected under human rights legislation.[13]

Meanwhile, the trials of the men accused of murdering Emanuel Jaques, and the trials of the *The Body Politic* officers arising from the 'Men Loving Boys Loving Men' article, drew nationwide media coverage that poisoned the environment in which gay and lesbian activists attempted to pursue their advocacy agenda. In early 1978, when sentencing the men found guilty of murdering Jaques, the presiding judge, in an act of appalling bigotry, stated, 'There are those who would seek legal protection for homosexuals in the Human Rights Code. You make me wonder if they are misguided. I wonder if there shouldn't be legislation to protect the people you seek to entice.'[14] The linkage of the murder with efforts to amend the code was also made by conservative politicians and, astonishingly, by the head of the Ontario Human Rights Commission. In a comment that shocked and infuriated lesbians and gays, Dorothea Crittenden, the chairman of the commission told a newspaper reporter that, because of the Jaques case, the time was not right for adding sexual orientation to the code.[15] Then, in January 1979, the trial of *TBP*'s publishers provided an opportunity for members of the religious right to whip up more backlash. They waged a vicious public attack on Mayor John Sewell after he spoke at a rally in support of *TBP*, condemning the charges against it as evidence of a police harassment campaign. Evangelist Ken Campbell produced a hurricane of vitriol by appearing on a popular Christian TV program, 100 Huntley Street, to relate his experience as a Crown witness at the *TBP* trial. As he spoke, the telephone number for the mayor's office flashed across the screen. The *Toronto Sun* aided Campbell, giving credibility to the campaign by publishing a front-page cartoon of Sewell being bashed by a telephone. The situation became so dangerously charged that Sewell was forced to enter and leave his office under police guard because of believable threats on his life.[16] The telephone campaign was followed by Campbell's 'Faith, Freedom and the Family' rally at City Hall, during which demonstrators carried placards linking Sewell and gay activist George Hislop with Jaques's murderers and with a U.S. mass murderer of male youths.[17]

This volatile, hate-filled climate turned Toronto's 1980 municipal elections into a battleground pitting Sewell, and the aspirations of the city's lesbian and gay communities, against the fear and paranoia of a substantial portion of the heterosexual population. The issue was posed in the media as the rise of 'gay power,' with its perceived potential for turning Toronto the Good into a modern-day Sodom and Gomorrah. Contributing to the general climate of hysteria was fear-mongering reportage of George Hislop's candidacy for a city council seat in a downtown ward containing a high concentration of lesbian and gay voters. Hislop was repeatedly portrayed as the gay candidate nominated by a power hungry lesbian and gay community, and dismissed as a single-issue candidate. Sewell, in turn, was cast as an accomplice in the gay power grab. A spillover from the U.S. media, the fear of gay power followed a CBS TV documentary, 'Gay Power, Gay Politics' that focused on San Francisco's lesbian and gay community, profiling Harvey Milk, the one openly gay member of the city council there. Canadian media picked up on the CBS story, speculating whether Toronto was becoming 'San Francisco North.'[18]

The anti-gay frenzy reached a feverish level when, two months before the election, Sewell attended the opening of Hislop's campaign office, giving a short speech expressing his hope that Hislop would be elected. Sewell's opponents lost little time in using the 'gay issue' to their advantage. 'I can see no good coming through this gay alliance,' said a prominent conservative councillor. 'Alliances with preferred or special minorities can only hurt the Office of Mayor.'[19] Sewell's mayoralty opponent, Art Eggleton, stoked the fire by stating, 'Sewell and Hislop are facilitating San Francisco-style gay power politics in Toronto.' He added that he did not want Toronto to become another San Francisco, where 'the gay community pushed its way into city hall ... I am a tolerant person but also traditional in my values. I can't agree with flaunting sexual preference.'[20] The strategy succeeded. Gay power was the main topic of conversation outside the halls where Sewell spoke. The campaign manager for one of Hislop's opponents for a city council seat reported receiving phone calls from 'gay bashers looking for someone who hates gays they could work for.'[21] By election day, it seemed as if the only issue for voters was the gay community's wanton lust for political power. Both Sewell and Hislop were defeated, and popular opposition to gay rights and so-called gay power was widely cited in the media as the reason.

The mainstream political campaign against Hislop and Sewell was restrained in comparison with that waged by a motley assortment of far-right and evangelical Christian organizations. Renaissance International alone distributed 100,000 copies of a tabloid, urging the defeat of Sewell and other municipal election candidates seen as being supportive of gay and lesbian rights. The day before the election, Renaissance published a two-page advertisement in the *Toronto Sun* attacking the gay community and calling for a vote for Toronto the Good.[22] Another group formed by fundamentalist Christians, calling itself Metro's Moral Majority, distributed a *Homosexuality Fact Sheet* door-to-door. One of its purported facts was that '1 out of 3 sexual assaults on children are committed by homosexuals.' Positive Parents, billing itself as a 'pro-family crusade against the radical homosexual lobby,' held a two-hundred-person 'decency' rally at City Hall, attended by Campbell, Salvation Army officers, and an allegedly reformed homosexual.[23] The League Against Homosexuals produced a widely distributed leaflet that screamed: 'Queers do not produce they seduce!' The league also called for the recriminalization of homosexuality as a 'crime against nature' for which a stiff mandatory prison term should be imposed.[24]

Emboldened by their success in the municipal elections, social and political conservatives used the gay issue against socially progressive candidates in the 1981 Ontario provincial election. Liberal and NDP members of the legislature, spooked by the municipal results, began backtracking from their previous support for the inclusion of sexual orientation in the Ontario Human Rights Code. The governing Progressive Conservatives appealed to a pro-family constituency and won a majority mandate. Positive Parents and the League Against Homosexuals again distributed literature targeting candidates who had supported gay rights. One Positive Parents leaflet stated, 'An N.D.P. sign on your lawn says you support homosexuals.' Christian fundamentalist organizations put forward anti-gay and anti-feminist viewpoints, primarily under the name of the Pro-Family Coalition.[25]

The events of 1980 and 1981 marked the arrival in Canada of a fully fledged family values movement that by then had flexed its muscles in the United States. In October 1982, Ken Campbell allied himself directly with the U.S. family values forces. He invited Moral Majority leader Jerry Falwell to speak at the first of a series of national crusades to 'liberate the oppressed,' such as 'women, children (born and unborn), and victims of drug abuse, alcohol or sexual disorientation.' Campbell launched a twenty-two-city campaign to ensure that Canada's new constitution and its charter of rights, then being finalized, did not enshrine 'godlessness.'[26] Within a few short years, the family values advocates would organize massively in several parts of Canada, to oppose the amendment of human rights codes to include sexual orientation, the legal recognition of same-sex relationships, sexual orientation anti-discrimination policies in schools, and other initiatives of the lesbian and gay rights movement.

SEVEN

Fighting against the Odds, Facing New Crises

Despite over a decade of advocacy, virtually no progress was made on amending human rights laws. The issue initially seized with such vigour as the way to achieve liberation was now prompting a debate about the advisability of continuing to pursue largely symbolic legislative reform in the face of renewed police harassment and religious right resurgence. It was also apparent that the early activist groups, while remarkably successful in many ways, had failed resoundingly in others. Many had struggled for years to survive and ultimately died. Efforts at building a national movement were faltering, and dissent and division over strategy were rampant. Then, in the early 1980s, another ingredient was added to this potent brew, as the death and devastation wrought by the arrival of AIDS became overwhelming. New exigencies diverted energies and financial resources away from traditional advocacy and community-building activities, and towards conducting AIDS awareness. Providing services for the growing legions of those who became ill vied with established advocacy agendas for resources and community support. If the mid-to-late 1970s had been a dark period, the early 1980s would quickly prove be cataclysmic.

Fighting against Discrimination

All the while that gay and lesbian activists were fighting against police repression and social conservative backlash, they continued to pursue their agenda for enactment of amendments to human rights laws. They did so with ingenuity and perseverance, even when they discovered that politicians generally paid far more attention to the opponents of gay and lesbian rights, or openly dismissed or ignored demands for legislated equality. Their efforts to secure sexual orientation amendments or remove discriminatory policies and practices proceeded on several complementary tracks. Lobbying and public action focused on the politicians who ultimately would need to amend the laws. Exposing and publicizing cases of discrimination, looking for means to establish positive legal precedents, pressuring human rights commissions to take a stand, and using all of these means to gain public support were the other tracks.

At the federal level, early success in securing a removal from the Immigration Act of the ban on gay and lesbian immigrants and visitors to Canada contrasted with political intransigence over ending discrimination and harassment in employment within federal jurisdiction. In 1974, the government released its Green Paper on Immigration, which proposed wide-ranging reform, including removal of the ban on gays and lesbians. Taking nothing for granted, however, gay and lesbian groups across the country mounted a concerted lobbying campaign directed to the members of a parliamentary committee charged with recommending legislative amendments. Success was achieved when the immigration ban finally was lifted in 1977 with the adoption of a more modern Immigration Act.[1] Yet, a number of high profile challenges to the Canadian Armed Forces' ban on gays and lesbians, while helping to bring media and public attention to an unjustifiable policy of discrimination, had no impact on changing government policy.

Two 1977 cases involving Pte. Barbara Thornborrow and Master Corporal Barbara Cameron were particularly instrumental in raising the issue of the gay ban in the public consciousness. Thornborrow's involuntary discharge from the armed forces followed a Special Investigations Unit search of her room and questions about her relationship with another woman. She acknowledged being a lesbian whereupon she was given the choice of being expelled after signing a document admitting her sexual orientation, or accepting psychiatric treatment. Thornborrow refused both options and contacted Lesbians of Ottawa Now. Together with Gays of Ottawa, they issued a press release, generating national media coverage. Thornborrow shortly afterwards was kicked out of the forces for being 'not advantageously employable.'[2] Cameron went public a few weeks later after she and eight other women at the military base in Argentia, Newfoundland were discovered to be lesbians and were expelled. The publicity generated by the Thornborrow and Campbell cases led to public pressure on the Department of National Defence to explain its actions, but not to a change in policy. Commenting following Thornborrow's expulsion, the chief of defence stated 'it is deemed necessary to discriminate against those who, having admitted or demonstrated behavioral traits such as homosexuality, might attempt to impose them on others, particularly youthful members.'[3]

Because of such official attitudes, the environment in the ranks of the military was poisonous. Rumours, gossip, and the use of informants fuelled terror and led to intimidation. One who endured such a climate was Darel Wood, expelled from the forces in 1978. She later related how the military's Special Investigations Unit planted informers in basic training so they could gain the trust of new recruits. Once someone was investigated for being gay or lesbian, they were ostracized. Wood recalled the three-month period between the investigation and her ultimate discharge as a time when she was treated like a 'leper.'[4] Another member of the military, Jacques Gallant, learned in 1976 that he was being investigated as a 'sexual deviate.' Later discharged from the forces, he appealed to the Federal Court, but it accepted the Department of National Defence position that civilian courts had no jurisdiction over military matters.[5]

When legislation establishing the Canadian Human Rights Act (CHRA) was proposed in the mid-1970s, lesbian and gay activists turned their attention to it immediately. The CHRA addressed discrimination in employment and provision of services within the federal government's jurisdiction, but excluded the RCMP and the armed forces. Sexual orientation was left out of the grounds of prohibited discrimination when the CHRA was introduced in Parliament in November 1976. During first reading of the bill, representatives of the National Gay Rights Coalition succeeded in obtaining support for a sexual orientation amendment from NDP MPs, a Liberal backbencher, and one Progressive Conservative MP, as well as a number of mainstream organizations. Opposition came from the armed forces, the RCMP, and the Department of External Affairs, all of which invoked fears about national security arising from their belief that homosexuals were highly susceptible to blackmail.[6] In the end, the CHRA was adopted without sexual orientation. When amendments were introduced in 1982 to protect the rights of people with disabilities and address sexual harassment in the workplace, the Liberal government once more adamantly ruled out adding sexual orientation. 'I am strongly opposed, and my party is strongly opposed, to this legislation,' commented the justice minister, Mark MacGuigan.[7]

At the provincial level, amending human rights laws to prohibit sexual orientation discrimination was irrevocably embedded in the public agenda in the period between 1975 to 1984, even if tangible progress, legislatively, proved elusive. One of the great achievements by activists in that regard was skilfully publicizing cases of discrimination to dramatize the need for legislative action. The cases put a human face to the demand, helping to shape public opinion and secure political support. The cases exposed the prevalence of homophobia and heterosexism, raising issues about preferred corporate image, appropriate role models, who should be authority figures, and about openly gay men working in charge of children and youth.

The most famous of the discrimination cases involved John Damien. For eleven long years, his struggle to gain reinstatement to the Ontario Racing Commission as a racing steward was a compelling example of why sexual orientation amendments were needed. Damien was fired in 1975 because he was homosexual, after having spent twenty-five years as a respected and competent jockey and horse racing professional. But once racing commission officials became aware Damien was gay, they concluded his orientation might lead to his being blackmailed. He was given the option of resigning in exchange for $1,200 and a letter of reference if he would not reveal the reason for his dismissal. He refused. The cash settlement was increased to $1,700. He refused again. The next day, he received a letter advising him that he was not being rehired, but no reasons were given.[8] Angered, Damien contacted Toronto GATE. They put him in touch with a lawyer, organized a defence committee, and held a press conference that gained national publicity. At a second press conference a month later, the newly formed Committee to Defend John Damien announced he was suing his former employers for $1 million.[9] Damien also launched a second suit against a doctor at the Fort Erie Race Track, alleging the doctor had violated professional ethics and the Venereal Disease Control Act by informing racing commission officials of Damien's homosexuality. Damien believed that disclosure prompted his firing.

The activists who supported Damien thought that he was the right person with the ideal circumstances to sway public opinion to secure a Human Rights Code amendment. Instead, the history of the case turned out to be one of frustration, legal delays, waning support, and personal pain. 'We had no idea of what we were getting into,' recalls John Wilson, who chaired the committee for several years. In the end, Damien and his small band of supporters were no match for the defendants, most of whom had their legal fees paid by the Ontario government.[10] Damien's defence initially met with enthusiasm in lesbian and gay communities. He spoke at public meetings and fund-raising events across Canada. His case generated enormous publicity, and was influential in winning some of the first political support in Ontario for an amendment to the code. In fact, his firing was raised by opposition MPPs in the Ontario legislature, and was cited by the Ontario Human Rights Code Review Committee its 1977 *Life Together* report. But the legal processes had slowed to a glacial pace, as the defendants used every delaying tactic at their disposal. Lack of legal progress kept Damien's case out of the news, depriving the committee of the publicity needed to do fund-raising. And media coverage waned following a retaliatory move in March 1976 by the defendants, who launched a defamation suit after *Weekend*, a magazine supplement to thirty-two newspapers across Canada, published a feature article on Damien's case. Although the suit was dropped a year later, it had a chilling effect on the media. Virtually no significant publicity was given to the case afterwards.[11] Sadly, Damien never did get the justice he sought. He endured bankruptcy, long periods of unemployment, and fears about becoming homeless. By 1986, Damien had become far too ill with pancreatic cancer to proceed with the lawsuits. Still, a symbolic victory was achieved in that year, shortly before Damien's death, when the original defendants finally agreed to an out-of-court settlement. They paid $50,000, the amount of one year's salary plus interest, into a trust fund for Damien in exchange for his agreement to end his suit against them.[12]

In Saskatoon, efforts to amend human rights legislation were boosted in September 1975, following the University of Saskatchewan's decision to ban Doug Wilson from placement in public schools and to remove him from the list of practice teacher supervisors because he was openly gay and involved with a gay liberation organization. The university claimed Wilson's presence in the public school system would be a 'disaster.'[13] Wilson fought back by filing a complaint of discrimination with the Saskatchewan Human Rights Commission, although the Fair Employment Act did not include sexual orientation as a prohibited ground of discrimination. He also made the incident known to the press, generating national publicity and an outpouring of support from the local lesbian and gay communities and straight civil libertarians. Wilson's case energized lesbian and gay activists on the prairies. A Committee to Defend Doug Wilson was established to raise funds for the legal efforts and conducted public education. The Human Rights

Commission, after completing a preliminary investigation, ruled the rights of gay people were protected under *sex* in the act and announced they would proceed with a formal investigation. Before they could do so, however, the university received a court injunction against the commission and a ruling that sex as defined in the act referred only to gender. The commission did not appeal and a short time later Wilson abandoned further legal action.[14] Nonetheless, Wilson's case, along with Damien's, was critical to the lesbian and gay rights movement nationally. They produced much-needed publicity, locally and across the country, about sexual orientation discrimination. For many people on the prairies, such publicity resulted in the first public discussion of lesbian and gay rights in their communities.[15]

Two British Columbia cases helped to create public awareness about sexual orientation discrimination during this era. The first involved a human rights complaint filed against the *Vancouver Sun* for refusing to publish an advertisement for Vancouver GATE's newspaper, *Gay Tide*. The second involved the dismissal of a gay man, Rob Joyce, from his position with a provincial government youth agency. The *Gay Tide* case is significant because for the first time in Canada, a human rights board of inquiry convened to adjudicate a complaint of sexual orientation discrimination, resulting ultimately in the first gay rights case heard by the Supreme Court of Canada. The BC Human Rights Commission argued that, although sexual orientation was not included in the provincial Human Rights Act, the *Vancouver Sun*'s advertising policy constituted discrimination without reasonable cause, pursuant to the act. The *Sun* had cast homosexuality as a threat to society, contending that any association with gay liberation would be offensive to many subscribers. On 12 January 1976, a board of inquiry ruled that the *Sun* had discriminated, fined the paper five hundred dollars, and ordered it to refrain from the same or similar contravention of the act in future. The historic decision stated that gays were a significant minority group persecuted by 'intolerant populations and institutions of government.' The *Sun* unsuccessfully appealed to the British Columbia Supreme Court, but the BC Court of Appeal subsequently overturned that decision, ruling that the *Sun* had reasonable cause not to print the advertisement, on the grounds that homosexuality was offensive to most people.[16] GATE appealed in turn to the Supreme Court of Canada. In a 6 to 3 judgment issued on 22 May 1979, that court found the *Sun* had reasonable cause to control the content of its advertisements, stating that the guarantee of freedom of the press in the Canadian Bill of Rights ensured a newspaper's right not to print material it wished to exclude.[17]

The Rob Joyce case revealed the vulnerability of gays in occupations where they counsel or assist youth, and how the perception of gays as corrupters of youth and children could damage careers and reputations. It began in 1982 when openly gay Joyce, who had received a special commendation from British Columbia's human resources minister, was fired by the British Columbia Corrections Association as a counsellor at a Vancouver youth hostel for juvenile prostitutes.[18] Hostel management accused Joyce of sexual misconduct with a client, although the accusation was never substantiated. Joyce protested and an internal corrections association investigation confirmed there were, in fact, no grounds to discipline, suspend or fire him, and no evidence to support the allegation. Subsequently, three human resources ministry investigations also found no evidence of wrongdoing while a provincial ombudsman's report actually recommended the ministry apologize to Joyce. They did not do so and never rehired him.[19] Instead, his name was placed on the government's child abuser registry and the provincial cabinet minister who had earlier commended Joyce repeated the sexual misconduct allegation during a radio program. Joyce, consequently, was unable to find other employment and was forced onto welfare.

With support from the Gay Rights Union, of which Joyce was a spokesperson, the Rob Joyce Legal Defence Fund was established. Litigation was initiated for wrongful dismissal and defamation. In November 1983, Joyce also filed a court petition for removal of his name from the child abuser registry, with which the government complied a few months later. But they refused to pay back wages or rehire Joyce, effectively leaving his reputation as a youth counsellor under a cloud of suspicion. Unable to find a job in his chosen field, Joyce continued his legal suits for as long as he could but dropped them in 1987 because he could no longer afford the costs. At that time, he described his then five years of proceedings as 'really gruesome ... They'd ask [during the examinations for discovery]: "What's a homosexual's reputation worth?"' Disillusioned, he lamented, 'One of the failures of the gay movement is that we haven't been able to provide adequate structures and defence funds so that people can fight protracted battles without losing their sanity.'[20]

Political Resistance to the Human Rights Campaigns

Mirroring the negative legal outcomes of the early human rights cases, the advocacy campaigns to secure legislative amendments forged ahead despite the odds against them, meeting almost universal political opposition. Yet, public support was shifting in favour of human rights protection for gays and lesbians, as evidenced by a 1977 Gallup Poll. It showed that 52 per cent of Canadians supported amending the CHRA to include sexual orientation, while only 30 per cent were opposed and 18 per cent gave no opinion. Significantly, however, majority support existed only among women and people under the age of forty-nine – hardly the profile of Canada's legislators at the time.[21] Disregarding the polling results, the federal government adamantly opposed amending the CHRA. Provincially, conservative political parties formed most of the governments by the early 1980s and catered to social conservative constituencies. As well, the rise of neoconservatism elsewhere, particularly the elections of Margaret Thatcher in the United Kingdom and Ronald Reagan in the United States, affected Canada both socially and politically. A deep and prolonged recession also put the political focus on economic rather than social issues, impeding sustained grassroots organizing for social change. In such a climate, it became more difficult for small bands of gays and lesbians spread thinly across the country to pursue an activist agenda. As Erin Shoemaker, a lesbian activist in Saskatchewan, has recalled about this period, 'We became a very conservative, rigid province, and lost a lot of educational and social services, everything. Jobs got tight. As a lesbian or gay person, I think a lot of us felt that we couldn't afford to take the kind of risks we had taken before.'[22]

In 1977, Quebec suddenly and unexpectedly became the first province to legislate a prohibition on sexual orientation discrimination. Only two years earlier, when legislation establishing the Chartre de droits, Quebec's human rights law, was introduced, sexual orientation was omitted and an amendment to add the term moved by the Parti Québécois (PQ) did not pass at the committee approval stage. The Liberal justice minister defended the omission by stating society was not ready for such an amendment, and that conferring legitimacy on homosexuality was not within the bounds of human rights legislation.[23] The PQ, despite their support for an amendment before forming the government, took a similar approach, initially dashing the hopes of lesbian and gay activists. After their election in November 1976, the PQ rebuffed calls for an amendment and even refused to meet with ADGQ to discuss the matter.[24]

But the political climate changed dramatically once Montreal police raided Truxx in October 1977. The angry community response, and widespread condemnation of both the raid and the police's heavy-handedness during the protest the night afterwards, caused unwelcome publicity for a government wanting to project a progressive image.[25] In the aftermath, ADGQ secured a commitment from the Quebec Human Rights Commission to recommend a sexual orientation amendment to the chartre, a gesture the government immediately embraced.[26] Acting with breathtaking swiftness, PQ justice minister Marc-André Bédard introduced a sexual orientation amendment on 7 December 1977 in the form of Bill 88. The PQ rushed the bill through the legislative process before any significant publicity could be generated and passed it on final reading at ten minutes before midnight on 15 December. Bill 88 was signed into law without fanfare four days later. Despite the manner in which a timid PQ government had proceeded, Bill 88 was a victory that lesbian and gay activists could legitimately claim arose directly from their efforts. A precedent had been set, a province had been forced to act. A momentous development for a still fledgling movement, it caused euphoria and optimism, becoming a symbol of what militant and visible lesbian and gay liberationists were capable of achieving. Buoyed by the exhilarating developments following these events, ADGQ activist Ron Dayman exulted, 'We in the gay movement have said it for years, and now we're proven right: gay rights will only come through public action. Public mass action which makes gays visible and which proves to the governments in power that gays are a significant force in our society, a force no longer willing to be ignored. The lobbying groundwork was important, but it was the militancy of gays in the streets which brought results.'[27]

Unfortunately, governments in other parts of the country ignored the historic legal change in Quebec and did not follow suit. In Atlantic Canada, virtually no progress was made, although Halifax's Gay Alliance for Equality organized for a sexual orientation amendment throughout the 1970s and early 1980s. Successive Nova Scotia governments remained unmoved. No concerted campaigns were launched in New Brunswick, Prince Edward Island, or Newfoundland. Ontario, on the other hand, was a fierce battleground. There, the Coalition for Gay Rights in Ontario (CGRO) formed in January 1975 to coordinate provincewide advocacy efforts in the face of a biligerantly anti-gay Progressive Conservative government. Almost immediately, three significant events propelled the Human Rights Code amendment issue into the public spotlight: John Damien was fired as a racing steward; the Human Rights Code Review Committee was established to advise the government on amending the code; and, a provincial election was held. All events were used by CGRO to generate publicity for and public awareness regarding an amendment. Following the election of a minority PC government, a Liberal private member's resolution and an NDP private member's bill were either defeated or not dealt with during May 1976. The debates about them angered activists because of a universal PC caucus opposition and homophobic comments made by Conservative members.[28] These actions prompted CGRO to adopt the slogan, 'Vote for Gay Rights, Vote against the Tories' during the 1977 election. It caught the attention of the media, which produced significant news coverage of gay human rights as an issue.[29] A period of backlash and extreme homophobia followed the 1977 election, which returned another PC minority government. The release in July 1977 of the Human Rights Code Review Committee's *Life Together* report recommending, among other things, that sexual orientation be added to the code, generated front-page headlines. This ground-breaking event was followed in rapid succession by homophobic hysteria fuelled by the sexual assault and murder of Emanuel Jaques, Anita Bryant's importation to Ontario of her Save Our Children campaign, and the criminal charges against *TBP* for publishing 'Men Loving Boys Loving Men.' Fears of paedophilia and of gay men as seducers and corrupters of youth, plus inflammatory media commentaries, created a poisonous political climate in which to continue to press for the introduction of a sexual orientation amendment.

Persevering despite this deluge, CGRO obtained the support of community and civil liberties groups, professional associations, trade unions, churches, women's groups, and others. They held rallies and demonstrations and undertook a new round of lobbying, including a first-ever meeting with a divided Liberal caucus in the fall of 1977. Evidencing the enormity of CGRO's challenge was the demand by some Liberals for exclusion of teachers and child care workers from the provisions of any amendment, a proposition CGRO rejected.[30] Then, in 1978, CGRO presented members of the legislature with its second brief, producing favourable comments in the press and from MPPs, but silence from the government.[31] The PCs, however, faced a political dilemma because of intense pressure to prohibit discrimination based on *handicap*, in anticipation of the United Nations Year of Disabled Persons; it did not want to prohibit sexual orientation discrimination at the same time. CGRO, recognizing the opening that an amendment to include handicap would create, forged a political alliance with groups representing persons with disabilities that were also lobbying vigorously for a code amendment. This led to the establishment, in early 1979, of the Coalition for Life Together, comprising gays, lesbians, and people with disabilities. Among its activities was a demonstration that featured gays, bisexuals, lesbians, and people with disabilities – many in wheelchairs – in front of the legislature to protest government inaction.[32]

Based on media reports of imminent Human Rights Code amendments, CGRO geared up in late November 1979, kicking off a new amendment campaign with a 'Gay Human Rights Day' rally attended by over two hundred people. Within days, the government – desperate to be seen as acting to outlaw discrimination against people with disabilities but not wanting to open up the code to amendment – tabled a bill intending to provide rights for disabled persons in a separate act. The ploy backfired, as the media, groups representing people with disabilities, and CGRO all slammed it. CGRO's Tom Warner commented that the PC government had taken a 'circuitous sleazy political route to avoid giving human rights protections to lesbians and gay men.'[33] CGRO organized a letter and telephone campaign directed at the three party leaders and publicly reconfirmed support for protecting people with disabilities through a code amendment. Groups representing people with disabilities called for the withdrawal of the bill. Faced with organized opposition, adverse media commentary, and a commitment by the Liberals and NDP to oppose the bill, the minority government withdrew it.[34]

Unfortunately, the political situation worsened within a few months. By the end of 1980, Liberal and NDP resolve had disintegrated. The homophobia witnessed in the Toronto municipal elections, and the hatred stirred up by religious right and other anti-gay groups, caused panic in the opposition parties, who now saw supporting rights for gays and lesbians as political suicide. Their panic was part of a wider reaction among liberals and progressives, shaken by the triumphs of Margaret Thatcher and Ronald Reagan and the rise of the religious right. They feared a global rightward shift in politics was also overtaking Canada. Consequently, during the run-up to the March 1981 Ontario election, support for lesbian and gay rights was jettisoned.[35] Worse still, during the election campaign period, Toronto police raided four bathhouses. The ensuing publicity about sexual activity in bawdy houses made politicians even more skittish about supporting lesbian and gay issues. Adding to the mix were right wing and Christian fundamentalist organizations with stridently anti-gay and anti-feminist views that worked actively in the election. Not to be outdone, the PCs ran on a much-touted pro-family platform.[36]

The PCs, returned with a majority government, soon introduced amendments to the code that did not include sexual orientation, prompting a new round of demonstrations and lobbying. CGRO protested at Queen's Park on the eve of the bill's second reading and appeared at the committee hearings to present a brief. Their presentation elicited a comment from the minister who introduced the bill that 'the government does not feel [sexual preference] should be enshrined as an acceptable or normal lifestyle.'[37] The government also ignored submissions from many organizations outside the gay and lesbian communities supporting CGRO's position. A Liberal amendment to add sexual orientation at second reading of the bill was defeated. The Conservatives' position angered gays and lesbians, who crowded into the legislature's public gallery to witness the final vote on the bill. When an amendment moved by the NDP at that stage was also defeated, three gay men rose in the gallery and shouted, 'This is a human rights omission!' They handcuffed themselves to the railing as other gay spectators began jeering the MPPs. Within minutes, security guards appeared with wire cutters, released the handcuffed protestors, and emptied the gallery after roughing up some of the spectators.[38] The protesters left the legislature resigned to the fact that achieving an amendment would take several more years of organizing.

In Manitoba, Gays for Equality (GFE) also soldiered on despite a climate of political hostility, generating publicity about discrimination against gays and lesbians when John Damien visited Winnipeg in November 1976. The visit featured a number of public events, including a demonstration on the steps of the Manitoba legislature.[39] The following year, the Manitoba Gay Coalition, comprised of ten groups, questioned candidates in the provincial election about amending the Human Rights Act, child custody issues, and legal recognition of lesbian and gay spousal relationships. One such intervention drew a dismissive remark from NDP Premier Edward Schreyer: 'I have no animosity to those who may be in that condition. It is not my impression that homosexuals are oppressed ... I say I've got more important things to worry about.'[40] As bad as things were under the NDP, they got worse when Schreyer's government was defeated by the Progressive Conservatives. Winnipeg activist Chris Vogel has recalled how gloomy the situation became, with the dominance of right-wingers in the PC government making lobbying for a sexual orientation amendment futile. Activists thus invested little effort in doing so throughout the PC government's four-year term.[41] Their hopes brightened somewhat in 1981, with the NDP's re-election. By then, the party had adopted a policy of including sexual orientation in the Human Rights Act. Encouraged, gays and lesbians renewed their lobbying, held demonstrations, submitted briefs, and sent in petitions. But the new government, led by Howard Pawley, remained reticent, stalling repeatedly on the issue. A May 1984 recommendation of the Manitoba Human Rights Commission for introduction of an amendment was ignored. Even the support of over sixty organizations, such as the Manitoba Teachers' Society, the Manitoba Association of Registered Nurses, and the College of Family Physicians failed to sway the government.[42]

Saskatchewan's NDP government was equally disinclined to act. When new human rights legislation in 1979 did not include sexual orientation, outraged lesbians and gays demonstrated at the legislature, joined by people with disabilities, seniors, and anti–nuclear development activists. They did not receive a warm welcome. An NDP MLA told them that homosexuality was a moral issue and that the government had received more negative than positive responses on the question of a sexual orientation amendment.[43] Conditions worsened after the 1981 provincial election, as the new Progressive Conservative government catered to fundamentalist Christians and the anti-abortion movement. The PCs adamantly opposed rights for gays and lesbians, and cabinet ministers periodically condemned homosexuality. Still, Saskatoon's Campaign for Human Equality and Regina's Equality for Gays and Lesbians Everywhere launched letter-writing campaigns, wrote briefs, and met with MLAs in order to keep the issue on the political agenda.

Next door, the Alberta Progressive Conservatives, first elected in 1971, held a virtual monopoly on the seats in the provincial legislature. While lesbian and gay activists realistically expected little progress to be made at the political level, they lobbied all throughout the 1970s and early 1980s in support of legislated human rights protection, mounting letter-writing and other campaigns. Hopes were raised briefly in 1976, after the Alberta Human Rights Commission recommended that sexual orientation be added to the Individual Rights Protection Act. The government, predictably, rejected the recommendation.[44] Resolving to press on with the issue nonetheless, activists coordinated and intensified their lobbying through the formation in April 1979 of the Alberta Lesbian and Gay Rights Association.[45] Later that year, however, the Alberta government sent a profoundly negative message, appointing a known opponent of gay and lesbian rights as chairman of the Human Rights Commission. The minister in charge of the commission defended the appointment with the claim that sexual orientation is voluntarily chosen, and therefore less deserving of protection from discrimination than involuntary characteristics such as race. Persons disclosing their sexual orientation, he contended, should expect discrimination because by flaunting their sexuality they may violate the rights of others.[46] Not surprisingly, the commission, in early 1980, recommended amendments to the act, from which sexual orientation was conspicuously absent. Lesbian and gay activists called for the resignation of the commissioners because they had backtracked from their position in 1976. 'We feel we've been stabbed in the back by the commission,' commented Doug Whitfield of GATE.[47] Renewed lobbying took place in 1984 after the commission, now headed by a more supportive chairman, renewed its call for an amendment. Publicity over the case of Claude Olivier, a group home supervisor fired solely because of his sexual orientation, also helped generate public support, although the government remained intransigent.[48]

On the West Coast, harsh political realities similarly offered little optimism. In the 1975 British Columbia election, the right wing Social Credit party trounced the NDP government. Social Credit's ideological bent and its conservative Christian supporters, together with what would become its amazing longevity, meant little progress towards a legislative amendment was made for nearly twenty years. The new government overhauled the human rights legislation, establishing a scaled-down and significantly less effective Human Rights Council, and abolishing the 'discrimination without reasonable cause' section that featured in the *Gay Tide* case. Coupled with Social Credit's disdain for human rights legislation generally was its hostility, often publicly expressed, towards homosexuality. Illustrative of such views was the comment made by a Social Credit backbencher during a legislative debate on lesbian and gay rights: 'There are many of us who don't believe in child porn (or) in child molesters; that is a sexual orientation that I think [the NDP MLA who had raised the subject] would reject himself.'[49]

Tribulations of the National Gay Rights Coalition

The strategic importance of securing further Criminal Code reform and of obtaining legislated human rights gave momentum to establishing, in 1975, a national coalition having those objectives. Thus was born the National Gay Rights Coalition (NGRC) that after 1978 became the Canadian Lesbian and Gay Rights Coalition (CLGRC). It struggled mightily to sustain itself but ultimately failed, disbanding in 1981 because of unresolved dissent and acrimony. Nonetheless, it was a bold initiative on the part of a fledgling movement, and remains an accomplishment unduplicated even today, originally consisting of twenty-seven member groups across Canada. The coalition's program for Criminal Code reform, using a liberation perspective, called for the repeal of sections dealing with indecent acts in a public place, loitering or wandering by a person previously convicted of a sexual offence, common bawdy houses, dangerous sexual offenders, soliciting, and the spread of venereal diseases. More explosively, it also called for abolition of all age of consent laws.[50] Far less contentious was the human rights platform calling for the inclusion of sexual orientation in, first, the Canadian Bill of Rights and, later, the Canadian Human Rights Act. It also called for the repeal of anti-homosexual provisions of the Immigration Act, and for an end to the ban on gays and lesbians in the Canadian military. In the end, it was the equality-seeking agenda and not the liberationist causes that dominated and defined the national coalition, with the latter serving primarily as fuel for bitter dissent. Over its short life, the coalition faced many challenges which, in the end, it simply could not overcome. As Ottawa activist David Garmaise, a key figure in NGRC, commented ten years after its demise, 'The word "coalition" is a misnomer. It was really an Ottawa lobbying office for national gay rights issues ... anything we tried to do in terms of co-ordinating anything across the country didn't really succeed. It was just too difficult.'[51] The NGRC remained a small, volunteer-based network of groups with diverse interests. As Miriam Smith has chronicled in Lesbian and Gay Rights in Canada: Social Movements and Equality-Seeking, 1971–1995, it struggled to address many problems, some of which are common to all grassroots organizing in Canada, others of which were unique to lesbian and gay organizing.[52] Many problems were intractable: vast distances made travel to meetings and conferences difficult and expensive; regionalism permeated everything; there was an inability to function effectively in two languages; divisions over Quebec independence remained unresolved; resources were meagre, and there was no full-time staff; sources of large-scale funding were never found; communications were primarily by mail; the majority of the member groups were exclusively or predominantly male, and most were from central Canada.

Gender issues also raged within the coalition, as lesbians and gay men struggled to unite around a common agenda. Many lesbians charged that the civil rights focus was too narrow and that it insufficiently addressed issues important to lesbians, such as building community. Positions on repealing pornography laws and abolishing age of consent laws were unacceptable to many lesbians (and some gay men). The structure and procedures of the group were condemned as hierarchic and weighted in favour of the male activists. Clashes over lesbian participation erupted as early as the 1976 conference, when lesbians formed a caucus and held separate meetings, engaging in extensive debate about their autonomy.[53] At the 1977 conference, women and men came together only during the plenary sessions, without any knowledge of the other's discussions. Gay men voted against resolutions proposed by the lesbian workshops and many lesbians voted against the amendment of the Criminal Code. Resolutions on voting powers, in particular, caused rancour and divisiveness. One stipulated that lesbian votes be prorated to give them 50 per cent of the total representation. A furious debate erupted that raged throughout the next year, culminating in a rescission motion in 1978 that left a legacy of recrimination and ill will.[54] Two resolutions on lesbian participation consumed five hours of discussion at the 1979 conference. Ultimately defeated, the resolutions stated there was a 'belief that ... CLGRC has actively sought to prevent, through legalistic or other means, the meaningful participation of women.' They acknowledged 'there is also a belief that the men who presently control the Coalition are so smugly complacent in their sexism that they could never loosen their grip on the reins of power.'[55] For Charlotte Rochon of Saskatoon, the problem was that CLGRC had become, by 1980, 'too much of a lobbying group. Purely political, and therefore alien to most lesbians. Women are more anarchistic. We organize in a looser fashion and we operate by consensus.'[56]

Contentious political issues remained unresolved and NGRC/CLGRC frequently endured debilitating battles over strategy and complaints that a small liberation-activist core from the largest cities controlled the agenda. In an article on the birth of coalition in 1975, Ken Popert commented, 'Five distinct groups defined themselves in various ways in the course of the [founding] conference. These can be conveniently tagged as religious, service-oriented, rights-oriented, anarchist and leftist.' Popert added that 'the civil rights grouping, which centred on GATE Vancouver, Winnipeg Gays for Equality, and Toronto GATE, easily dominated the formal conference proceedings.'[57] Toward the late

1970s, the tensions caused by the presence of these distinct groups within a single activist organization opened an unbridgeable schism between those wanting to pursue civil rights activism and others – fractured into several splinters – wanting a broader mandate focused on sexuality issues, social activism, or education. From the outset, angry debates erupted over the coalition's mission, making the annual national conferences battlegrounds for the conflict between working for legislative reform *and* pursuing lesbian and gay liberation objectives in a broader context. By 1978, these conflicts over strategy were tearing apart the fragile coalition.

Halifax's Robin Metcalfe assessed this dynamic in a 1978 position paper in which he stated, 'there is confusion about the relationship between the NGRC on the one hand, as a coalition of groups to achieve certain limited, defined goals, and the entire Canadian and Quebecois lesbian/gay liberation movement, on the other, with its wide range of activities and directions.'[58] The board of directors of the Saskatoon Gay Community Centre, in a 1979 letter published in the coalition's newsletter, lamented:

> We had always dreamed that the NGRC, since it provided our only national forum, could be a broadly-based, action oriented, vital coalition recognizing the variousness of our community and tapping our vast resources to further our struggle in *all* of the areas where our liberation must take place – in the area of civil rights, yes, but also socially, educationally, culturally, that broad political spectrum that covers every aspect of our lives. The NGRC has, in our experience, been so much less than that: narrowly civil libertarian, central Canadian dominated, anti-lesbian and woman, generally, and intolerant of dissent.
>
> Our time, energies and resources are much better spent in building the truly grassroots, truly lesbian feminist-gay liberation movement that is our dream. We believe that a new lesbian and gaymens liberation movement which attempts to meet more fully the diversity of our needs can only enhance and compliment the existing civil rights grouping. Our commitment is to the building of that other movement. That is our task.[59]

Because of its many divisions and weaknesses, the national coalition was on its deathbed by 1980. Membership had dropped from more than fifty groups to twenty-one, eleven of which were from Ontario. There was only one francophone group and no lesbian groups whatsoever. Only ten member groups and sixty-seven individuals attended the conference that year, whereas other conferences had attracted nearly two hundred people. At the final plenary, delegates unanimously approved a winding-up resolution, with the official demise occurring a few months later following a mail ballot of groups still holding membership.[60]

Despite its many problems and short history, CLGRC did have a number of successes. Foremost among them was the amendment of the Immigration Act in 1977. Another was bringing public attention to the homophobic policy of the Canadian Armed Forces. Two national days of protest in 1977 focusing on sexual orientation discrimination had shown that cooperative action across the country was possible, as pickets and public forums were held in several cities. CLGRC also succeeded in establishing a profile on Parliament Hill, managing, as David Garmaise notes, to 'raise a lot of issues and talk to a lot of politicians.'[61] And it helped significantly to establish gay and lesbian rights as an issue about which the national media would report. In the words of Ottawa activist John Duggan, 'we were part of the movement as a whole breaking the isolation because of getting articles onto Canadian Press because they were seen as being of national interest. They weren't just local issues. And this helped, I think, break the isolation for people who don't live in the main cities [because] the local newspaper ... would carry the articles and radio stations would carry them.'[62]

Following the death of CLGRC, the Canadian Association of Lesbians and Gay Men (CALGM) briefly attempted to establish itself as a replacement. Refusing to bill itself as a national coalition or even as a representative group, CALGM lasted only for about a year and then quietly died. Its one significant achievement was a presentation to the parliamentary committee that considered changes to the Canadian constitution. In December 1980, CALGM called on the committee to include sexual orientation in a constitutional charter of rights.[63] Historically, CALGM symbolized a brief transitional phase in which contentious elements of liberation advocacy were jettisoned in favour of exclusively equality-based demands more palatable to the mainstream. Demands such as abolishing the age of consent and repealing the pornography laws were not taken up. As Miriam Smith notes, these issues 'had been the proud banners of gay liberation in the early days of NGRC, demonstrating that, at the federal level, the member groups of the coalition were not prepared to moderate the full implications of gay liberation, as they defined it, to turn themselves into an "acceptable" lobby.'[64] CALGM, having no such qualms, focused on equality rights to the exclusion of other issues. As we shall see in Part Three, this solidifi-cation of equality rights, *sans* gay liberation, would soon weaken the influence that die-hard lesbian and gay liberationists had exercised on the movement as a whole throughout the 1970s.

The Demise of Liberation Activist Groups

But there was also another reason for the change in the make-up of the now decade-old lesbian and gay activism. Most of the activist groups spawned in the ferment of the early 1970s proved unable to survive. By 1980, GATE Vancouver's energies were sapped and it ceased to exist, having failed to sufficiently broaden its membership base.[65] Always a small group of militant activists, GATE's membership, recalls founding member Roedy Green, 'was so grim nobody wanted to hang out with them.' In Green's estimation, the group had drifted 'far, far too out on the edge to capture the mainstream. They just alienated everybody. They were just too rabid.'[66] GATE's role was taken up for a short time by the Gay Rights Union, formed in 1982. According to one if its members, Richard Banner, the union stressed public action and incor-porated feminist and trade union principles. It was active until about 1988.[67] Toronto GATE died around 1981 after some tumultuous years during which it was permeated with conflict and dissent. Founding member John Wilson notes, 'There always tended to be all kinds of divisions in GATE, sort of factions going on here and there. It's amazing that it actually held together as long as it did, considering some of the differences were quite heated at times.'[68] Toronto GATE was followed briefly by Gays and Lesbians Against the Right Everywhere and Lesbi-ans Against the Right. These groups adopted similar strategies, main-taining a highly visible, in-the-streets presence. In Montreal, ADGQ went through periods of great activity followed by dormancy. After the anger over the 1977 Truxx raid dissipated, association membership fluctuated, reaching, at its peak, a couple of hundred members, and at its low, only seven or eight. Over the subsequent years, ADGQ pub-lished a newsletter that later became *Le Berdache*, the first francophone political publication for gays and lesbians. After that paper died in 1986, ADGQ went into decline, disbanding in 1988.[69]

In smaller communities, groups associated with 1970s activism sur-vived much longer, but only by changing the focus of their activities. By the end of the 1970s, Gays for Equality, Winnipeg had ceased to have its earlier public profile but remained alive, conducting public education and speaking out when the need arose.[70] Gays of Ottawa (GO) had maintained a high level of political action during the 1970s only because of a small core of committed liberation activists. That core gradually shrank and political action became a less prominent feature of GO's activities by the early 1980s. As GO activist John Duggan recalls, 'One of the things, I think, about Gays of Ottawa is that we were always a relatively few number of hardcore people. The membership was never that active.'[71] Paradoxically, though, as GO member Lloyd Plunkett remembers, the community expected them to be there 'whenever a crisis happened in Ottawa.'[72] Similarly, the Gay Alliance for Equality in Halifax, following a heightened period of political action in 1977–1978, focused on other priorities. The majority of GAE members were not politically active, notes long-time activist Robin Metcalfe, so it was difficult to gain support for political advocacy.[73] By the end of the 1970s, GAE had become almost exclusively devoted to running a community centre and a bar.

In addition to the movement's many irreconcilable differences over strategy, and the difficulty of sustaining liberation activist groups across the country, many activists began to argue that fighting the backlash directed by the police, media, and religious right organizations should take precedence over seemingly futile campaigns to secure human rights amendments. Scarce resources and precious energies should be directed to more urgent needs, they contended, rather than being wasted or sapped on elusive, and limited, legislative change. A 1979 article in *The Body Politic* written by Michael Lynch, then one of Toronto's leading human rights activists, had even gone so far as to declare 'The end of the human rights decade.' Lynch argued that 'containment of totalitarian power, particularly that of the police' had to become the new strategy. He concluded that the ambiguity of the human rights strategy and its attractiveness to both conservatives and radicals were problematic: pursuing human rights amendements would lead ultimately to the dominance of conservative voices and assimilation with heterosexuals on their terms, rather than the liberation sought by more radical proponents.[74] Tellingly, few mourned the passing of CLGRC. *TBP*, in fact, editorialized that the coalition had 'outlived its usefulness' and was 'a vestige of an era when mobilizing gay women and men in public action for human rights was seen by most gay activists as the most productive, if not the only, way to build our movement and communities.' The movement, *TBP* asserted, was developing 'other means to consolidate our organizations, to reach out to gay people in our communities, and to reach cities, towns, and rural areas that we have never reached before.'[75] Five years later, Stan Perksy, a Vancouver activist, expressed similar concerns. He believed the movement had erred in failing 'to see that the principles, methods and especially the goals of gay liberation are not the same as those of lobbyism' around legislative amendments. Lobbyism had as its aim, Persky declared, 'assimilation at a formal level.'[76]

The Emerging Health Crisis: Responding to AIDS

Adding to concerns about the desirability of pursuing human rights activism was the realization that, as the 1980s got underway, the lesbian and gay movement was confronted with a new and devastating onslaught. It left in its wake illness, death, and new organizing exigencies, as well as new manifestations of homophobia, prejudice, and discrimination. There were calls for repressing liberated sexuality, especially the curtailment of promiscuity and celebratory or recreational sexuality, and the scapegoating of gay men as the cause of a deadly epidemic. Acquired Immune Deficiency Syndrome (AIDS) was something that no one could have anticipated, and for which no one was prepared. Awareness of it as an emerging health crisis began first only in the largest U.S. cities, but gradually spread elsewhere until, before long, fear and paranoia became rampant. Gay men in ever increasing numbers began to be ill with an array of diseases. They were dying quickly. The summer of 1981 saw the first U.S. media reports on a rare form of cancer, Kaposi's sarcoma, that had been seen previously in North America only in rare cases involving people over fifty years of age. Coverage of its sudden appearance among several gay men who had had multiple and frequent sexual contacts led to Kaposi's sarcoma being ingrained in the public consciousness as 'gay cancer' or a 'gay plague.'[77] These first media reports created the impression that promiscuity, drug use, and the affects of medication to treat parasitic infections, to which gay men were believed to be particularly vulnerable, were the causes of Kaposi's sarcoma. The sexual freedom on which lesbian and gay liberation had been based was accused of causing an epidemic sweeping the gay community that, through bisexuals as conduits to heterosexuals, would threaten everyone. The Canadian media followed suit. In August 1982, a Canadian Press wire story referring to the so-called gay plague was picked up by a number of newspapers.[78]

The first death from AIDS in Canada is thought to have been in 1979, although it was not then diagnosed as such. There were four other deaths in 1980 and six in 1981.[79] AIDS awareness among Canada's gay and lesbian communities began principally because of the media reports picked up from the U.S. until *TBP*, in a September 1981 article on the new 'gay cancer,' reported on developments in American cities. In its next issue, *TBP* printed its first detailed article on the health aspects of AIDS.[80] Later, *TBP* chronicled how gay men in New York City were among the first to fuel the hysteria surrounding KS, noting with alarm that major U.S. gay publications were promoting the mainstream view of AIDS as a gay disease. *TBP*, committed to putting forward a gay liberation analysis, lamented that anti-sex hysteria was beginning to set in, symbolized by a pronouncement in the March 1982 issue of the *Advocate*, the largest U.S. gay publication, that 'Our lifestyle can become an elaborate suicide ritual.'[81] *TBP*'s liberationist stance on AIDS was clearly articulated in a November 1982 article by Michael Lynch. He reported on the paranoia and panic sweeping through gays in New York City, who 'began to fear sex itself, and even to feel guilty just for being gay.' Lynch scathingly described such response to AIDS as being similar to that of 'helpless mice.' He lamented the fact the 'power to determine our own identity' – seized so aggressively by lesbian and gay liberationists in the 1970s – had been given back to the medical profession from which it had been only so recently wrenched. Despite the advances of the previous decade, Lynch commented, the panic that took hold upon the arrival of AIDS 'could never have set in so quickly and so deeply if within the hearts of gay men there weren't already a persistent, anti-sexual sense of guilt, ready to be tapped.' Self-oppression seeded by the homophobia and heterosexism of a society that labels homosexuality abnormal, perverse, and immoral was rising to the surface again. Concluding his article, Lynch summarized the challenge that lay ahead: 'The thrust of gay liberation, even if the term does feel nostalgic in 1982, remains that we make our own lives, that we do not sign ourselves over to the panic-mongering journalists and doctors.'[82] Other articles in *TBP* over the next several months similarly challenged the rapidly solidifying misperceptions about gay men and AIDS.[83]

Not everyone welcomed *TBP*'s liberationist rejection of anti-sexual and anti-promiscuity stances on AIDS. One U.S. gay man who had AIDS angrily accused *TBP*'s articles of confusing 'medicine and morality,' for voicing fear about panic and backlash instead of engaging in 'rational discussion about the health hazards of promiscuity.' Promiscuity, he asserted, 'is killing us.'[84] Walter Bruno, a 1970s gay activist, responding to one *TBP* article at this time, lashed out by charging, 'If homosexuals courted each other seriously, refraining from sex until they knew each other intimately, we might have a chance to track this disease down and stop it. But oh! mercy! beware the reactionary in our midst.'[85] Daniel C. Willoughby, a doctor in Vancouver, accused *TBP* of creating a reassuring atmosphere of nonchalance. He demanded *TBP* issue an 'apology for their frivolity in the handling of the subject,' declaring that 'to encourage promiscuity would hardly seem healthful advice.'[86]

Regardless of the conflicting viewpoints on the linkages between promiscuity and AIDS, the horrifying reality of death and disease sustained the panic and paranoia. By the fall of 1982, a fully fledged health crisis was underway, with 527 reported cases in the United States, nearly 75 per cent of them gay or bisexual men. Canada had fourteen reported cases in September 1982, ten in Montreal, two in Toronto, and one each in Vancouver and Windsor.[87] AIDS was taken beyond the mere discussion of cold statistics in Canada's mainstream media in 1983 after Peter Evans, a twenty-eight-year-old gay man in Ottawa, decided to give AIDS a human face by outing himself. His action produced some of the first positive media exposure focusing on people with AIDS.[88] By that time, Quebec became the first province to establish an agency to deal with AIDS, the Comité SIDA du Québec.[89]

Community activism on AIDS issues emerged in early 1983 as an urgent priority in Canada's larger cities. AIDS Vancouver, Canada's first community-based AIDS group, was formed in January that year. It distributed educational information in bars and bathhouses, started a phone line, and held a large public forum.[90] The AIDS Committee of Toronto was founded in June.[91] Montreal's Collectif d'intervention communautaire auprès des gais, a gay social services community group, established the AIDS Task Force, a fundamental concern of which was to ensure that 'we should be shaping the information [distributed to the gay community] and not putting our lives in the hands of the medical establishment.'[92] Political action, patient support, fundraising, and public education became focused on AIDS and the people who were dying from it. The still very limited community resources were put into fighting illness and death, conducting education, and researching the causes of AIDS. Little was left for small, grass-roots community groups working on other issues. Trying to achieve lesbian and gay liberation and pursuing human rights advocacy were de-emphasized.

That liberation politics were by no means dead was witnessed by the fact that it was also 1983 in which organizations propelled by the militancy of people living with AIDS began to organize themselves. At the second National Forum on AIDS in Denver, Colorado, these individuals put forward the phrase *people with AIDS* in an attempt to change the way the illness was seen and how the people who had it were viewed. A conference statement from twelve attendees who had AIDS read, 'We condemn attempts to label us as victims, which term implies defeat, and we are only occasionally patients, which implies passivity, helplessness and dependence upon the care of others. We are people with AIDS.'[93] It was a statement of liberation consciousness finding expression in a completely new context. Later known as the Denver Principles, the document became a manifesto for organizing by people with AIDS all over the world.

Lesbian and gay liberation consciousness also influenced the response to AIDS in other critical ways. Community organizations launched in the 1970s during the exuberance of liberation politics were instrumental in establishing the first AIDS groups in a number of Canadian cities. Miriam Smith, in *Lesbian and Gay Rights in Canada*, observes that lesbian and gay liberation activists were now becoming key organizers of the response to AIDS.[94] One example was the formation, in January 1984, of the first major AIDS community organization in Montreal as a division of Gay Montreal. It soon became the Montreal AIDS Resource Centre/Association des resources Montréalaises sur le SIDA.[95] Activists in Gays of Ottawa, particularly Bob Read, conducted the first AIDS education in that city, and helped launch the AIDS Committee of Ottawa. A Manitoba Gay Coalition forum on AIDS in August 1983 led to the Village Clinic becoming the focus for AIDS awareness and health services in Winnipeg.[96] It was a pattern that would be repeated in many cities over the next few years, as gay and bisexual men across Canada became ill with AIDS-related diseases, or people living with AIDS migrated from the larger cities with well-established gay commercial scenes to return to the smaller cities where they had family and friends. Often in these smaller cities, out and proud lesbian and gay liberationists, who had bravely pioneered the first activism and community building in the previous decade, and who were the only publicly visible members of queer communities, were called upon to leap into the breach once more, to organize in response to the gravest crisis yet seen.

EIGHT

Liberating Communities, Changing Consciousness

Not everything about the late 1970s and early 1980s was doom and gloom. Lesbian and gay organizing actually gained strength and increased in visibility as the concepts of community and culture focused on a common sexual orientation firmly took root, as did lesbian and gay pride. Even in the midst of a host of challenges and crises, progress was made on a number of fronts. Visibility and a fierce resolve to fight back against adversity gained currency not only among activists but also among so-called non-political gays and lesbians. Increasingly, more and more of the latter identified with the gay is good ethos of liberationists and their notion of community, even if they demurred at the militancy and radicalism that catapulted such concepts irreversibly into the dialectic of social activism and onto the agenda of social change. Same-sex sexuality and identity were affirmed and flaunted. Significant organizing took place in smaller and rural communities as pioneering groups formed in every part of Canada, led by courageous trailblazers determined to break down isolation and fear, create safe spaces, build community, and instil a more positive consciousness. Queer culture advanced. Lesbians and gays of colour, additionally, were beginning to challenge the attitudes and behaviours of whites, and to address racism in gay, lesbian, and bisexual communities, moving community development and advocacy into new areas of concern. The movement set in motion by the brave few in the early 1970s could not be stopped, despite the efforts of the state, church, and political elites, or the ravages of AIDS.

An Explosion of Community Development

Grass-roots community development exploded in the late 1970s and early 1980s, and the exuberance of liberation became more public, manifested through such events as Vancouver's Gay Unity Week, an annual held every August that began in 1976. Starting in 1979, Montreal had Gairilla, a week of events that later became Gai-e-lon la, to coincide with la fête nationale celebrations at the end of June. Montreal's 1980 events attracted over ten thousand people.[1] Toronto's lesbian and gay pride celebrations were revived in June 1981, when over one thousand people participated in the day's events. It was also in that year that Edmonton's pride events were started in the aftermath of the police raid on the Pisces Sauna. But the early 1980s also were notable for the rapid expansion of lesbian and gay community groups in many cities, and the emergence of lesbian and gay business sectors in the largest ones. *TBP* in 1981 listed groups in every province except Prince Edward Island. Organizations had cropped up in such places as Kamloops, Red Deer, Brandon, Mississauga, North Bay, and St John's. Youth groups had been founded in several cities, as had groups representing parents of lesbians and gays. Religious and recreational organizations began to proliferate. Half a dozen cities had gay/lesbian radio or community cable television shows. The first organizations representing gays, lesbians, and bisexuals in the professions outside academia – social workers and lawyers – had formed.

Volunteer-based community groups offered a range of social services, seeking to create community centres and safe social environments in which gays, lesbians, and bisexuals could gather and conduct both public education and political advocacy. These groups helped to transform their communities, and served as the local symbols of the international lesbian and gay liberation movement. In doing so, they also helped to demonstrate the existence of a market that could be served by local businesses. In Winnipeg, for example, activists involved with Gays for Equality helped launch Giovanni's Room, a bar and restaurant, in 1982. Gio's in turn helped spawn Winnipeg's Gay Community Centre by renting out rooms for various activities; profits from Gio's were used for several years to support the financial viability of the Centre.[2] Gays of Ottawa was now operating an expanded and thriving community centre for social activities, political action meetings, and the operation of a phone line. Similarly, in Halifax, the Gay Alliance for Equality expanded in 1976 to run weekly dances out of the Turret – an old building in the downtown – that were so successful GAE was able, a year later, to lease the building and turn it into the Gay Community Centre.[3]

At the same time, there remained a noticeable disparity between the options available to gays and lesbians in larger urban centres and those attempting to survive in many smaller ones. On the one hand, the need for safe, alternative places to meet and socialize lessened, at least for gay men, in Canada's larger cities, as gay-owned businesses were established. Bars and taverns became increasingly more upscale and more routinely owned by gays. They were clean, safe, and upfront about being gay establishments. In contrast with earlier times, they were brightly lit, attractively decorated, and viewed gay and lesbian sexuality in a positive way. Vancouver, Toronto, Montreal, and other cities began to see an expansion of discos and after-hours clubs appealing to a younger crowd. One of these new-style establishments was the Roost, opened in Edmonton in late 1977. Its owner, Dow Hicks, had been active in the community-run Club '70 and that experience had convinced him that 'the market was there and we just had to figure out how to tap it.'[4] Then, in the early 1980s gay and lesbian–owned businesses diversified beyond bars and dance clubs. Gay restaurants opened, a welcome development in a time when, for the most part, looking for a pleasant place to have a meal meant seeking out straight-owned eateries that would not harass or tell homosexuals to go elsewhere. Business owners began forming associations of collective interest, with the first, Toronto's Lambda Business Council, being formed in 1978. The Greater Vancouver Business Association emerged in the mid-1980s.

The needs of smaller communities were dramatically different. Community building in such places faced many problems and threats, not the least of which were the risks involved with being out of the closet or a community activist. Those who fell into the latter category were sometimes shunned by or isolated from the very communities they were attempting to help. Harold B. Demarais was one of those individuals, working tirelessly in the mid-to-late 1970s to build a visible and positive gay and lesbian community in Windsor. As an activist and media spokesperson Desmarais was considered a troublemaker by more closeted gays, who wanted nothing to do with him because they felt he was rocking the boat. He was socially ostracized by a group of gay men who had access to power and money. Nonetheless, he and others in Windsor Gay Unity persevered, holding dances for awhile that required enormous amounts of work but helped foster a sense of community.[5]

Another successful organizing effort was the West Kootenays Gay Group, based in Nelson, British Columbia, in the early 1980s. It had members in communities throughout the province's southern interior, holding regular meetings and potluck suppers, as well as running a phone line. A 1983 article published in *TBP* noted, 'Gay people who live [in the West Kootenays] ... are developing gay networks that are beginning to emerge from underground as organizations with names, addresses, phone numbers and services to offer. The services are mainly social: introductions to the gay community, sponsorship of parties and discussion groups and so on. Sometimes there is a local crisis line, if the community is large enough, and some peer counselling is attempted.'[6] Elsewhere in British Columbia, the Island Gay Society established branches in communities on Vancouver Island, with the Port Alberni branch opening a community centre and producing a newsletter. *Flagrant*, an Island lesbian publication put out by a collective during the early 1980s, contained news, poetry, and commentary. Also functioning was the Rural Lesbian Association, listed with a post office box in Rushkin. Typically, gays and lesbians living in small and rural communities in British Columbia at this time, as was the case across the country, felt isolated and vulnerable, with no real sense of belonging to a community. Margie Cogill, who lived in small BC communities throughout the 1970s, remembers never having heard the word 'lesbian.' Eventually, she met another woman with whom she fell in love, but neither of them had any idea there were other women like them. They thought they were unique. It was not until out-of-the-closet entertainer Heather Bishop did a concert in the town in which Cogill lived, and asked Cogill and her lover whether there were other lesbians in town, that the two women came to a realization of who they were.[7]

In Alberta in the late 1970s and early 1980s, Calgary's Gay Information and Resource Centre, through the heroic efforts of Doug Young and Robert Harris, put gays and lesbians in smaller communities in touch with one another and placed the group's newspaper, *Gay Horizons*, on news-stands throughout the province.[8] The Saskatchewan Gay Coalition, formed in December 1977, was dedicated to fighting discrimination, doing outreach, networking, and conducting education; this group did some truly marvellous work at reaching out to small and rural communities. Making contacts discreetly with gays and lesbians living in small communities or on farms, coalition organizer Doug Wilson travelled throughout the province, meeting with small groups and building up a mailing list that grew to about 750 names. The coalition's newsletter helped isolated individuals keep in touch with larger gay communities and concerns.[9] In Manitoba, Gay Friends of

Brandon, formed in the late 1970s, held potlucks and other social events and ran a phone line.

In Ontario's Near North, Charlie LaFrenie attempted to organize in a climate of hostility, where notoriety as a gay or lesbian could and did lead to discrimination and harassment. LaFrenie, through an advertisement in local newspapers, announced formation of the Gay Information Centre in Collingwood in 1979, causing a sensation fanned by considerable media interest. The first gay or lesbian group in the area, it became a subject of both curiosity and controversy. Sadly, the publicity led to LaFrenie's dismissal from his employment with a local hotel. More trouble ensued when an infuriated local cleric asked the town council to ban the group. Although the council refused, on the basis that the group was not illegal, LaFrenie was subjected to vicious harassment in the community and eventually moved away. The group he founded collapsed shortly afterwards.[10]

In an attempt to reach out to individuals throughout northern Ontario, and in smaller and rural communities elsewhere, CGRO launched Operation Outreach in 1980. Assisted by a grant of four thousand dollars received from an inter-church funding agency, Robin Hardy was hired as a grass roots organizer for six months. This initiative led to the birth of Gays of Thunder Bay and aided in reconstituting the Gay Association of Sudbury, later renamed the Sudbury All Gay Alliance (SAGA)[11] SAGA tried to change Sudbury, described by Lloyd Wagner as being at that time 'a very cold and lonely place' for gays and lesbians, by holding dances three or four times a year in community halls.[12] The dances were an alternative to the only bar, the Nickel Range – which locals called the 'Nickel Strange' – where gays, transvestites, bikers, and drug dealers hung out. 'You had to wear rubber boots to go into the washroom,' recalls Steve Brown, another SAGA member.[13] SAGA's focus was social, and it funded itself through dances and donations. It had many highs and lows, reaching a zenith in the mid-80s with an annual budget of thirty to forty thousand dollars. Wagner, a SAGA stalwart, states that this enabled it, for a brief but heady period, to spend thousands of dollars on charities and to provide financial support for gays in North Bay and Timmins. In North Bay, another community in northern Ontario, Cate Lazarov and Val Fournier initiated the founding of the Caring Homosexual Association of North Bay in November 1980, and immediately ran into difficulties with the broader community. A minister's wife complained about the association using the Women's Centre for its meetings and use of the space was withdrawn. Lazarov and Fournier also were driven out of the centre despite having been active in it for some time. Efforts to find other meeting space resulted in many rejections. In the process, the Roman Catholic Bishop of North Bay declared gays and lesbians could not have access to church premises. Eventually, a woman came forward and offered the association meeting space, and from out of it the group functioned until about 1982.[14]

It was equally difficult for gays, lesbians, and bisexuals in Quebec to live openly outside of Montreal and Quebec (the city) during this period. Those in communities such as Abitibi or Sept-Isles, or in the Gaspé continued to be isolated and vulnerable.[15] One group, L'Association gaie de l'Ouest québécois, in Gatineau-Hull, formed in 1979, ran into blatant homophobia when their landlord locked them out of their office, stating he did not want queers in his building. Following relocation, the group lasted for a few years.[16] Groups also formed in Charlevoix, Lennoxville, and Sherbrooke in the early 1980s. While bars, restaurants, and other establishments existed for gay men in several Quebec communities, lesbians had few options and were even more isolated and invisible, notes Montreal activist Louise Turcotte. She recalls that lesbian groups did form for awhile in Trois-Rivières, Quebec, and Drummondville, but did not last long. In addition, there was a 'back to the country' movement of lesbians from Montreal during the 1980s.[17]

A small group of rural gays and lesbians in New Brunswick and Northern Maine launched Northern Lambda Nord in January 1980 to provide a social environment for people living in nearby communities. The group published a newsletter circulated widely in those areas. According to Jacques Lapointe, a Canadian who helped to found the group, 'You've got to be extremely courageous to be gay in rural areas, but it is a chosen lifestyle.'[18] Atlantic Canadian lesbians and gays wanting to organize into visible communities faced a number of daunting challenges. A few fearless individuals attempted to maintain visibility, like James Duplessis, who for many years was the only publicly out gay in Saint John, New Brunswick. In fact, there were no meeting places at all in that city after the closing of a bar frequented by gay people, which is remembered as 'really seedy.' Survival meant becoming part of a group or circle of gay and lesbian friends. Dances started in 1979 and, hosted by two lesbians, Carol and Stella, were among the few available options for several years. Saint John's first community group, born in 1983 out of the efforts of John Markidis and a small group of volunteers, was the Lesbian and Gay Organization of Saint

John. It ran bimonthly dances and an office, offered a range of services, and published a newsletter until about 1985, after which it fizzled out and slowly died.[19]

Elsewhere in New Brunswick, Fredericton Lesbians and Gays, founded in 1979, also organized dances and published a newsletter. In Moncton, surrounded by the New Brunswick Bible belt, violence and homophobia gave impetus in June 1981 for the establishment of the first gay and lesbian group there. Don Cormier and a group of gays decided visibility was the best response to a rash of bashings and harassment in an outdoor cruising area where men had been stabbed and attacked with baseball bats. Some of the men were fired after their employers received phone calls identifying them as gay.[20] Cormier and his friends organized a picnic to be held in a city park on July 1. But after the local media picked up the story, a storm of protest prompted the city council to unanimously pass a new by-law they hoped would force cancellation of the picnic by requiring all groups larger than forty people to obtain a permit to use the park. Undeterred, the city's gays and lesbians held their picnic anyway, congregating in the park in small groups. Gais et Lesbiennes de Moncton/Gays and Lesbians of Moncton grew out of that controversy in early 1982, and immediately met with resistance from the heterosexual community. Noella Richard, the first president, states they had to call about fifty places for a dance venue before they found one that would rent to gays.[21]

The impact of lesbian and gay liberation was also felt in various cultural and artistic industries. Gay theatre in English Canada moved into an important new phase in the 1970s, when Sky Gilbert started doing plays with gay themes. One, *Buddies in Bad Times*, became the name of a theatre company Gilbert founded in 1977, along with Rhubarb! – a festival focusing on new works, including those by gays and lesbians. Edmonton's Brad Fraser wrote *Wolfboy* in 1979, a play about the emerging homosexual relationship between two youths in a psychiatric hospital; it was performed for the first time at the 25th Street Theatre in Saskatoon.[22] In publishing, a 1977 compilation of prose and poetry by Vancouver's Stan Persky, *Wrestling the Angel*, dealt with being gay as a factor in the development of his political theory. John Alan Lee wrote about the sexual liberation of gay men in Toronto in his 1978 book, *Getting Sex: A New Approach: More Fun, Less Guilt*. It described the places frequented by gay men and the means they used to find sexual partners.[23] The first English-language book about the Canadian lesbian and gay liberation movement, *Flaunting It! A Decade of Gay*

Journalism from The Body Politic, edited by Ed Jackson and Stan Persky, was published in 1982.

Queer art and music also burgeoned during this period. In art, five members of a Toronto collective called ChromaZone organized exhibitions during the early 1980s. One collective member, multimedia artist Andy Fabo, gained a wide following for using images of gay male sexuality in his early works.[24] Similarly, JAC, a Toronto artist collective formed in 1980, and whose name was an acronym created by the initials of three gay men who comprised it, held a number of workshops and showed their works in a popular gallery. Vancouver's Kiss & Tell collective, in the mid-1980s, began producing photography, multimedia exhibits, performance art, and books. Consisting of Susan Stewart, Persimmon Blackbridge, and Lizard Jones, their works dealt with issues of sexual orientation, gender, and marginality. Lesbian art was frequently profiled in Vancouver festivals.[25] Music, especially music produced by lesbians, also began to blossom. Sara Ellen Dunlop, in 1975, recorded original songs on her own label through her own company and later helped found a popular women's rock band, Mama Quilla II.[26] Concerts featuring lesbian entertainers proliferated in cities across Canada, often organized by Toronto's Womynly Way Productions, serving as an affirming source of lesbian culture at a time when options for women were sorely limited. Other lesbian pioneers in music, Ferron and Heather Bishop, blazed new trails because of their openness about their sexuality.[27] Gay male entertainers bursting onto the musical scene at this time included David Sereda and the Nylons, an *a cappella* group formed in 1978.

The need to provide news, information, and analyses from liberated gay and lesbian perspectives, and to counteract the still largely negative presentations of the mainstream media, led lesbian and gay activists to begin publishing magazines and periodicals of their own. In Montreal, ADGQ produced Gais du Québec, in September 1977. By June 1979, it had become a newspaper, *Le Berdache*, which was published until 1982. It was succeeded by *Le petit Berdache* in February 1983, until it also folded in January 1986.[28] A group of activists who left ADGQ founded *Sortie* in September 1982. Distributed throughout Quebec, *Sortie* saw sixty-two issues until it ceased appearing in 1987. Louise Turcotte launched *Amazones d'hier: lesbiennes d'aujourd'hui* as a lesbian-only publication in March 1982.[29] Also founded in that year was the lesbian publication *Ça s'attrape*. Other important regional papers launched in this era were Ottawa's *GO Info*, which converted from a newsletter to a monthly newspaper in 1982. An Atlantic Canada newspaper, *Gaezette*, grew out of the newsletter of the Gay Alliance for Equality, and was published ten times a year. Similarly, *Angles* grew out of the Vancouver Gay Community Centre's *GCC News*, becoming an independent newspaper in 1985. *Perceptions*, a magazine-format publication from Saskatoon, first appeared in 1982. *Pink Ink* started in 1983 as a national publication with a mission to generate 'important dialogue on such issues as peace, racism, pornography, culture and our history.' Unfortunately, it folded after only five issues. A group from *Pink Ink* went on to produce *Rites*, a national magazine dedicated to being a forum for the 'rites and rituals of our culture, lusts and desires.' Publishing from 1984 to 1992, *Rites* promoted lesbian and gay liberation, feminism, and progressive social change. It strove to give expression to the connections between 'lesbian and gay oppression and the oppression of all women and the experience of other oppressions such as class, race and age.'[30]

Lesbian Visibility and Organizing

Meanwhile, lesbian liberation, as distinct from lesbian and gay liberation, flourished in the late 1970s and early 1980s as lesbians continued to struggle for visibility, forming organizations separate from those of both gay men and straight women. Autonomous lesbian organizations emerged across the country, with diverse missions and varying degrees of success. An important impetus for the creation of the new lesbian groups was the fact that, within women's organizations, efforts at keeping lesbians closeted, at low profile levels of involvement, continued and, in some cases, intensified. In Halifax, for example, Lynn Murphy recalls that such efforts forced lesbians to leave women's organizations, following which it became apparent 'just how much work had been done by the lesbians and what a kind of blow this was ... to have that not available anymore.'[31] Montreal's Louise Turcotte also remembers, 'We knew that in [the] 70s, who were the feminists, they were called lesbians.' But as the women's groups became more mainstream, lesbians became less and less welcome in them. Turcotte attributes much of the subsequent anti-lesbian sentiment to growing dependency on government funding to keep women's organizations afloat.[32] Similarly, Liz Massiah, active in Alberta in the mid-1980s, recalls that many lesbians involved in women's groups felt they could not be out. One group, in fact, actually put out a feminist magazine by a collective that was mostly lesbians who would not discuss that fact.[33]

At the same time, many lesbians found it extremely difficult to work within primarily gay male organizations because of disagreements around issues such as the age of consent, pornography, and sex in public places. The sexism of many gay men was also problematic. So too was the preponderance of gay sexual imagery in what were supposed to be gay *and lesbian* spaces, the refusal of gay men to take up issues advocated by lesbians, and gay men's lack of commitment to establishing organizational structures and processes to give lesbians power and position. One group that struggled with such issues with a fair degree of success was Gays of Ottawa. But changing the organization to make it more welcoming and inclusive of lesbians was not easy. Much debate and tension ensued. 'It was tough,' states Marie Robertson bluntly. She remembers that 'it was a struggle sometimes, you know, just as a woman and feeling isolated. And I would say, for me it was more a feeling of feeling isolated as opposed to blatant sexism that was abusive to me, or nobody ever said to me, "Marie, you go and make the coffee." That didn't happen to me. But feeling very isolated.'[34] Barb MacIntosh, who served as GO's president for two years in the 1980s, agrees that, in the early years, the relationship between women and men 'wasn't too smooth.' About 90 per cent of the members were men for most of the 1970s, although the number of women grew to be about 20 per cent by 1980. For MacIntosh, 'the conflict came from the differences in the men's and women's communities themselves. You know, when women first started getting involved in GO, the men were used to it being their organization. They weren't used to working with women, and they didn't know where women were coming from, and what kinds of things we wanted and what we cared about. There was conflict because it was a learning process.'[35] Some progress was made in 1982 with adoption of a resolution requiring half of GO's board of directors to be women. Other factors contributing to the dramatic increase in lesbian involvement in GO were the commitment shown by some men to make it an organization in which women would feel comfortable, the absence of alternatives for lesbians in Ottawa, and the realization that creating a positive social environment for women would most likely be achieved by working in GO.

Unfortunately, other organizations did not have such accomplishments. Most gay men remained appallingly disinclined to accept any responsibility for changing the situations in which they dominated. Expounding on the problem of the imperviousness of gay males to repeated lesbian demands for change, Robertson declared in a 1976 article:

> The problem is obviously much deeper than the superficial male chauvin-
> ism in the movement: the meatballs who insist on saying '*man*kind,' 'him,'
> 'he' when referring to both sexes. I perceive a clear conflict of interest. Gay
> liberation, when we get right down to it, is the struggle for gay *men* to
> achieve approval for the only thing that separates them from the 'Man' –
> their sexual preference ... The point is that if you [men] were not gay you
> would be part of the powerful, prestigious male ruling class that op-
> presses women, whether you choose to face that reality or not. Your birth
> as males defines that; you don't.[36]

For Jean Hillabold and other politically aware lesbians in the Gay
Community of Regina during the early 1980s, the use of sexist language
by gay men was an important issue that the men simply refused to
address. Hillabold recounts how one lesbian member undertook to
challenge the men on this point, with little success:

> She also challenged the men on their use of the word 'girl' for female
> people of any age. They didn't refer to each other as boys, well, occasion-
> ally but not always. They were men but then there were girls ... She had to
> continually confront them on this. They would say 'Oh well, whatever.'
> Some man would say, 'I met this girl, I really enjoyed working with this
> girl,' and she would say, 'How old was this girl?' and he would say, 'Oh,
> 55' and she would say, 'That was a woman.' He would reply, 'Oh well,
> whatever, woman, whatever.' They didn't see the importance of such
> things.[37]

The difficulties many lesbians have had with gender stereotyping of
women, in the form of drag, also was not understood by the men.
Hillabold recalls that they didn't understand that drag is not a form of
entertainment that most lesbians care to see. 'They would ask me if I
could get a lot of women to show up for the drag show. I would say,
well, frankly, no. I could let them know that it's occurring, but no, I
don't think large numbers of women would come. We could dress this
way if we wanted to, but most of us in the lesbian community have
considered that option and rejected it. It represents a feminine role that
we rejected long ago.' Hillabold also attributed the historic problem of

lesbians and gay men working together to different family and economic statuses, and to men's insensitivity to the fact that women often
are not as well off financially, or have parental responsibilities. 'I am a
single parent. They would do things like having an emergency board
meeting that they would plan two hours in advance. They would
phone me to say, "Jean, we are having this meeting in two hours, can
you show up?" I would say, "No, I can't find a babysitter in that length
of time, if you give me twenty-four hours' notice I probably could." So,
they would say, "Oh, too bad." So they would make important decisions in which I couldn't participate.'[38]

Christine Donald, reporting on a 1982 lesbian workshop's discussions on the relationship between lesbians and gay men in mixed
groups, emphasized another concern, as follows:

> The extent to which women feel alienated from political events reflects
> their feelings of powerlessness in the face of a male-dominated society.
> Too often this pattern is repeated in mixed lesbian and gay male-groups.
> But the process of change must be two-sided: the women need to speak
> now, and the men to listen ... [And we] resent the conditioning that makes
> us collude with men in discounting our own experience, our own skills,
> that makes us feel strangers to power and the use of money. We particu-
> larly resolved to resist the role of mother to the men (making it all right for
> them, tidying up their emotional gaffes, helping out whether we are
> overtaxed or not, not asking that we be satisfied in the process – 'the
> mommy response,' one woman called it).[39]

Reflecting on the difficulties lesbians have had in working with gay
men, Louise Turcotte and Nancy Tatham, during interviews, cited the
unwillingness of men not only to share power but to abandon their self-
centredness when defining issues around which to organize. Turcotte
stressed that, in order to work with lesbians, gay men had to imagine a
different kind of group from those in which they had been involved
historically. They needed to share power with lesbians and let the
women do what they wanted to do within the groups. As long as gay
men did not confront their own social position, nor compromise on
what the political agenda would be, things never worked out.[40] Tatham,
a prominent organizer in Kingston's lesbian and gay community for
nearly two decades, is critical of gay men for not being interested in
issues that don't affect them. In her experience, 'When you're doing
work on an issue that is of importance to [gay men] you are wonderful

and, you know, can do no wrong. And they'll, they'll take every minute and every ounce of sweat that you've got. And then when you sort of wave your hand and say, "Can we shift over here?" of course, you know, how it appears to me personally, that's when you see who all falls away and the very few, if any, that are left at that point.'[41]

The dominance of male sexuality and imagery has been equally troublesome. Line Chamberland, recalling the problems lesbians faced working with gay men in ADGQ, cited misogyny and lesbian resentment of the men's tendencies to project a more masculine image as part of their sexuality.[42] Echoing those sentiments, Maureen Irwin recollects that both physical images of gay male sexuality and the perceived cavalier manner in which gay men engaged in sex created major problems for lesbians working within mixed organizations in Edmonton. 'The sexuality and how they act it out and the depiction on walls – there are a number of lesbians who are into leather and other things and go for this – but the women I knew [didn't] and so it was very upsetting, and the men wouldn't take down the pictures and all this kind of stuff ... [And] the men wanted the right to fuck publicly, or in the parks, and all that kind of stuff, and we had a real hard time, a lot of people still have a really hard time with that.'[43] Similarly, many of the fights with the men in GO during the 1970s were over the dominance of male sexuality. One such incident focused on an art exhibit described by Marie Robertson as having had 'cocks for days.' When a woman on the GO board, an incest survivor, announced that the women were going to remove the art for their women's night events, 'The men just didn't get it.'[44] Sexual imagery of a different kind caused a furore within GAE in Halifax. A wall mural painted by a gay man in the Turret, the group's bar, featured two headless, bare-breasted women with lightening going from nipple to nipple. Women spraypainted it, which the men then claimed was destruction of property. Another dispute erupted because gay men refused to respect the need for lesbians to have their own spaces when they converted a place in the Turret known as 'the women's corner' into a stand-up cruising area for men. At another time, drag queens started using the women's washroom, which caused problems for the women.[45]

Not surprisingly, autonomous lesbian organizations began to spring up to free lesbians from the problems encountered working with straight women and gay men. These groups were strongly influenced by but also differed significantly from those subscribing to lesbian separatism, which never really took root in Canada. In fact, many Canadian lesbians expressed public disagreement at this time over the feasibility of lesbian separatism. One of those critics was Jane Rule, who wrote in 1982, 'Because I live in a world of children, women, and men, both by choice and in any public place, it makes no sense to me to exclude any of them from my concern and conversation. It may be that men (and women) in power will destroy the world. I cannot think that our best defence is to lump all men in that category and then stop speaking to them, particularly as increasing numbers are trying to listen as well as to speak about issues that concern us.'[46] Speaking over a decade later about why a separatist movement did not develop in Canada, Marie Robertson commented, 'Well, I think that it was only in large cities like Toronto where you would hear that voice the most ... [In smaller communities] there's not the luxury of doing that ... I don't think that the support for that movement was nationwide ever, period. And it was certainly not even Ontario-wide ... Toronto was the place where that noise was coming the most, and the feeling was not shared.'[47]

The desire for lesbian autonomy, on the other hand, generated ferment in communities across the country, with lesbian collectives springing up to run phone lines, publish newsletters, hold cultural events, put on women-only dances and challenge both feminist and gay liberation groups. Calls for an autonomous lesbian movement were heard at a 1976 conference in Kingston hosted by the Queen's Homophile Association: 'The Not-So-Invisible Woman: Lesbian Perspectives in the Gay Movement' was initially planned on the assumption that deciding the relationship of women to the gay movement should involve both women and men. At the opening plenary, however, Francie Wyland, a member of Wages Due Lesbians, successfully introduced a motion calling on the women attendees to meet alone as a group, without men being present, to decide the direction that the conference would take.[48] The group advocated strongly for an autonomous movement, arguing that lesbians were 'fighting for control over *all* our lives, in order to have sexual choices.' This meant more than fighting solely for civil liberties, or 'a little world of our own (the lesbian ghetto).' It meant struggling to build lesbian power, which 'always means lesbian autonomy from those who have more power than us, including straights, but above all from men, *even gay men.*'[49]

The Kingston conference became a formative event in the history of lesbian organizing, leading to other national conferences and fostering the formation of lesbian groups. One delegate remembers that it 'started things brewing for lesbians.' Other national lesbian conferences followed in the fall of 1976, and in 1978 and 1979. One group formed after Kingston was the Atlantic Provinces Political Lesbians for Equality (APPLE). (One member later recalled that after a discussion about 'equal to who and all that stuff' the name was changed to Atlantic Provinces Political Lesbians for Example.) It held social events and was one of the main groups that organized women's coffee houses once a week. They also engaged in some political activity, such as taking their banner to International Women's Day marches, and operated a phone line. It was a group focused primarily on process, says one of its founders: 'We operated collectively and were more worried [about] the process than we were about the product ... Process was very important. So when we got together we'd often sort of, you know, be sitting in someone's living room all kind of, you know, our arms all kind of around each other talking about each other's problems before getting on with the politics. We kind of wanted to clear the air first. At the time, I found it all kind of supportive.'[50] APPLE lasted until about 1980 or 1981. After the national lesbian conference in 1978, the group also produced two issues of what was intended to be a permanent, national lesbian publication, called *Lesbian Canada Lesbienne*.

Several lesbian groups came and went in Toronto in this era. Following the closure of Toronto's women's centre in 1975, a group of women leased a house that for a few months was the location of a number of organizations, including *The Other Woman* and Wages Due Lesbians. It later became an informal meeting place for discussions and parties. In December 1975, the Three of Cups formed as a social space for lesbians, holding coffee houses profiling performers, writers, poets, and others. Gay Women Unlimited, established in 1976, lasted for a couple of years, providing a meeting place and social alternatives to bars and dances. Still another group was the Lesbian Caucus of the Gay Alliance Toward Equality, which existed from 1976 until shortly after the formation of the Lesbian Organization of Toronto (LOOT). Launched in 1977, LOOT was an umbrella organization open to any lesbian who wanted to join. 'Every lesbian is inherently a member of the Lesbian Organization of Toronto,' proclaimed one of its leaflets. Before long, the LOOT centre became a place for various groups to meet, and was the location of a phone line, a weekly drop-in, and a library. Activities included publication of a newsletter, dances, Sunday brunches, and coffee houses. Unfortunately, by 1981, LOOT could no longer sustain itself and ceased to exist.[51] LOOT's peer counselling and contact activities were taken up by Lesbian Phone Line, which functioned from 1981 to 1984.[52]

In Montreal, difficulties within Labyris in the spring of 1976 caused a split from which Gay Women of Montreal and the Montreal Lesbian Organisation were formed. Both groups had short lives but offered social alternatives for lesbians while they existed.[53] Francophone lesbians in Montreal, by February 1977, had founded a collective, which was mostly a social centre, called co-op femmes. It provided a space for meetings, art exhibits, music, and dances.[54] Louise Turcotte notes that co-op femmes had a lot of political information and discussion, and organized around feminist (but not specifically lesbian) issues like abortion and child care. Nevertheless, it was the place to be for francophone lesbians, who as a group did not have an organization of their own. More and more women in co-op femmes eventually wanted it to take on lesbian issues, and there was some criticism expressed about its not calling itself a lesbian group. While this generated a debate within the group around the use of 'lesbian' in its name, Turcotte has stated that most of its members did not want it to come out as a lesbian centre so as to be able to receive grants for funding. They also were afraid of being recognized in the part of the city where they were located as a lesbian meeting place.[55] Eventually, problems developed within co-op femmes and, after three or four years, it disappeared. There were no rules of procedure or hierarchy, which were rejected as being masculine. There were many divisions along ideological lines. According to Line Chamberland,

> There was a tension between, political tension and splitting, splitting that's still there, between what we called the lesbian feminists and the radical feminist separatists, lesbian separatists. Here they called themselves radical feminists, but their position is more like the separatist one. They did not want anything to do with the gays, the men, they don't want to deal with the institutions, all of their political work was with the other lesbians and the lesbian community. The lesbian feminists were more inside the feminist movement and doing some work in the lesbian community and the feminist movement.[56]

Attempts to form an autonomous lesbian organization in Ottawa also met with success for a time, embodied by the Lesbians of Ottawa Now (LOON) in 1976. One of its founders, Marie Robertson, recalls that the women who formed LOON were 'mainly a lot of bar dykes.' This caused tension between them and the 'politically correct feminists at the [women's] centre.' Before long, LOON left the women's centre, never to return, and began meeting at GO's centre.[57] Another LOON stalwart, Rose Stanton, remembers that its primary objective was to provide a social climate for women, by running run a phone line, holding dances, and organizing other events. But it also worked with gay men in efforts to have sexual orientation added to the Ontario Human Rights Code. LOON was very informally structured, such that in Stanton's recollection, the women who 'took up the space made the decisions.'[58] She attributes its demise in 1979 to a number of factors: 'the exhaustion of the organizers from working on national conferences, running weekly dances, and finding a place to hold dances. But the coup de grace was the ideological issue of separatism ... Discussions about separatism polarized LOON to the extent that it ceased to exist as an organization.'[59]

On the Prairies, the Womyn's Collective, founded in Calgary in 1977, held its first all-woman dance to respond to the fact that other gay community dances and events were about 99 per cent men. The collective held meetings, dances, consciousness-raising groups, barbecues, and other activities, such as women's drop-ins. It later also established the Lesbian Information Line.[60] Calgary's Lesbian Mothers Defense Fund, launched in the early 1980s, held the province's first lesbian conference in 1983, called 'Shattering the Myths,' that drew women from Edmonton, Lethbridge, Red Deer, and Saskatchewan.[61] Meanwhile, in Edmonton, the first large, long-term organization for lesbians, Wommonspace, was started in January 1982 by Jeanne Rioux and six others following the departure of lesbians from Edmonton GATE.[62] According to Lorna Murray, a long-time Womonspace organizer, women counsellors and social coordinators in GATE decided they were doing all the work but the men made all the decisions. So they dedicated themselves to forming a group to put on events just for women that would function on more of a feminist and collective model.[63] Regina's Lavender Social Club was born about the same time, its primary activity being monthly dances for women. A short time later, the desire for alcohol-free events in nonsmoking venues gave impetus to the Lesbian Association of Southern Saskatchewan (LASS). Founded by Beth Traynor and a small group of other women in early 1983, LASS made it clear from the beginning 'that alcohol [consumption] was a real issue. There needed to be some place away from the bar for the women to meet.'[64] Sue Cook, another LASS founder, felt the group was important because 'for a couple of us, our energy came from the fact that we were also in women's organizations, and when it came to things like International

Women's Day we were representing issues that were dear to our hearts but there was no lesbian representation.'[65]

Not all automonous lesbian organizing was focused on creating meeting spaces and social activities for lesbians, however. Some innovative and groundbreaking activities promoting political objectives and asserting the public visibility of militant, out lesbians featured prominently in a number of cities at this time. Lesbians were instrumental in organizing and maintaining International Women's Day committees and formed contingents in International Women's Day marches across the country. As well, the first specifically lesbian pride event, distinct from gay pride activities, was held in May 1981, as part of the Binational Lesbian Conference, when two hundred women marched through downtown Vancouver.[66] Dykes in the Street followed it on October 7, in Toronto. The next year, lesbians organized protests against the right in Montreal, Toronto, Vancouver, and five communities in British Columbia. Lesbians against the Right (LAR), formed in 1981, organized Toronto's Dykes in the Streets event, and dedicated itself to protesting the emergence of a right wing backlash against gays and lesbians. LAR participated in community forums and demonstrations, giving visibility and a political voice to lesbians. Until its demise in 1983, LAR endeavoured to be grass roots, to forge 'links between lesbians and the gay movement, the women's movement, the antiracist movement, the labour movement, the reproductive-rights movement, the antinuclear movement, and antipoverty organizations.'[67]

Diversity within Rapidly Changing Communities

Another significant development in the late 1970s and early 1980s was the increasing diversity of the gay, lesbian, and bisexual communities. Gays and lesbians with disabilities were beginning to assert a presence, as were gays and lesbians of colour. The result was the emergence of the first groups by and for members of these communities and the raising of awareness about barriers to access, the prevalence of stereotypes, and the impact of racism and discrimination within gay and lesbian communities. Gays and lesbians with disabilities remained largely isolated from and ignored by the larger queer communities and issues of access and accommodation were seldom addressed, even by the activists who so vigorously promoted liberation and social change. At the same time, the numbers of people of colour in bars, clubs, and other commercial establishments were growing each year, but they were generally isolated and marginalized. Most lesbian, gay, and bisexual community organizations did not have *any* people with disabilities, gays, lesbians, or bisexuals of colour, or aboriginal people involved with them.

Groups specifically for gays, lesbians, and bisexuals with disabilities formed during this period. The first, the York Rainbow Society for the Deaf, later renamed the Toronto Rainbow Alliance of the Deaf, began in about 1977. The Alliance formed after Ray Barton ran across a group for gay deaf people during a visit to San Francisco. He was able to draw upon a loose network of gay men who patronized a popular pub, those who attended private parties, and friends he met at a school for deaf people. From its inception, the group provided social events and other activities. In 1980, it hosted, for the first time in Canada, the international convention of Rainbow Societies.[68] Another group breaking new ground in this period was Calgary's New Horizons. It was the brain-child of Jean B., active in both the gay/lesbian and disabled communities in Alberta, who decided in 1980 that there needed to be a social club for gays and lesbians with disabilities. She approached a gay male friend, also disabled, whose house had a ramp for wheelchairs. A society was set up and meetings were held at his house once a month. They advertized the group in a community newsletter and, for about five years, had six to twelve people involved. Things started to drop off after that, however, and Jean and her friend decided not to continue with the group, so it folded in 1986.[69]

Isolation and marginalization typified the experiences of lesbians and gays of colour in this period. Roy Hallett, a white gay man active in the Queen's Homophile Association in the late 1970s in Kingston, has recounted the difficulties of a gay Asian friend attempting to fit into the city's gay community. People ignored him, Hallett stated, and he felt awkward being the only nonwhite person at gay events.[70] Moreover, a researcher would be hard-pressed to find on advocacy agendas any issues of direct concern to native gays and lesbians, or to gays, lesbians, and bisexuals of colour, or even any discussions of racism at the several national and regional conferences during this period. Reprehensibly, as will be shown below, racism on the part of individuals who were publicly identified with the struggle for sexual liberation also poisoned the environment within the movement, igniting explosive debates over race and sexuality.

Probably the first group to proactively deal with questions of race was Wages Due Lesbians. They held a 1976 international conference of the Wages for Housework campaign, attended by Canadian, English, and American women who were Black, white, lesbian, and straight. Black women had a high profile at the conference, and discussions of oppression and the need for autonomous organizing of Black lesbians were featured.[71] But the climate even among activists was generally more negative, as evidenced by a raging debate over race and sexuality among gay men that erupted in the pages of *TBP* in the early 1980s. The debate challenged some of the notions held by liberationists about the extent to which free sexual expression could itself become a form of oppression. The first round began in 1983, when Ken Popert wrote an article following from the decision of the *TBP* collective not to publish an advertisement for a sex magazine called *White Assed Super Pricks*, which boasted on the cover that it was 'Unethnic.' Popert was critical of the decision, claiming the magazine 'could be *making fun* of the racial aspects of gay male porn.' He then went on to assert that having a sexual preference for men of a certain race was comparable to having a fetish for men with moustaches. Claiming that 'There is an important distinction to be made between me and my sexuality,' Popert contended, 'If my sexuality is racially tinged, it is not because I am a racist, but because I have grown up in a society which attached great importance to race.' He then angered many people by attempting to justify his arguments using a liberation analysis, asserting, 'Gay liberation, before anything else, stands for the integrity and inviolability of sexual desire, the right of men and women to choose their sexual partners according to their needs. No matter how well intended or how good the end, we can never allow anyone to prescribe our sexuality.' Popert concluded by stating, 'Racism will go out of our sexuality when racism goes out of society, and not before.'[72]

Popert's views were assailed in letters to *TBP* printed in subsequent issues. Tony Souza responded by noting that applying Popert's argument to homophobia and heterosexism would mean that all those fighting for gay liberation should 'give up on acting individually and collectively' and 'wait for society to change.' Eng K. Ching wrote that gay liberation 'provides me with the condition from which I act towards the end of all oppression. By refusing to act against racism in our homosexuality, we let straight society define our sexuality and also block the further advances of gay liberation.' Richard Fung, one of the few people of colour involved in lesbian and gay activism at this time, commented, 'For me, as for all non-white gay men and lesbians, racism is a central issue in our lives, whether in our daily relations with a wider society, our interactions within the gay ghetto, or finally, in bed.'[73]

To deal with both the racism and homophobia they experienced, to facilitate coming out of the closet, and to establish welcoming meeting places, organizations for people of colour began to form in the early 1980s. The first was Gay Asians of Toronto (GAT), started as a peer discussion group in 1980 by Richard Fung and Gerald Chan after Chan wrote an article about being gay and Asian that was published in a magazine serving Toronto's Asian community. Fung, who had been active in *TBP* and other Toronto groups, attended an international gay and lesbian conference and was energized by the experience of caucusing with other gay Asians. Fung and Chan contacted each other and placed an advertisement in *TBP* for a support group, later being joined by Nito Marquez and Tony Souza. These four individuals began holding regular discussion groups that eventually led to the establishment of GAT.[74] Among GAT's purposes were: promoting unity and mutual support among gay Asians; organizing social, cultural, educational, and recreational activities for its members; providing culturally sensitive social and support services; and advocating on issues relevant to their community's concerns.[75] In 1982, GAT led Toronto's Lesbian and Gay Pride Day Parade as the honoured group; GAT activist Alan Li gave the keynote speech. Spectacularly, GAT's parade contingent featured a lion dance that wound its way through Chinatown – the first public expression of same-sex orientation within the city's rapidly growing Asian community. From 1983 onwards, GAT held CelebrAsian, an event celebrating the anniversary of the group's founding, which featured entertainment, fashion shows, and other activities. In 1984, Fung again broke new ground with the production of a video, *Orientations*, profiling gay and lesbian Asians, including Asians in drag and leather, working class people, and professionals. But Fung also showed Asians as sexual beings, thus dealing head-on with the problems they faced in coming out as gays and lesbians, and with the attitudes of the dominant white gay and lesbian communities. One young Asian man in the video commented that racism in the gay community was common: 'Sometimes, when you are in a bar, they make you feel so unattractive.'[76]

Black gays and lesbians in Toronto also began to organize around this time, through the efforts of gay men such as Doug Stewart and Derych Glodon and lesbian activists Sylmadel Coke, Debbie Douglas, and Carol Allen. Zami, the first group in Canada for gays and lesbians who are Black and West Indian, was founded in 1984. The name Zami was chosen because it is an East Caribbean word for lesbian sex. Zami fulfilled social, political, and supportive roles, including peer counselling and discussion groups. In the same year, women 'who felt the need to meet, give support, and organize around being lesbians of colour' formed Lesbians of Colour (LOC). LOC's activities included weekly meetings at which discussions were held on various aspects of being lesbians of colour. The group also held social events such as potluck dinners, dancing, and picnics.[77] LOC's involvement in public events included participation in workshops on racism at the Lesbian Sexuality Conference in 1984.

What is thought to be the first group for Native gays and lesbians in Canada also appeared during this period, in Saskatoon. Founded in the late 1970s, the Gay Native Group was listed in *Gay Saskatchewan*, the newsletter of the Saskatchewan Gay Coalition, as late as October 1979, but disappeared shortly thereafter. There was also an Aboriginal gay alcoholics anonymous group, in the mid-1980s, in Vancouver.[78] Generally, however, Aboriginal lesbians and gays remained largely invisible, or, if visible, marginalized. The organizations and meeting places of the broader gay, lesbian, and bisexual communities were almost exclusively populated by white people of European descent who had little awareness of or contact with Aboriginal peoples. It would take another decade or so before groups of Aboriginal gays and lesbians would form to assert their presence and promote their own particular advocacy and education agendas.

Progress Nonetheless

By the end of 1984, lesbian and gay liberation, born with such promise and enthusiasm fifteen years earlier, was under siege on all sides. Some of its leading activists, such as Michael Lynch, had even declared in 1982 that the movement, as contemplated in the early 1970s, was dead. Indeed, the profound difficulties of translating a sexual liberation perspective into an agenda for social and legislative change, as we have seen, appeared insurmountable. Pervasive homophobia and heterosexism, together with a rejuvenated political right wing bolstered by the emerging social conservative movement, impeded legislative action to remove sexual orientation discrimination. The police forces of the country continued to wage war on gay sexuality, and engaged in new campaigns of repression and harassment. Many factors had combined to prevent lesbian and gay liberation from becoming the mass movement its progenitors had fervently hoped would arise. There were frequent accusations that liberation really meant libertarianism, and fundamental disagreements with feminists on issues such as the age of consent and pornography. Deep schisms had emerged between liberationist and equality-seeking agendas that were more conflicting than unifying, despite the carefully articulated strategy of using human rights advocacy in the short term to obtain liberation in the long term. The first attempt to forge a national movement of gays and lesbians had failed resoundingly. Groups that promoted gay and lesbian liberation advocacy had largely died out. The seeming inability of gay men and lesbians to find either common ground or mutually agreed organizational structures was not permitting them to work in common cause on any significant scale. Nor did an autonomous lesbian movement emerge nationally. Then, just when it seemed the situation could get no worse, the advent of AIDS caused illness, death, collective grief, and rampant paranoia, forcing beleaguered and poorly resourced community groups to recast their advocacy agendas, to redeploy their energies to confront the new and devastating crisis.

Yet, the liberationist activists of the early 1970s were being proven right in many significant respects. The pursuit of legislated human rights, despite the conflict between liberationists and mere equality-seekers, was creating awareness among the public and the media about the effects of homophobia in the areas of employment, access to services, and housing. The campaigns to achieve legislated rights, as Denis LeBlanc stated, were part of a 'strategy of getting visible, of letting our brothers and sisters know they were not alone' (see chapter 3). Another gay liberationist, Ken Popert, writing in *The Body Politic* in 1975, had accurately predicted that 'the effectiveness of civil rights is much less important than the effectiveness of the public campaign that demands those rights. Of all the questions raised by gay liberation, the issue of civil rights is the one which attracts the greatest support, from gays and straights alike. By a campaign for civil rights, we can penetrate the media and advance the reeducation of the public on the subject of homosexuality.'[79] What was not clear by the mid-1980s was whether the human rights campaigns would lead to the long-term achievement of liberation that many of their leading activists sought. It remained to be seen whether Popert's optimistic prediction was coming true in the changed circumstances of a decade later: 'It cannot be emphasized too strongly that the campaign for civil rights is a means not an end. When the state officially recognizes in law the rights of a minority, this means only that it has been compelled to acknowledge that minority as a political force. The gay struggle will not be ended when sexual orientation takes its place in the rights codes of the ten provinces; on the contrary, the struggle will be lifted to a new level.'[80]

The problem by the mid-1980s, in so far as liberation activists like Michael Lynch and Stan Persky were concerned, was the suspicion that, despite the efforts and intentions of liberationists, the attainment of civil or human rights had in fact become the end, not the means. Whether the movement would be taken to a new level, as Popert forecast, was hotly disputed. Nonetheless, through the publicity generated by fighting back in the face of police repression or advocating for human rights protection, the consciousness of gays and lesbians continued to change and more and more closets emptied in all parts of the country. Despite the hostility and intransigence of the politicians, the issue of rights for gays and lesbians was, by the early 1980s, firmly implanted on the public agenda. And, paradoxically, while sexual liberation was condemned following the arrival of AIDS, and the ethos of liberation cited as a cause of the epidemic, the consciousness imbued by gay and lesbian liberation and the activists schooled in it shaped much of the response to the disease. Similarly, lesbian and gay liberation proceeded inexorably at the grass roots level as gay and lesbian communities became increasingly visible, and much more diverse. Liberation was spreading to smaller communities and rural areas. There was a resurgence of gay and lesbian pride – a fundamental tenet of lesbian and gay liberation. Groups were forming for lesbians and gays of colour, and for religious and recreational purposes. Even the rise of gay and lesbian businesses was attributable to the impact of lesbian and gay liberation, as was the thrilling vibrancy of a slowly maturing queer culture. Despite backlash, dissent, and crises, it could not be said, based on the evidence, that lesbian and gay liberation was dead.

PART THREE

Between Queer and the Mainstream, 1985–1999

NINE

Victory in the Human Rights Campaigns

By the late 1980s, the lesbian and gay movement was proceeding along two parallel tracks. The first track (examined in this chapter and in chapter 10) was almost exclusively rights oriented. The second track (explored in chapters 11, 12, and 13) continued liberationist tactics of pushing the envelope in areas of sexual expression, community standards, fighting against police and state harassment of queer sexuality, rejection of victimization and vilification, and assertion of visibility and pride. As Gary Kinsman observes in *The Regulation of Desire*, lesbian and gay liberation at the end of the twentieth century 'must be situated within a broader context of sexual and social struggles: one characterized by struggles over the Charter of Rights and Freedoms and equality rights on the one hand, and intensified sexual policing and the continuing denial of our actual sexualities and relationships on the other.'[1] Exploring the two separate tracks of lesbian and gay activism begins by noting that, following the traumatic events chronicled in Part Two, lesbian and gay liberation, beginning in about 1985, entered a long phase in which it appeared to have virtually disappeared as a significant social movement seeking radical change. The advocacy focus shifted overwhelmingly towards pursuit of legislated equality rights. Liberationist activists moved from being in a position of dominance in the human rights campaigns to that of a vocal minority hoping to exert influence. The trend was seen first in the efforts to secure human rights code amendments, and later in the attempts to gain legal recognition of same-sex relationships. As had been feared by Lynch and Persky (see chapter 7), equality rights became seen by most of those espousing them as ends in and of themselves, rather than merely means to an end (i.e., liberation). A key factor was assumption of leadership by activists not imbued with the liberation analysis of the 1970s, individuals more decidedly middle class, professionals (especially lawyers), and bureaucrats who embraced heterosexual models and mores.[2] Secondly, the coming into effect, in 1985, of equality rights guaranteed by section 15 of the Canadian Charter of Rights and Freedoms profoundly moved the yardsticks, politically, judicially and socially. Charter rights bolstered the argument that gays, lesbians and bisexuals merely sought equality with heterosexuals. Advocacy tried to position gays, lesbians, and bisexuals as ordinary citizens who, despite their sexual orientation, were reflective of mainstream values and mores. This did not involve addressing far less respectable, infinitely more controversial sexuality issues, rejecting oppressive social mores, or changing repressive sex laws. And it was imminently better, in the view of equality-seeking activists, to take up the Charter as a cudgel, and to fight in the august confines of the courts and the legislatures, than, in the fashion of the 1970s, to take to the streets with picket signs and noisy demonstrations.

Charter-ing a New Course

The first track of the lesbian, gay, and bisexual movement – equality-seeking rights advocacy – gained momentum in 1981, after a constitutional agreement was reached between the federal government and all provinces except Quebec. The Constitution Act, 1982, which included the Canadian Charter of Rights and Freedoms, came into effect after receiving the approval of the British Parliament. Section 15 of the Charter, which assured equality and nondiscrimination, and provided a means by which discriminatory laws or government policies could be challenged in the courts, came into force on 17 April 1985. While not specifically including sexual orientation as a prohibited ground of discrimination, section 15 was broadly written so that the rights guaranteed by it are not restricted to the specifically enumerated grounds. Accordingly, the existence of enumerated grounds does not detract from the section's general prohibition on discrimination, meaning that it could be – and soon was – interpreted by the courts as applying to analogous but not enumerated grounds such as sexual orientation.[3]

As legal and other scholars have noted, the impact of the Charter on the legal status of gays, lesbians, and bisexuals has been profound. Kathleen Lahey, in *Are We 'Persons' Yet?*, noted that 'the number of cases decided in favour of lesbian and gay applicants under the rubric of

Marie Robertson (left) and Rose Stanton (right) of Ottawa carry a banner in the lesbian contingent of the gay rights demonstration held during the 1976 conference of the National Gay Rights Coalition in Toronto. The coalition held seven such national conferences between 1975 and 1981.

Mike Johnstone (left) of Gays of Ottawa talks to a reporter at a demonstration in front of the Supreme Court of Canada in October 1978. The participants were supporting Vancouver GATE's case accusing the *Vancouver Sun* of discrimination for refusing to run a classified advertisement for the newspaper *Gay Tide*.

Lesbian marchers lead off the 1984 Lesbian and Gay Pride Day parade in Toronto. The annual Pride events, held in late June to mark the anniversary of Stonewall, were revived in 1981 in response to massive police raids on gay bathhouses that year.

Demonstrators outside the offices of Canada Customs and Revenue in Toronto in 1987 protest the seizure and detainment of books and periodicals destined for Glad Day Bookshop and other gay and lesbian bookstores.

In July 1991, Queer Nation holds a 'Queer without Fear' march in Toronto against homophobic violence. The march was part of a concerted strategy of high-visibility activism designed to assert a more militant direction for a movement that was, by then, dominated by equality-seeking assimilationism.

Members of Windsor's lesbian and gay community carry a banner announcing their Pride Day during the Lesbian and Gay Pride Day parade in Toronto, 1992. Groups from all over Ontario participate in Toronto's Pride event, now one of the largest in the world.

Kristyn Wong-Tam, of Lesbian Youth Peer Support, speaks on homophobia in the education system at the Out in the Classroom conference organized by the Coalition for Lesbian and Gay Rights in Ontario and held in November 1991. The conference addressed strategies for fighting homophobia in the schools.

The 1993 Dockards Demonstration by the Nova Scotia Persons with AIDS Coalition at Canadian Forces Base, Halifax, protested the homophobia of the Armed Forces and demanded the amendment of the Canadian Human Rights Act to include sexual orientation.

Campaign for Equal Families activists rise in the Ontario Legislature and shout 'Shame!' following the defeat of Bill 167, the first legislation to legally recognize same-sex common law relationships, 9 June 1994. From left to right: Eleanor Mahoney, Patricia Dewhirst, Tom Warner, Bob Gallagher, Mary-Woo Sims, Susan Ursel.

Members of the Campaign for Equal Families lead off Toronto's 1994 Pride Day parade, giving it a more political and angry tone than in previous years, following the Ontario Legislature's defeat of Bill 167.

Lesbian and gay youth participate in the first Lesbian and Gay Pride Day parade in London, Ontario, in 1994. The parade took place in a climate of homophobia heightened by the London mayor's refusal to issue a proclamation for the day and the police witchhunt against gay men arising from Project Guardian.

1994 marked the first Lesbian and Gay Pride Day parade in London, Ontario. The placard in the centre of the photo suggests the growing diversity of queer communities everywhere.

This Pride march in New Glasgow, Nova Scotia, in June 1996 took place following a long campaign by a local anti-gay member of Parliament, Liberal Roseanne Skoke, that generated national media attention for her religious-based opposition to amending the Canadian Human Rights Act to include sexual orientation.

These queer community broadcasters in Calgary produced radio programs for local gays, lesbians, and bisexuals. From left to right: Gene Rodham, Freedom FM (now defunct); Michelle Wong, Dykes on Mykes; and Stephen Lock, Speak Sebastian. This photograph appeared on the cover of the 12 June 1997 issue of *Fast Forward Weekly* magazine.

Toronto mayor Barbara Hall participates in From All Walks of Life, an AIDS fundraiser in the late 1990s. Over the course of the decade, the fight against AIDS expanded to include organizations specifically for people of colour and two-spirited peoples and attracted significant political and mainstream support.

"sexual orientation" remained shockingly small until the courts began to apply the equality guarantees of the Charter of Rights and Freedoms to those "sexual orientation" clauses [that have been inserted into human rights code].'[4]

Noting that lesbian and gay activists of the 1970s expected their human rights campaigns and court challenges to fail, but pursued them because they could be used to mobilize lesbians and gays, Miriam Smith states that,

> The Charter fundamentally altered the equation. For the first time, there was the possibility that lesbians and gays could obtain actual legal protection and defence of their rights in a broad range of areas. In this sense, the Charter created a new avenue for the achievement of substantive policy success. Although the organizational weaknesses of the lesbian and gay rights movements meant that the communities were initially slow to pick up on it, eventually, this new political opportunity was seized on and new organizations such as EGALE were created. However, the Charter also created a new discourse of rights talk. The defining feature of rights talk is its positivistic approach to law, meaning that the law is taken seriously on its own terms as a means of achieving social change. The meaning frame of gay liberation had assumed that the defence of the rights of lesbians and gays – which, in the seventies meant their freedom to pursue their sexuality without harassment from state and society – could best be achieved by the creation of lesbian and gay community and community institutions. Legal guarantees were not enough. The goal of gay liberation was to build a social movement, and to use the movement to ensure that legal rights would be enforced and would be meaningful in the real lives of lesbians and gays. In contrast, the meaning frame of rights talk assumes that the law is sufficient protection and that changing the law is the primary goal of political organizing.[5]

But it was by no means clear in the early days of the Charter the extent to which it would advance equality for gays and lesbians. This area of Charter jurisprudence had yet to evolve. The evolution was prompted by the fact that, to prepare for the advent of the Charter's equality rights, the federal and provincial governments were obligated to review all legislation and to introduce any amendments necessary to ensure compliance. Accordingly, in January 1985, just weeks before section 15 took effect, the federal Progressive Conservative government issued a discussion paper, *Equality Issues in Federal Law*. The paper addressed sexual orientation issues, including the ban on gays and lesbians in the armed forces and the RCMP. Criticized as profoundly unsatisfactory by lesbian and gay activists and other civil rights advocates, the paper included homophobic and stereotypical representations, without any counterviews. In particular, it appeared to accept the rationale purported by the RCMP and armed forces as justification for their bans on homosexuals in their ranks.[6] Still, the door had been opened, and gay and lesbian activists quickly seized the opportunity, taking advantage of the formation of the Equality Rights Subcommittee of Parliament that followed release of the discussion paper. It held hearings across the country soliciting public opinion on section 15 issues and was specifically mandated to examine sexual orientation as a prohibited ground of discrimination. Approximately 250 individuals and representatives of organizations made submissions. Many were lesbians and gay men stressing the need for protection under the Charter.[7]

In October 1985, the subcommittee recommended adding sexual orientation to the Canadian Human Rights Act, removing the ban on gays and lesbians in the armed forces, and changing federal government security clearance guidelines. It also called for Criminal Code amendments establishing a uniform age of consent for all sexual acts.[8] In a March 1986 statement, Justice Minister John Crosbie committed to 'take whatever measures are necessary to ensure that sexual orientation is a prohibited ground of discrimination in relation to all areas of federal jurisdiction.'[9] This raised expectations that the federal government would act on the recommendations. The RCMP, in fact, announced in 1988 that it had lifted its ban on homosexuals, taking the position that homosexuality by itself was not proof of unreliability or a bar to obtaining a security clearance.[10] The armed forces, on the other hand, remained belligerently resolute in their opposition, causing the government to stall repeatedly on amending the CHRA. The military maintained that, under section 1 of the Charter, the ban was a reasonable limit on the protection ordinarily afforded by the Charter's equality rights. Such intransigence, combined with vociferous opposition within the federal PC Party meant that, despite repeated assurances by Crosbie and his successors over the next few years, no action was taken on amending the CHRA and the ban on gays in the military remained in place. (The government did act on the various Criminal Code amendments.)

Illustrative of the opposition within the governing party were comments made by PC MPs in 1986 during debate on a private member's bill to amend the CHRA, introduced by NDP MP Svend Robinson.

One MP vomited a hateful barrage of bigotry and ignorance: 'Can you feature a fairy RCMP constable trying to arrest a lumberjack with a powder puff? Can you imagine a lesbian RCMP fairy at the scene of an armed robbery screaming: "Stop, surrender, or I'll hit you over the head with my purse?" If fairies were not hired they would cry discrimination.'[11] Another Tory MP warned direly, 'homosexualism is anti-biological. It is committing biological suicide. It is anti-medical, it is hygienic insanity. It is a crime against humanity whether medical or moral.' Raising the spectre of AIDS, he then declared, 'gays are the first to be stricken' but in time, 'others become infected.' Condemning the opening up of 'this bombshell of so-called human rights' for homosexuals, he thundered, 'it is human suicide.'[12] Despite the expression of such views, Prime Minister Kim Campbell, in her book *Time and Chance*, noted that the PC government had accepted in 1991 that sexual orientation was a prohibited ground of discrimination under the Charter. But bringing the armed forces and the Tory caucus on side proved daunting. At one point, in fact, the chief of defence prepared and then did not issue an announcement changing the policy. As word of the pending announcement got out to the national media, Tory caucus members rebelled and the government and military brass retreated.[13]

Campbell recalls an 'almost casual disdain in jokes and comments' about gays and lesbians made even by caucus members thought to have moderate views.[14] John Crosbie also later revealed that his commitment to act on the subcommittee's recommendations unleashed 'an unholy row in the Conservative caucus,' lamenting that some caucus members were 'reactionaries and fundamentalists.' He related how his frosty reception at a PC policy convention contrasted with vigorous applause for 'a young minister of the Fundamentalist Christian Assembly Church in Abbotsford, B.C.' who opposed a sexual orientation amendment.[15] There was also an unofficial PC caucus committee on family values, consisting of about thirty-five MPs, and supported by six cabinet ministers, that vigorously fought any enactment of gay rights legislation. Believing Canada would be 'better off' without the Charter, that court decisions resulting from it had been 'strange and aberrational,' they contended: 'The demand for individual rights at all costs is disruptive to the family and society.' They sought the entrenchment of the importance of the family in the preamble to the constitution and the introduction of a legislative definition of a traditional family.[16]

Petitions, letter-writing campaigns, and briefs presented to Parliament calling for a CHRA amendment had no effect, so to enlist judicial support gays and lesbians launched court cases. The first such case, *Haig v. Canada*, began when Graham Haig, an Ottawa gay activist, and Joshua Birch, a former captain in the air force, challenged an armed forces directive under which Birch became ineligible for promotions, postings, or further military training because of his sexual orientation. Birch, denied a Canadian Human Rights Commission investigation into the policy because sexual orientation was not included in the CHRA, assisted by Haig, asked the courts to declare that the CHRA infringed the Charter. In June 1992, the Ontario Court of Appeal did so, declaring the CHRA was to be 'interpreted, applied and administered as though it contained "sexual orientation" as a prohibited ground of discrimination,' and read in that term; in other words, the CHRA was to be read as if sexual orientation was specifically included in it.[17] The government did not appeal, letting the decision stand as a precedent that would soon be cited in a number of other cases.[18] The most significant case was that of Michelle Douglas. She launched a constitutional challenge and a lawsuit using Charter arguments after first having her security clearance removed and then being expelled from the armed forces because she admitted to being a lesbian and displayed an 'apparent strong loyalty to members of the gay community.'[19] Douglas charged that Administrative Order 19-20, which provided for the expulsion of gays and lesbians from the Canadian Armed Forces, was inconsistent with section 15 of the Charter because it discriminated on the ground of sexual orientation. She also argued her dismissal violated her right to freedom of association, and claimed that once it became clear she would not be disloyal to Canada, and was not a security risk, the armed forces carried on its investigation anyway. An adjudicator agreed, ordering that Douglas be retroactively granted a top secret security clearance and be reinstated to her position. The armed forces did not comply with the decision, however, and in 1992, the Supreme Court of Canada, ruling on an armed forces appeal, concluded that an administrative tribunal's ruling could not bind government. Douglas fought back with a lawsuit seeking compensation and an application to the Federal Court of Canada to rule that the military's policy violated the Charter. 'They put me and others through hell,' she said. 'I would like to see some form of compensation, even if it's only a public apology.'[20] Just as the suit was about to be heard, the armed forces capitulated and, citing *Haig*, negotiated a settlement.[21] Shortly thereafter, the federal government relented and finally lifted the ban against gays and lesbians in the military.

Provincial Human Rights Campaigns

The arrival of Charter rights also led to the amendment of provincial human rights laws, although in most cases it took several years to occur. Too frequently, politicians procrastinated or pandered to bigots and religious zealots, rather than bring their legislation in line with the Charter and the growing body of jurisprudence it was generating. Concerted lobbying campaigns remained essential, complemented and strengthened by court decisions and the findings of human rights tribunals applying the Charter in cases of sexual orientation discrimination. Nonetheless, the legal and judicial foundations had been laid, and the politicians were ultimately forced to act, first in Ontario, and later in other provinces. Over the period between 1986 and 1999, as a result, the human rights laws of all provinces, one territory, and federally, were amended to prohibit sexual orientation discrimination.

The road to victory in the era of the Charter began in Ontario, when the Progressive Conservatives, who governed continuously for some forty years, suffered a stunning rebuke in the 1985 election. Reduced to a minority of seats, they were toppled within a few days of forming a new government. The Liberals under David Peterson took office after signing an accord with the New Democratic Party. In October 1985, NDP MPP for Ottawa, Evelyn Gigantes, introduced a private member's bill that set the stage for the adoption of a sexual orientation amendment.[22] The timing was fortuitous. Early in 1986, the Liberal attorney general, Ian Scott, introduced various statutory amendments in the form of Bill 7, An Act to amend certain Ontario Statutes to conform to s. 15 of the Canadian Charter of Rights and Freedoms. Taking a minimalist stance on what was thought necessary to comply with the Charter, Bill 7 did not initially include a Human Rights Code sexual orientation amendment. However, the Coalition for Gay Rights in Ontario (CGRO) seized the opportunity, submitting a brief to the Standing Committee on the Administration of Justice, arguing that adding sexual orientation to the code was necessary to comply with section 15 of the Charter. Shortly thereafter, Evelyn Gigantes moved an amendment to Bill 7, which was adopted at the committee review stage, and became part of the bill.[23]

Trouble, and the near defeat of the amended bill, lay ahead. Over the summer, churches and right wing political groups mobilized under the name of the Coalition for Family Values (CFV), led by an evangelical minister. CFV professed its commitment to 'basic moral and family values,' attacking the sexual orientation amendment as leading to a 'change in the fabric of our society.'[24] Other groups mounting similar opposition were REAL Women and Big Brothers of Canada. In early October, CFV distributed a letter to fifty thousand Ontario households, urging recipients to protect their families by telling their MPPs to vote against Bill 7. The letter drew heavily on fears of child molestation and the employment of gays by social agencies, schools, day care centres, and group homes, condemning 'the use of legislation to interfere with the moral choices and values of Canadians.' Meanwhile, the Ontario Conference of Catholic Bishops declared, 'Any law that leaves the door open to such a life-style [homosexuality] will cause great harm to society.' In early November, CFV wrote to all MPPs decrying the Bill 7's negative impact on schools, churches, religious institutions, marriage, and social values. A CFV spokesperson asserted it would be 'immensely unfair to a much larger segment of Canadians to be forced into courts to defend their moral values and standards.'[25] Queen's Park was flooded with petitions from churches and other angry expressions of opposition. Alarmed by the opposition, many Liberal MPPs began to waver. The media world became rife with reports that a free vote would be held, raising the prospect of defeat of the amendment on third reading.[26]

Scrambling to counteract the influence of their opponents, the Coalition for Gay Rights in Ontario, now joined by the Right to Privacy Committee (RTPC), launched their own letter-writing campaign, and the Metropolitan Community Church of Toronto sent a letter of support to Premier Peterson from forty clergy of various denominations. More publicly, about twelve hundred people attended a CGRO-RTPC rally just days before the vote on the final reading, at which members of the three mainstream political parties spoke in support of Bill 7.[27] Finally, on November 21, the government announced that Liberal MPPs would be asked to support the amendment rather than voting according to their conscience. Angered by that decision, and claiming Bill 7 would grant gays 'special rights,' CFV bombarded Queen's Park with a last-ditch telephone campaign.[28] The ensuing debate in the legislature dragged on for six days, infuriating the many gays and lesbians who sat, hour after hour, in the public gallery listening to homophobic diatribes. While MPPs from all three parties spoke in favour of the sexual orientation amendment, MPPs condemning the bill dominated, asserting it would undermine the traditional family and weaken family values. They quoted letters from churches, cited religious prohibitions against homosexuality, fulminated about child molestation, and asserted that gays and lesbians should not be teachers or child care workers. Some complained that the amendment would lead ultimately to legalizing gay marriages and same-sex adoptions.[29] Nonetheless, on third reading, Bill 7 was adopted by a vote of 64 in favour and 45 opposed.

Jubilant gays and lesbians packed into the public gallery, defying stodgy legislature protocol, stood up and burst into applause. Their exultations were matched in communities around the province. A long and bitterly fought campaign was finally over. Noted CGRO activist Harold B. Desmarais years later, 'I never in my wildest dreams thought I would live in a province where sexual orientation was included in the human rights code in my lifetime. I figured the best I could hope for was that I was ... working on a foundation that others could build on and that, if not for me, perhaps for the next generation. I never expected it to actually happen in my lifetime, I really didn't. I was flabbergasted that it did.'[30]

The next human rights campaign began quite unexpectedly in the Yukon. The catalyst was the election of an NDP government committed to new human rights legislation including sexual orientation. The promise arose directly from behind-the-scenes lobbying of closeted lesbians active in the party and a meeting between Helen Fallding, a lesbian activist, and an NDP member of the legislature.[31] Unlike other parts of Canada, however, there were no lesbian or gay organizations in the Yukon, no long history of public lobbying on the issue, and no real means to confront the homophobia of opponents. Predictably, the government's announcement became a flashpoint for opposition politicians and social conservative advocates. The Progressive Conservative opposition leader condemned it, as did Anglican, Baptist and Pentecostal clergy.[32] A group called the Movement Opposed to Homosexual Extra Rights (MOTHER) claimed the intended law would legitimize homosexuality. Most of the opinion columns and letters printed in the *Whitehorse Star* were hostile. One article raised the spectre of homosexual recruitment of children.[33] Complicating matters was the fact that the NDP formed a precarious minority government. When the human rights bill was introduced, they did not gain the support necessary to proceed to a vote, and initially abandoned it. Instead, they issued a White Paper intended to stimulate public debate on the inclusion of sexual orientation. During the ensuing community consultations, no submissions were received from individuals known publicly to be gay or lesbian; only one submission was made by a group of anonymous gays. The churches and MOTHER on the other hand kept up their assault, asserting that the Yukon was being taken over by homosexuals and child molesters. Fortunately, the government reintroduced its legislation in early 1987 and passed it, with sexual orientation included.[34]

While the political circumstances in Ontario and the Yukon were propitious, the climate in Manitoba worsened and gay and lesbian activists there became increasingly pessimistic. The NDP government, nearing the end of its first term, had taken a pounding in public opinion polls over its attempts to legislate French language rights in the province. That backlash bolstered the NDP's historic reticence to act on the controversial issue of gay and lesbian rights. As the government's popularity plunged, activists feared the Tories might win the next election, further prolonging any action. So gloomy were the prospects that Winnipeg activist Richard North began a hunger strike in March 1985 to focus public attention on government inaction. Throughout the next fifty-nine days, North appeared at the Legislature every morning, delivering open letters to the attorney general's office and the NDP caucus chair. Sometimes he included letters from prominent members of the NDP and professional associations, the results of public opinion polls and relevant statistical information, copying the local media. Ultimately, however, North ended his strike because he experienced vision problems, without having moved the government to act.[35]

Fortuitously, the re-election of the NDP and the arrival of section 15 of the Charter changed the situation positively within a short time. The Lobby for Inclusion of Sexual Orientation in the Manitoba Human Rights Act (LISO) seized the opportunity to organize a lobbying campaign.[36] Adding impetus to their efforts was a court's ruling that the human rights act was not broad enough to provide protection from discrimination on grounds not specifically enunciated, such as sexual harassment and sexual orientation. These events prompted the government, in the spring of 1987, to introduce Bill 47, creating a new human rights code that made specific reference to the principles underlying the Charter and that included sexual orientation as a prohibited ground of discrimination. LISO responded with a successful postcard and lobbying campaign and formed a coalition with other groups supporting the legislation. About sixty nongay groups called for the inclusion of sexual orientation, a critical development that lobby organizer Margie Cogill later noted: 'We couldn't have done it alone. Of course, they were a great boost to the morale of the gay community. And they gave credibility to our claim that we were not just an isolated fringe group. That gave the government courage to put the amendments forward.'[37] One

NDP MLA noted, 'the broadly-based group of supporters of the amendments, which included the United Church, was well-organized and made a fine showing at the public hearings held after second reading.'[38]

Still, oppositional deputants reflecting fundamentalist Christian views mobilized for the legislative committee hearings on Bill 47. MLAs otherwise received almost no letters opposing the inclusion of sexual orientation. Cogill recalls the 'church groups and hate groups that just over and over said the same thing about hellfire, damnation, and sinfulness and all of this. And it was a most amazing process to me to see the hate that there is and the lack of understanding, the lack of knowledge, the lack of tolerance, and the very narrowness that there is within certain segments of society. And it was a very painful process.'[39] Considerable opposition, also existed in the Legislature, among the Progressive Conservative opposition and a significant number of NDP members. The PCs were particularly hostile. 'There wasn't one Conservative that would support us, or understand our point of view, or work with us. Not one,' Cogill remembers.[40] Liberal leader Sharon Carstairs, who supported the amendment, lamented in her book, *Not One of the Boys*, that the debate was 'a low point for me in terms of any kind of respect I had for members of the Tory party. I couldn't believe the venom that spewed from their mouths.' One PC member 'read nauseating materials in the House, including sections from a book declaring that homosexuals have unprotected sex in order to deliberately spread the AIDS virus. He asked us all if we wanted Winnipeg to become the AIDS capital of Canada.'[41] Another PC MLA told Carstairs the sexual orientation amendment was treated with 'lots of snide comments and laughter.' As well, the Roman Catholic Archbishop had made representations to members of the legislature, urging them to vote against the amendment, and this had greatly influenced members with strong religious beliefs.

Support within the NDP was not universal, adding to the government's problems, since it held only a one-seat majority. According to Cogill, an 'old guard' element in the government caucus was staunchly opposed. In the end, to secure the support of some reticent NDP members, the government amended the bill to state that it 'neither condones nor condemns the lifestyle of those it intends to protect.' It also defined sexual orientation as 'heterosexual, homosexual or bisexual, and refers only to consenting adults acting within the law.'[42] With these concessions, victory occurred in July 1987, when a new Manitoba Human Rights Code was adopted at three a.m., observed by 35 lesbian and gay rights supporters in the public gallery. The bill was supported by 29 New Democrats and Carstairs (the sole Liberal MLA), and opposed by 24 Progressive Conservatives.[43]

In Nova Scotia, both the Human Rights Commission and the Progressive Conservative government steadfastly resisted adding sexual orientation to the Human Rights Act long after the equality rights sections of the Charter came into effect. The commission rejected a 1988 recommendation from their staff that sexual orientation be added to the Human Rights Act. At another point, a commissioner claimed during a meeting with Lesbian and Gay Rights Nova Scotia (LGRNS) that gays are 'a plague upon the earth.'[44] However, the commission gradually changed its stance, and in September 1990, approved a policy to protect lesbians, gays, and bisexuals from discrimination on the grounds of sex. It directed that in all places where the act referred to *sex* it would be interpreted also to mean *sexual orientation*, citing section 15 of the Charter and the recommendations of the parliamentary subcommittee.

At the political level, Attorney General Ron Giffin caused a public uproar in 1986, following release of the recommendations of Parliament's subcommittee on section 15 of the Charter, by asserting the government would resist attempts to 'force' police forces to hire lesbians and gays. Giffin opined that gays create morale problems in police forces, and that he was upholding the fundamental moral values of society. He threatened to use section 34, the notwithstanding clause of the Charter, to prevent being compelled by the courts to hire gay and lesbian police. 'I honestly wonder if we aren't being carried away with individual rights,' he pondered ominously.[45] Additionally, Halifax activist Robin Metcalfe recalls that Premier John Buchanan 'was a major obstacle.'[46] Maureen Shebib of LGRNS expressed a similar view in a 1989 interview in *Rites*: 'What became very clear (and just confirmed what most of us have believed for a long time) is that the only real opposition to us, and the one man blocking the legislation, is the Premier.'[47] Victory finally resulted following Buchanan's resignation. His successor, Donald Cameron, introduced a sexual orientation amendment shortly after taking office. But the bill was flawed because of an exemption provision applying to groups like Big Brothers and the Boy Scouts.[48] The Gay and Lesbian Alliance, LGRNS, and the Nova Scotia Persons with AIDS Coalition lobbied to improve the legislation. Enlisting support from two dozen other groups, they succeeded in forcing removal of the exemption provision and extension of protection for persons with AIDS. On 27 June 1991, the amended Human Rights Act was adopted by the legislature.[49]

Throughout 1990 and 1991, a case of discrimination involving Eric Smith had helped provide further impetus for lobbying efforts. Smith was a teacher in Shelburne, a small Nova Scotian community, who had tested positive for the HIV virus. The information became public when a receptionist in the clinic disclosed his result to others in the community. School officials, urged on by parents, barred Smith from teaching. As events progressed, it became apparent that being known as a homosexual was as much an issue as AIDS in the minds of many in the community. Angered by what had happened, the Nova Scotia Persons with AIDS Coalition mounted a publicity and letter-writing campaign directed at the government and the teachers' union. In the end, Smith agreed to an arrangement whereby his salary was continued but he was not allowed back into the classroom. Wilson Hodder, of the coalition, later recalled that, despite the outcome for Smith personally, his case generated national media attention and helped to increase awareness locally about the difficulties confronted by people living with AIDS. It further dramatically illustrated the need for a Human Rights Act amendment.[50]

Next door in New Brunswick, lesbian and gay activists, spurred by developments in other provinces and the success of Charter advocacy, began to organize for an amendment of the province's Human Rights Act. To do so, Francis Young, Hal Hines, and four other people constituted the Human Rights Committee of Fredericton Lesbians and Gays in the autumn of 1987.[51] The committee, soon transformed into the provincewide New Brunswick Coalition for Human Rights Reform, encouraged by the election of a Liberal government in 1988, launched what Young has described as a 'quiet lobbying strategy adapted to the largely rural nature' of the province.[52] They prepared a brief documenting incidence of violence and discrimination against gays and lesbians, and held meetings with politicians. Support was obtained outside the gay and lesbian communities to counteract religious organizations and the right wing, antibilingualism Confederation of Regions (COR) party, which was then making political inroads. A media kit was assembled and a questions and answers document on sexual orientation discrimination prepared for members of the Legislature.

According to Claude Olivier, another coalition activist, their members deliberately avoided generating publicity about their demand until publication of the provincial ombudsman's 1990 report calling for sweeping changes to the Human Rights Act. The issue heated up when, predictably, the sexual orientation recommendation became the focus of hearings before a legislative committee in early 1991.[53] The coalition appeared before the committee, as did AIDS New Brunswick and the New Brunswick Federation of Labour. Two opposing submissions were heard, from the COR party and a Christian minister. COR asserted that 'certain types of sexual orientation are considered criminal acts and others carry a high of degree public health concern.' The minister claimed 'the government has an obligation to promote sexual intercourse within marriage and to discourage it outside marriage,' and must discharge that responsibility 'by making it legal for people to discriminate against people who are having sexual intercourse outside of marriage.'[54] Adoption of the amendment was delayed by a provincial election in which the Liberals were voted back in. Afterward, the coalition had to mount a campaign to counteract reports that a statement might be added to the act that including sexual orientation did not constitute condoning homosexuality. Successful in their efforts to have such a statement omitted, the coalition renewed its lobbying efforts in earnest when a bill amending the act was finally introduced in the spring of 1992.[55] The PCs and New Democrats supported its final form. It was opposed only by COR, whose members claimed moral considerations could not be divorced from human rights laws and linked homosexuality with bestiality. Fortunately, forty-two non-gay organizations publicly supported the bill. It passed on 13 May 1992 by a vote of 34 to 8.[56]

In western Canada, the election of NDP governments, following several years of right wing Conservatism influenced by fundamentalist Christians, led to amendments of human rights codes in British Columbia and Saskatchewan. In the former, activists had faced, in the late 1980s, a hostile, right wing Social Credit government led by a fundamentalist Christian, Bill Vander Zalm. As a result, they had largely abandoned efforts to pressure the government to amend the human rights law to include sexual orientation. Pursuing any concerted campaign in such a climate was thought futile. More encouragingly, by the mid-1980s the opposition NDP stated publicly that it would amend the Human Rights Act if elected to government. The NDP's Colin Gabelmann even introduced a private member's bill intended to achieve that objective, which Social Credit MLAs defeated.[57] When the NDP took office following the 1992 election, it acted quickly on its commitment, introducing Human Rights Act amendments that included sexual orientation. The NDP strategy to move quickly and avoid either public consultation or outcry succeeded in having the new legislation adopted by the legislature on 12 June 1992.[58]

In Saskatchewan, the Progressive Conservative government of Grant Devine had also remained staunchly opposed to lesbian and gay rights while in office throughout the 1980s. The Tories deliberately did not add sexual orientation to the Human Rights Code in 1985, when they brought in other amendments to conform with section 15 of the Charter, despite a lobbying campaign by Gay Community of Regina, nor in 1989, when they introduced further amendments. 'We've written off this government in terms of human rights,' responded Saskatoon gay activist Peter Millard.[59] As problematical for activists was the fact that, during most of this period, the NDP remained disappointingly silent, not bothering even to raise the omission of sexual orientation as an issue during the debates on the 1989 amendments. Nonetheless, in anticipation of the election of an NDP government, the Campaign for Human Equality (CHE) mounted a new lobbying effort in 1990 that targeted NDP politicians. Their efforts were bolstered when NDP leader Roy Romanow, at long last, stated publicly that an NDP government would add sexual orientation to the province's human rights law.[60]

Romanow's announcement made lesbian and gay rights a prominent issue in the 1991 election. The PCs and their religious right supporters used it against the NDP and Romanow. They also used Romanow's support of abortion rights against him in his Saskatoon riding.[61] The Coalition in Support of the Family circulated 170,000 copies of a booklet raising the spectre of 'sweeping special rights for homosexuals and lesbians' if the NDP were elected, and ran newspaper advertisements having a similar message.[62] The coalition also condemned abortion, day care, welfare, 'rabid feminism,' and socialists. They picketed Romanow at campaign meetings, accusing him of being anti-life and pro-gay. Following the NDP's election to government, CHE renewed its lobbying but found the NDP initially reluctant to act. Romanow's cabinet was split on the question, and social conservative activists continued to agitate effectively. An unpleasant surprise occurred when the NDP justice minister, reacting to the *Haig* decision, stated that Human Rights Code amendments would be delayed. He speculated that, instead, a bill might be introduced to prohibit discrimination in general rather than listing specific grounds such as sexual orientation. CHE condemned the announcement. The Saskatchewan Human Rights Commission responded by declaring it would accept sexual orientation complaints using *Haig* as the rationale. In contrast, the efforts of REAL Women Saskatchewan and the Coalition in Support of the Family seemed more persuasive. They and other social conservative groups mounted an intensive letter-writing initiative in newspapers. They flooded communities, especially in rural areas, with leaflets claiming human rights legislation was never intended to protect behaviour such as homosexuality, that only 'innate, morally neutral birth characteristics' should be protected from discrimination. They also decried the prospect that employers and landlords would no longer be able to exercise choice based on deeply held personal views.[63]

It took nearly two years before the Romanow government sufficiently overcame such opposition, finally introducing, in 1993, Bill 38, which at long last added sexual orientation to the code. But to placate critics, the government added a last-minute provision stating that such action did not protect persons who engaged in activity prohibited by the Criminal Code (the paedophilia and incest amendment). Bill 38, adopted on June 22 by a vote of 38 to 10, was opposed only by the PC members of the legislature, although 25 NDP MLAs thought to be opposed were absent for the vote.[64] The decisive outcome did not end social conservative agitation, however, and efforts continued in hope of whipping the population into righteous outrage. The Coalition in Support of the Family collected 50,000 signatures on a petition calling for a plebiscite on the issue.[65] The president of the Christian Heritage Party filed an unsuccessful human rights complaint alleging the amendment made the Bible hate literature and undermined religious freedom. And, during the 1995 provincial election, the new PC leader promised to repeal the inclusion of sexual orientation.[66] Fortunately, the NDP was re-elected and all efforts at repeal have failed.

Newfoundland followed Saskatchewan in amending its human rights legislation, although little progress had been made in the 1980s. Beginning in 1985, the Gay Association in Newfoundland (GAIN) and other groups had lobbied resistant Progressive Conservative and Liberal governments. GAIN submitted briefs to the legislature in 1985 and 1987 and conducted a petition and letter-writing campaign focusing on amending the Human Rights code to comply with the Charter. They were supported by the province's human rights commission. Unmoved, the government introduced 1988 code amendments that omitted sexual orientation.[67] The Liberals, under Premier Clyde Wells, also refused to accept that the Charter prohibited sexual orientation discrimination, citing the fact that the federal government had not yet amended its human rights act, and claiming the need to await judicial decisions under the Charter. Wells and his government ministers went on to make a series of negative public pronouncements about a sexual orientation amendment. Newfoundland activists recall that the justice minister claimed sexual orientation, as a legal term, was too vague and that concerns existed about gays and lesbians being teachers and child care workers.[68] Compounding the situation was a climate of hostility growing out of revelations of sexual assault involving young males by a prominent Roman Catholic priest and of physical and sexual abuse against boys who were wards of the Mount Cashel orphanage. Sexual acts in both cases became associated with homosexuality in the media, in evidence presented to the two public inquiries established to investigate them, and in the public consciousness.[69] Despite this hostile climate, Gays and Lesbians Together, formed in September 1990, kept lobbying, distributing a brief to members of the legislature during Gay Pride Week in June 1991 and holding a press conference calling for an amendment. These actions, in conjunction with the official declaration of pride week by St John's mayor, garnered considerable media attention. But a subsequent meeting with the justice minister reconfirmed the government's opposition.[70]

Introducing a sexual orientation amendment was repeatedly raised at provincial lobby sessions held by Newfoundland women's organizations. At the 1992 women's lobby session, lesbian activist Brenda Ponic talked privately with Premier Wells about the issue, without success. During the formal session, she vigorously challenged Wells, describing ways in which lesbians face discrimination and arguing the need for a sexual orientation amendment. According to a transcript of the session, Wells responded: 'There's a lot of people in this province and in this nation who disagree strongly with the opinion that you just expressed. I mean you mentioned one of them. The Salvation Army ... has a particular point of view ...'[71] The Human Rights Commission also exerted pressure on the government. It announced in 1993 that, based on *Haig*, it would extend protection from discrimination to gays and lesbians by reading in sexual orientation to the Newfoundland legislation. The commission then used that approach to deal with a complaint of discrimination filed by Brian Nolan, a gay man in St John's. Nolan accused the police of wrongful arrest and harassment. He claimed police arrested him for no reason and called him a 'faggot.' In a separate action, the Police Complaints Commissioner subsequently agreed there was no just cause for the arrest and that homophobic slurs had been uttered.[72] In August 1995, a judge ruled in response to a government challenge of the Nolan complaint that the commission had the legal authority to exercise reading in. The justice minister appealed, arguing that the legislature, and not the courts, should decide whether the law affords protection from sexual orientation discrimination. At the same time, he indicated the government would bring in 'appropriate legislation' to address the issue.[73] A breakthrough finally came in November 1997, after Brian Tobin, who replaced Wells as premier, announced the government would amend the code to include sexual orientation. All parties supported the action, and a bill amending the code was adopted on December 9.[74]

In nearby Prince Edward Island, little was done to lobby the government to amend the Human Rights Act until 1986. The PEI government at that time wanted to review the act to deal with discrimination because of political affiliation. In a bold move, two women calling themselves the Lesbian Collective presented a brief urging inclusion of sexual orientation along with the other ground. The action had no effect on the politicians but Lee Fleming, an out lesbian active in various community endeavours, remembers it led to the first article on lesbians and gays ever to be printed in the Charlottetown *Guardian Patriot*. Other media coverage followed for a short time, generating enough interest to increase the membership of the Lesbian Collective and establish a lesbian phone line.[75] But it was not until ten years later that progress was made on the legislative front. A few months after taking power in 1996, Progressive Conservative premier Pat Binns advised a constituent in a letter, 'We do intend to move ahead with legislative changes to the human rights act, including prohibition and [sic] discrimination on the basis of sexual orientation.'[76] His government acted in 1998, when sexual orientation was included in a number of amendments to the human rights act adopted by the legislature.

By 1999, Alberta and the Northwest Territories (now the Western Arctic and Nunavut) were the only jurisdictions that had not amended their human rights legislation. While the NWT has yet to act, Alberta, in that year, reluctantly accepted the findings of a Supreme Court of Canada decision that effectively amended provincial legislation on the ground that its exclusion of sexual orientation contravened the Charter. A Charter challenge was necessary because, for nearly three decades, the Alberta government had adamantly refused to amend their human rights legislation. Undeterred and amazingly tenacious, lesbian and gay activists repeatedly submitted briefs, mounted letter-writing drives, and held meetings with members of the legislature. In January 1985, just prior to section 15 of the Charter taking effect, thirty-two Alberta gays and lesbians met with a PC Party caucus committee reviewing amendments to the Individual Rights Protection Act (IRPA). Unimpressed, the PCs reconfirmed their opposition, and sexual orientation was excluded from IRPA amendments adopted later that year.[77] Public statements opposing a sexual orientation amendment were regularly uttered. In a 1989 speech, one cabinet member declared he could not support such a move if it meant that admitted homosexuals would be allowed to teach in schools. Another minister told a conference of the Alberta Federation of Women United for Families that 'two homosexuals do not constitute a family.'[78] IRPA amendments enacted in 1990 also omitted sexual orientation. The government's intractable position reflected its need to placate a strong social conservative constituency. The PC convention in 1993 went so far as to vote against amending provincial laws to protect gays and lesbians from discrimination. Tellingly, a skit performed at the convention had as a character a limp-wristed gay French waiter.[79]

The hostile political climate meant it fell ultimately to Delwin Vriend to begin protracted litigation, ending with a Supreme Court of Canada decision that forced a change in Alberta law. Vriend was fired in 1991 from his employment with King's College, a Christian institution in Edmonton. Although he had disclosed his sexual orientation when offered a job in 1987 and was told it would not be an issue, the college fired Vriend, by then an out gay activist, when his sexual orientation became known publicly. The college justified the dismissal by claiming 'homosexual practice goes against the Bible, and the college's statement of faith.'[80] A defence fund for Vriend was established and a complaint was filed with the Alberta Human Rights Commission. The Gay and Lesbian Alliance wrote letters to MLAs, citing the case as an example of the need to amend the IRPA. When the commission refused to deal with his complaint, claiming it had no jurisdiction in the case, Vriend launched a legal challenge arguing that the IRPA's failure to include sexual orientation contravened section 15 of the Charter.[81]

Even more troubling than the commission's refusal to deal with Vriend's complaint was a statement of the chief commissioner, Fil Fraser, that the commission would not call on the government to introduce an amendment. Outraged, lesbian, gay, and bisexual activists picketed the commission and called for the chief commissioner's resignation.[82] It was only after nearly two years of publicity about the Vriend case that the commission finally issued a statement supporting the inclusion of sexual orientation in the IRPA. Led by a new chief commissioner, it announced it would no longer wait for government action and would investigate complaints of sexual orientation based on the principle established in *Haig*.[83] In response, the provincial minister responsible for the commission lashed out, publicly refuting its decision and declaring homosexuals have more rights than anybody else.[84]

Vriend's legal challenge claimed the commission violated his Charter rights by refusing him a service because of his sexual orientation. On 2 April 1994, a judge ruled that, in accordance with *Haig*, sexual orientation must be read into the IRPA, and found Vriend had been the victim of sexual orientation discrimination.[85] But Vriend suffered a setback when, on appeal by the government, the Alberta Court of Appeal concluded in February 1996 that the government did not have to amend the IRPA and overturned the lower court decision. In a 2 to 1 judgment, the justices ruled that the legislature, and not the courts, must determine the issue. Astonishingly, the majority decision also purported that homosexuals were treated no differently than heterosexuals in the IRPA because neither group is mentioned in it.[86] The Alberta government, bolstered by the appeal court's decision, omitted sexual orientation when it amended the IRPA in May 1996, despite intense lobbying by over one hundred groups.[87]

The Supreme Court of Canada agreed to hear Vriend's appeal, which was argued over two days in November 1997. Indicating the importance of the case, Vriend was supported by the Canadian Association of Statutory Human Rights Agencies and eleven other human rights and advocacy groups, including EGALE. Intervening against Vriend were the attorney general of Ontario, the Focus on the Family Canada Association, the Evangelical Fellowship of Canada, the Alberta Federation of Women United for Families, and the Christian Legal Fellowship. In its arguments, the Alberta government claimed the IRPA was neutral on sexual orientation and, therefore, everyone was treated equally on that basis, and that it should be legislatures, and not the courts, that determine whether the Charter's equality provisions should be reflected in provincial human rights laws.[88] The Court issued its judgment on 2 April 1998, finding unanimously that the IRPA's omission of sexual orientation infringed or denied rights guaranteed by section 5 of the Charter. The justices also ruled that such discrimination was not demonstrably justifiable under section 1. Seven of the eight justices agreed the most appropriate remedy was to read in sexual orientation to the IRPA.[89]

The Supreme Court's decision unleashed a venomous torrent of homophobic hatred. Outside the legislature, the most visible opposition came from the Canada Family Action Coalition – led by a Christian minister claiming support in up to one thousand churches – that ran full-page advertisements in two daily newspapers. The Alberta Civil Society Association broadcast advertisements on several radio and television stations, claiming the decision would infringe religious freedom and undermine the family.[90] A popular radio show was flooded with calls from listeners expressing fears about gays adopting children or schools teaching children to be tolerant of gays and lesbians, and with recitations of scripture and Biblical justifications for refusing to protect gays and lesbians from discrimination.[91] Some gay activists bore the brunt personally. Edmonton activist Murray Billett received hostile phone calls and letters, and feared for the safety of his family. Michael Phair, Edmonton's only openly gay city councillor, was barraged with negative and threatening calls, prompting him to publicly express his fear and that of others in the gay and lesbian communities. 'I've been told that I should be shot, and other gays and lesbians should be shot, that I should never have been born, and that there's no place in this province for people like me,' he revealed. One caller threatened to mutilate Phair's genitalia.[92]

Vociferous criticism of the Supreme Court decision was also voiced by political conservatives worked into a feverish state over unelected judges usurping the role of legislatures. Many PC caucus members, led by Provincial Treasurer Stockwell Day, a social conservative champion, publicly urged invoking the notwithstanding clause of the Constitution, under which the legislature could vote to override the decision for five years. Premier Ralph Klein and MLAs, mainly from rural areas, were deluged with angry phone calls. Many callers urged use of the notwithstanding clause, while others merely read 'church bulletins or scripted comments verbatim over the phone.'[93] Klein's office reported about one thousand calls, with two-thirds opposing the Vriend decision. Stockwell Day reported about 1200 calls, most of which were negative. In the end, the Klein government did not invoke the notwithstanding clause, despite opposition form about one-third of the caucus. The last provincial bastion of legally permitted discrimination in housing, employment, and access to services had fallen.

Amending the Canadian Human Rights Act

During the late 1980s and early 1990s, the Progressive Conservative government of Brian Mulroney could not obtain the necessary support of its caucus and party members for adding sexual orientation to the Canadian Human Rights Act (CHRA). The most concerted, but ultimately doomed, attempt was made by Kim Campbell when she was justice minister. Writing in *Time and Chance*, she stated she attempted to allay concerns of opposing MPs by promising to prohibit discrimination in employment and access to services while not granting legal recognition to same-sex relationships. An important consideration for Campbell was her 'hostility to the doctrine of extension,' under which the courts not only determine the constitutionality of laws but prescribe how they must be written or the specific actions that government must take.[94] Within that context, Campbell tabled CHRA amendments in December 1992 that included sexual orientation but at the same time announced that marital status would be defined in a way that did not include same-sex relationships. 'I don't know of a jurisdiction in the world that recognizes same-sex marriages,' she said as justification.[95] Gay and lesbian activists criticized the manoeuver, as did members of the Tory Family Caucus.[96] Campbell's bill, in any event, died once she was moved from justice to defence in a cabinet shuffle. The government soon dropped it from their list of legislative priorities.[97] By June 1993, Campbell was prime minister, and by September, the Conservatives had been annihilated in an election, being reduced to only two seats. The bill to amend the CHRA died on the order paper when Parliament was prorogued.

The prospects for a CHRA amendment brightened during and immediately following the 1993 federal election, but then soon faded. In response to an election questionnaire sent out by EGALE, Liberal leader Jean Chrétien expressed support for the CHRA amendment but claimed the issue of same-sex spouses needed more study.[98] The Liberals' election platform also promised to introduce legislation prescribing tougher sentencing for those convicted of committing crimes motivated by hate on the basis of sexual orientation or other specified grounds, such as race or religion. After the election of the Liberals, Justice Minister Allan Rock announced in December 1993 that the government would amend the CHRA. He also pledged that the government would review entitlements to benefits by same-sex partners.[99] Amendment of the CHRA was also included in the Liberal's first speech from the throne. But the government soon got cold feet, as opposition within its caucus mounted and virulent objection by social conservatives to the hate crimes legislation organized.[100] The promised hate crimes provisions of the Criminal Code were introduced as Bill C-41 in September 1994, and the inclusion of sexual orientation faced fierce resistance. 'Homosexuality is statistically abnormal, it's physically abnormal and it's morally immoral,' declared Liberal MP Tom Wappel. His cohort, Roseanne Skoke, opined that homosexuality was not supported by 'Canadian and Christian morals and values,' and that homosexuality 'is undermining the inherent rights and values of our Canadian families and it must not and should not be condoned.'[101] Wappel, Skoke, and fellow Liberal backbencher Dan McTeague led a public campaign against the sexual orientation provision of Bill C-41, and were joined by about a dozen other MPs. Fortunately, in the end, the bill, with sexual orientation included, was passed by Parliament in June 1995.[102]

Religious and social conservative groups, active since mid-1985 in organizing against a CHRA amendment, intensified their efforts as the prospect of such amendment became more likely, given the evolution of Charter litigation. REAL Women, the anti-feminist, family values bulwark of the social conservative movement, had been particularly vociferous over the years. It peddled the line that 'Many people would be hurt by "sexual orientation" equality laws. Athletic associations, colleges, university campuses, churches, schools, day-care centres, boy's clubs, parents of school-age children, Children's Aid Societies, counselling agencies and all professions in physical contact with the public.' REAL Women accused such legislation of giving gays and lesbians 'special rights recognizing in law their lifestyle and behaviour.' They claimed that as 'alcoholism, or compulsive gambling, for example, do not qualify for such protection, neither should other deviant behaviour such as homosexual activity.' Homosexuality, the group asserted, is a disorder of 'psycho-sexual development' that can be 'reversed' through treatment and Christian counselling. Playing on fears of paedophilia and child molestation, REAL Women claimed homosexuals cannot procreate and therefore 'must recruit – often the young,' seek sex 'in the young age group,' and resort to prostitution as they grow older. For added measure, the group's literature accused gays of engaging in 'bestiality and other perversions,' spreading AIDS, and being influenced by paedophiles and advocates for child pornography.[103]

Another active group, the Evangelical Fellowship of Canada, mounted a fund-raising and petition campaign in 1995 that declared ominously that 'inclusion of sexual orientation could affect the freedom of speech and religious freedom of many Canadians who believe homosexual practice to be immoral.'[104] Later, once a CHRA amendment was introduced, REAL Women and the Evangelical Fellowship were joined by the Canadian Conference of Catholic Bishops, which warned that amending the CHRA would lead to the social legitimization of relationships the church could not condone. Another group, the Coalition of Concerned Canadians, ran a full-page national newspaper advertisement opposing the sexual orientation amendment. Describing themselves as being dedicated 'to clarifying and reinforcing the continuing importance of the traditional family in Canadian Society,' they proclaimed the CHRA amendment 'is the product of myth and is a serious threat to marriage and family.'[105] Supporting these groups in Parliament were Liberal caucus family values champions and the Reform Party (later the Canadian Reform Conservative Alliance, or the Canadian Alliance), which contributed to the government's reticence to amend the CHRA. The Reform Party actually issued a policy statement in late 1994 declaring that, if elected to govern, they would not only oppose adding sexual orientation, they would remove from the CHRA all 'divisive' characteristics such as race and religion. A simple statement that the 'fundamental human rights of all Canadians are protected,' in their view, would be sufficient.[106]

The turning point came in March 1996, when CHRC Chief Commissioner Maxwell Yalden publicly castigated the government for inaction. The rebuke produced a round of embarrassing publicity about the government's failure to deliver on its promise. The next day, Chrétien announced that a bill amending the CHRA would be introduced.[107] In late April, Justice Minister Allan Rock introduced Bill C-33, emphasizing it would not deal with benefits for same-sex couples, marriage, or adoption. Then, to appease family values MPs and social conservative groups, the bill was amended to add a preamble stating the government 'recognizes and affirms the importance of family as the foundation of Canadian society and that nothing in this act alters its fundamental role in society.'[108] To further placate opponents, the government announced a free vote would be held. Reform MPs also attempted unsuccessfully after first reading to have *family* defined in the preamble of Bill C-33. They introduced twenty-nine amendments, all of which were defeated. Finally, on 9 May 1996, Bill C-33 was adopted in the House of Commons, on a vote of 153 to 76, ending the long and tortuous campaign commenced by gay and lesbian activists over two decades earlier.[109]

The Apparent Demise of Lesbian and Gay Liberation

With the adoption of the federal legislation, and the enactment of sexual orientation amendments provincially, the lesbian and gay movement had reached an historic turning point. At the same time, the conflict and tensions between liberationist and assimilationist objectives were intensified, even as the distinctions between the two became more blurred. These outcomes arose principally because of the dominance of human rights advocacy and the prominent roles of some liberation activists in the various human rights campaigns. It seemed that, somewhere along the way, the fight to achieve legislative change as a necessary step on the road to liberation had been abandoned. The end sought by the movement seemed to have become equality, not liberation. It was a case of perception becoming the reality for most observers and many of the participants.

But as we shall see in subsequent chapters, lesbian and gay liberation, in fact, had not disappeared. Nor was it dead, although searching for evidence of its existence solely from the vantage of the human rights campaigns of the 1980s and 1990s would inevitably result in its being hard to discern. Yet, undeniably, victory in the battles to amend human rights laws, particularly in political climates not especially disposed towards recognizing rights for gays and lesbians, and in the face of fierce social conservative opposition, was powerfully symbolic, and vindicated the strategy put forward by liberationist activists in the 1970s. Visibility had been asserted because of the publicity generated by the demonstrations, presentation of briefs, use of the media, and other means. The heterosexual public was more aware, and better educated about gays, lesbians, and bisexuals. The demands and aspirations of gays, lesbians, and bisexuals were firmly implanted on the political and public agendas. Thousands and thousands of queers all over Canada had been able to see others like them on television, in newspapers, and in the streets, and been able to find the strength to come out of the closet. Where liberationists differ from assimilationists, even today, however, is by recognizing that, in practical terms, legislative amendment alone would not significantly change the everyday lives of gays and lesbians nor remove the homophobia and heterosexism that oppresses them.

Nonetheless, despite the success of the human rights campaigns they had launched with such militancy in the 1970s, the victories were bittersweet for liberationists. They accentuated the inherent conflict always present in the human rights strategy and had, in the short term at least, actually strengthened the equality-seeking assimilation they so fundamentally opposed – at the expense of liberation advocacy, especially respecting issues of sexuality. More troubling still were the pronouncements of academics such as Didi Herman, who in her 1994 book, *Rights of Passage*, cast lesbian and gay liberation activists in CGRO as essentially having sold out to liberalism in the pursuit of questionable legislative change, rather than fostering a truly liberationist advocacy. Focusing on the Bill 7 campaign in Ontario, Herman argued that an unintended consequence was to 'leave unchallenged liberal principles and contribute to the entrenchment of problematic concepts such as the minority rights paradigm. At the same time as some lesbians and gay men were being politicized into a lobbying campaign, the identity they were being asked to take on was that of the "minority" subject of liberal human rights laws.' Herman criticized CGRO for not infusing the debate on Bill 7 with alternative ideas of sexuality and pursuing a strategy that was 'an abandonment of the field to liberals and the right.' She claims the fact that CGRO chose to be 'a voice of lesbian and gay liberalism implicitly meant that the organization was not speaking for feminist, socialist, and other progressive lesbians and gays men,' who became 'increasingly marginalized from the "public face" of the lesbian and gay movement.'[110] Herman's argument is, however, that of an academic, rather than an activist. It is difficult to see – even taking into account the ascendancy of equality-seeking assimilationism – how pursuing any strategy other than that undertaken by CGRO would have resulted in advancing the movement. Would it have been better to articulate what Herman proposes but to lose the Bill 7 campaign? That outcome would surely have removed the possibility of any support from elected, albeit liberal, politicians, in turn strengthening the influence and impact of the religious right, who would have been seen as scoring a huge victory.

Admittedly, the flip side of the victories was unquestionably the short-term entrenchment of equality rights activism and the marginalization of liberationist causes. Nowhere was this truer than in the federal lobbying efforts to secure a CHRA amendment in the mid-1990s, which focused exclusively on equality rights using the Charter as the instrument for achieving legislative change. It was, in the words of Miriam Smith, 'rights talk' in full measure. As she notes, 'Rights talk equates legal change with social change and neglects the deployment of rights as political resources. While the gay liberation movement focused on challenging dominant social codes and viewed demands on the state as a means of mounting this challenge, equality-seeking in the eighties and nineties is increasingly focused on challenging state policy as an end in itself.' Rights talk, Smith correctly contends, 'privileges legal victory over societally directed challenges.'[111] At the federal level, particularly since the advent of the Charter and the arrival on the scene of Equality for Gays And Lesbians Everywhere in the late 1980s, calls for – or even references to – liberation have been completely absent from human rights advocacy. An EGALE leaflet from the early 1990s noted it was 'working towards equality for gay men and lesbians under Canadian law' by 'seeking to challenge the Charter of Rights and Freedoms.' There was no reference to challenging repressive sex laws, or their enforcement, and, surprisingly, no discussion of challenging and combatting homophobia and heterosexism. EGALE's pitch, instead, was to 'citizenship': 'If you feel that you are as good as any other citizen and that you want the benefit of the law as well as its responsibilities, you are a potential member of EGALE.'[112] Citizenship and equality, not liberation and overcoming oppression, now, more clearly than ever, became the public message of the gay and lesbian movement. It had eclipsed the more radical liberationist message, both within and outside of queer communities, and was now ready to take command of another issue – relationships recognition – that could have been, but lamentably was not, fought on liberationist terms.

TEN

Legal Recognition of Same-Sex Relationships

Even as federal and provincial human rights laws were being amended in the 1990s, the legal recognition of same-sex spousal relationships gained ascendancy. Further legislative change to achieve that end seemed logical, at least to the white, able-bodied, middle-class, urban, equality-seeking activists who dominated the movement. The achievement of equality with heterosexuals could now be extended into a new realm of the law and public policy, through the effective use of Charter litigation. Yet, seeking legal recognition of spousal relationships was even more fraught with difficulties than amending laws to prohibit discrimination in employment, housing, and access to services. These challenges were to divide the gay, lesbian, and bisexual communities, and fuel the perception that equality-seeking assimilationism was the totality of the movement. Liberationists of the 70s and 80s despaired at the new direction and its uncritical embracing of same-sex spousal relationships in the heterosexual mode. Virtually vanished from the discourse of queer advocacy were liberationist and feminist critiques of the heterosexual nuclear family and liberationist scepticism over attempting to fit queer relationships, in all of their diverse and often radical forms, into the constraints of oppressive state-sanctioned coupledom based on monogamy, inequality, and sexism. Lamentably, the new agenda sought to establish gays, lesbians, and bisexuals as mainstream, to comfortably accommodate them within the middle-class Canadian family. Drag, leather, SM sex, pornography, promiscuity, and blatant flaunting of queerness were eschewed as embarrassments and as inimical to the new, more respectable public persona of the gay, lesbian, and bisexual communities. Issues related to coming out of the closet – still a risky decision for many – and combatting systemic homophobia and heterosexism were sidelined.

Legal Recognition of Same-Sex Relationships: A Problematic Issue

The current battles over relationship recognition have their roots in the mid-1980s, as many more gays and lesbians began publicly declaring that they were in same-sex relationships. This process brought them into conflict with laws and regulations restricting all spousal benefits and responsibilities to heterosexuals. Many, including professionals who had never before felt the need to be activists, became angered and politicized, transforming both the nature and public face of gay, lesbian, and bisexual activism. Added to this impetus was the changing legal situation arising from the amendment of human rights laws and the rulings of the courts on the impact of the Charter. These developments created a patchwork of legal contradictions. An employer could not, in law, refuse to hire a bisexual, gay, or lesbian person but could refuse to designate that person's same-sex partner under spousal benefit and family support policies. Yet, gays, lesbians, and bisexuals were required to pay into such plans, subsidizing the relationships of their heterosexual colleagues, whether married or common law. Discriminatory laws and policies were challenged, especially those relating to receipt of spousal benefits, division of household assets, spousal support, and child custody.

   Still, many philosophical dilemmas and practical considerations weighed against pursuing the recognition of same-sex relationships. Not all lesbians, gays, and bisexuals have jobs with benefits packages. Those who do not would not prosper personally from campaigns to secure spousal benefits. Also left out would be persons who are not in relationships, who, because of taxation and mandatory contributions to benefits plans, could justifiably claim economic disadvantage due to being uncoupled. In addition, campaigns for inclusion in mainstream family structures meant acceptance of a particular concept of family originally imported from Britain and Europe and modified only to accommodate same-sex relationships. Family structures prevalent in other cultures would be excluded. Persons living together but receiving social assistance or disability benefits as individuals could have their benefits reduced by being deemed to be in spousal relationships. Others who were in relationships but did not live together under the same roof could be excluded for failing to meet the cohabitation requirement.

Charter litigation and the lobbying associated with obtaining legal equality between same-sex and opposite-sex relationships were particularly problematic for the minority of liberationists still active in the gay and lesbian movement. Such advocacy meant largely accommodating same-sex relationships within the existing heterosexist and still essentially patriarchal social and legal status quos. It required a strategy of assimilating same-sex relationships into tax systems, pension plans, employment benefits, and family support laws originally intended to privilege marriages in which male spouses were the breadwinners and wives were dependants. Instead of seeking to liberate sexuality and relationships from the oppression of the family, activism became focused on asserting that gays, lesbians, and bisexuals *are* family, and obtaining legal recognition of *equal families*. Liberationists were dismayed at the refusal of spousal rights proponents to argue for a redefinition of the way in which benefits are provided by the state, such as universally to individuals or on the basis of economic need or dependency. Liberationists also recoiled at, and condemned, the obsessive advancement of arguments expressing the need for state legitimization and validation of same-sex relationships that, thereby, make them respectable.[1] Christine Donald, of the Coalition for Lesbian and Gay Rights in Ontario (CLGRO), noted in a 1998 interview, 'the danger of the equal rights thing is not looking carefully at who you want to be equal with ... I don't see much there [in the behaviour of heterosexuals] that I want to copy, I really don't.'[2] For Nikki Gershbain, writing in *Xtra!* in 1997, the rise in prominence of advocacy for legalizing same-sex relationships symbolized 'the dilution of the socialist gay vision that emerged in the 1970s and 80s,' resulting in the politics of gay and lesbian difference being 'transformed into a desire to promote gay and lesbian sameness.'[3] As Kathleen A. Lahey noted in her excellent presentation of the difficulties associated with relationship recognition politics, a key problem with the new advocacy is 'that it leaves intact the social, economic and sexual hierarchies that initially justified these structures and created this seemingly safe space for queers within larger structures of appropriation and oppression.'[4]

Fundamentally, the relationships recognition issue was seized by predominantly affluent, urban, and white gays, lesbians, and bisexuals and then presented as *the* issue of primary importance to *all* members of the queer communities. Virtually no lesbians and gays of colour, low-income gays and lesbians, or those with disabilities were involved, and their experiences and perspectives were, accordingly, not reflected.

Within queer communities in the larger urban centres that were, by the early 1990s, as diverse and multicultural as Canada itself had become, arguing for acceptance of same-sex relationships within a legal framework embodying the dominant white, Anglo-Saxon tradition meant excluding many for whom the nature of family and relationships were culturally different. A movement truly committed to social change, rather than mere accommodation, would have advocated for recognition of a multiplicity of family structures that took into account social, economic, and cultural differences. Such a movement would not have uncritically accepted, even tacitly, that the dominant family structure of Canadian society is fundamentally acceptable save for its unfortunate lack of inclusion of same-sex couplings. Black lesbian activist Carol Allen, in an article published in 1992 noted:

> If we want benefits the approach we want to getting them must take the bigger social and economic picture into consideration. We need to be sure that our arguments are inclusive rather than exclusive of those whose family structure is different. Some of us live in collective houses with people we consider our 'family.' Some of us are non-monogamous, others are monogamous and don't live together, still others have relationships which don't look like anything mentioned here. If this is the reality for some, why should we promote legal strategies aimed at securing benefits that will apply only to *some* lesbians and gays?[5]

The spousal benefits agenda also did not speak to the more pressing needs of people of colour. Kwame Stephens, a Black gay man active on queer issues with white gays in the late 1990s told *Xtra!*: 'It struck me that the agenda of white gay men is very difficult. They're fighting for rights. We've got pension rights now, for example. Who will reach out for those rights? The white, mainstream guys who feel comfortable. But for the black guy whose dealing with the comfort level [with his sexuality], he's not going to reach for that. The closet cases are the black guys. They have more need for homophobia education across the board.'[6]

The issue of legally recognizing same-sex marriage has been particularly contentious. On that subject, Nikki Gershbain commented in her article in *Xtra!* that 'the gay marriage issue goes beyond the problem of matrimony to test our entire vision of our society. There was a time when gay men and lesbians were on the vanguard of sexual liberation, which they saw as part of a larger project of social and economic justice.' The issue was an example, in her view, of how 'gay men and lesbians have been reinvented for the neo-conservative 1990s,' an era when being a gay activist no longer automatically meant being left wing and 'the radical edge of sexual liberation has been diffused.'[7] Many activists schooled in liberation politics similarly spoke out about the direction taken by rights advocates of the 1990s. 'Marriage is not something we have ever lobbied for, nor would we. It's a philosophical question. Is marriage an institution that is particularly appropriate for same-sex relationships?' asked CLGRO's Tom Warner in a 1998 article also published in Xtra![8] In an earlier discussion of the subject, Warner wrote, 'It is time to purge ourselves of the belief that our relationships must be legitimized or validated by heterosexuals. We should not care whether they think we are respectable. The belief that we need to be legally married to be equal to heterosexuals is simply another insidious form of internalized homophobia.'[9]

Similarly, Jeff Dodds, writing in Perceptions in 2000, commented: 'Perhaps it stems from years of finding strength in not being sanctioned by the state that I'm suddenly discomfited by the idea that they [the federal government] think I need their legitimization to feel better.' Dodds then went on to observe that 'the marriage agenda is being pushed by affluent gays and lesbians without a strong basis of grass-roots support.' In contrast, he noted, 'Twenty or thirty years ago it [the movement] was about being accepted for who we are, not an effort to be assimilated into the broader population. I don't want the right to marry because that is not my culture. I don't want to be considered the same as heterosexuals because I am not.' Dodds, identifying more urgent issues affecting the daily lives of gays and lesbians, voiced concern that 'for many in our community, the issues are more personal: issues like good physical and mental health, systemic homophobia in institutions who are supposed to provide care, issues around poverty, incidence rates of suicide and drug and alcohol abuse that are dispro-portionately high, and so on. I don't see the recognition of our relation-ships by the federal government as being particularly meaningful in changing these realities.'[10]

Yet other activists, like Brent Hawkes, pastor of Toronto's Metropoli-tan Community Church, have been clear in wanting to see same-sex marriages legalized. 'Any discrimination that is ingrained in law needs to be changed, because it gives the impression to society that it is acceptable to discriminate.'[11] Many people in the gay, lesbian, and bisexual communities see such legalization as a form of social accept-ance. As one lesbian identified only as Rachel observed in Xtra!: 'It's about legitimacy and equality. It's my guess that with marriage, there will be less gay-bashing, less self-recrimination.'[12] And even some early gay liberation activists, like Chris Vogel, believe that achieving the legal recognition of same-sex marriages is critical in the pursuit of equality in all its forms.[13] Vogel and his partner, Richard North, launched the first challenge of the marriage laws in 1974.

More recent challenges to marriage laws have included the 1992 case of Pierre Beaulne and Todd Layland, who attempted to obtain a marriage licence but were told that it was illegal for two men to marry. They launched an action in the Ontario Court General Division alleging that the provincial law governing the issuance of marriage licences violated section 15 of the Charter. In March 1993, a panel of judges ruled in a 2 to 1 decision that marriage can only take place in law between a man and a woman, and that Beaulne and Layland had not been discriminated against because of their sexual orientation.[14] Subsequently, a Quebec gay couple, Michael Hendricks and René Leboeuf, commenced a court case in the fall of 1998 disputing the definition in the Quebec Civil Code restricting marriage to two persons of the opposite sex. The action, filed in the Quebec Superior Court, has not yet been determined.[15] And, during 2000, a gay couple, Michael Leshner and Michael Stark, initiated a challenge to the Ontario law governing the issuance of marriage licences.[16] Later that year, Brent Hawkes announced to considerable media fanfare that he would be using an old provision in Ontario law, the publishing of the banns, both to perform same-sex marriages, and, he asserted, to have them legally recognized.[17] On another front, the NDP government of British Columbia, prompted by lesbian and gay activists and a rising number of court cases seeking issuance of marriage licences under provincial law, launched a Charter challenge of the federal legislation that restricts marriage to opposite-sex couples in 2000.[18]

Irrespective of the diverging opinions among activists, there has been, undeniably, an urgency and attractiveness to waging campaigns to secure legal recognition of same-sex relationships, at least insofar as ensuring the same rights and responsibilities as exist for common law heterosexual relationships. Even a liberationist group such as the Coalition for Lesbians and Gay Rights in Ontario (CLGRO) has not been able to decline taking up the issue, and organized for legislative reform, finding, in the process, that its liberationist principles became compromised and challenged. Taking up the battle necessarily involved obtaining judgments from the courts and support from politicians within conservative legal and legislative frameworks and middle-class notions of family. Yet, there was also a need to confront entrenched anti-homosexual attitudes and pervasive heterosexism validating and per-petuating bias in favour of granting special, privileged status to heterosexual relationships, especially marriage. The campaigns of fam-ily values proponents and social conservatives seeking to influence or control public policy also demanded a response. Few liberationists, no matter how sceptical of or ambivalent towards relationship recogni-tion, were able to ignore such dynamics. The dilemma thus created for liberationists remains unresolved more than a decade after the first spousal benefits campaigns were organized.

Attempting to Forge a Consensus

CLGRO became the first organization to develop a comprehensive, consensus-based position on relationships recognition, with a focus on lobbying for legislative change. CLGRO members themselves provided the impetus for the new strategy, identifying relationships recognition as a priority following the amendment of the Ontario Human Rights Code. To plot a strategy, CLGRO hosted a 1989 conference, 'On Our Own Terms.' Speaking at the conference from a liberationist perspec-tive, Chris Bearchell challenged those in attendance to 'strive for some-thing more than mere equality' with heterosexuals. *Spouse* is not a term well suited to the reality of same-sex relationships, Bearchell observed, as spousal relationships are generally based on dependency or 'an unrealistic expectation of exclusivity.' With the advent of gay liberation, gays and lesbians, in Bearchell's view, were free to create their own forms of relationships, recognizing that some spousal entitlements pe-nalize people who are not in relationships.[19] In the end, CLGRO emerged from the conference with a fragile consensus that struck a balance between those who wanted to attain equality with heterosexual rela-tionships and the liberationist view argued by Bearchell and others. Specific legislative changes were to be sought within a framework based on an optional system of self-designation of a spousal relation-ship, recognizing that all persons should have the right to determine the nature of their own personal relationships in accordance with their personal values and beliefs. This issue was seen as being essentially one of freedom of choice.[20]

Between 1989 and 1994, CLGRO articulated its position and slowly gained support within the broader communities, trying to steer a middle course. It acknowledged that many rejected the traditional, hetero-sexual models of relationships and family as patriarchal, oppressive, and discriminatory towards single persons or those living alternative lifestyles. At the same time, CLGRO stated that many others wish to live in much the same way as their heterosexual friends and relatives, while still others have views that fall somewhere in-between these two positions. The group's stance was that persons wanting all the rights and benefits and all of the obligations and responsibilities for their same-sex relationships as are applicable to heterosexual relationships, should be able to obtain them in law. Those choosing not to do so should be able to simply opt out. To convey that position, CLGRO articulated a statement of principle that read: 'All people, regardless of sexual orientation, have the right to determine for themselves their primary personal relationships and to have those relationships sup-ported and recognized in law and by social institutions.'[21] To achieve their objectives, CLGRO called for the establishment of an optional partnerships registration system and amendment of the definition of spouse and marital status in various provincial laws.

Then, in a development that liberationists of the 1970s would never have foreseen, CLGRO membership received an influx of lawyers, civil servants, and other professionals who were interested in relationship recognition but not particularly committed to liberation or issues re-lated to sexuality. These individuals, through a CLGRO working group, put together over a two-year period a groundbreaking brief, *Happy Families*, which set out precisely how dozens of Ontario laws should be amended to achieve recognition of same-sex relationships in the same way as heterosexual common law relationships were recognized. While these developments were beneficial in many ways – CLGRO now had more people and resources, plus legal expertise that could not other-wise be obtained – it introduced a tension within the organization. Two distinct perspectives emerged between those who wanted to maintain a liberationist approach and others for whom legislative amendment was a sufficient objective in and of itself. An agitated debate took place within CLGRO's working group in early 1991, when Tom Warner and Christine Donald circulated a policy document intended to amplify the position taken at 'On Our Own Terms' to address CLGRO's preference for a basis, other than relationship status, for apportioning social ben-efits. The statement read: 'CLGRO believes that, whereas our prefer-ence would be that benefits be made available on an individual basis (with allowances for the dependence of children, the aged and the disabled), whenever benefits are available to heterosexuals living in couples, these same benefits also must be made available to same-sex couples on the same footing.' As recorded in the minutes of the working group, 'The policy statement generated much heated debate. There seemed to be several people who were uncomfortable with the issues of dependency and alternate family structures that underlined the statement.'[22] As will be seen later, these tensions helped pave the way for the establishment of a separate equality-seeking organization dedicated exclusively to attaining the legal recognition of the same-sex relationships. This organization abandoned any pretext of pursuing lesbian and gay liberation objectives.[23]

The Rocky Road to Bill 167

Armed with the fragile consensus formed at 'On Our Own Terms,' and struggling constantly to manage the many conflicts and dissents over strategy, CLGRO began lobbying to have some seventy provincial laws amended. Just prior to the 1990 provincial election, CLGRO set out its position in general terms, together with a summary of recent human rights and Charter cases, in a letter to all members of the legislature. Then, to the surprise of nearly everyone, the New Democratic Party won the election. Shortly afterwards, the new government announced the extension of spousal benefit coverage (but not survivor pensions) to public service employees in same-sex relationships. Pension benefits, they argued, were precluded by the provisions of the federal Income Tax Act, which recognized only opposite sex spouses. The NDP also heightened expectations by announcing 'this government's review of all pertinent laws and policies pertaining to spousal benefits.'[24] The announcement sounded like a commitment to amend the laws; however, within a short time, a spokesperson for the Ministry of the Attorney General told the press that the review might not lead to legal reform, as it was only 'preliminary ... an identification process.'[25] In fact, the government was nervous about acting on same-sex benefits, and timidity took hold in reaction to strident opposition within the NDP caucus. Bob Rae, in *From Protest to Power*, recalled there was a 'lack of enquiring signals' from cabinet members content to let the study continue. There was also the desire to have courts force the issue. 'My own hope was that enough cases would work their way through the courts that opinion in the caucus and the province would move.'[26] The cabinet's reticence meant that virtually nothing happened over the next two years.[27]

But obstacles other than NDP caucus resistance also confronted CLGRO. For quite some time, the only pressure exerted on the government came from CLGRO and a small group of NDP party activists. Most MPPs weren't hearing from constituents supporting the measure. This provided the excuse for dismissing relationship recognition as being important only to a concentrated downtown Toronto constituency. In addition, the flukey, unexpected NDP electoral victory and the government's long shot chance at re-election – they gained office with only 37 per cent of the votes cast, the smallest popular vote plurality ever for a majority government in Ontario – put an urgency on the need for quick action. CLGRO, accordingly, urged the introduction of legislation well before the next election, anticipating an outpouring of anti-gay venom from the religious right once amendments were introduced. With that objective in mind, it increased its efforts throughout 1992, beginning with its *Happy Families* brief.[28] CLGRO and members of the Lesbian Gay and Bisexual Committee of the NDP lobbied and met with key cabinet ministers. They protested Attorney General Howard Hampton's prolonged failure to even meet with them to discuss the issue, staging a sit-in at his office. This action heightened media attention but prompted a statement from Hampton about the lack of unanimity within the lesbian and gay communities on the question, the complexity of the issues involved, and the scores of laws that would need to be changed. He added, 'governments can only take on so many agendas at once.'[29] In September, CLGRO generated national media coverage over a Human Rights Board of Inquiry decision, based on Charter arguments, that the Ontario government had discriminated against Michael Leshner, a government employee, by refusing to recognize his same-sex partner for survivor benefits under the pension plan. CLGRO spokesperson Tom Warner called upon Hampton 'to accept the finding in this case, to reject any advice to appeal to the courts and, in addition, to proceed immediately to amend provincial laws.'[30] Ultimately, the government did not appeal, although the Leshner decision marked the beginning of sustained religious-right opposition. Hampton and the Human Rights Commission were deluged with angry reaction orchestrated by church groups across the province. As a countermeasure, CLGRO mounted its own phone and fax campaign.[31]

The fall and winter of 1992 also featured unsuccessful CLGRO efforts to secure Liberal Party support to offset NDP back bench opposition. A meeting between CLGRO and Liberal Leader Lyn McLeod proved disappointing. McLeod expressed opposition to amending the definition of 'marital status' and to granting adoption rights to same-sex couples. In December, CLGRO delivered to Queen's Park seven thousand post cards from individuals throughout Ontario calling on Bob Rae to amend provincial laws.[32] Then, as the situation seemed most hopeless, Marion Boyd succeeded Hampton as attorney general. Shortly after taking office, she met with gays and lesbians in the NDP and expressed support for bringing in legislation. Still, government delay continued. The cabinet's planning and priorities committee considered a submission on legislative changes in March 1993 but deferred making a decision. In May, CLGRO provided the committee with its own proposed omnibus bill, with no apparent effect.[33] In June, Boyd raised the stakes in a speech in which she committed to introducing a bill.[34] But it was not until December that ministry staff presented Boyd with a list of bills under development for the following spring, on which was found 'Same Sex Spouse Review.'[35]

Although CLGRO advocated an omnibus bill to amend all laws defining 'spouse' and similar terms, there was yet no indication of just how extensively any government bill would amend the various laws. It was suspected from media reports that the NDP, if they acted at all, would take a minimal approach, removing discrimination in the provision of certain benefits, but excluding family law and adoption rights.[36] In fact, Bob Rae confirmed in his memoirs that there was consideration of a compromise approach. This was not pursued, he states, because of 'a reluctance to see this as an issue that required accommodation and compromise.' He also blamed the lesbian and gay community, which 'demanded the whole loaf, or nothing.'[37] The latter position reflected the fact that adoption was a 'no compromise' issue for most of those pushing for legal reform. Leaving it out would have been a concession to homophobia and heterosexism, as the presumption was (and is) that gays, lesbians, and bisexuals cannot be good parents or role models. And it would have split the gay, lesbian, and bisexual communities along gender lines, as the right to adopt was a critical issue for lesbians. Accordingly, CLGRO rejected compromise, taking the position in September 1992 that 'we cannot divide our human rights into sections and then bargain with the government over which ones will be implemented.'[38]

The issue of amending laws was given added public exposure during a 1993 by-election in a downtown Toronto constituency with a large gay, lesbian, and bisexual electorate. To the astonishment of many, Lyn McLeod made same-sex rights an issue in her party's campaign. She wrote to Rae, chastising his government for breaking its promise. She went on to say, 'If you will agree to bring legislation forward immediately I will do everything possible to facilitate passage ... and in the unlikely event that the courts have not yet finally settled the matter within two years, please be assured that a future Liberal government will move swiftly to take the action which I am requesting you to take immediately.'[39] McLeod's letter, circulated widely in the media and among gays and lesbians, created the impression the Liberals supported legislative change, a perception that would later come back to haunt McLeod and her party.

Within weeks of winning the by-election, Liberal Tim Murphy introduced a private member's bill – Bill 45 – intended to bring Ontario laws into line with the Leshner decision. If passed, it would have afforded same-sex benefit rights but would not have amended family law or permitted same-sex couple adoptions.[40] The real value of Bill 45 was not so much the limited rights it proposed to grant, but the opportunity it provided to keep pressure on the NDP. It therefore was seized upon as a focal point for lobbying, serving as a means to gauge support and opposition in each of the three parties in the legislature. At second reading in early June 1993, most NDP members voted for the bill, but only five Liberals did so, including McLeod. All Progressive Conservatives opposed it. Ordinarily, at that point Bill 45 would have proceeded to hearings before a legislative committee, but it was dead on delivery. The Liberal caucus was riven with dissent over McLeod's by-election statements, and many of that party's MPPs, especially those from rural ridings, were angry. They saw the bill as a vote-losing proposition. Committee hearings never took place, and the bill vanished from the legislative agenda.[41] With time running out in the NDP's term, and fury building in the gay, lesbian, and bisexual communities over the government's stalling, CLGRO held a sit-in outside Bob Rae's office on 21 February 1994.[42]

Meanwhile, social conservative forces began organizing with more vigour upon the arrival of Bill 45, claiming it represented 'an attack on freedom of religion' and the right to express the view that Christianity 'does not condone homosexuality.' In November and December 1993, thirty petitions were read in the legislature, most being from church congregations in small towns or rural areas. One petition bearing 2,200 signatures from the Family Coalition Party claimed, 'The Ontario legislature is out of control,' and asserted, 'Marriage and the family are the rock all civilizations are structured on.' Well-organized, face-to-face encounters with churchgoers opposed to gay rights confronted MPPs from rural and suburban ridings.[43] Catering to this constituency, the PC Party, during a 1994 by-election in the rural riding of Victoria-Haliburton, used same-sex rights to attack both the NDP and the Liberals. Newspaper advertisements charged same-sex benefits were 'a new priority' for the NDP and that 'Lyn McLeod has been pushing it personally for months.' After the PCs won the riding, many in the media and the Liberal caucus cited the reason as opposition to same-sex benefits.[44]

At the end of February 1994, Marion Boyd finally announced a bill would be introduced, but did not provide details. She also acknowledged some caucus opposition to the bill. A short time afterwards, Rae went on record publicly, stating his government would give same-sex couples all the rights enjoyed by heterosexual spouses.[45] The stage for a huge battle was now set and, wasting no time, NDP caucus dissenters and social conservative advocates became more vocal. Boyd began equivocating, claiming the bill's introduction could not be guaranteed before the legislature adjourned for the summer. The media reported that none of the options presented for consideration at a caucus meeting had been supported. According to Rae, there was 'extraordinary resentment from those who simply didn't see this as a priority, particularly with an election year looming.' Ominously, a free vote on the bill was suggested that, Rae noted, 'created problems because it ended up allowing a bitter and divisive public debate.'[46] Compounding the problems was a full-scale backlash outside the Legislature. A letter from the Roman Catholic Archbishop of Toronto imploring Catholics to write letters to MPPs to oppose same-sex rights circulated in churches and produced massive media coverage.[47] The Canadian Federation of Independent Business condemned the initiative as a further attack on the already beleaguered small business community and the taxpayers.[48] A *Toronto Sun* business columnist charged that 'in politically-correct Ontario ... only the middle-class has no rights' in a column with a headline that screamed: 'Open your wallets: Same-sex benefits will cost untold millions.'[49] Neoconservative polemicist David Frum exclaimed, 'This is supposed to promote non-discrimination; it looks a lot more like a good old-fashioned NDP grab for other people's money.'[50]

Shattered Consensus and Equal Families Ascendancy

The prospect of an actual bill, and the massive opposition of social conservatives, mobilized the gay, lesbian, and bisexual communities in an unprecedented manner. An influx of volunteers and a resolve to achieve victory immeasurably bolstered organizing in support of the legislation. But the influx also precipitated the shattering of CLGRO's consensus position and caused CLGRO's forfeiture of the leadership of the campaign. A new entity, the Campaign for Equal Families (CEF), was formed out of CLGRO's working group on relationship recognition, and adopted as its slogan, "We Are Family." CLGRO activists had serious misgivings about the CEF strategy and rhetoric, but remained active in the campaign in order not to abandon an issue they had succeeded in bringing to the point of having a bill in the legislature, and to maintain a united front publicly. In particular, Tom Warner became the CEF co-chair, along with Mary-Woo Sims, who had been active in CLGRO's working group. But CLGRO activists were massively outnumbered, and relations between a minority of liberationists and the vast majority of equality-seekers within CEF remained rocky.

Significantly, while liberationists cringed, 'We Are Family' tapped a deep-rooted desire on the part of individual gays, lesbians, and bisexuals – still reviled and viewed as deviant – to achieve mainstream respectability and legitimacy, to have same-sex relationships seen as the same as heterosexual ones – as conventional families – and to be valued in the same way. It was a powerful motivator for the masses of gays, lesbians, and bisexuals who were not politically aware and who had no analysis beyond wanting to make their lives better and to have discrimination removed. For liberal heterosexuals, We Are Family and the Campaign for Equal Families were reassuring. Same-sex relationships could be accommodated because they fit into, rather than threatened, the family structure. At the same time, the massive organizing of social conservatives under the family values banner engendered anger in the gay, lesbian, and bisexual communities generally, and strengthened a resolve, even among liberationists, to fight back on whatever terms would succeed in persuading the legislature to change the laws. As Miriam Smith has observed, 'the nuances of CLGRO's position were lost from view in the extensive mobilization behind the slogan "We are Family" ... The option of treating lesbian and gay couples differently from straight couples with respect to some aspects of relationship recognition, a position that had been proposed by the Ontario Law Reform Commission, or of making relationship recognition optional through CLGRO's system of relationship registration, were eclipsed from view in the public debate.'[51] Instead, as one CEF publication articulated, the reassuring message was that gays and lesbians 'continue to find partners, form families and create a refuge of stability and warmth for ourselves. We believe our efforts should be as honoured and respected as those of other people. Recognizing our families takes nothing away from other people's families, but it does add to well being in our society. And it helps end the discrimination we have experienced for too long.'[52] Another CEF leaflet overburdened with the assimilationist, equality-seeking rhetoric that liberation activists find offensive, craven and pleading, asserted: 'the Equality Rights Amendment Act [the NDP's same-sex rights bill] is a significant step forward in the struggle to achieve equality, respect and dignity in Ontario.' The legislation should be supported, it claimed, because 'recognizing same-sex relationships is a humane and decent step.'[53]

Tellingly, however, CEF was both remarkably successful and spec-tacularly ephemeral. Between the middle of May and the end of July 1994, it opened an office, recruited over one hundred volunteers, raised over $93,000, and hired four staff, including the two campaign coordi-nators, Bob Gallagher and Louise Stuart. CEF-type organizations also sprang up in several communities around the province. Press confer-ences, community rallies, and letter-writing campaigns were held. MPPs were lobbied and the public support of trade union leaders, members of the arts and cultural communities, clergy, and others was obtained. But once the NDP bill was defeated, CEF quickly dissipated. Warner and other CLGRO activists then exited CEF.[54] And within a year, despite its profile and success in the spring and summer of 1994, CEF had ceased to exist. CLGRO, on the other hand, trudged on, still promoting liberation analysis of relationships recognition and other issues.

Bill 167

On 19 May 1994, Marion Boyd introduced Bill 167 for first reading. Its provisions would not have granted legal recognition to same-sex mar-riages, but, if adopted, would have amended 'spouse' and 'marital status' in fifty-six provincial laws. CLGRO's *opting out* and domestic partner registration provisions were not included.[55] The fate of the legislation remained uncertain from the outset, especially as a free vote would be permitted, thus increasing the likelihood of its defeat. The NDP caucus still had many dissenters and significant opposition party support did not exist. MPPs from rural and suburban ridings were increasingly outspoken in their opposition. One, an NDP back-bencher, declared he would not support Bill 167 because 'every time you walk down the street people would say "There goes that guy that supports the queer people."' He added, 'the majority of people see it as a sexual-deviation issue.' MPPs from all parties were flooded with phone calls, letters, and petitions from fundamentalist Christians and others who opposed the bill. One Conservative MPP reported receiving calls 'from at least a dozen ministers upset about the whole thing.'[56] Lyn McLeod immediately backtracked from her earlier commitments to support a limited same-sex rights bill, declaring Bill 167 would be 'a redefinition in law of the family,' and 'I don't think we're ready for that as a province.' PC leader Mike Harris flew to Toronto especially to join the members of his caucus in voting against the bill.[57]

Bill 167 barely passed first reading by a vote of 57 to 52 and would not survive for long. Only four Liberals supported it, and one indicated he would vote against it at second reading. Ten NDP members voted against it. In addition, another twenty MPPs were absent, most of whom were opposed but were expected to be present at second reading. In desperation, the NDP retreated, declaring the bill would be amended in hope of securing Liberal support. The proposed definitions of spouse and marital status would be withdrawn and replaced with a new term, *domestic partner*, and the right of same-sex couples to adopt children would be removed.[58] The strategy didn't work. McLeod charged the government could not be trusted to follow through on the amendments. And the gay, lesbian, and bisexual communities felt abandoned and betrayed – by both the government and the Liberals.[59] Not surprisingly, on 9 June 1994, Bill 167 was resoundingly defeated on second reading. Erupting in anger following the vote, nearly two hundred gays and lesbians crowded into the public galleries screamed 'Shame! Shame! Shame!' until they were forced by security guards to leave. They continued their demonstration on the steps inside the legislature's main foyer, fists clenched defiantly in the air, their screams of 'Shame!' and 'Shame on Lyn!' echoing through the building. Ontario Provincial Police officers, wearing white latex gloves – to protect themselves from being infected by AIDS – and carrying truncheons, roughly shoved the demonstrators off the foyer's steps and out the front door. These crude actions caused further outrage and provided graphic images for newspaper and television news coverage. That evening, ten thousand members of the community took to the streets to angrily protest the bill's defeat.[60] While such action allowed the community to vent, the political reality was that, with the death of Bill 167, legislative action to legalize same-sex relationships in Ontario seemed unlikely in the near future.

New strategies would have to be pursued if the issue was to be kept on the public agenda.

Fighting in the Courts

Even before Ontario's political campaign was launched, individuals across the country had begun going to the courts and human rights tribunals in pursuit of legal recognition for their same-sex relationships. Indeed, the fact of such cases was one reason CLGRO embarked on the process that led to Bill 167. Once that legislation was defeated, the advocacy focus shifted almost exclusively to litigation to force government action. Most cases focused on gaining benefits for same-sex partners of employees, but others sought survivor benefits under insurance policies or challenged child custody and adoption laws. Within a decade, a significant volume of jurisprudence, too numerous to recount here, had been produced.[61] Suffice it to say here that, as a result of Charter litigation, discriminatory laws, regulations, and policies were struck down, creating pressure on governments to ensure that laws relating to spousal relationships were brought into line with the rights guaranteed by the Charter.

Of the myriad cases brought forward, the Supreme Court of Canada (over the course of a decade) heard three, resulting eventually in the equality provisions of the Charter being applied to same-sex common law relationships, although not to the legal recognition of same-sex marriages. The first case, *A.G. Canada v. Mossop* (1993) was not argued on Charter grounds; rather, it was based on statutory interpretation of *family status* as defined in the Canadian Human Rights Act, which at the time did not include sexual orientation. The Court in that case ruled that Parliament had not intended same-sex relationships to be included within the statutory definition of family status. The other two cases, *Egan v. Canada* and *M. v. H.*, expanded the equality rights guaranteed by section 15 of the Charter. First, in *Egan v. Canada* (1995), the Supreme Court held that sexual orientation discrimination is prohibited but did not recognize a same-sex relationship for government pension benefits. Later, in *M. v. H.* (1999), the court went further, ruling that same-sex common law relationships must be treated equally under the law with heterosexual common law relationships.

Of course, fighting in the courts does not easily lend itself to promoting lesbian and gay liberation analyses of relationships and the role of the state in regulating them, even if the litigants subscribed to such views, which virtually none of them appeared to do. Seeking positive court decisions in the context of recognizing relationships, in fact, has represented the epitome of equality-seeking assimilationism. Typically, litigating same-sex relationship cases, as MacDougall has noted in *Queer Judgments*,

> sets up its own stereotype of a single standard for all to conform to if the expectation of protection from discrimination is to be realized. In several cases where courts have considered the meaning of family or relationships in the homosexual context, for example, they have looked for virtual identity with the heterosexual model. To be questioned is the assumption that heterosexual stereotypes of family or relationships are the only ones that are worth protecting. It is important to remember that part (though not all) of being a homosexual is *homo*-sexuality. Homosexuality by its very nature is never going to be formally equal to heterosexuality, and vice versa.[62]

Unfortunately, this important distinction generally has been absent from the positions put forward by both individual litigants and the gay and lesbian groups that have supported them as intervenors in key cases. Rather, as MacDougall points out, same-sex couples 'go out of their way to show that their relationship *is* like that of an opposite-sex couple.'[63]

As with the lobbying to obtain amendments of laws dealing with recognition of spousal relationships, court cases, especially the high profile pronouncements of the Supreme Court of Canada, generate massive media coverage. Lawyers for the litigants and spokespersons for equality-seeking groups applaud the decisions as milestones towards achieving tolerance and equality. But in doing so, they trumpet the We Are Family mantra, downplaying or negating altogether the very real differences that exist between heterosexual and homosexual sexuality and relationships. Instead of trying to preserve and protect the aspects of queer sexuality that are different and special, while removing discrimination against same-sex relationships, they promote the 'sameness' of same-sex and opposite-sex relationships. Not only has this created the misimpression of homogeneous views in gay, lesbian, and bisexuals communities, but liberationist options have been effectively foreclosed. In turn, momentum is created for amending laws to bring them into line with the pronouncements of the courts, so that same-sex relationships are treated, in all respects, in the same way as opposite-sex relationships.

Legislative Recognition of Same-Sex Relationships

The success of Charter litigation and of equality-seeking advocacy has in recent years led to the amendment of laws regulating spousal relationships in most parts of Canada. British Columbia's NDP government was the first to amend laws to extend legal recognition to same-sex relationships, proceeding incrementally rather than by way of omnibus legislation. It began in 1995, with the amendment of Adoption Act regulations to permit single persons, including homosexuals, and same-sex couples to adopt. Despite proceeding administratively to avoid a rancorous public debate, opposition was voiced by members of the BC legislature, mainly Liberals. Petitions protesting the amendment and bearing a few thousand names were presented in the legislature.[64] Following this initial foray, the government of Glen Clark introduced two bills in 1997 changing the definition of spouse in the Family Relations Act and the Family Maintenance Enforcement Act such that same-sex couples became subject to child support, custody, and maintenance requirements. Almost immediately, religious groups mounted a campaign to defeat the bills. The Roman Catholic Archbishop of Vancouver, calling on Catholics to send letters and faxes and to make phone calls in protest, denounced homosexual relationships as 'gravely immoral' and the bills as attacking the sacredness of marriage and weakening the fabric of society. Joining the archbishop were heads of the Conference of Mennonites, the Akali Singh Sikh Society, the Orthodox Rabbinical Council, and the Council of Muslims of Canada. Fortunately, these efforts did not succeed in generating large scale public opposition. On 22 July 1997, the Family Relations Act amendments were adopted by a vote of 59 to 9.[65] Continuing its gradual approach, in 1998 the NDP amended provincial legislation to provide explicitly for pension benefits for surviving same-sex spouses of public sector employees.[66] And, on 14 July 1999, Bill 100, Definition of Spouse Amendment Act, 1999, was adopted. It amended the definition of spouse in a number of acts, including those governing funerals and cemeteries, estates of deceased persons, and wills.

Of course, the BC government did not act without pressure from the gay, lesbian, and bisexual communities, principally exerted through the December 9th Coalition, composed of members of a number of community-based advocacy groups. It formed in 1992 in response to the manoeuvring of federal justice minister Kim Campbell to exclude same-sex relationship recognition from Canadian Human Rights Act amendments. Miriam Smith notes in *Lesbian and Gay Rights in Canada* that, like other groups, the December 9th Coalition 'has reflected the tensions of rights talk, the tensions between equality as similar treatment, and the diversity of views on relationship recognition in the lesbian and gay communities.'[67] It has supported the right of gays and lesbians to marry but has also adopted a more inclusive concept of family, based on emotional interdependency. The coalition also participated actively in consultations with the provincial government in 1992 concerning amendments to the Human Rights Act, holding a provincial conference that recommended specific changes, at which agreement was reached on calling for the legal recognition of same-sex relationships.

Newfoundland, as part of the amendments to its Human Rights Code in 1997, extended the application to pension plan provisions that comply with registration requirements under the federal Income Tax Act. But other, more far-reaching laws remained unchanged.[68] The first omnibus amendment of provincial laws occurred in Quebec in 1999 following years of lobbying by gay and lesbian groups, pressure from the Quebec Human Rights Commission, and initial foot-dragging by the provincial government. The campaign began in 1991, when the Coalition des organismes de Montréal métropolitain called on the governing Liberals, as part of a review of the Quebec civil code, to legally recognize same-sex relationships for both common law and marriage purposes.[69] A further boost occurred in 1994, when the Human Rights Commission recommended that Quebec follow the lead of Ontario, which was then debating Bill 167. Disappointingly, however, it also timidly stated that same-sex couples should not be allowed to adopt children. The justice minister immediately ruled out any action, noting, 'It is a project that is encountering certain difficulties in Ontario for all kinds of reasons. There is no intention here in Quebec to move in the same direction.'[70] It was not until 1996, following the election of a new Parti Québécois government, that political action of any kind was taken: Bill 133, recognizing same-sex spousal benefits in the private sector, was adopted. About the same time, the government announced public hearings on extending full legal recognition to same-sex common law relationships, but hearings were postponed until the fall of 1998, following the re-election of the PQ.[71] In the meantime, to intensify the pressure on the government, the Coalition pour la reconnaisance des conjoints et conjointes de même sexe was formed, consisting of ten gay and lesbian groups and supportive organizations from outside the gay and lesbian communities. The fact that the Charte des droits et libertés de la personne du Québec proscribed all forms of discrimination on the basis of sexual orientation was argued to support demands for legislative action.[72] Finally, in early 1999, the PQ introduced omnibus legislation amending twenty-eight provincial laws and eleven regulations establishing the same legal recognition for all common law relationships, whether opposite- or same-sex. With the support of the opposition Liberals, the amendments were adopted on June 10.[73]

Unlike other parts of Canada, Quebec did not endure a campaign by churches and social conservatives denouncing the legislation. Réal Ménard, an openly gay MP in the Bloc Québécois, noted in a 1996 essay that the church and clergy 'while not unimportant, are far from having the kind of influence that churches still do in some rural English-Canadian communities.' He also noted that, atypically, 'Quebec has no polarization between left and right ... The result is there is no organized "conservative" movement. Without it, no anti-homosexual public discourse has been able to emerge. The church in Quebec has not raised any noisy objections to recognition for same-sex couples.'[74] This state of affairs contrasted sharply with the situation in Ontario, where the election of the Progressive Conservatives under Mike Harris in 1995, with strong support from both neoconservatives and social conservatives, created an inauspicious political environment for pursuing the issue. There, CLGRO and other gay and lesbian groups abandoned as futile efforts to obtain legal recognition of same-sex relationships by legislative amendment.

Instead, Ontario activists launched a number of legal challenges in the hope that courts applying the Charter would force an otherwise unsympathetic government to act. That opportunity eventually arose during the 1999 provincial election, when the Supreme Court of Canada released its decision in the *M v. H* case, finding that the definition of spouse in Ontario's Family Law Act (FLA) contravened the Charter. It gave the government six months to bring the law in line with the Charter. If the government did not do so, the offending section would become invalid. In response, Premier Harris indicated his government would comply, but gave no details as to just what that would mean legislatively. The government had several options, including, do nothing, invoke the notwithstanding clause of the Constitution, amend only the FLA, or amend only some laws, while leaving others unchanged. Over the ensuing months, CLGRO pushed for amendment of all provincial laws, not just the FLA. They met with the attorney general and mounted a postcard campaign urging Harris to honour his commitment by amending the definition of spouse in all laws. Instead, the government introduced Bill 5, creating a new category, *same sex partner*, through which same-sex spouses were granted all the legal rights and responsibilities as for common law heterosexual couples, by amending sixty-seven provincial laws. The government also made it clear that it wanted to preserve 'the traditional family' and that the laws were being amended only because the Supreme Court was forcing them to do so. In fact, Bill 5 was ridiculously called An Act to Amend Certain Statutes as a Result of the Supreme Court Decision in M v. H.[75]

CLGRO, while condemning the government's rhetoric and reasoning as offensive, called nonetheless for quick adoption of the legislation, to avoid a repeat of the Bill 167 debacle. There was no desire to give the religious fundamentalist and social conservative forces time to mobilize, the result of which might well have been the weakening of the government's resolve. Significant opposition existed within the Tory caucus and a small number of Liberals were thought to be opposed. Given that Bill 5 went much further than what might have been expected from a political party historically and strongly opposed to rights for lesbians, gays, and bisexuals, a party which openly appealed to a family values constituency, CLGRO decided to claim victory.[76] They obtained agreement from the Liberals and the NDP to vote in favour and to not insist on public hearings. 'It achieves a level of equality with common-law relationships for opposite-sex couples and that is what we are focusing on,' commented CLGRO's Tom Warner.[77] Consequently, Bill 5 was adopted in a remarkable one-day sitting on October 27, and given Royal Assent the next day. The changes to the FLA took effect on November 20, the date marking the end of the six-month deadline set by the Supreme Court, and the changes to the other laws took effect on 1 March 2000.

Bill 5's adoption was clearly a victory for gays, lesbians, and bisexuals, but there was little celebration. That was partly due to the way in which the government had framed the legislation to appease their core constituency. But there was also dissatisfaction on the part of activists committed to an exclusively equality rights perspective. Liberationists generally focused on the result achieved by the legislation, and cared little about the terminology deployed – same-sex partner as opposed to spouse. As Brenda Cossman observed in *Xtra!*, 'given the history of controversy in the gay and lesbian community about whether we should be going after spousal rights – "partner" isn't a bad compromise.'[78] But equality rights advocates, particularly those in EGALE, condemned the legislation for establishing a 'separate and unequal' regime. Bill 5, they argued, created a 'discriminatory distinction' that treats 'same-sex relationships as inferior to opposite-sex relationships' and which 'sends a clear message that same-sex relationships are qualitatively different than opposite-sex relationships.' EGALE supported an action by the lawyers for M, in *M v. H*, for a ruling by the Supreme Court as to whether Bill 5 conformed with the Court's decision by adding 'same sex partner' to the FLA rather than amending 'spouse.' EGALE President Laurie Arron noted, 'let's ensure that the legislation provides what the Supreme Court judgment requires: simply equality – nothing more, nothing less.'[79] Similarly, M's lawyer, in a letter published in *Xtra!*, lambasted Bill 5 for creating a 'segregated approach that invites discriminatory thinking.' Claiming the government had not complied with the decision in *M v. H*, she declared, 'Equality is not just a question of dollars and cents. It is a matter of dignity.'[80] Liberationists, on the other hand, bristled at the thought that the movement had been reduced to the level of obtaining 'dignity' for gays and lesbians through court decisions. Liberationists never thought gays and lesbians lacked dignity. For them, undertaking campaigns to win dignity merely gives credence to the claim by heterosexual elites that they are the only ones who can rightfully determine what is and is not respectable, moral, or dignified. Liberationists see asking the state to confer dignity as casting queers in the role of supplicants seeking benediction and redemption, grateful for finally being lifted from the foulest depths of degradation and despair.

Following *M v. H* the efforts to achieve legal recognition shifted to other provinces. In Alberta, the government moved to foreclose recognition of same-sex relationships in 1999 by specifically restricting the definition of *common law relationship* to heterosexual couples. 'If we need to take it to the Supreme Court ... then I guess we have to do that,' vowed Fred Dickerson of Edmonton's Gay and Lesbian Community Center in reaction to the new law.[81] Going even further, the legislature adopted the Constitutional Referendum Amendment Act, 1999, which requires a referendum before any legislation is introduced, pursuant to the notwithstanding clause of the Charter, which declares a law or provision of a law operates notwithstanding the rights guaranteed by the Charter. Lesbian and gay activists denounced the new referendum law. 'It's quite clearly directed at the pariah minority of the day which happens to be us,' commented Julie Lloyd of Equal Alberta.[82] Given the strength of social conservative and religious right forces in Alberta, any submission to a referendum of legislative amendments dealing with same-sex rights is likely to create a vicious climate of hatred, homophobia, and hysteria. For those seeking legalized same-sex marriages, the new law was even more draconian. It specifically exempted from the referendum requirement 'any Bill or provision of a Bill within the jurisdiction of the Legislature that relates to who may marry.' Not only would no public vote on the subject of marriage be tolerated, the Alberta government remains free to invoke the notwithstanding clause to override a court decision recognizing same-sex marriages.[83]

Despite the resistance of the Alberta government, three other provinces responded, in 2001, to the *M v. H* decision by introducing legislation granting legal recognition of same-sex relationships in varying degrees. On 1 June 2001, the Nova Scotia legislature adopted amendments to provincial laws recognizing same-sex relationships in the same way as common law heterosexual ones. The legislation also provided for the registration of such relationships with the provincial Office of Vital Statistics as *domestic partnerships*, making Nova Scotia the first jurisdiction in Canada to introduce such a legal system. Unfortunately, the legislation was seriously deficient in that it excluded amendments that would have granted same-sex couples the right to adopt children.[84] Adoption rights also proved to be an obstacle in Manitoba. On 27 June 2001, the timid NDP government secured passage of a bill that amended only ten laws and excluded adoption rights. Bill 41 provided legal recognition to same-sex relationships for the purpose of medical benefits, pensions, and spousal support, but left untouched more than seventy other laws dealing with spousal relationships. Angry lesbian and gay activists protested outside the Manitoba legislature on June 17, demanding that same-sex couples be given the right to adopt. 'We need a government of leaders, not followers,' declared one of the protesters, lesbian activist Noreen Stevens, who was in the midst of attempting to adopt a child with her same-sex partner.[85] Adding to the pressure on the government, a petition circulated during Pride Week, signed by two thousand people and the vast majority of presenters before a legislative committee considering Bill 41, called for extending the legislation to include adoption rights. These efforts did have some impact: the government appointed a committee to prepare a report on the issue and committed to introduced additional legislation at a later date based on the committee's findings. The outcome in Saskatchewan was significantly different. There, the NDP-Liberal coalition government introduced a bill that amended twenty-four laws to recognize same-sex couples under provisions dealing with common law relationships, including the right of a partner in a same-sex relationship to adopt their partner's children. The bill was quickly enacted and, surprisingly for lesbian and gay activists, was supported by five members of the right wing Saskatchewan Party.[86]

Efforts were also underway, beginning in the late 1980s, to amend federal laws and regulations dealing with civil service employee plans, taxation, and public pensions, as well the benefits plans of companies, banks, and crown corporations operating under federal laws. EGALE, from its founding in 1985, established itself as the primary organization leading the drive for amendment of the federal laws.[87] In doing so, it made no pretense of subscribing to lesbian and gay liberation principles. Its focus was unabashedly on 'fighting for equality' and 'fighting for justice in the courts.' Dominated by lawyers, civil servants, and other professionals, it distinguished itself from the former Canadian Lesbian and Gay Rights Coalition by avoiding any involvement in what Brenda Cossman, writing in *Xtra!*, has described as 'Less respectable issues, like censorship, sexuality, and age of consent.' (Recently, EGALE did become an intervenor in support of Little Sister's book store in its challenge of customs censorship). As she observed, 'EGALE has been successful, precisely because it is mainstream; precisely because it presents a relatively unthreatening face. It is a decent, fit and proper face of the gay and lesbian community. It is the face of respectability.'[88]

In respect of relationship recognition, EGALE's efforts picked up steam following the 1993 federal election, when Liberal Justice Minister Allan Rock spoke positively about introducing the CHRA amendment and, as the logical next step, granting same-sex benefits. Rock began to backtrack in the spring of 1994, however, after condemning as 'unduly provocative' the Ontario NDP's Bill 167, then being hotly debated.[89] Divisions in the federal Liberal caucus, and among the members of Parliament generally, impeded progress. Some MPs urged Rock to define family based on emotional and financial dependency, the rule used in Australia. Others vociferously objected to both the amendment of the CHRA and the legal recognition of same-sex relationships.[90] Significantly, in September 1995 MPs of all parties voted decisively to defeat a private member's motion introduced by openly gay Bloc Québécois MP Réal Ménard that would have granted legal recognition to same-sex couples. Two subsequent private member's bills introduced by Ménard suffered the same fate.[91]

The position of the federal government over time was to acquiesce case-by-case to decisions by courts and tribunals, rather than to introduce comprehensive legislation. This minimalist stance led, in May 1999, to the amendment of a statute that establishes the federal civil service pension plan, following a judgment by the Ontario Court of Appeal. The court held that, under the Charter, the federal government discriminated against the same-sex partners of employees by refusing them survivor pension benefits. Indicative of the resistance existing within the government caucus, six Liberal MPs voted against the bill, and the government, having only a slim majority, had to rely on opposition support to secure its passage. Similarly, Liberal MPs joined with the Reform Party in June 1999 to support a resolution upholding the definition of marriage as being exclusively between a man and a woman.[92]

Momentum for a comprehensive legislative amendment picked up in the early months of 1999 when activists in the Foundation for Equal Families, which had emerged out of the Bill 167 campaign, grew tired of Liberal stalling and launched an innovative Charter challenge. Their objective was to have the courts force the government, through a positive decision in a single legal suit, to amend fifty-eight federal laws. 'We frankly would have wanted a legislated solution where the (federal) government simply said, "We will do what's right." They just haven't done it,' stated the foundation's Michelle Douglas at a press conference.[93] As part of the campaign, EGALE and the Foundation for Equal Families, joined by CLGRO and other groups, vigorously sought support within the mainstream Canadian family, through the distribution of thousands of postcards directed to the prime minister that, in the words of foundation spokesperson Bob Gallagher, featured a photograph of 'a nice little dyke family.'[94] At about the same time, some movement towards comprehensive legislative change was seen within the Liberal caucus. Encouraged by both the Supreme Court decision in *M v. H* and the adoption of legislation in Quebec, government MPs began to publicly promote the introduction of a federal omnibus bill.[95] Shortly thereafter, federal justice minister Anne McClellan disclosed she was preparing omnibus legislation; an estimated thirty lawsuits respecting federal legislation and a growing body of jurisprudence, including by the Supreme Court of Canada, meant that the time had come to act.[96] The government finally did so in February 2000 by introducing Bill C-23, the Modernization of Benefits and Obligations Act, which amended the definition of *common law partner* to establish for same-sex relationships all of the same rights and responsibilities as existed in law for common law opposite-sex relationships. Adopting a classic assimilationist stance, Kim Vance, EGALE's president, welcomed the legislation, stating, 'The time has come for us to assume our place in Canadian society fully recognized as the equals that we are.'[97]

Immediately, opposition in Parliament and among social conservatives geared up to attack Bill C-23. Seeking to cast their homophobia in a more progressive light, Reform Party MPs and some Liberal backbenchers criticized the legislation for not recognizing nonspousal, economically dependant relationships, such as siblings who live together, or cohabitants who do not have a sexual relationship. Several Liberal MPs with social conservative views threatened to vote against the bill.[98] To placate expressions of concern within and outside Parliament that Bill C-23 would lead to legalizing same-sex marriages (it would not have done so), Justice Minister McLellan later introduced an amendment that added a definition of marriage that included only opposite-sex couples. In the end, Bill C-23 was adopted on 11 April 2000 by a vote of 174 to 72, with 17 Liberal MPs joining the Reform Party to vote against it.[99]

Not included in Bill C-23 were overdue amendments to the Immigration Act to recognize same-sex relationships. Advocacy on that front had been intensified in the 1990s, and the first legal challenge occurred in 1992 when Bridget Coll, a lesbian from Ireland, applied to be recognized as the *life companion* of her same-sex partner, Christine Morrisey, who agreed to sponsor her. When the application was denied, Coll and Morrisey went to court seeking establishment of same-sex partners as a new category within the *family class* of immigrants. The case did not go forward after immigration officials approved Coll's application under the separate *independent class*.[100] The Lesbian and Gay Immigration Task Force (LEGIT), founded in 1991 in Vancouver, embarked on concerted lobbying to change immigration policy, submitting a 1992 brief to the immigration minister documenting seven cases of same-sex relationships that were not being recognized. Pointing out that four countries recognized sponsorship rights for members of such relationships, LEGIT called upon Canada to follow suit.[101] When LEGIT was rebuffed by immigration officials, they secured a meeting with then Minister of Justice Kim Campbell. She advised Canadian visa officers that recognition of same-sex relationships was a humanitarian issue falling within the family reunification policies. But policy is not legislation, so LEGIT, EGALE and CLGRO, among others, continued to lobby for Immigration Act amendments. They achieved some success in 1999, when the government, responding to a recommendation of a task force reviewing the act, announced that same-sex relationships would be specifically recognized as part of a wholesale updating of the act.[102] However, the bill died when a federal election was called in the year 2000. Although reintroduced by the re-elected Liberal government, it had not been adopted at the time of the time of writing this chapter.

Although there have been significant victories in the pursuit of statutory recognition of same-sex couples, the debate over the desirability of such campaigns continues unabated. The wholesome, reassuring appeal to the mainstream, according to Foundation For Equal Families activist Bob Gallagher, is deliberate, strategic, and 'subversive.' 'Bringing queer families into the tradition of the family is far more disruptive than staying outside in our own little bubble, doing your own little thing, which doesn't really affect anybody else.'[103] Others, however, strenuously disagree. In the aftermath of Bill C-23, activist Steven Maynard, writing in Ottawa's *Capital Xtra!*, lamented that, while obtaining same-sex benefits was important, 'by pursuing benefits for same-sex couples only, our movement misses the unique opportunity to demonstrate the power of nominally queer issues to speak out and embrace many people whose relationships and living arrangements do not conform to dominant models or even slightly modernized ones.' In the rush to embrace spousal benefits and the right to marry, Maynard noted that there has been 'far too little discussion ... about how this will actually limit the freedom of many queer people by propping up punitive distinctions between those who will be deemed legally and socially acceptable and those who will not ... Once upon a time, the lesbian/gay liberation movement struggled for things like same-sex benefits, but did so with a vision premised on setting free not only gays and lesbians, but all those who lived in queer and unconventional ways.'[104]

Without doubt, the achievement of legally recognized same-sex relationships federally and in some provinces, and the advocacy that has helped secure such an achievement, has widened the ideological gap between liberationists and assimilationists. Looking solely at this issue or at that of human rights code amendments examined in chapter 9, it would be easy to conclude that liberation politics are dead. Media attention and the resources of gay and lesbian groups have been principally devoted to equality issues, with, by comparison, only occasional mention of or attention given to sexuality issues. On the other hand, looking at the divide from a broader perspective, it is by no means clear that accommodation of same-sex relationships within the legal framework of heterosexual orthodoxy will, in the long run, fundamentally change queer sexuality or the diversity of queer relationships. Fears that it will seem unfounded, although the outcome of same-sex relationship advocacy, at least in the short term, has been the marginalization of the unconventional relationships about which Maynard wrote. Equally important, as we shall see in the next four chapters, the amendment of a few laws has not eradicated homophobia and heterosexism. The efforts of rights advocacy have not significantly diminished the zeal of the police, state regulators, and social conservatives in their campaigns to curtail or repress expressions of same-sex sexuality. Coming out, feeling safe, and being visible are as difficult for many gays, lesbians, and bisexuals today as they were more than three decades ago, and continue to require the deployment of the now 'old' liberationist strategies used so effectively since the early 1970s.

ELEVEN

AIDS Radicalization, Queer Nation, and Identity Politics

The late 1980s and early 1990s saw a reradicalization of lesbian and gay advocacy within the contexts of ever more militant responses to AIDS and the emergence of more diverse and more decidedly post-Stonewall groups of activists. Massive AIDS organizing, proceeding in parallel with the efforts to amend human rights laws and to establish legal recognition for same-sex relationships, created a vast network spread across Canada of organizations providing services for people with AIDS, conducting preventive education, and advocating for funding and government action. As AIDS and HIV cases increased dramatically, thousands of closets emptied, and new forms of homophobia had to be combatted. Over a relatively short period of time, HIV/AIDS forced whole sectors of society to take notice and to respond in ways that gay and lesbian liberation, as an abstract, never would have been able to do. At the same time, both the ethos and organizing strategies of lesbian and gay liberation helped radicalize the advocacy that became associated with AIDS as well as the education campaigns and the support and treatment systems that such advocacy fostered. Arising out of this tempest, a new generation of queer activists also burst onto the scene. Influenced by AIDS radicalism and vigorously assailing the assimilationist thrust of equality rights activism, a new generation, calling themselves 'queer,' attempted to forge a new agenda for social change. The queer activists bore striking similarities to the lesbian and gay liberation militants of two decades earlier – even though they sought to distance themselves from both the liberationist and the assimilationist camps. In particular, queer activists rejected what they saw as the 'identity politics' of the 'old' movement, in which the identities of gay, lesbian, or bisexual were so important. They advocated more fluid concepts of sexuality and identity that rejected both the necessity of labelling and the attempts to achieve a new, respectable identity that too frequently sought to impose stifling conformity.

Liberationist Influences on AIDS Organizing

Data published regularly on AIDS cases helped to drive home the message that urgent community and government responses were needed. Ottawa's Laboratory Centre for Disease Control reported the number of Canadian cases as of 1 December 1986 at 788. Chillingly, 663 of the total were gays or bisexuals, of whom only 331 were still alive. All provinces except Prince Edward Island had reported cases by that time, although none were reported in the Yukon or the Northwest Territories.[1] AIDS support groups also emerged in virtually all parts of the country, to fulfil the needs of acknowledging the existence of AIDS, of providing treatment and support for people living with AIDS, and of conducting public education about it. It was no longer a health crisis confined to the United States or the big cities of Canada.

The new AIDS groups cropping up across the country often had their beginnings within existing gay and lesbian community organizations. Lesbian, gay, and bisexual activists in those groups, schooled in the liberation politics of the 1970s, once more assumed positions of leadership and visibility, bringing to a new, more urgent battle, the skills and perspectives honed previously in community-building pursuits. A 1986 listing of community groups in *The Body Politic* gives testimony to the extent to which these established activists helped launch the new AIDS movement. The contact for the AIDS Information Committee in St John's, Newfoundland, was listed as gay activist Wally Upward. Halifax's Metro Area Committee on AIDS showed the GAE Gayline as the contact. The AIDS Committee of London could be reached by calling gay activist Richard Hudler. Elsewhere, AIDS Regina, founded in 1985, initially operated out of the Gay Community Centre. A meeting of community activists led to the formation of AIDS Calgary in 1984–5 and one of the first key organizers for the new group was gay activist Stephen Lock. Members of Edmonton's Gay Alliance Toward Equality had, by 1985, also formed an AIDS committee within their group that eventually led to the formation of the Edmonton AIDS Network. Similarly, the Hamilton AIDS Network for Dialogue and Support was started in 1986 by members of Hamilton United Gay Societies. And during

1987 and 1988, AIDS New Brunswick was launched at the instigation of gay activists in Fredericton, and SIDA Moncton grew out of an initiative of Gay Liberation of Moncton.[2] The result was that, by the early 1990s, AIDS support groups had spread to nearly every urban community in Canada. Larger Canadian cities had established a number of different AIDS organizations. Among them were hospices and groups providing free meals and low income or rent-geared-to-income housing.

During the first few years of the crisis, small bands of activists conducted education and advocacy in the midst of tremendous ignorance, resistance, fear, and denial. Those involved with gay and lesbian organizing were plugged into developments in the U.S. and were among the first to understand the need to put community support structures in place. Because these people were out and visible, the media and other members of the community turned to them for information and assistance. And, as they had done in pursuit of lesbian and gay liberation in the early 1970s, they often dragged their communities along with them. In Montreal, for example, the early AIDS activists contended with a perception among francophones that AIDS was not their issue. Observed an article in *The Body Politic* in 1985, 'Francophone gays are said to believe AIDS is a risk mainly to English-speaking men who travel frequently to New York and San Francisco.'[3]

The low level of public awareness and a lack of acknowledgment of AIDS as an issue to be addressed, especially in communities outside North America's largest cities, were obstacles to organizing and conducting education in the early years of the crisis. According to Regina activist John Edgar, in 1985 death from AIDS was 'very rarely acknowledged' and was 'still very much a closeted issue.'[4] The Kingston AIDS Project, started in 1986, had to combat a sense that there was no need to deal with AIDS in a small city. Gay men living there felt 'it isn't going to happen to me.' By 1990, however, some well-known members of the gay community became seriously sick, which led to a change in perceptions.[5] Maurice Michaud, active in Gay Liberation of Moncton, remembers, 'It took awhile for the message to come through.' The notion was that AIDS was a big city issue.[6] Claude Olivier of AIDS New Brunswick similarly recalls that, as late as 1990, not much discussion of AIDS took place in Fredericton because it was 'still a little bit of a taboo subject among gays here ... It was kind of hush-hush.'[7] The founders of AIDS Calgary, Stephen Lock recalls, had not actually met a person with AIDS at the time the group formed. Although the group knew that people with AIDS existed in the city, they 'were not saying anything.' In fact, only a handful of people anticipated the arrival of AIDS in Calgary at the time. Within three or four months of the founding of AIDS Calgary, however, the first HIV-positive person came forward.[8] Similarly, not much happened organizationally in Edmonton until the first AIDS case was diagnosed there in July 1984.[9]

Ignorance and resistance also had to be overcome in Windsor, according to gay activist Jim Monk, although that city had some of the earliest reported cases. Because of Windsor's proximity to Detroit and the impact of U.S. media coverage, Monk, a long-time gay activist involved locally and with CGRO, was forced to deal with media inquiries on the issue as early as 1982. Nonetheless, in the community, 'People found ways to diminish that two people are dead. And we thought the way the media was reacting was homophobic and was trying to undo all of the advances that we had made for gay rights recognition and was going to scare away people from coming out, and all kinds of things. It was quite a nightmare.' Still, as more awareness was gained, Windsor's Lesbian and Gay Community Services Group set up a condoms committee that ultimately led to the formation of the AIDS Committee of Windsor. Gradually, local public health officials and the United Way expressed interest, and people started volunteering for AIDS awareness work. These developments put even more responsibility on the city's activists. 'The people who volunteered were looking to the gay leadership for what to do,' Monk notes. For the first five years or so, 'the dominant voices were the people in the Lesbian and Gay Community Services Group.'[10]

Educational materials on AIDS, particularly materials aimed at gay men, did much over the years to spread the word about the necessity of practising safe sex. The concept of safe sex contrasted sharply with the alternative views put forward by religious organizations and conservative forces – that AIDS education should focus on abstinence and monogamy; that talking about, and thereby 'condoning,' certain sexual practices should be avoided. Safe sex was rooted in the lesbian and gay liberation view of sex as healthy and natural and was promoted by the gay, lesbian and bisexual activists who became so many of the early AIDS advocacy pioneers. Integrally linked with the safe sex message was the rejection of guilt, self-loathing, and shame associated, in the homophobic and heterosexist mainstream, with homosexual acts. It was, in fact, largely gay activists such as Ed Jackson, a former member of the editorial collective of *The Body Politic*, who developed explicit educational materials for AIDS organizations that discussed how to use condoms, to engage in safe or risk-reduced oral and anal sex, and sadomasochism. Jackson, while education coordinator with the AIDS Committee of Toronto, gained considerable notoriety in the media for championing education materials that eroticized safe sex practices and made them seem fun, and that used street vernacular, rather than clinical terminology, to describe genitalia and various sexual acts.[11]

The initial influence of gay liberation activists began to wane and to be challenged toward the end of the 1980s, as government funding for AIDS groups became more common. The groups, increasingly well financed by grants, asserted independence from the lesbian and gay community organizations that launched them. Health and social service professionals became more involved, and began to rival community activists for leadership and influence. AIDS organizations consequently grew ever more disconnected from the needs of gay men with AIDS, whom they saw as clients, and from the advocacy agendas of lesbian and gay organizations. Priorities shifted to conducting research and education, developing prevention strategies, and raising funds to provide services. Rejection of radical advocacy and a don't-rock-the-boat outlook took root.[12]

Grass-Roots Advocacy and a New Militancy

Dissatisfaction with the established AIDS groups, and their increasingly mainstream aspirations, soon emerged as an important element in the evolution of grass-roots advocacy. Politicized people living with AIDS started, in the mid-1980s, to organize in separate groups focused on their most urgent needs. They empowered themselves, refused to be marginalized and victimized, and decided to take control of their lives and the AIDS advocacy agenda. The Denver Principles provided the philosophical framework for organizing. New entities, coalitions of people living with AIDS (PWAs), catapulted themselves into community organizing and public consciousness. The first of these new groups, the PWA Coalition, appeared in Vancouver in early 1986 after a group broke away from AIDS Vancouver. Its activism focused on forcing Health and Welfare Canada to approve a new drug, AZT, for use in Canada. Spokesperson Kevin Brown was instrumental in drawing public attention to the need for access to the drug. In 1987, the group received its first federal government funding. By 1990, it had firmly established itself in the community.[13]

A similar group, the Toronto PWA Coalition, was founded in early

1987. Later renamed the PWA Foundation, its organizing imperative was securing financial assistance to permit PWAs to live without being in abject poverty and function as best they could in the everyday world.[14] Montreal's Comité des personnes atteintes du VIH du Québec also started in late 1987, growing out of dissatisfaction with C-SAM (Comité SIDA Aide de Montréal), which was seen as too focused on education and health issues. There was also a fundamental philosophical disagreement between the founders of the new group and C-SAM over whether PWAs 'were simply the recipients of services or full-fledged members with rights.'[15] A similar disagreement led to the 1986 creation of the Nova Scotia Persons with AIDS Coalition after PWAs became alienated from the (Halifax-based) Metro Area Committee on AIDS. According to AIDS activist Wilson Hodder, the split arose because the AIDS committee had made education its primary focus when gay men in the group wanted it to take up direct treatment issues.[16] By the early 1990s, two other PWA groups had also formed: the Persons Living with AIDS Network of Saskatchewan, in Saskatoon, and People Living with HIV/AIDS Network of New Brunswick.

The second major change in AIDS organizing was the emergence of militant, treatment-based activism in the late 1980s that, in the way in which it articulated its demands and the strategies it pursued to achieve them, drew upon the radical liberation activist tradition of a decade earlier. According to Gary Kinsman, a gay liberationist involved in this radicalization of AIDS activism, the new movement was a response to the depoliticized nature of most AIDS groups. Working-class people in particular felt alienated from the professionals in service or medical fields who now dominated such groups.[17] This new AIDS activism was initially launched by ACT UP – AIDS Coalition to Unleash Power, of New York City. It soon spread to other North American locations, with groups using the same or similar names appearing in such places as Vancouver, Ottawa, Montreal, Toronto, and Halifax. They transformed AIDS advocacy and impacted the broader gay, lesbian, and bisexual community, helping to launch the queer nationalist movement, which is presented later in this chapter. ACT UP Montreal was formed in 1988 and lasted until about 1990.[18] ACT UP Vancouver started in 1990 in response to the lack of political action on the part of AIDS Vancouver and the PWA Coalition. During its brief existence, it organized demonstrations and other actions to protest the lack of leadership on AIDS by the right wing and homophobic Social Credit government of British Columbia.[19]

In 1987, a group of veteran gay activists and other politicized people with AIDS began discussing the formation of a new advocacy group in Toronto. It included gay men who had had extensive experience with grass-roots gay political action during the heyday of liberation politics in the 1970s. Taking the name of AIDS Action Now! (AAN), it was formalized by early 1988 into a highly effective, very visible advocacy group.[20] Since then, it has had a measure of success and longevity not enjoyed by other groups in the ACT UP mold. AAN gained strong support from the community because of its willingness to take up political issues, particularly access to new drug treatments, that others had shunned. Evert A. Lindquist and David M. Rayside noted in their 1990 study, 'AIDS policy in Canada: Community activism, federalism, and the new politics of disease,' that AAN drew upon the activist traditions of the 1970s and early 1980s to launch a new AIDS action agenda: 'Drawing upon an enormous reservoir of activist energy and anger about political inaction, AAN! added a militant political wing to the community group constellation. The group ... raised the profile of a number of treatment issues, believing that the medical and public health establishments were concerned only with the not-yet-infected. They raised concerns about the difficulty or impossibility of obtaining new promising treatments for AIDS, the narrow and exploitive methodologies used in drug experimentation, and the inadequacy of patient care in Toronto hospitals.'[21]

AAN, supported by Montreal's Action SIDA, led a protest at the 1988 National Conference on AIDS that culminated in the burning in effigy of the federal health minister, Jake Epp. During his time as minister, Epp ignored calls for a national strategy on AIDS, including substantial federal funding to fight the growing crisis. In fact, community activists could not recall ever having heard Epp, a staunch family values advocate, utter the word 'AIDS.' Calls for his resignation had become a regular feature of AIDS advocacy. The effigy burning at such a high-profile event succeeded in embarrassing the Progressive Conservative government of Brian Mulroney. Epp announced shortly afterwards that federal funding would be increased to $129 million over five years. It marked the first step in the eventual establishment of a National AIDS Strategy that, in 1998, was made permanent by the Liberal government of Jean Chrétien – but only after sustained and vigorous pressure campaigns by AAN and other groups.

AAN was also instrumental in forcing Bob Rae's NDP government in Ontario to establish a government-funded drug plan providing costly drugs to people with AIDS and other catastrophic illnesses. Through demonstrations, press conferences, and lobbying over four years, AAN scored a huge victory when the Trillium Drug Plan was announced after a long period of delay and stalling.[22] A pivotal event occurred at the NDP's provincial conference in November 1994 when AAN held an angry demonstration. Afterwards, two AAN activists, Greg Pavelich and Brent Southin, had an unscheduled meeting with Rae to advise him that unless the government announced the drug plan before World AIDS Day on December 1, he would be burned in effigy at a demonstration.[23] On November 30, Rae announced the government's new comprehensive drug plan. AAN spokesperson Glen Brown, in declaring victory, commented, 'This is the culmination of the pressure we've put on the government on this issue. The announcement came as the direct result of our pressure.'[24]

At the end of the 1990s, AIDS advocacy again entered a period of change. Many of the once small, volunteer-based organizations had become large bureaucracies, with big budgets, sizable staff, income derived from government grants, lucrative fund-raising campaigns and, increasingly, corporate sponsorships. The AIDS Committee of Toronto, for example, had a 1998 budget of $2.3 million. Private donations accounted for revenues of $1.3 million, government grants represented nearly $800,000, and the remainder came from other sources.[25] The demographics of AIDS, and medical advancements, also changed, and changed the form and nature of community advocacy. The number of total cases started to decrease in the mid-1990s. New treatments, especially 'drug cocktails,' were permitting people with HIV and AIDS to live longer and more productively. But the number of new HIV infections reported annually was increasing, especially among intravenous drug users, heterosexual women, young gay men, and Aboriginal people. Also alarming was the fact that the median age of those infected with HIV had declined from thirty-two years in 1982 to twenty-three years in 1996.[26] Philip Berger, a Toronto doctor long in the forefront of the fight against AIDS, outlined in a 1998 article the new challenges then confronting AIDS activists. The battle against AIDS in Canada 'now means confronting addiction and poverty,' he observed.[27] Not surprisingly, the specific concerns of gay and bisexual men were becoming less of a priority and the dominance of gay activists was being reduced.

People of Colour and Gays and Lesbians of the First Nations

One other important way in which AIDS advocacy changed, beginning in the late 1980s, was that white gay males in urban centres gradually ceased to be the only individuals at whom AIDS education and services were being targeted. As AIDS cases increased and the identifiable same-sex communities became more culturally and racially diverse, the particular needs of people of colour and First Nations peoples moved to the forefront. Community-based AIDS groups came under frequent criticism for their inability or unwillingness to provide education and services for, or to meet the treatment needs of these communities. There was an urgent need for sensitivity to cultural conventions about sexuality that are different from those of European ancestry. Funding and organizational commitments were needed to conduct education and outreach in other languages and in places other than the bars and clubs that were associated with the white male community.[28] These exigencies gave rise to new groups aimed at dealing with AIDS among people of colour and the First Nations that were separate from the large and well-established AIDS groups. An important element of such organizing, just as it had been for lesbian and gay liberation groups, was to change attitudes both within and outside of the various communities to be served. Homophobia and heterosexism needed to be confronted, positive identification with same-sex orientation and same-sex acts needed to be fostered, and visibility and overcoming oppression needed to be promoted.

The first of the groups to form was the Black Coalition for AIDS Prevention (Black CAP), in Toronto in 1989. Gay activists, especially Doug Stewart, were instrumental in helping to launch Black CAP. Working with the culturally diverse Black communities in Toronto, Black CAP committed itself to dealing with the 'impact of racism, sexism, heterosexism, homophobia, classism and other forms of discrimination in our lives as Black people living with or affected by HIV/AIDS.'[29] A similar group in Vancouver, the Black AIDS Network (BAN) was formed in the early 1990s. 'Blacks come from a world where the rate of HIV infection is high,' stated Ron Parker of BAN in 1996. He also indicated that significant numbers of immigrants and refugees come to Canada with the HIV virus, while others unknowingly engage in behaviours, such as unsafe sex, that put them at risk. Thus, there was a critical need to conduct education and to provide services specifically for these communities.[30]

AIDS among the large Asian communities of Toronto resulted in 1990 in the launching of the Gay Asians AIDS Project (GAAP) by the AIDS Committee of Toronto and Gay Asians Toronto (GAT). Impetus for the project grew out of the experiences of gay Asians who were being diagnosed with AIDS. GAT member Dr Alan Li saw that 'there were problems accessing services that would understand Asians' special needs, including how to deal with the impact of AIDS on one's family, acceptance in the Asian community and strong ethnic ties.'[31] GAAP conducted education, provided prevention counselling and support, conducted advocacy, and carried out other activities. It addressed homophobia in Asian communities and an attitude among gay Asians which, in the words of GAAP co-chair Herbert Hsu, meant 'there are still a lot of gay Asians who can't identify themselves with us.'[32] In 1994, GAAP, the Chinese AIDS Alert Project, and the Vietnamese AIDS Project joined forces to form the Asian Community AIDS Services.[33] Gays Asians of Vancouver Area, in 1991, initiated the founding of Asian Support AIDS Project to conduct education and meet prevention needs. ASAP's Henry Koo commented in 1995 that 'from the Asian perspective, we are where the white community was in the early '80s' in terms of understanding AIDS or acknowledging its presence in the community.[34] Toronto's Alliance for South Asian AIDS Prevention (ASAP) was also founded in 1990. Accessing South Asian communities to conduct AIDS education and provide information presented ASAP with a number of challenges, including overcoming cultural conventions that 'generally regard any discussion of sex or sexuality as taboo ... [and confronting that persistent] mythic perception of AIDS/HIV as a white homosexual problem.'[35] Before long, ASAP was conducting extensive education in South Asian communities, including publishing information in Bengali, Gujarati, Hindi, Punjabi, Tamil, and Urdu. In 1995, it became ASIA – the Asian Society for the Intervention of AIDS.

Similarly, AIDS organizations for First Nations peoples, including those for two-spirited (gay or lesbian) people, formed independently of the mainstream AIDS groups. Native people who were HIV-positive or who had AIDS were reticent about approaching existing organizations or did not feel welcome in such groups. Susan Beaver of Two-Spirited People of the First Nations (TPFN) noted in a 1992 article, 'It's really hard for us to practice our culture within lesbian and gay organizations. Increasingly, those who are HIV-positive or who have AIDS are moving closer to their communities, their roots. This is very important to the healing process.' Frederick Haineault of Vancouver's Healing Our Spirit group commented, '[the mainstream groups are] basically geared to gay white middle class males. I know a number of our people who've approached them and haven't connected with them at all.'[36] The Edmonton Feather of Hope Society, Canada's first organization dealing specifically with AIDS/HIV issues among First Nations people, was started in 1990 by Ken Ward, an HIV-positive man, after initially contacting the AIDS Network of Edmonton and learning that there were no native staff members in it. 'That's when I knew there should be an organization dealing specifically with this issue [AIDS in Native communities],' he stated.[37] By the late 1990s, a network of Aboriginal AIDS organizations had been established. From its office in Ottawa, the Canadian Aboriginal AIDS Network conducted initiatives to create awareness of AIDS in Aboriginal communities and to pressure the federal government to give more attention to the issue. 'Indigenous people are the ones that are being severely impacted by the disease,' noted the network's executive director Kevin Barlow in a 1997 article. 'We realize we need to be responding more heavily to try and curb growing cases and to care for those people that are now living with the disease.'[38]

Cultural differences in respect of how homosexuality is viewed among First Nations also were being addressed by such organizations. The challenge was complicated because no uniform view of homosexuality existed among First Nations peoples and attitudes in many cases have been influenced by European colonization and Christianity. The Edmonton Feather of Hope Society, for example, has stated one of its objectives as 'To educate Aboriginal people in a manner that is appropriate to each community.'[39] Other priorities were dealing with the low self-esteem of many gay and lesbian Aboriginals and issues related to addictions and childhood abuse.[40] Homophobia, both internalized and that exhibited by heterosexual Aboriginals, presented other challenges. Gilbert Deschamps, a community development worker with TPFN, has stated, 'There's a lot of internalized homophobia among two-spirited people. There's low self-esteem, high risk behaviour and suicide.'[41] Conducting AIDS education on the various First Nations reserves also posed other challenges. In some cases, Albert McLeod of the Manitoba Aboriginal AIDS Task Force (founded in 1991) has noted, the presence of television created the impression that AIDS is a white man's disease: 'You don't see many Canadians dealing with AIDS on TV, let alone aboriginals. It's usually on the American channels.'[42] In contrast, in the early 1990s, the most remote Native communities far away from urban centres did not know very much about AIDS at all. For that reason, Toronto's TPFN 'focused almost exclusively on AIDS education in Toronto and on the reserves.'[43] Among the educational initiatives undertaken has been the pioneering work of actor, playwright, and activist

Evan Adams. He toured Aboriginal communities in the late 1980s and early 1990s, performing his play, *Snapshots*, a true story of a First Nations man with AIDS who eventually died. Acceptance of the man's homosexuality, and coping with that revelation, also were important elements of the play.[44]

Queer Activism

In the early 1990s, lesbian and gay advocacy was briefly transformed as queer activism burst onto the scene, propelled by a militant new generation that grew up in the post-Stonewall and post-AIDS era. 'A new generation of activists is here,' wrote Allan Berube and Jeffrey Escoffier in the Winter 1991 edition of *OUT/LOOK*, a national lesbian and gay quarterly published in the United States. 'They have come out into communities devastated by the AIDS epidemic and into political consciousness through the struggle against AIDS.'[45] Describing themselves as 'queer,' rather than gay, lesbian, or bisexual, these new activists were determined to be confrontational and to achieve inclusiveness of all marginalized peoples. The rise of the 'nation of queers' was at one in the same time reminiscent of some gay liberation front groups of the early 1970s, and a rejection of the assimilationist activism that had taken root in the 1980s. According to Berube and Escoffier, queer nationalists were 'trying to combine contradictory impulses: to bring people together who have been made to feel perverse, queer, old, outcast, different, deviant, and to affirm sameness by defining a common identity on the fringes. They are inclusive, but within boundaries that threaten to marginalize those whose difference doesn't conform to the new nation.'[46] Short-lived and never able to resolve its inherent contradictions, queer nationalism, like the gay liberation front movements, nonetheless changed the gay, lesbian, and bisexual communities. Queer nationalists rejected the identity politics of the gay and lesbian movement, claiming that labels such as gay, lesbian, bisexual, and community promoted by now mainstream activists were intended to integrate, homogenize, and make respectable those who were once sexual outlaws.

Unfortunately, queer nationalism, despite its initial promise and radicalism, failed dramatically to become a sustainable, broadly based coalition of the marginalized and the excluded it purported to be.[47] Eschewing political strategies and traditional forms of activism, queer nationals asserted their difference principally through their attire, and by wearing badges and stickers with 'queer' on them. Black leather, shaved heads, or spiked hair dyed brilliant colours, and facial and body piercing were among their trademarks. But, while they changed the fashion of younger gays, lesbians, and bisexuals, queer nationals, in an organizational sense, accomplished very little.[48] As Barry D. Adam has observed in *The Rise of a Gay and Lesbian Movement*, 'Queer Nation combined spontaneous high energy and an anarchistic internal dynamic that resulted in a wave of high-profile challenges to heterosexism but also in the division and dissolution of many groups after a couple of years. Despite a new freshness and resolution brought to the post-Stonewall movement, queer nationalism contained its own set of contradictions. Its claim to an identity that is more inclusive than gay or lesbian inevitably stumbled over a new series of oppositions and exclusions.' In the end, Adam concludes, 'Queer Nation turns out not as the overarching unifier but as yet another fraction in the overall mosaic of contemporary gay and lesbian organizing.'[49]

The first group to formally use the name Queer Nation emerged in New York City in April 1990. It grew out of discussion groups on homophobia and visibility issues, with members of ACT UP being among its founders. Consisting of youth describing themselves as queer, and older AIDS activists, they launched a visibility campaign in response to a rash of gay bashings in the East Village. One of their pamphlets screamed, 'I HATE STRAIGHTS.' By the summer of 1990, they had attracted considerable media attention. But, as their numbers increased, the task of achieving consensus became more difficult. By 1992, Queer Nation New York no longer existed.[50] Nevertheless, the success of queer nation in New York City fostered the formation of similar groups elsewhere. Queer Nation Toronto started in the fall of 1990 and lasted for about two years. The queer nation groups formed in Montreal, Ottawa, and Vancouver were equally short-lived.

Queer Nation Toronto grew quickly, attracting as many as two hundred people described in one news report as 'divisive, eclectic ... [and] action-oriented.'[51] Queer Nation Toronto was best known for posters appearing in downtown Toronto with messages such as, 'Queers are here, get used to it' and 'Gays bash back.' During its brief existence, Queer Nation Toronto held demonstrations against gay bashings, the religious right, anti-abortion events, the war with Iraq, and censorship. Notable among these efforts was a huge 1991 night-time demonstration, 'Queer Without Fear.' They staged 'kiss ins' and confronted heterosexism by gathering en masse at straight bars and clubs to assert a visible same-sex presence. Steven Maynard, active in Queer Nation Toronto during its formative days, wrote in 1991 in *Fuse* magazine, 'We seized the label "queer" away from bigots and bashers, printed it in big, black, bold letters, and proudly stamped it on our shirts and on the streets. We raised our Queer voices to shut down Christian fundamentalists and to remind everyone "we're here, we're queer and we're not going away." And we shoved our queer tongues down each others' throats in front of unsuspecting suburban shoppers who made the mistake of venturing into the heart of our downtown territory.'[52] But, as Maynard also noted, 'In many ways Queer Nation embodies some of the possibilities and problems of lesbian/gay politics in the past few years, particularly concerning the contested roles of "identity" and "community."' Queer nation responded to the fact 'our agenda has narrowed from a broadly conceived lesbian/gay liberation to one of marking out the fairly limited boundaries of the queer nation and defending these borders,' he added. Yet, queer nationalism was itself predicated on identity and community – that of being queer members of a *nation*.

Like the many groups that preceded them, queer nation organizations, riven with dissent and disagreements over how to deal with sexism and racism, soon dissipated and eventually collapsed. Women and people of colour, despite the group's professed commitment to inclusiveness and fighting oppression in all forms, drifted away because their voices were 'lost in the frenzy of mostly white, mostly male meetings.' Lori Lyons, active in Queer Nation Toronto, observed after its demise that the group, in addition, 'never had the political depth to resolve its own contradictions. We had no strategy for creating our new inclusive nation, nothing to consolidate the myriad of people who brought their anger to our doorstep.' The personal priorities of the members clashed, and there were no processes for reaching consensus. Noted Lyons, 'Such confrontations split the group, all too often along race and gender lines. People began to leave, insulted at the attacks on their personal visions. These ex-Nationals, along with assimilationist gay men and lesbians, created a formidable backlash to Queer Nation's radical politic.'[53] Yuki Hayashi has also written about the alienation she felt as the queer nation group she belonged to 'progressively became mired in factionalizing, splintering and drawing of lines.' What had started as an inclusive, high-energy movement of feminists, AIDS activists, anti-racists, peace advocates, and other social activists, dwindled and died.[54] Queer Nation Ottawa was also roundly criticized for not dealing with racism. Tonia Bryan lambasted the group, writing in 1992 that,

> Queer Nation has stalwartly avoided the inclusion of a critique of the racism of its own organization. Queer nationals seem to be more comfortable mentioning the word racism in the most ambiguous ways possible, and still these white gays and lesbians claim to 'care' about my rights as a Black Lesbian??? ... Fighting racism and or homophobia means fighting the many faces of domination as it manifests itself in society. This also means taking a hard look inside oneselves in order to identify ways in which we have internalized the systems that seek to destroy us. Stop lying to yourselves about a canadian multicultural utopia that exists only on paper. REALLY examine how you as white, gays and lesbians make decisions everyday that enable you to benefit from Canada's system of institutionalized racism, in ways that I, a Black lesbian, never will.[55]

The Ottawa group, formed in February 1991, also encountered resistance from activists and others in the gay, lesbian, and bisexual communities over its radical tactics. Calling for the outing of closeted gays and lesbians who demonstrated homophobia or supported it in others, in particular, made many people uncomfortable. Other tactics included demonstrations, conducting 'Queer Ins,' displaying same-sex affection at shopping malls and other public places, and at overwhelmingly straight social spots, such as bars and discos. Its manifesto asserted, 'We are a Queer Nation of unapologetic lesbians, gays and bisexuals of diverse races, abilities, ages, creeds, classes and cultures working together to collectively eliminate homophobia and promote and celebrate the visibility of queers by employing non-violent direct action.'[56] But, like queer nation groups elsewhere, Queer Nation Ottawa quickly failed to sustain itself.

The Rise of Queer and the Challenging of Identity

Looking back from the perspective of nearly ten years, it is clear queer nationalism never did take root as a transformative social movement, and became, instead, a brief, if academically interesting, blip in the history of the broader gay and lesbian movement. Still, it did leave an important legacy. Culturally, queer nationalists popularized the use of 'queer' to be more inclusive of sexual minorities and other marginalized peoples, as a replacement for the more cumbersome, 'gay, lesbian,

262 BETWEEN QUEER AND THE MAINSTREAM

bisexual and transgendered people.' Queer space, queer culture, queer theory, queer studies and queer communities have become familiar in the contemporary lexicon. But queer nationalists also unleashed a new variation of the old debate about identity and the purpose of pursuing a liberation strategy. By adopting queer they reclaimed and politicized a derogatory term commonly used in the days before lesbian and gay liberation. It represented the belief in an identity that is more ambiguous and more fluid than gay, lesbian, or homosexual. As one queer theorist has stated, 'Queer ... exemplifies a more mediated relation to categories of identification.'[57] Similarly, Tom Patterson, writing in Vancouver's *Angles*, stated in 1991, 'The accepted rhetoric today is to call ourselves the lesbian and gay community or communities. It's hard to believe community has any significance left. The term itself has been stretched out of meaningfulness.' Questioning the widespread use of community, and the implicit comparison of lesbians and gay men to other minorities, Patterson argued, 'we are not another minority, we are in every minority. We are everywhere. We are not concentrated in a few neighbourhoods – we are only most visible in a few neighbourhoods ... Every person who wants sex could be a queer.'[58]

Despite the fast demise of the queer nation groups, the challenging of identities based on sexual orientation that they fostered has continued in the emerging field of queer theory, mainly through academic discourse. Some queer theorists have argued that deconstructing normative models of gender identity – a key element of lesbian and gay liberation analysis – itself ultimately achieves only the legitimization of gay and lesbian identities, with undesirable results. Queer theorists challenge the appropriateness of even advocating for such identities. In issuing that challenge, they believe they are proceeding from a sense of disenchantment with lesbian and gay liberation. Annamarie Jagose, a queer theory academic at the University of Melbourne, Australia attributes the disenchantment to a 'deepened understanding' of how heterosexist privilege is maintained and reproduced. She argues that queer consciousness questions 'how the marshalling of lesbian and gay identities might inadvertently reinforce that heterosexual hegemony they are programmatically opposed to.' What's more, she believes such consciousness adopts a critical approach to 'the putatively causal relation between a secure identity and an effective politics.'[59]

Queer nationalists, and the young queers in all their diversity who followed, expressed skepticism about, or rejected outright, the identity politics first formulated in the 1970s. As we examined in Part One, asserting a gay (or lesbian, or bisexual) identity in the early years of lesbian and gay liberation was absolutely essential to the formation of a positive sense of self and an affirmation of a healthy and completely natural alternative sexuality. It was necessary to achieve visibility, to challenge the notion of presumed and compulsory heterosexuality, to throw open the doors of the multitude of insidious closets in which gays and lesbians were imprisoned, and to force social and sexual change. At the same time, the assertion of such identity introduced a contradiction in that, in the long term, a key objective of lesbian and gay liberation is to make possible greater sexual freedom, a more fluid sexuality for everyone. As gay liberation polemicist Allen Young wrote in his essay 'Out of the Closet and into the Streets' in the early 1970s, 'Gay, in its most far-reaching sense, means not homosexual, but sexually free.'[60] Like the inherent but necessary contradiction in the strategy of pursuing human rights to advance the cause of liberation, there is a tension induced over time between promoting new identities of gay, lesbian, bisexual, transgendered, and so on while pursuing the goal of sexual freedom for everyone. Rights advocacy and promotion of identities, perhaps inevitably, become conservative influences that eventually impede and then outrightly resist the more radical objectives of liberation and sexual freedom. A synergy of rights attainment and identities that are respectable and non-threatening to the heterosexual mainstream takes hold, and becomes itself constraining and oppressive, marginalizing those who do not, or refuse to, conform. Queer nationalists, by seizing upon and exposing these troubling dynamics – even while paradoxically asserting another quite different identity – unleashed a much-needed debate that is still engaging activists and theorists a decade after the queer nation groups burst onto the scene.

Bert Archer, a writer whose columns have appeared in Canadian gay publications, has been one of those who has attacked the notion of rigid lesbian and gay identities. Commenting on the subject in 1998, Archer declared the gay liberation movement of the 1970s a failure and denounced what followed it – a gay 'territorialism' – as permitting 'no room for ambiguity' in sexual matters. Rather than the liberation of all people, the objective, wrote Archer, had become forming 'a parallel society to the mainstream, alike in everything but the sex of their partners.'[61] Archer condemned the territorialist approach as presenting an image of people interested in marrying, having children, and obtaining spousal benefits, who see themselves as being 'quite different from the immature gays of the 70s who wore a lot of leather, or a lot of lace, and made what they did in bed, or the alleys or the slings, a primary concern.' Instead, he noted the territorialists have portrayed themselves as the 'mature gays' who in effect disenfranchised all of the others.[62] (*Assimilationists* could well be substituted for *territorialists*, for the sake of our discussion of the differences between liberationists and equality-seekers.)

Archer developed his analysis further in his 1999 book, *The End of Gay (and the Death of Heterosexuality)*. He postulated that despite the great progress and victories of the lesbian and gay movement, and the enormous benefits that queers have derived from them, the movement has ignored or forgotten 'the possibility of a sexual attraction that is neither primarily nor exclusively based in anatomy nor especially relevant to your sense of self.' He then speculated that we are approaching 'the end of gay' and, inevitably, the end of the movement of gays and lesbians for sexual liberation, one indication of which is the changing attitude of youth towards their sexuality:

> People, generally younger people brought up on the notion that not only was there such a thing as sexuality but that sexuality of all sorts was okay (as long as there was some latex involved somewhere), are starting to notice that their hearts and loins are not described very well by these only now solidifying sexual designations. Though there has always been a fair amount of sexual experimentation among adolescents, in the past few years they've been not only having sex with members of their sex as well as its opposite, but consciously not acknowledging – in light of extensive familiarity with the concept of sexual identity – the significance of their actions on any concrete definitions of their own identity. Whatever their current or eventual sexual habits, more and more of them are chafing at definition, not only at gay and straight but at bi, too, simply not wanting to be pegged down.[63]

The problem with Archer's analysis, and with queer theorists generally, is that it proceeds from an initially quite insightful critique of the more problematic outcomes of the identity politics fostered by gay liberation to a reach a dubious conclusion that the gay and lesbian movement has been transformed by 'post gay liberation' dialectic and consciousness that declare gay, lesbian, bisexual, and even heterosexual identities to be passé. It is by no means clear that everyone is becoming freer to have both same-sex and opposite-sex relationships without labelling or reprisal, as Archer would have us believe. The suspicion remains that reticence over being labelled or pegged is really a reticence to be known as gay, lesbian, or bisexual because of the still negative attitudes held by society generally towards same-sex relationships. There seems little evidence to suggest that there is any reluctance to be labelled a heterosexual. Heterosexuality, despite Archer's clever subtitle, is neither dead nor even close to death. Moreover, until heterosexism and homophobia have disappeared (an unlikely prospect) there will not be – indeed, cannot be – an end of gay, although, as in the past, gay may be given some other name to distinguish it from the norm of heterosexuality. The risk presented by the queer theorists' views is that the rejection of identity in respect of sexuality might simply create a larger, if somewhat more comfortable, closet in which no adverse consequences will arise – so long as the possibility of sexual relations with members of the opposite sex remain possible and exclusive homosexuality is rejected as labelling.

TWELVE

Queer Community Standards
and Queer Spaces

Despite the dominance of equality-seeking rights activism, the second track of the lesbian and gay movement proceeded apace, addressing issues of sexuality in the late 1980s and throughout the 1990s in a manner firmly rooted in earlier liberation politics. This included celebrating sexuality, eroticism, and pornography, resisting state regulation and police repression – and especially challenging the notions of community standards, of public and private, and of consent regarding sexuality and sexual behaviour. This period also saw the public articulation of the alternative mores and standards of the queer communities, manifested in *queer spaces*, that are quite different in matters of sexuality from the heterosexual majority. Fierce battles were waged over how sexuality should be expressed, the Criminal Code sections dealing with obscenity and pornography, and the censorship practices of Canada Customs.

More clearly reflective of the militancy and sexuality radicalism of lesbian and gay liberation, this second track, over the years, succeeded in pushing the envelope socially and legally, forcefully challenging the notion of community standards of tolerance. Not surprisingly, engagement in this brand of sexual politics put liberationists in conflict once more with many feminists and with the equality-seeking assimilationists within the movement, as well as with the police and the state. This arm of the movement also generally agitated for its objectives without strong or visible public support from the broader lesbian, gay, and bisexual communities. There was no national coalition or network, such as had existed with the National Gay Rights Coalition in the 1970s, demonstrating commitment for such actions and providing a forum for forging cross-country consensus and coordination. EGALE especially did not stake out any significant positions on sexuality issues and, other than its intervention in the court challenge mounted by Little Sister's in its anti-censorship case, provided no meaningful support to campaigns challenging outdated sex laws. It also avoided taking a definitive position on the age of consent. Consequently, the campaigns on these issues were largely localized, even when they challenged national policies or the Criminal Code. And they much less frequently attracted the positive attention of either the mainstream or the lesbian, gay, and bisexual communities than did the equality-seeking campaigns.

The Anti-Censorship Campaigns

As we have seen in parts One and Two, an important objective of lesbian and gay liberation, from the beginning of the movement, has been freeing sexually expressive materials from state censorship and repression. Resisting censorship thus continued to be a critical issue for liberation activists from 1985 onwards. It was a formidable task, given that governments sought to tighten prohibitions on pornography to address concerns of a host of constituencies, most notably religious groups, social conservatives, and women's organizations. Beginning in late 1984, the federal government set up the Special Committee on Pornography and Prostitution, known as the Fraser Commission. It examined the assertion that pornography is harmful because it leads to an increase in sexual assaults, concluding that two types of harm could be attributed to pornography. The first type, according to the commission, is to members of the public who are involuntarily subjected to pornography. The second, it claimed, is caused by pornography's undermining of the right to equality for women. In April 1985, the commission released its report based on six months of public hearings across Canada. The report, while not precisely defining pornography, drew a distinction between material that is 'merely sexually explicit' with no 'appreciable amount' of violence or degradation and that which makes a connection between sex and violence, degradation or abuse in 'such a way as to suggest approval of that abuse.'[1] It recommended removal of *obscenity*, with its connotations of moral outrage and indecency, as a term in the Criminal Code, and proposed instead that a new section be created which grouped various existing sections under a new category relating to *pornography*. At the same time, the commission urged caution in the drafting of these new sections to ensure that 'the definition of the prohibited conduct, material or thing is very precise.' It set out a three-tier system to deal more severely with pornography depicting children, or in which those depicted were harmed, and less severely with depictions of adult consensual sex.[2]

The Mulroney government attempted to amend the obscenity laws based on the Fraser Commission report in a 1986 statute, Bill C-114. Immediately, an outcry was heard from civil libertarians, human rights activists, journalists, and editorial writers because of the bill's puritanical and repressive features. In particular, concern was expressed because the proposed law ignored a Fraser Commission recommendation for exempting from criminal prosecution erotic material found in adult magazines such as *Playboy* because they were acceptable to contemporary Canadian standards. Even more troubling were Bill C-114's definitions of *sexually violent behaviour* and *degrading pornography*, and a definition of pornography as *'any visual matter* showing vaginal, anal, or oral intercourse, ejaculation, sexually violent behaviour, bestiality, incest, necrophilia, masturbation or other sexual activity' (emphasis added).[3] The public response was so overwhelmingly critical that the government eventually never enacted the bill, thus bringing to an end attempts to legislate new obscenity laws.[4] The result is that the Criminal Code definition of obscenity, except for a 1993 amendment to section 163 dealing with child pornography, is the same today as it was in 1959. Nonetheless, the positions taken by the Fraser Commission have had a profound influence on judicial decisions and social attitudes over the last decade and a half.

Complicating matters further have been the policies of Canada Customs (discussed later in this chapter) and a particular judgement of the Supreme Court of Canada, *Regina v. Butler*, which ruled on pornography in a manner that has had significant impact. The *Butler* decision expanded the community standards test to include the exploitation of sex in a degrading and dehumanizing manner that is perceived by public opinion to be harmful to society, and especially to women.[5] The Supreme Court also ruled in *Butler* that the obscenity section of the Criminal Code was a justifiable infringement of the freedom of expression provisions otherwise guaranteed by the Charter: 'There has been a growing recognition that material said to exploit sex in a "degrading or dehumanizing" manner will necessarily fail the community standards test, not because it offends against morals but because it is *perceived* by public opinion to be harmful to society, particularly women' (emphasis added). The justices then went on to say, 'The courts must determine as best they can what the community would tolerate others being exposed to on the basis of the degree of harm that may flow from such exposure. Harm in this context means that it predisposes persons to act in an anti-social manner, in other words, a manner which society formally recognizes as incompatible with its proper functioning.'[6] Consequently, in obscenity cases, the Criminal Code can override the freedom of speech guarantees of the Charter. Problematically for anti-censorship advocates, *community standards* are left for the courts to determine in particular cases. Such determination is made in reference to a hypothetical 'national standard' based on what judges believe members of 'the community' would tolerate. There is no distinction between communities, between what be may acceptable in, say, downtown Toronto as opposed to a small town, or between the lesbian, gay, and bisexual community relative to the broad heterosexual one.

The *Butler* decision was hailed as a great victory by some feminist organizations, particularly the Legal Education and Action Fund (LEAF), which had intervened in the case assisted by US anti-pornography advocate Catherine MacKinnon. But gay and lesbian liberationists, as well as academic experts and civil libertarians, generally condemned the decision as setting as dangerous precedent. Gay and lesbian liberationists feared it would set the stage for a renewed series of attacks against same-sex pornography. In fact, *Butler's* impact and the problem of determining community standards soon were driven home dramatically in two cases involving sexually explicit same-sex materials sold by Glad Day Bookshop in Toronto. The first case, decided on 15 July 1992 by an Ontario court justice, found as obscene twelve items of sexually explicit gay male material destined for Glad Day that had been seized by Canada Customs. The judge ruled they portrayed casual sex and sex – anal penetration – that was not 'human' (as opposed to dehumanizing sex as contemplated in *Butler*) and would harm the community.[7] Then, a judge in a second case involving Glad Day also drew upon *Butler* to determine that a lesbian fiction magazine, *Bad Attitude*, containing a fictional fantasy article about consensual SM sex involving two women, contravened the Criminal Code.[8] The concept of social harm embodied in *Butler* featured prominently in the case. In his February 1993 judgement, the judge opined that, based on *Butler*, had the protagonist been male, society would recognize the actions as harmful to the community. The issue of sexual orientation was deemed irrelevant.[9]

The *Bad Attitude* case was the first attempt to secure a judicial distinction between queer community standards and those of the broad heterosexual community, as defined by judges. Glad Day witnesses contended that material such as that in *Bad Attitude* should be considered differently from heterosexual pornography – that the community standards for gays, lesbian, and bisexuals were different from those of the heterosexual mainstream. They argued that depictions or representations of sexual acts between members of the same sex are not degrading or dehumanizing because the social status and power of the individuals are equal, unlike relationships between men and women. Another objective was to show that lesbian pornography was being subjected to selective law enforcement and harassment when considered in the context of what community standards tolerated for heterosexual sex.[10]

The charges against Glad Day and the court decision that followed unleashed outrage, a round of protests, and a renewed debate about pornography in the lesbian, gay, and bisexual communities of Toronto. Lesbians in leather featured prominently in a demonstration of over one thousand people the night after the charges were laid. The comments of activist Sue Golding were typical. She characterized the police action as 'not just an attack on lesbian sexuality, but an attack on all forms of sexual expression, and indeed, expression itself.'[11] Lesbian activist Chris Bearchell, shortly after the conviction of Glad Day, commented, 'It is a sad comment on our times that a moral panic about sexual imagery is led by feminists; that their energy is channelled into an anti-sex backlash that hits queers and sex workers first and hardest. In the face of a problem that demands justice and power over their own lives for the abused, this brand of feminism perpetuates fear and intolerance instead, while it diverts attention from real causes of violence.'[12] Bearchell's criticism was directed to the many feminists, including lesbians in the vanguard of the anti-pornography fight, who had no qualms about the *Butler* decision or the rightness of their views. Susan G. Cole, for example, was clear that the SM themes of *Bad Attitude* could not be defended: 'I saw women hurting each other. I saw a radical lesbian expression of the traditional, male domination-and-surrender theme. Is that okay? No.'[13] For Cole, the appeal of such lesbian pornography is attributable to the fact 'there is so little lesbian representation, we're desperate for anything. If other images were available, I don't think it would be appealing.' The depiction of SM in pornography, she argued, was simply a reflection of the dominant view of sexuality, in which there is no equality for women, where sexuality is based on male dominance and female submission. As she wrote in her 1989 book, *Pornography and the the Sex Crisis*:

> Many gay and lesbian activists have criticized any analyses that tend to question sadomasochistic sexuality. They bemoan the absence of sexual pluralism in society and the vulnerability of sexual minorities who have been denied their personal freedom. Those espousing sex liberalism say these dissidents are the real revolutionairies challenging sexual norms. But contrary to their personal claims about their sexuality, the practitioners of sadomasochism who inflict and experience humiliation and pain in closely scripted encounters are not at all sexual dissidents, but proponents of the dominant sexual ideology ... So-called 'tops' and 'bottoms' in the lesbian sadomasochistic sexual construct fiddle with roles but they do not challenge the construct ... They call themselves liberators, radical perverts, sexual outlaws or anything else, but they are really some of the most eloquent proponents of the sexual status quo.[14]

The solution for Cole respecting sexually explicit materials that subordinate women is law that provides a strong 'civil remedy' that empowers women victimized by pornography to act to seek redress and compensation.

But, as Bet Cecill, a longtime lesbian community activist in Vancouver has noted, efforts at finding concensus among women, straight or lesbian, on issues like pornography and SM were difficult and painful. Some women tried to demystify the topic and engage in rational discussion, she believes, but many more saw violence in a relationship as being the same as SM. Cecill's own positions on sexuality, censorship, and sexual imagery, more closely aligned with those of gay liberationists than with feminists, put her into conflict with other women. And she acknowledged in a 1992 interview that her views differ dramatically from those of other feminists:

> There's a fundamental disagreement, I mean this absolutely fundamental disagreement, about the place of and the influence of mass-produced sexual representation, some of which is absolutely, disgustingly mysogynist. I have no argument with that. It *is*. My differences come in how I define that ... and often I don't think I can define that. So much of what you do with sexual representation, or so much of the impact, is what you bring to it, what you know about it, you know? And if your idea is that heterosexual intercourse is inherently oppressive, and there are women who

believe that, then you're gonna see, you know, two people fucking, and its submissive, you know, and he's doing it to her, and all of the rest of it. In my opinion, there is nothing inherently oppressive in that and about a whole bunch of other things ... We had plenty of rape and torture and murder and pillage and assaults on women long before we had mass-produced imagery of any kind, so the arguments that this [sexual imagery] causes men ... to do nasty things to women, I think, is really thin. If you take that stuff all off the face of the earth ... we'd still have the same problem.[15]

Reflecting on the differences between feminism and gay liberation on matters relating to sexuality, Chris Bearchell and Denis LeBlanc wrote, in 1991, 'Gay liberationists break down some of the taboos, or at least extend their limits, by creating a culture that talks relatively comfortably about sex. They recognize and express solidarity with the rights of other sexual minorities, such as prostitutes, and support the rights of women. Gay liberation differs from some liberal and radical feminists over freedom of sexual expression and in its opposition to censorship.'[16]

Jean Hillabold, in a series of articles recently published in *Perceptions*, has attempted to put into perspective the debates that raged in the 1980s and later, noting that, 'Lesbians, in particular, are still feeling the aftershocks [of the feminist "sex wars"], and are still divided on the issue.'[17] Hillabold believes that 'feminists needed a scapegoat and an achievable goal' and, in the 1980s, siezed upon pornography as the enemy, and its eradication as a solution. 'If this form of brainwashing could be purged from Western culture, androgyny and equality would supposedly flourish everywhere. As an added bonus, being against porn meant feminists could join forces with fundamentalist Christians who wanted sex to be kept out of sight.'[18] Hillabold sees these 'Victorian reformers' as reminiscent of the social purists of the late nineteenth century that were discussed in Part One: 'White heterosexual college-educated women of the "mainstream" feminist movement ... picketed the book and video stores that sold "filth," lobbied for tougher censorship laws and sought to rescue the "victims of patriarchy" who worked in the sex biz,' she notes. But as bondage and discipline and other forms of sadomasochism became increasingly prevalent and butch/femme roles made a comeback in queer communities, 'self-identified dykes, women "of color," and working class women increasingly organized apart from, or in opposition to, white educated feminists who argued for the regulation of porn, prostitution and violence by various branches of government.' The polarization of 'sex positive' and anti-pornography agendas intensifed as a result.[19]

By the 1990s, the debate on sexuality and pornography included the views of more than just middle-class white activists. Tomiye Ishida, of Vancouver, who described herself as a parent, lesbian, former sex trade worker, political person of colour, and feminist, stated in 1996, ' Honouring our lusts strikes a chord for sexual liberation, but how far can we honour them? In a world where all were equal, oppression and exploitation could not exist. But let's face it, we live in a world founded on oppression.' On the subject of sexuality, pornography, and consent, Ishida observed:

> Feminists have done much to bring forward the issue of power in an effort to address violence against women in relation to the sex industry and the manufacture of hetero pornography. Unfortunately, their calls for state regulation of the sexism and violence in porn have been co-opted by conservatives to provide moral legitimacy for their own campaign against sexual explicitness.
>
> Gay porn does not reproduce women's subordination as hetero porn does. And not all prostitutes are victimized. But we cannot simply struggle for the unfettered liberation of sexual desires, disregarding power relations. Nor can I buy into the concept of an essentially violent, predatory male sexuality.
>
> We must struggle for the power to affirm a diversity of sexualities; to define, to represent, and to celebrate our different consensual sexual desires where difference is not marked by disadvantage.[20]

For these and other reasons, the response to the raids on Glad Day and the judgment in the *Bad Attitude* case were affirmations of the volatile and contentious natures of the politics of sexual liberation that continued to be features of queer community activism even while more respectable issues such as human rights code amendments and spousal benefits were attracting the most media and mainstream attention. So too were other challenges to the pornography laws, focused on the Customs Act and the Customs Tariff, first introduced in the 1800s, and amended in 1986 and 1987, respectively. The acts give customs officials sweeping powers to seize, censor and ban books and periodicals coming into Canada.[21] Beginning in 1984, Canada Customs began forcing foreign publishers of gay sex magazines to censor their publications if they did not want them to be seized at the border. This resulted, for several years, in magazines appearing with white pages with the word 'censored' printed across them after customs officials had objected to their content. In other cases, black dots or markings were placed over photographs, and white spaces appeared in the texts. Even articles dealing with safe sex practices such as education about AIDS were subjected to this form of censorship. Eventually, to overcome harassment, some publishers found printing houses in Canada to produce the materials – without having to leave blank pages or white spaces!

Changes to the laws were required following a 1985 Federal Court of Appeal decision that the provisions permitting the seizure or banning of books found to be immoral or indecent were too vaguely restrictive of the freedom of expression rights guaranteed by the Charter.[22] In response, in May 1985 the Mulroney government introduced 'temporary' amendments to Tariff Item 99201–1, in the form of Memorandum D9-1-1. The unconstitutional element was replaced with a prohibition on materials that, echoing the language of the Fraser Commission, contained 'sexual acts that degrade or dehumanize any of the participants.'[23] But the new memorandum changed little in practice. It allowed for the seizure or banning of any publications containing 'depictions or descriptions of anal penetration, including depictions or descriptions involving implements of all kinds.' Sexual material would also be prohibited if it aroused 'immoderate or unwholesome desire.' Worse, customs officials were given the authority to use their personal judgment as to whether or not materials qualified as obscene based on these criteria.[24]

Legal challenges to customs' authority under Memorandum D9-1-1 began in 1987, when Glad Day Bookshop and the Canadian Committee Against Customs Censorship disputed the banning of a book, *The Joy of Gay Sex*. It was placed on the banned list because it depicted acts of anal intercourse, and immediately ceased being available for sale. By contrast, *The Joy of Sex*, a comparable sex manual for heterosexuals, was never placed on the list and was sold in bookstores across the country.[25] A judge ruled in 1989 that *The Joy of Gay Sex* was not obscene.[26] Canada Customs, in response, minimally amended Memorandum D9-1-1 to state that materials dealing with anal intercourse would be allowed only if they were not erotic or 'prurient in nature.' This ignored the spirit of the court decision and in practical terms did not change significantly the customs policy.[27] In fact, the harassment of gay and lesbian bookstores intensified, a move seen by bookstore owners as retaliation. Magazines were destroyed or held until they were no longer saleable.

One shipment of art books from Europe arrived at Glad Day as 25 kilos of shredded paper and cardboard. The financial losses incurred by an estimated four to five-hundred seizures to that time were onerous. Glad Day owner Jearld Moldenhauer accused customs of intimidation tactics to force the store to exercise self-censorship: 'You have to understand that detainments and seizures are done for one reason only: to force you to internalize the censorship mentality. I refused to do that.'[28] The tactics of customs, upheld historically by the courts, towards Glad Day and other gay and lesbian bookstores is, as Bruce MacDougall notes in *Queer Judgements*, typical of how censoriousness and censorship 'operate on two levels, the general and the specific. At the specific level they operate to forbid or constrain or condemn a particular instance of expression. At the general level they disapprove of anybody who might be associated in some way with the particular censored expression and expect at least self-censorship from that person.'[29]

By 1990, Canada Customs was seizing nearly 75 per cent of books and magazines shipped to bookstores serving gays, lesbians, and bisexuals. Before long, lesbian as well as gay male pornography also was targeted. *Macho Sluts*, a best-selling fiction collection by openly SM lesbian Pat Califia, was the book that Little Sister's in Vancouver most often had detained by customs.[30] Books by such authors as Jane Rule, Allen Ginsberg, William S. Burroughs, Christopher Isherwood, and Pier Paolo Pasolini were among those seized. One large American distributor, for which about 15 per cent of sales was to the gay or lesbian market in Canada, reported in 1994 that its shipments were regularly seized. Distributing to over 150 countries, he noted, 'Canada is the only country that we deal with that will actually remove books from a shipment and take them away.'[31] One of the largest detainments in history involved shipments from his press in 1993.[32] By contrast, and indicative of the targeted nature of the customs actions, a 1990 survey of nongay booksellers revealed that they rarely had their books and periodicals detained.[33] It was also clear that political support existed for such harassment. Minister of National Revenue Otto Jelinek, a Progressive Conservative, stated in 1993, 'The majority of Canadians – maybe they're the silent majority, they're the normal people who don't speak out so loudly – they don't want this stuff coming in.'[34]

Amid this climate, Little Sister's Book and Art Emporium decided, in December 1986, to fight back. The catalyst was detainment of 548 books and seventy-seven magazines. The store's owners responded by issuing a press release and holding a demonstration in front of the offices of the Vancouver MP who was then the cabinet minister responsible for Canada Customs. The publicity attracted the support of the British Columbia Civil Liberties Association.[35] In 1987, Little Sister's and BCCLA went to court over the detainment of two issues of the *Advocate*, the largest gay news and opinion publication in the United States, because customs officials claimed it had suggestive advertisements. Just weeks before the trial date, customs conceded that an error had been made, and the case ended. Little Sister's intensified its resistance in 1990 by launching a Charter challenge of customs' authority. They argued that the seizure and destruction of materials at the border represented a form of prior restraint on freedom of speech and that, in policy and in practice, Canada Customs was homophobic and discriminated against gay and lesbian literature. The government's application to have the challenge dismissed was rejected by the British Columbia Supreme Court. Then, two weeks before the court case was to commence in October 1994, customs announced that Memorandum D9-1-1 had been revised to remove anal penetration from the list of prohibitions.[36] Little Sister's forged ahead nonetheless, determined to challenge the constitutionality of the legislation under which the memorandum had been issued. The judge released a decision in January 1996, ruling that customs officials contravened the Charter in the *administration* of the regulations governing obscene materials. Unfortunately, he did not rule on whether the relevant sections of the Customs Act and Tariffs Act are unconstitutional.[37]

The outcome of the *Little Sister's* case at this level disappointed bookstores and did not stop customs' harassment. As Little Sister's Janine Fuller noted, without a ruling on the constitutionality of the legislation, 'Nothing changes as a result of this decision.'[38] A few weeks after the judgment, consequently, Little Sister's was back in court, seeking an injunction to stop the harassment by customs, and to seek costs. The store scored a victory in March 1996 when the BC Supreme Court ordered the federal government to pay Little Sister's $170,000 towards its legal costs of $261,000. The judge also ordered customs to remove Little Sister's from its 'lookout' list.[39] But the border seizures did not stop. Books with SM themes bound for Glad Day were seized in late 1997 and early 1998 because they dealt with 'sex with violence.'[40] Even non-SM materials, such as an issue of *OG* (*Oriental Guys*) were detained, as was a shipment of art books, before being ultimately cleared.[41] Similarly, two gay erotica books were detained in the fall of 1998. 'It seems like they're picking up the pace,' lamented Glad Day's manager.[42]

The legal fight suffered a setback in April 1998 when the BC Court of Appeal, in a 2 to 1 decision, dismissed Little Sister's appeal. The majority of judges held that customs' authority to ban and seize materials is unconstitutional, but they rejected arguments that materials destined for gay and lesbian bookstores should not be judged by the same standard used for heterosexual materials. Little Sister's had contended that *Butler* should not be applicable because there was no risk of harm to gays and lesbians presented by the seized materials, as the power and relationships in same-sex situations are different from those of heterosexuals. The justices disagreed, holding gay and lesbian obscenity is prohibited under the law 'because it is obscene, not because it is homosexual.'[43]

Little Sister's appealed to the Supreme Court of Canada, and its case was argued in March 2000. Intervening on the side of the bookstore were a range of groups: EGALE, the Canadian Conference of the Arts, and – surprisingly, given their earlier support for *Butler* – the Women's Legal Education and Action Fund (LEAF). These groups argued that the *Butler* decision should not apply to same-sex pornogrpahy, as it is based on a concept of harm to women as depicted in heterosexual pornography.[44] Countering such arguments was an intervention from a new, international feminist group, Equality Now, which argued that customs was correct in seizing materials destined for Little Sister's. Claiming pornography is sex discrimination, Equality Now contended that gay and lesbian pornography 'advances and promotes self-hating, aggressive, violent, non-consensual sexual behavior as positive, normal, and liberating.' It expounded that 'gay male pornography contributes to the homophobic rejection of gay men and lesbian women, and their sexuality, by normalizing male aggression generally and encouraging the subordination of one individual to the domination of another.'[45]

On 15 December 2000, the Supreme Court of Canada issued a profoundly disappointing judgment that resolved none of the major issues raised by Little Sister's. All nine judges agreed that Little Sister's had been targeted and harassed by customs, and subjected to 'treatment [that] was high handed and dismissive of the appellants' right to receive lawful expressive material which they had every right to receive.' They also found that 'it is fundamentally unacceptable that expression which is free within the country can become stigmatized and harassed by government officials simply because it crosses an international boundary, and is thereby brought within the bailiwick of the Customs department.' But all of the justices also resoundingly reaffirmed the *Butler* decision's harms-based test for pornography, and stated that it must apply equally to same-sex and heterosexual expressions of eroticism and pornography. As for the power given to Canada Customs to carry out its censorship, a majority of six judges ruled that, with one limited exception, the legislation did not violate Canada's consititution. The exception was the *reverse onus* provision under which it fell to the importer to demonstrate that the material was not obscene. Henceforth, the Court ruled, the Crown, through customs, must determine 'whether it can establish on a balance of probabilities that the expressive material is obscene.' The power of *prior restraint* exercised so zealously by customs in respect of shipments to gay and lesbian bookstores – the ability to detain materials at the border – was found to be not unconstitutional. Equally troubling, particularly given the Court's condemnation of the treatment meted out to Little Sister's by customs, was the majority conclusion that differential treatment was made 'at the administrative level in the implementation of the legislation' and could be resolved at that level. In contrast, a minority of three judges found 'the flaws in the Customs regime are not the product of simple bad faith or maladministration, but rather flow from the very nature of prior restraint itself.' The appropriate remedy, in the view of the minority, was to strike down the prior restraint provision.[46]

It is the opinion of the majority of justices that prevails, however, with the result that after fifteen years of litigation little had changed. In fact, a Canada Customs official was quoted, after the *Little Sister's* decision, as saying, 'The Supreme Court has reaffirmed our obligation to detain obscene material at the border.'[47] With *Butler* also reaffirmed, to be applied according to the 'national standard' of what the community would tolerate, it seems likely seizures will continue, and more lengthy and expensive court challenges will need to be launched. In the months leading up to the Little Sister's decision, Customs continued to maintain its vigilance against gay and lesbian materials, widening its net to include After Stonewall, a gay bookstore in Ottawa. In July 2000, books dealing with SM and forced sex, destined for After Stonewall, were seized at the border.[48] Should other court challenges be launched, however, there is little reason to believe, based now on both the *Butler* and *Little Sister's* cases, that if they were to involve the seizure of materials dealing with SM, they would be successful. Ominously for such cases, the majority of justices in the *Little Sister's* decision noted in reference to *Butler*:

The material [to be obscene] must also create a substantial risk of harm which exceeds the community's tolerance. The potential of harm and a same-sex depiction are not necessarily mutually exclusive. Portrayal of a dominatrix engaged in the non-violent degradation of an ostensibly willing sex slave is no less dehumanizing if the victim happens to be of the same sex, and no less (and no more) harmful in its reassurance to the viewer that the victim finds such conduct both normal and pleasurable. Parliament's concern was with behavioural changes in the voyeur that are potentially harmful in ways or to an extent that the community is not prepared to tolerate. There is no reason to restrict that concern to the heterosexual community.[49]

Pornography dealing with consensual SM, in the view of the Supreme Court it would seem, is dehumanizing because it would cause harm to those who view it and therefore is obscene. Customs remains relatively unfettered in its power to seize material it considers 'on a balance of probabilities' to be obscene. In addition, arguing that queer community standards, rather than the national (heterosexual) standards, should be used to judge pornography produced for gays, lesbian, and bisexuals, would seem to have little chance, at least for the forseeable future, of succeeding. Battles over pornography and the state's censorship and repression of it are, accordingly, destined to remain hot issues on the advocacy agenda of lesbian and gay liberation for quite some time. Engaging in such battles will require the abandonment of equality-seeking arguments, seeing as equal treatment with heterosexuals under repressive sex laws will be futile. Instead, it will require, as was begun to be seen in the *Little Sister's* case, the vigorous, sustained promotion of liberationist perspectives that lead to more sexual freedom, including in particular freedom to produce and distribute sexually explicit materials, whether same-sex or heterosexual in nature. The battles won't be short, or easy, but they must be engaged.

The Child Pornography Law

Another front in the pornography battle opened following the hasty adoption of controversial child pornography legislation in the run-up to the 1993 federal election. The result was a new law, section 163.1 of the Criminal Code, that critics claimed would lead to abuse and arbitrariness in enforcement. Adopted in June 1993, Bill C-128 received unanimous support from all political parties. It made illegal possession of written materials or visual representations depicting, portraying, describing, advocating, or counselling sex with children, defined as 'sexual activity with a person under the age of eighteen years that would be an offence under this Act.' Child pornography included pictures of 'a sexual organ or the anal region of a person under the age of eighteen years.' The new law caused great concern among civil libertarians, the arts community, the media, and some lesbian, gay, and bisexual activists. The *Globe and Mail* repeatedly condemned it.[50] The *Toronto Star* also editorialized against the bill, the process by which it was approved, and the 'cynical politicking' that led to its adoption. As the *Star* pointed out, the new law would submit adults to criminal prosecution for portraying sexual relationships between sixteen- and seventeen-year-olds, even though sixteen-year-olds can marry with parental consent.[51]

Legislators ignored the many expressions of concern and supported Bill C-128 with fervour. Speaking for the minister of justice during third reading of the bill, a Tory cabinet minister cited the Fraser Commission findings and *Butler*, as well as the Tory party's 'family caucus,' for the bill's coming to fruition. Other MPs supporting the bill specifically cited *Butler*.[52] Some MPs, notably Liberal Thomas Wappel, wanted to give police broad authority to deal with groups like the North American Man-Boy Love Association (NAMBLA). The parliamentary secretary to the minster of justice spoke at length about NAMBLA during debate on the bill.[53] This concern led to the inclusion in the definition of child pornography of any written material or visual representation that advocates or counsels having sexual relations with persons under the age of eighteen that would be criminal. Under other sections of the Criminal Code, that could include sex with a prostitute under the age of eighteen or consensual anal intercourse between a person over that age and one who is under it.

Some lesbian and gay activists expressed alarm over section 163.1. They feared it would be used to disproportionately target gay men, drawing upon the widespread association of homosexuality with paedophilia and child molestation, particularly among the police and in the judicial system. CLGRO approved a Bill C-128 backgrounder in September 1993 that stated, 'It is fairly obvious, though, that the carrying out of this law will not be equitable. It is intended to be used against paedophiles with the happy optional extra of catching some lesbians, gay men and bisexuals in the net – just as the decision in *Butler*, intended to protect women against the effects of straight male pornography, was first used against a lesbian magazine.'[54] CLGRO's document recalled that 'hysteria against paedophilia has traditionally been used against lesbians and gay men, by accusing us all of being child-molesters.' It added that 'the recurrence of antipaedophile moves at this time [i.e. Bill C-128] is clearly part of the backlash. The right wing feel we have gained too much ground and are seeking a solid-looking position from which to fight back, to push us back.' The backgrounder condemned the use of the term *child* in the new law to describe persons in their teens and *child pornography* to describe pornography depicting those over the legal age of consent. Furthermore, CLGRO observed, while studies have shown that 95 per cent of abusers are heterosexual men, often persons known to the child (fathers, brothers, uncles, etc.), the attack on paedophiles reflected in Bill C-128,

> is not accompanied by the corresponding condemnation of child abuse by family members; no major measures have been undertaken to prevent rape and abuse of children within the family ... Nor is concern shown for improving the treatment of young people by adults, increasing the autonomy of children/young people, or giving them increased power for self-definition or control over their own actions. Legitimate concerns can be expressed about the sexual exploitation of youth by adults, gay and straight, but these are not met by simply forbidding sexual activity. Open discussion of sexuality in the schools, etc, are generally opposed by those who support Bill 128 and such legislation.[55]

CLGRO also jointly published an educational leaflet with a group called Forum 128, established to oppose Bill C-128. *Young People and Sex* was distributed widely. Its primary purpose was to alert individuals to the provisions and far-reaching implications of the new law, noting that 'it will take years for the courts to determine its constitutionality.'[56] EGALE, on the other hand, took a minimalist approach to C-128, calling on gays, lesbians, and bisexuals to ask Liberal and NDP candidates (but not Conservatives) in the 1993 federal election why their party supported it. EGALE did so only from the perspective that it was a 'law that was widely condemned by civil libertarians as a threat to *freedom of expression*' (italics added).[57]

CLGRO's position on the child pornography law generated considerable controversy among gay and lesbian activists. A headline run in *GO Info*, then Ottawa's main gay and lesbian newspaper, on a story reporting CLGRO's adoption of the backgrounder claimed CLGRO endorsed paedophilia, a position it had not, in fact, taken. Enormous pressure was exerted on CLGRO activists, in particular Tom Warner, by other activists who argued that speaking out about Bill C-128 would be portrayed in the media as gays and lesbians supporting paedophiles, and would adversely impact equality-seeking efforts. Especially concerned were members of the CLGRO working group on relationship recognition and activists outside CLGRO who were then in the throes of lobbying the Ontario government to introduce a same-sex relationship bill. Ultimately, CLGRO did not rescind its position. Warner and others in CLGRO believe that this was one of the reasons that led eventually to a new organization, the Campaign for Equal Families, being formed once Bill 167, the Ontario relationships recognition legislation, was introduced in the legislature. CLGRO's experience was an indication of how profoundly difficult it is to attempt to stake out a position that is critical of particular aspects of a law dealing with an explosive issue like child pornography. As Brenda Cossman would later write, in *Xtra!*, in the context of the near hysteria that erupted following a court challenge of the new law, 'Speaking out against the child pornography law has become sacrilege. It runs into a wall of public hostility and outrage that seems almost prerational. Amidst the current hysteria, simply speaking out against the child pornography law makes you a paedophile.'[58] At a time when advocacy groups for gays, lesbians, and bisexuals were focused on seeking acceptance within the mainstream, and the respectability that goes with such acceptance, it is not surprising that no other established queer groups joined CLGRO in its criticism of Bill C-128.

Not long after its adoption, Bill C-128's potential for abuse was vividly demonstrated when charges were laid against an artist, Eli Langer, over paintings he exhibited at a gallery. The works portrayed adults and children in various sexual acts, including masturbation and anal intercourse.[59] The ensuing court case, in the Ontario Court's General Division, focused on the issue of artistic freedom, with the Canadian Conference for the Arts, the Canadian Civil Liberties Association, and PEN Canada intervening to challenge the constitutionality of section 163.1. During the trial, witnesses for the Crown, including a psychologist at Warkworth Penitentiary, testified that Langer's work would be sexually arousing for paedophiles and would be seen as justifying adult-child sex. Artists testified on Langer's behalf, praising the quality of his work and its artistic merit.[60] In April 1995, Justice David McCombs found that Langer's work indeed had artistic merit and did not condone child sexual abuse, but rather lamented the reality of it. He ordered Langer's work returned to him, ruling its seizure an unwarranted violation of the Charter right to freedom of expression. But the judge did not rule on the constitutionality of the child pornography law itself, and, although Langer appealed the part of the decision saying section 163.1 did not violate constitutional rights, the Supreme Court of Canada refused to hear the case.[61]

One controversial provision of section 163.1 banning possession of pornographic materials was contested in a sensational court challenge launched by a sixty-five-year-old man, John Robin Sharpe. Upon returning from the United States, Sharpe had in his possession a manuscript containing short stories he had written under a pseudonym that was seized by Canada Customs. Sharpe was charged with possessing and distributing child pornography under section 163.1. He initially scored a victory when, in January 1999, Justice Duncan Shaw of the British Columbia Supreme Court struck down part of the section as unconstitutional – generating a public fury and attacks on the judiciary. The judge stated the charges presented a profound invasion of freedom of expression and personal privacy, thus violating the Charter. Noting other sections of the Criminal Code protect children from abuse and exploitation arising from pornography, the judge held that the possession prohibition goes too far by outlawing such personal belongings as books, diaries, and pictures. He did not, however, find that all parts of the law are unconstitutional.[62] As soon as the decision was publicized in the media, a torrent of outrage from neoconservatives, religious organizations, and anti-pornography groups led to demands that the judge resign. He was subjected to a barrage of hate messages, and even a death threat. In Ottawa, opposition MPs demanded the federal minister of justice invoke the notwithstanding clause of the Constitution so that the decision would not stand. The government did not do so, but did file an appeal. After the BC Court of Appeal upheld the judgment, the case was appealed to the Supreme Court of Canada and argued in January 2000.[63]

In its submission to the Supreme Court, the Government of Canada argued that the BC appeal court 'seriously underestimated the gravity of the risk of harm to children in comparison to the restriction of the rights of those who want to possess child pornography.' It went on to state, 'It is also clear that visual representations, including those not made using actual children, are used to reinforce distortions, to fuel fantasies and to groom other children for sexual purposes.'[64] At issue in the case was Sharpe's contention that the materials seized were 'works of the imagination' and did not involve real children. On 28 January 2001, the Supreme Court justices upheld the constitutionality of section 163.1, and 'clarified' its provisions by creating very limited exemptions from its application. Materials that are self-authored, self-produced materials entirely for personal use, and visual recordings (videos, photographs, et cetera) for private use were ruled lawful provided they did not themselves describe or depict unlawful activity. Baby photographs, depictions of casual kissing and hugging, and educational, scientific, or medical works also were ruled lawful. The *artistic merit* provision of the law, the court said, 'must be established objectively and should be interpreted as including any expression that may reasonably be viewed as art.' The majority judges added that the *public good* defence afforded by the legislation 'should be liberally construed.' But, as Brenda Cossman noted, 'That the court even had to say all this is a stunning example of just how broad the definition of child pornography is.'[65] Expounding on the harm-based premise of the child pornograpraphy law, the majority of justices noted: 'In adopting s. 163.1(4), Parliament was pursuing the pressing and substantial objective of criminalizing the possession of child pornography that poses a reasoned risk of harm to children. The means chosen by Parliament are rationally connected to this objective. Parliament is not required to adduce scientific proof based on concrete evidence that the possession of child pornography causes harm to children. Rather, a reasoned apprehension of harm will suffice.' Still, a minority of three justices thought the majority went too far. 'Child pornography is harmful whether it involves real children in its production or whether it is a product of the imagination,' they opined.[66] Canada's draconian child pornography law, as a result, remains virtually intact, and is likely to be the subject of ongoing debate and further legal challenges.

Project Guardian

It was not long after CLGRO released its criticism of the new child pornography law that one of its concerns proved prescient. The new law was used in London, Ontario under the pretext of capturing paedophiles, but in fact resulted in 'the happy optional extra of catching some lesbians, gay men and bisexuals in the net.' It occurred in November 1993, after a London teenager pulled a bag of videos from a river where he was fishing and took them home. His mother saw them and turned them over to the police. Using section 163.1, the police launched what they initially called Operation Scoop, which later became Project Guardian. Two men were eventually charged with and convicted of child pornography offences. But over the next few months, dozens of other men were charged with various offences not related to child porn. Gay men were rounded up and arrested after photographs from the videos were shown to students, social workers, and street youths to obtain identification of the individuals in them. Eventually, the list expanded beyond the men in the videos. The result, by May 1994, according to a London police press release, was 521 interviews, eleven search warrants, and the arrest of thirty males. The police also said 'fifty-five victims, ranging in age from eight to seventeen years' had been 'identified.' The charges, 243 on 1,252 counts, included making and possessing child pornography as well as various other sexual and drug-related offences.[67]

The police campaign entered high gear in late May 1994, after some eight hundred videos were seized from the apartment of Buryl Wilson, a high school teacher. Using this incident, the police issued a press release stating, 'This seizure and the resulting investigation will, no doubt, lead to many cities and towns throughout this province. Experience has shown us that this serious problem goes well beyond London. It is a widespread, underground connection of individuals who indiscriminately victimize children for their own pleasure.'[68] London's Chief of Police Julian Fantino then held a sensational press conference, using the seized videotapes as a backdrop, to call upon the provincial government to set up a task force to deal with 'child exploitation.' The Ontario government complied by funding what then became Project Guardian. According to government documents, by the time it wound down in 1996 the project had cost taxpayers $1.57 million not including undisclosed amounts relating to surveillance, witness relocation, and radio communications.[69] By October 1995, Project Guardian had laid 482 charges, 61 dealing with pornography and 249 with other offences involving various sexual activities: obtaining the sexual services of a person under the age of eighteen (190 charges) and having consensual anal intercourse with a person under age eighteen (59 charges).[70] The fact that all of the reported cases involved men and youth or boys fuelled the suspicion of activists that the sole focus of the 'project' was homosexuality. No discernible interest was shown by the London police throughout the duration of Project Guardian for the exploitation of young women and girls by older heterosexual men. The police also habitually described the younger persons involved with consensual sexual acts as 'children' abused and victimized by older predators. The media accepted the police version and carried many stories about child sexual exploitation, as if consenting acts and sexual assault were the same thing. The fact that many of the alleged victims did not see themselves in that role, but rather as consenting participants, was dismissed as irrelevant. One prosecutor told a judge during a trial that the defendant 'directly contributed to the degradation and psychological destruction of his victims and his legacy is that they progressed *to a higher level of homosexual activity*' (emphasis added).[71]

Alarmed by these police tactics and the number of arrests, the gay community led by activists Richard Hudler, Clarence Crossman, and journalist Joseph Couture, plus the Homophile Association of London Ontario (HALO), issued a public statement decrying what they called a witch hunt developing out of the investigation. HALO produced a leaflet, distributed widely in the community, refuting police assertions, repeatedly picked up by the media, that there was a 'ring' of any kind: 'There is no ring of adults passing around boys. There is an informal network of youth – none of whom know all the others. It is the youth who have made connection with various men – few of whom know any of the others.'[72] The group also set up a court watch program to provide legal assistance to those arrested and to monitor the cases.

It became apparent over the course of Project Guardian that inconsistencies existed in witness testimonies. Serious questions were also raised about police methods. The mother of an eight-year-old boy reported by police to be the youngest victim of the ring publicly stated there had been no abuse and denounced the police for persuading her son to make false statements against a man accused by police of fondling him and another boy. The other boy in the alleged incident also denied that fondling took place.[73] Most damning of all, the eight hundred videotapes seized from Buryl Wilson turned out not to be child pornography. They included mainstream American and European films, documentaries, and commercially available pornography. Although Wilson was eventually charged, it was for possession of 8-millimetre films, photographs, and magazines that had no connection to the videos so prominently displayed by Fantino during his child pornography ring press conference.[74] A serious blow to the credibility of police assertions was dealt on 19 March 1996, when Crown attorneys withdrew all pornography charges against Wilson. (He was also charged with indecency and prostitution-related offences.)

Joined by CLGRO, HALO criticized London police attitudes and the targeting of gay men in a joint September 1996 brief, *On Guard: A Critique of Project Guardian*, which called the investigation a witch hunt designed to portray gay men, in the public consciousness, as paedophiles:

> We have used the phrase 'witch-hunt' from time to time in reference to this investigation. The appropriateness of this word lies for us in the fact that a simple accusation of being a witch was enough to cause permanent suspicion and discredit for a woman or man during periods in Western history when there were witch trials. Often the only way a person could demonstrate their 'innocence' was through death in a 'Catch-22' trial.
>
> The modern equivalent to witch-stigma is pedophilia. Men charged with sexual involvement with teenagers, even those who are of legal age to give consent for particular sexual acts, are routinely described by the police and media as being involved with 'children' and 'young boys.' Anyone who speaks up to say that things are not as black and white as they are being presented is also stigmatized.[75]

In the end, the alleged child pornography ring, later refashioned as a child explotation ring, that Fantino had cited as the rationale for establishing Project Guardian, proved not to have existed.[76] Still, the damage had been done, and relations between London's gay community and its police were poisoned for a long time after Project Guardian had ceased.

Challenging the Age of Consent

The other wing of the fight to support the right of young people to sexual self-determination has been challenging the still discriminatory age of consent legislation. A generally negative climate for same-sex activity, especially as it relates to young people, has persisted notwithstanding further Criminal Code amendments adopted by Parliament in 1985, which took effect 1 January 1988. Under those reforms, the old gross indecency offence was repealed and 'buggery' was replaced with 'anal intercourse.' The age of consent was lowered to fourteen years for most acts committed in private by two unmarried persons. Sex was also deemed legal if it involved a consenting individual over the age of twelve and under the age of fourteen and an accused over the age of twelve and under sixteen, and the difference in the ages of the individuals was not more than two years. The notable exception was anal intercourse, which remained illegal for unmarried persons under eighteen.[77] Lowering the age of consent also was countered by the introduction of an offence, punishable by up to five years in prison, where a person obtains, or attempts to obtain, the sexual services of a person under the age of eighteen, 'for consideration.' A conviction could be rendered where there had been sex in exchange for food, housing, clothing, money, drugs, or alcohol. It was this provision London police used during Project Guardian to target gay men involved with consensual sex with males between the ages of fourteen and eighteen.

The higher age of consent for anal intercourse was ultimately found to violate the Charter. In a case known as *Carmen M*, involving a heterosexual couple, a judge in the Ontario Court General Division ruled in 1992 that no evidentiary basis existed 'to conclude there is any legislative purpose in prohibiting consensual acts of anal intercourse by or with young persons aged 14 to 18.' She also found no harmful effect on the public or the individual in respect of a consensual act, and that it was difficult to conclude that such an act 'invokes the moral outrage of the community.' In addition, she stated, the absence of a defence of consent was an infringement of Charter rights. Yet, while acknowledging that there may be an effect of the decision on same-sex situations, she declined to rule in respect of them. The federal government appealed.[78]

The Ontario Court of Appeal granted the Canadian Foundation for Children, Youth and the Law, the Canadian AIDS Society (CAS), and CLGRO intervenor status in 1994. The foundation argued that the unavailability of the defence of consent to those under eighteen constituted age discrimination contrary to section 15 of the Charter. CAS and CLGRO contended the anal intercourse law contravened section 7 of the Charter because it deprived young gay men of their liberty and security of the person. They also held that singling out anal intercourse for special regulation contravened section 15 on the ground of sexual orientation, and that such contravention can not be demonstrably justified in a free and democratic society under section 1. Their factum contended that section 159 of the Criminal Code 'is phrased to distinguish anal intercourse from all other sexual conduct, to make this conduct seem more suspect and morally questionable than vaginal or oral sex.'[79]

In a 26 May 1995 decision, the Ontario Court of Appeal struck down section 159. All three justices found that it discriminated because of age. One justice (the only woman) ruled that the law 'arbitrarily disadvantages gay men by denying to them until they are eighteen a choice available at the age of fourteen to those who are not gay, namely, their choice of sexual expression with a consenting partner to whom they are not married.' A successful sexual orientation challenge thus had to await another case.[80] In a separate case, a Federal Court justice also opined, on 24 February 1995, that section 159 is unconstitutional. He dismissed the government's argument that a different age of consent for anal intercourse is justified to fight HIV transmission and found that the limitation was not reasonable and that there was no legitimate purpose to be served by it.[81]

To date, the federal government has not introduced Criminal Code amendments to comply with these decisions. CLGRO raised the issue with the federal minister of justice, Anne McLellan, in a May 1998 letter in which it expressed 'profound concern' over government inaction. Noting social conservative groups were lobbying to increase the age of consent, CLGRO called for immediate introduction of a Criminal Code amendment to 'establish a uniform age of consent for all sexual acts at 14.' In a February 1999 response, McClellan signalled a likely increase by stating, 'Any provision for a minimum age of consent to sexual activity (heterosexual or homosexual) has, as its major policy purpose, the protection of children from exploitation by adults. As you are no doubt aware, concerns had been raised in this regard prior to the recent cases dealing with section 159, as to whether current Criminal Code protections were sufficient to protect children.'[82] In fact, a government announcement made in late 1999 called for a review of the law, with a view to raising the age of consent for all sexual acts to sixteen or even eighteen. The need for review was presented in the context of protecting children from abuse. Ironically, whereas liberationists fought in the 1970s for abolition of the age of consent, the fight in early part of the twenty-first century now seemed destined to be about opposing that it be raised.

Policing Queer Communities

As the events in London attested, one of the oldest issues raised by lesbian and gay liberationists – police homophobia and harassment – continued to be volatile and controversial. In recent years, policing Canada's queer communities has been characterized by both notable progress to achieve a better rapport through formal liaison processes and renewed concerns over targeted and harassing enforcement. The issue has generated heated passions, with conservative gays and

lesbians and assimilationist activists attempting to emphasize that police homophobia and harassment are largely things of the past, that
police repression of lesbian and gay sexuality has not been a significant
issue since the early 1980s. Instead, they assert, the focus must now be
placed on building processes to liaise with, and educate, police. Incidents involving the enforcement of the Criminal Code, to regulate the
conduct occurring in bars, bathhouses, and public places are dismissed
as not being gay issues. Police actions in such places should no longer
be characterized, they assert, as harassment of gay, lesbian, and bisexual communities, since heterosexuals also are, or at least potentially
can be, charged with offences under those same provisions of the law.
And there is little questioning by conservatives and assimilationists of
the moral values that underlie the laws, particularly that sexual conduct must be restricted to places that are 'private,' or that homophobia
still motivates the actions of police in their vigilant seeking out of queer
sexuality. Liberationists, on the other hand, have sought to address
such issues and have continued to call for the repeal of oppressive sex
laws that criminalize consensual sexual activity, whether same-sex or
heterosexual, under the guise of enforcing morality.

Turning first to police liaison initiatives, it is clear that varying degrees of progress have been made to improve relations with the police
in cities such as Ottawa, Vancouver, Edmonton, and Calgary, although
incidents of police homophobia and widespread mistrust of police by
gays, lesbians, and bisexuals remain prevalent. In Ottawa, a formal
police liaison process was initiated in 1989 following a series of gay
bashings, through the Ottawa-Hull Lesbian and Gay Task Force on
Violence that, in 1991, became a permanent Ottawa-Carleton Police
Liaison Committee for Lesbian, Gay, Bisexual and Transgendered Communities. It later issued a report on police relations containing forty
recommendations. While not all were accepted, the police responded
positively by agreeing to document anti-gay and anti-lesbian violence,
establishing a dedicated gay bashing line and issuing statements condemning gay bashing. A bias crime unit was also set up to investigate
crimes involving hate, such as gay bashings.[83] The committee has grown
over the years, to the point where, by 2000, according to David Pepper,
a gay man hired by the force to be director of community development,
'The chief has publicly denounced hate crimes and the liaison committee is directly accountable to him.' Carroll Holland, active in the committee since its inception, has been so positive about the liaison process
that she dismissed as having 'their mindsets in the '80s' members of

queer communities who believe that working with the police is, in the more radical terms used by *Capital Xtra!*, 'antithetical to being queer.'[84]

The results of liaison processes in Edmonton and Vancouver have been more mixed. Gay and Lesbian Alliance member Liz Massiah noted in 1997 that formal liaison in Edmonton, begun five years earlier, was not being taken seriously by most police officers. While senior management was supportive, middle management was not, and no significant commitment had been made to conducting education on sexual orientation issues. In addition, there were at that time no out lesbian and gay cops in the city.[85] Progress was made in Vancouver in 1995 after the police launched a public relations campaign encouraging gays and lesbians to join the force. Police also joined an anti-homophobia poster campaign with the Gay and Lesbian Centre. By the end of the year, weekly police drop-ins at the centre were held and sensitivity training sessions on homophobia were developed for officers. Unfortunately, the success of these initiatives was tainted by renewed mistrust of police after homophobic incidents involving police officers became known publicly. One featured police abuse of a prominent AIDS activist, John Kozachenko, who was called 'faggot' and 'queer' when being held in custody.[86] More positively, Vancouver's chief of police made an important symbolic gesture of goodwill towards the city's queer communities when he led a small group of openly gay police officers in the 1997 pride parade. He also told the media that he was committed to 'providing fair, equitable police service to all the people in the city,' and, as an employer, 'to send a strong message to our employees that they'll be treated fairly and equitably by the same standards.'[87]

Calgary's police liaison initiative was reinstituted in 1996, over a decade after the first unsuccessful effort. The Calgary Gay and Lesbian Community Police Liaison Committee strove to promote communication, education, and awareness, identify and resolve crime and concerns about safety, and increase police awareness on community issues.[88] Information on gay and lesbian issues became part of diversity training for police officers and a study was made of gay bashing incidents. Education was conducted on how officers should respond to domestic abuse in same-sex relationships. Calgary's police chief appeared on the front cover and was interviewed in the November 1997 issue of the city's gay paper.[89] But within the Calgary police force, homophobia and heterosexism continued to create problems for gay and lesbian officers. A closeted gay male officer who did not know any other gay officers noted in a 1997 magazine interview that negative perceptions existed in upper management. 'There is no real direction from up top as far as acceptance and [having] some policies on it.' In the same interview, a closeted lesbian officer stated, 'We need to be very strong women. We need to be tough. Basically, perceptions are that you are either sleeping with your partner, so you're a slut, or you're gay if you're not sleeping with your partner.'[90]

In contrast with the experiences of these other cities, Toronto and Montreal have witnessed ongoing organizing against police harassment, and policing issues have continued to dominate community advocacy much more so than the establishment of police liaison processes. Efforts to improve relations between the queer communities and police in Montreal consisted, in the early 1990s, mainly of periodic meetings between members of the community and the police in response to a series of murders of gay men and acts of police harassment and violence. The situation worsened in the early morning of 15 July 1990, when police raided the Sex Garage, a loft party attended by over three hundred people, mostly gay men and lesbians. Partiers accused police of beating them with nightsticks, using homophobic verbal abuse, and making threats of violence. Eight people were arrested.[91] Angry gays and lesbians responded with a sit-in for two hours on Ste Catherine Street. The next day, during a demonstration outside a police station, more than seventy police officers in riot gear attacked two hundred lesbians and gay men, arresting forty-eight protesters. One demonstrator was hospitalized after being taken into the police station. He claimed police kicked him in the shoulder and spine, clubbed him twice in the groin, and threw him against a wall. Other demonstrators said that police, wearing latex gloves, clubbed and choked them with their sticks.[92] A new group, Lesbians and Gays against Violence, was formed in response to these events and to address police brutality and homophobia, and some of its members served on the police's minority relations committee.[93] Another group, started in 1993, La Table de concertation des lesbiennes et gais de grand Montréal, called for a Quebec Human Rights Commission inquiry into the unsolved murders of a number of gay men and the increase of violent acts against members of the community generally. The commission agreed, issuing a 1994 report that, among other things, called for improved relations between the police and lesbians and gay men.[94] Some improvement did occur thereafter. Encouragingly, by 1999, a number of Montreal's gay and lesbian police officers reached the point of being able to come out of the closet, with a contingent of them marching that year in the gay pride parade. One of the officers, Patrick Lavallée, lived openly in a same-sex relationship with fellow officer, André Proulx, and headed a thirty-member Assocation for Gay Police Officers and Firefighters in Quebec.[95]

Police liaison, in a formal and ongoing sense, did not develop in Toronto until the mid-1990s, and even then remained ad hoc and without roots in the activist communities. After the various raids on gay bathhouses in the early 1980s, the idea of liaison was rejected by most of the city's activists. Some community members did meet periodically with police to discuss community issues and participated in police education forums. And a neighborhood committee involving police and gay community members was eventually established and has functioned for several years in the downtown Church-Wellesley area. A handful of lesbian and gay community members also did collosal work conducting training sessions on sexual orientation for police officers. More typical of the policing climate in Toronto, however, have been periodic harassment and targeted enforcement. Police homophobia greeted the 1991 appointment of Laura Rowe to the Toronto's Police Services Board after she publicly identified herself as a lesbian. The result was, according to one press report, 'a smelly smear campaign' designed to discredit her. Stories were leaked to the press that she was suspected of being involved in criminal activity. Another report alleged a child had been sexually abused in her home. Fortunately, Rowe was cleared of all suspicion after a police investigation. These actions, Rowe later noted, were caused by fear on the part of police officers. 'They were terrified of having a lesbian on the board.'[96]

Homophobia among Toronto police officers continued to cause concern throughout the 1990s, both within the police force and outside of it. An openly gay police officer, Constable Brian Aguiar, stated publicly in 1991 how shocked he was at the attitudes he encountered. 'They [used] abnormal methods to make life miserable at work,' he said. There also were acts of harassment, like finding pink feathers in his gun and having supervisors pursue trivial complaints to the maximum extent permitted. During a roll call, he was 'bombarded with a barrage of insults' because others thought he might have AIDS.[97] More dangerous for Aguiar was the fact that he found himself working alone more than would normally be the case, including being assigned to patrol duties at night without an another officer accompanying him. 'Other officers don't want to work with you because you're gay,' he was told. On one night patrol, another officer, upon seeing an effeminate man, stated the man 'should be shot and pissed on.'[98] Sadly, little seems to have changed in the ensuing years. As late as 1999, Aguiar was commenting in the media that being gay or lesbian on the force was 'hell.' 'Everyone's in the closet, pretty much,' he lamented. Hostility and lack of career advancement remained obstacles. 'There's too much harassment and discouragement, and not enough support.'[99] Lesbian police officers have also faced daunting challenges if they attempt to come out. Judith Nosworthy, a lesbian officer with the Toronto police, has spoken publicly about the negative impact of a small group of homophobic officers.[100] Nevertheless, some progress was made in 2001, when Nosworthy was appointed as the first full-time liaison officer to the lesbian and gay community.

Equally problematic have been a militant Toronto police union long believed by many community activists to be a hotbed of homophobes, and a craving for respectability among growing legions of gays, lesbians, and bisexuals willing to tolerate police crackdowns against undesirable sexual behavior. Members of the police union, in recent years, have been aggressive in visiting gay and lesbian bars, bathhouses, and licensed social events. Using the provisions of the liquor licensing law to enter such places, they have laid bawdy house, indecency, disorderly conduct, and other charges. Such actions have been vigorously denounced by militant activists in the community for whom they are echoes of the police harassment more typical of earlier decades. Such actions are also seen as being consistent with what Susan Eng, the former chair of the Toronto Police Services Board, described in a recent *Globe and Mail* article as a police subculture in which 'police buy into the social heirarchies the rest of us deny exist. The police subculture makes a distinction between people the police will do things *for* and people they do things *to*.' Police believe that there are certain 'criminal classes,' observed Eng, add that 'the public buys into this: A significant proportion see themselves as those the police will do things for and not to – they see themselves as upstanding citizens who need protection from the criminal elements.'[101]

Eng's analysis succinctly describes the dynamics at play in recent years between Toronto's police and certain types of behaviour within the gay community, as well as the sharp divisions that have emerged within the queer communities over police actions. Many police still tend to view the sexuality happening in queer spaces as criminal, as well as disgusting and socially undesirable. Within the lesbian, gay, and bisexual communities there also exists a growing element who see themselves as 'respectable,' professionals and business people living in upscale neighborhoods. These upstanding citizens don't go to (or don't publicly admit going to) sex clubs or bathhouses or engage in sex in public places, which are presumed to be frequented by gays and lesbians who are not respectable, whose behaviour 'gives gays and lesbians a bad name.' These so-called respectable gays want the police to do things for them, like keeping their streets safe from drug dealers and prostitutes, and free from the homeless and destitute. In exchange, they support police actions against the bars, bathhouses, and other establishments, even if, on occasion, police conduct may be excessive or targeted. As Eng stated, 'The people police do things for may be willing [to] overlook these [police] misdemeanours. As far as the officers are concerned, it is only those people they do things to who criticize them – and those people don't have much power.'[102] In contrast, a tenacious but admittedly small band of Toronto activists still largely see the queer communities as being in the category of people the police do things to, and continue to speak out, and organize against, police raids and other actions.

It was against this backdrop of conflicting attitudes that a series of police raids on Toronto queer spaces, bars, and bathhouses, took place in recent years focusing on sexual conduct or other activity deemed to be in contravention of the Criminal Code or the liquor licence laws. But unlike the police crackdowns of the 1970s and early 1980s – especially unlike the police raids on bathhouses in 1981 – forging community consensus was difficult, and considerable efforts were made to marginalize or dismiss the concerns raised by those who spoke out. The events began in 1996 after a raid on Remington's, a gay strip club that led to bawdy house and other indecency-related charges against nineteen staff, dancers, and customers. Primarily known for its male strippers, Remington's had private booths where dancers performed for customers for pay. The indecent theatrical performance charges arose from the 'Monday Night Sperm Attack,' during which dancers ejaculated on stage.[103] Police justified their raid by citing recent raids on two straight strip clubs, during which charges had been laid due to 'lap dances' performed by female strippers for male customers. A 1997 Supreme Court of Canada decision upheld the legality of municipal bylaws prohibiting lap dancing, which it deemed an indecent theatrical performance. Police officials argued that gay establishments therefore were not being singled out. Yet, while the charges caused alarm in some quarters, little was done to organize a community response. Initial attempts at forming a coalition to reform the bawdy house laws, consisting of members the National Leather Association and Maggie's, a prostitutes' rights group, did not come to fruition. Instead, city council-lor Kyle Rae and Bob Gallagher, a gay activist who worked in the office of another city councillor, attempted to manage the issue through meetings with police officials, and media statements criticizing the deployment of police resources for the action, but generally downplaying its significance. Gallagher, featured along with Rae in a *Globe and Mail* news story, dismissed fears of a repeat of the 1981 raids. 'There was some concern at first that this was the tip of the iceberg. But I think since then there have been some very encouraging sounds coming from the police. It's clear a lot of senior people in the department are leery about backing this kind of operation.'[104] Rae told *Xtra!*, 'I can't believe they've spent money on this kind of activity when ... it's consenting adults. I can't get [the police] to clean up the crack dealers in Allan Gardens. Where's the panic in the community saying we need to clean this up? There isn't any.'[105] But these public pronouncements were devoid of any suggestion of targeted policing or homophobia within police ranks. It was also hard to sustain community interest, as the trials of the accused dragged on for three years. In mid-1999, the Crown quietly dropped its bawdy house charges against eleven dancers and four customers. However, charges of keeping a common bawdy house and permitting an indecent theatrical performance were continued against the manager.[106] Finally, in December 1999, a judge of the Ontario Court of Justice found that Sperm Attack Mondays 'exceeded the contemporary Canadian community standard of tolerance' and pronounced the manager guilty of the charges.[107]

A radically different response, and a return to advocacy more clearly rooted in lesbian and gay liberation analysis, resulted from police actions in the summer of 1999 following four separate police visits to the Bijou, a self-described 'porn bar' in downtown Toronto in which men engaged in consensual sex in dark rooms and at a 'slurp ramp.' Nineteen bar patrons were arrested for committing indecent acts. The owner was charged with liquor license offences. During the police actions, a Bijou employee was handcuffed, taken into custody for several hours, and strip-searched. He was charged with obstructing a peace officer after assisting some Bijou patrons to escape to avoid arrest.[108] Large and angry community meetings protested the raids. From this uprising came the June 13 Committee, a new group dedicated to lesbian and gay liberation principles and to monitoring police actions, organizing community responses, and advocating for changes to the sex laws. At a press conference, the committee, joined by CLGRO, called for the dropping of all charges against those arrested at the Bijou, and criticized the misuse of police resources for such actions. Meetings between police officials, gay businesses, and councillor Kyle Rae, along with the public pressure exerted by community activists, resulted in the eventual dropping of the charges against all Bijou customers.[109]

Backlash and hositility was generated towards the undeniably large-scale community organizing that took place in the aftermath of the Bijou raids, indicative of the conservatism that had gripped Toronto's community, and the desire to maintain an image of respectability. The resurgence of activism in defence of liberated sexuality, and the condemnation of police harassment, were portrayed as minority views and throwbacks to the now bygone days of gay liberation militancy. A campaign was launched to dismiss the militant responses and to marginalize and discredit the June 13 Committee and others who spoke out against the police. Prominent in that campaign was *fab*, a gay entertainment and lifestyle magazine with a decidedly conservative and assimilationist bent. Refusing to find fault with the police or even to characterize the actions at the Bijou as raids, *fab* became a forum for those wanting to trash the more radical voices in the community and defend the police. In a lengthy feature interview in *fab* with Kyle Rae shortly after the Bijou raids, Rae commented,

> There are some people who are one-tune activists and that is they have only one way in which they think issues can be resolved, and that is by confrontation. Some people want to reconstruct the victim, right. We're victims again. There's other people who want to get angry and have a demonstration. That's what I used to do in '81 but now we've had changes to the Ontario Human Rights Code, we've got an Ontario Human Rights Code that we're included in, we have a Charter of Rights and Freedoms. The world isn't 1981 anymore but there's a bunch of dinosaurs who can only react in one way and have taught people that this is the only way that we can achieve what we want. When in fact, it isn't. You've elected me and I'm now at the table making decisions and working with the City, with the police, with the community trying to resolve them.[110]

Anti-activist in its editorial views, *fab* continued its attack on police critics in a second feature article a few weeks later in which the author, John Kennedy, referred to 'alarmists' in the community, and quoted Brent Hawkes of the Metropolitan Community Church as saying, 'Times are changing and we have to change our tactics, change our style to what's more effective today. As the community gets more rights and feels less and less threatened, they're not going to jump behind the first person who wants to start a protest.' As for activists who condemned the Bijou raids, Hawkes advised the broader community, 'Be careful that the extremes in our community don't cause people to be paranoid. Those who play the paranoia card do our community a real disservice.' The article also quoted both Hawkes and Rae as debunking concerns expressed by the June 13 Committee, CLGRO, and others that the community needed to remain vigilant over the increasingly likely prospect of a raid on a bathhouse. Rae declared emphatically that 'there is absolutely no interest on the part of the police to go into the bathhouses ... there is no one who is going near the bathhouses.'[111]

fab editor John Kennedy added his voice in a regularly published column in which he accused those protesting the raid on the Bijou of being 'a vocal minority.' 'People were grandstanding and suggesting that we deserve special rights under the law and that we're not going to sit back and let the police tell us what to do. Nonsense. The equal rights we fought so hard for come with equal responsibilities.'[112] Another *fab* writer, Rob Wilson, struck a similar note, proclaiming, 'Even though the overwhelming majority of gay men reacted to the fuss [over the Bijou] with a giant yawn, a small but vocal group of activists used the opportunity to antagonize the cops and demand the right to have sex anywhere they please. Years and years of fighting for legal equality and trying to convince society that gays don't want special rights – just equal rights – quickly went down the drain.'[113] Others joined the chorus, including John Coulbourn, a former Albertan living in Toronto, who wrote about the Bijou in Calgary's *Outlooks*, stating, 'I'm not sure it is a gay issue at all, in light of the fact that similar charges had been brought in Quebec, against the straight owner of a straight swingers' club where men and women had public sex.' Instead, he opined, the issue was one for 'libertarians of all bents and persuasions who feel that what consenting adults do in the exclusive company of other consenting adults is none of anybody's business but their own.'[114]

But in fact the June 13 Committee, CLGRO, and others protesting the raid did not seek 'special rights,' and did not argue that the issue was exclusively a gay one. They took a liberation approach that sought greater sexual freedom and amendment of laws that are used, in a selective or targeted way against gays, prostitutes, and heterosexuals whose sexual activities (so-called swingers' clubs, SM, et cetera) are outside the mainstream social mores. In a leaflet circulated after the raids, the June 13 Committee demanded that 'the charges against the

Bijou patrons and staff be dropped, that the raids stop, that police be accountable to the community, *and that the vague, outdated laws governing private consensual sex be reformed'* (emphasis added).[115] Moreover, the allegation that protesting the police actions in the Bijou case had set back hard-won equality gains was preposterous. The amendment of Ontario laws to recognize same-sex relationships occurred in the midst of the protests and, in fact, Tom Warner, who was a spokesperson for the June 13 Committee, was also a spokesperson for CLGRO during the efforts to secure adoption of the relationship recognition bill.

Significantly, despite the views expressed by Rae, Hawkes, and writers in *fab*, police continued a policy of harassment. Throughout the summer and fall of 1999, police issued warnings to four Toronto gay bars that resulted in the closing of backrooms used for sexual contact. Three of the four bars catered to leather and SM crowds.[116] In April 2000, the owner of the Barn, a bar with a leather and SM clientelle that for several years had been the venue of 'naked night' parties for members of Totally Naked Toronto Men Enjoying Nudity (TNT Men), was charged with permitting disorderly conduct, in contravention of the Liquor Licence Act. The charge followed a visit by police to one of the naked night events.[117] The charge was laid although no sexual acts were observed (or permitted by the organizers). Similarly, charges relating to liquor licence offences were laid in November 2000 against another leather/SM bar, the Toolbox, after police visited a naked night held there.[118]

Community anger was rekindled after five male police officers, in the early morning of 14 September 2000, visited the Club Baths, where three hundred women were participating in the Pussy Palace, a popular lesbian bathhouse event that been held annually for three years. The officers knocked on closed doors, took down the names of women at the event, and were 'intimidating and imposing' according to Women's Bathhouse Committee member Janet Rowe. The fact that the event was licensed provided the opportunity for the police visit and, ultimately, for laying charges against two event organizers: three counts of disorderly conduct, and one count each of failing to provide sufficient security, serving alcohol outside the prescribed area, and serving liquor outside the prescribed hours. The lawyer for the women promised a vigorous defence: 'I will be asking the courts to stay the proceedings on the basis that the police investigation violated constitutional norms under the Charter of Rights and Freedoms.'[119] In response, Kyle Rae, no longer trying to deny the possibility of a bathhouse raid, issued a scathing press release denouncing the action as a 'panty raid' and a waste of police time and resources. Within days, other politicians and community spokespersons also spoke out against the raid. Several hundred people attended a community protest meeting, following which about four hundred marched on police headquarters. A second demonstration about a month later, billed as a Panty Picket, attracted over one hundred people. A Women's Bath House Legal Defense Fund was struck, that quickly raised more than $10,000 for the legal challenge.[120] Predictably, *fab* dismissed all these events, characterizing as 'the overstatement of the year' a June 13 Committee statement in a press release that the raid on the Pussy Palace was 'the worst attack on a bathhouse in 20 years.' *fab* claimed once more that the 'gay community largely reacted to the incident with a collective yawn.'[121] On 31 January 2002, a judge of the Ontario Court stayed the charges, criticizing the police for violating the constitutional right of privacy of the women at the Pussy Palace.[122]

Given the worsening relations and the increased police harassment, it is no surprise that many lesbian, gay, and bisexual activists reacted with alarm in late 1999 at the prospect that Julian Fantino would be appointed chief of Toronto's police. The causes were varied: the record of Project Guardian in London, while Fantino was chief there; his strained relations with Toronto's Black community over his release of race-based crime data while having been on the Toronto force previously; his reputation as a cop's cop; and his vocal opposition to civilian oversight of police actions, expressed principally in his disparaging of the Special Investigations Unit, which investigated activities like police shootings. With the likelihood of Fantino's appointment looming, CLGRO, the June 13 Committee, and about a dozen other groups representing youth, anti-poverty activists, and people of colour, held a press conference, circulating an open letter urging that he not be appointed.[123] However, Fantino ultimately was appointed and then spent considerable time meeting with members of the gay, lesbian, and bisexual communities in a public relations effort to overcome the legacy of his term as chief in London. Predictably, some within the communities moved quickly to embrace the new chief. One of those, noted an article in *Now* magazine, was 'a member of the Church-Wellesley committee who's more concerned about cracking down on crackheads than community policing or whether Fantino's going to close neighbourhood bathhouses in one of those law-and-order binges of his when he takes over.' This gay man, who later became the chair of the neighbourhood committee, was quoted as saying he wanted Fantino to know 'there is a moderate voice in this community.'[124] *fab*, in an exclusive interview with Fantino shortly after his appointment, gave the chief a chance to attack CLGRO and the other groups which had spoken out. 'A lot of it is quite unfair, erroneous and devoid of fact,' Fantino claimed. 'I don't think it was useful to engage in rhetoric when passion was inflamed.' Later in the article, Fantino expressed 'faith in the [gay and lesbian] community, in its depth of caring and leadership. We can't allow radical elements of any community to jeopardize our efforts to understand each other.'[125] One of the meetings Fantino did have during those early days was at a gay restaurant, hosted by the Fraternity, a group for gay professionals and business people in which, not surprisingly, 'radical elements' were hardly represented.

Certainly, little occurred during the first year of Fantino's leadership of the Toronto police to indicate that anything on the scale of Project Guardian was in the offing in the city. But the raid on the Pussy Palace, and Fantino's rush within the days immediately following it to once more denounce 'rhetoric' that is inflammatory were not encouraging for the long-term prospects of improved relations with the gay, lesbian, and bisexual communities.[126] Activists also awaited an indication that homophobia on the part of individual police officers was being addressed, and that the climate for gays and lesbians within the police force was improving so that more of them would feel free and safe to come out. It seemed apparent that the differences and conflicts between more radical liberationists and the accommodation politics of conservative activists would continue to play out, without resolution, concerning Toronto's police using sex and liquor laws to target and harass expressions of queer sexuality.

Fighting for Queer Space and Queer Values

Liberationists, in addition to challenging archaic and sex-negative laws and the repressive actions of the police, have, over the last fifteen years, also advocated for the concept of queer space and queer community values. As we have seen, same-sex activity committed other than in private in the most restricted capacity, is still viewed by police, the justice system, and by a significant proportion of the heterosexual majority, as criminal, deviant, antisocial and repugnant. Advocating for queer space is a defiant response. An important element of such advocacy is the assertion that, in queer space, the standards of tolerance of the lesbian, gay, and bisexual communities should prevail, not those of the heterosexual mainstream. Through such advocacy, the sexual politics of lesbian and gay liberation were recast for the 1990s. Asserting the right to engage in liberated sexuality in queer spaces, or even simply the expression of 'queerness,' was positioned in a much broader, more ideological context. Lesbian and gay liberationists asserted the right to have sex and/or be nude in certain places determined by the state to be public. Queer space, they argued, applied to any place gays, bisexuals, lesbians and transgendered people congregate in significant numbers, enabling them, rather than the dominant heterosexual society, to determine acceptable and unacceptable behaviour. Bars and clubs, gay bathhouses, secluded places in parks late at night, rooms used by gay, lesbian, and bisexual groups for meetings, and even highly public events such as Pride Day become places that are 'queered.' They are transformed and redefined.

Displays of drag, leather culture, and sadomashocism in public but queered places, or at public events where gays, lesbians, bisexuals, and transgendered people gather, are acceptable to those present as celebrations of sex-positive and gender-bending diversity. Nudity in queer spaces becomes a glorification of the human body in all of its ages, shapes, sizes, and beauty. Sex in queer spaces becomes liberating. As Gerald Hannon suggested in an article supporting gay sex in public but secluded places, 'Though no one I spoke to (not the police, not city councillors, not parks department managers, not citizens' groups like Park Watch) would concede that consensual sex is a legitimate park activity, I think we have to begin by declaring that it is, and then decide as a community when and where it is appropriate.' (Hannon, however, did not use the term 'queer space.')[127] Attempts by the state or heterosexual social institutions to assert or reassert authority over queer spaces have been fiercely resisted. So, too, have efforts of those within gay, lesbian, and bisexual communities who see such queer manifestations as setting back the cause of 'equality and acceptance.' Desperate for accommodation within the mainstream, assimilationists denounce various activities, even when occurring in queer spaces, as giving gays, lesbians, and bisexuals 'a bad image,' and support their curtailment, including by means of police action.

The concept of queer space, and the debate over which community standards should govern it, featured prominently in court cases arising from the bawdy house and indecent theatrical performance charges against Remington's. The trials raised the issue of community standards of tolerance, both in respect of the broad community of heterosexuals and within the gay, lesbian, bisexual, and transgendered communities. The police and prosecution argued that the activities in the club, which legally is a public place, went beyond community standards of tolerance. The defendants claimed what went on in Remington's did not violate gay community standards. According to the testimony of veteran gay activist George Hislop, the act of ejaculation on stage would not be seen by gays as indecent, shocking, or offensive.[128] Sociology professor and gay activist Gary Kinsman testified that sexual expression was important to the gay identity and community. He pointed out significant differences between gay and heterosexual erotic performances: women dancers in straight strip clubs are victims of the discrimination and social oppression faced by women in society generally because of pervasive sexism. The situation for male performers is much different, he noted. 'There is not a generalized relationship of oppression or sexism [among men], but rather a relationship of equality.'[129] Unfortunately, the judge in the case dismissed as lacking credibility all of the gay community activists who spoke about queer community values and standards of tolerance, ruling instead that Sperm Attack Mondays exceeded the contemporary Canadian community standard of tolerance. Queer space, as a legal concept, had been rejected, at least for the time being.[130] Similarly, as previously discussed, the Supreme Court of Canada, in the *Little Sister's* case, gave short shrift to any notion of a standard for queer communities, in respect of pornography, that differs from that for heterosexuals.

Queer space, and the desire to push the enevelope in respect of community standards of tolerance, have stirred controversy in lesbian, gay, bisexual, and transgendered communities. Debates raged in Toronto following the raids on the Bijou over what should, and should not, be permissible in gay bars. It was for many simply a demand to have 'the right to have sex anywhere they please,' and was cast, quite wrongly, in some of the public meetings as an issue promoted only by older sex-crazed white men. Similarly, lesbian and gay pride events, at least in Toronto, have generated heated confrontations over queer space and queer values. Topless lesbians have led the charge, arguing that that there is a sexist double standard in society about women appearing bare-breasted in public when men are able to be bare-chested anywhere without comment or condemnation. Women who do so are considered to have committed indecent exposure, are obscene, and risk criminal sanction. Tomiye Ishida, writing in *Capital Xtra!* in 1997, noted, 'The issue arises in the interpretation of the law regarding what constitutes "indecent exposure." Decent or indecent, sexual or non-sexual – a moralistic and subjective judgment.'[131] Increasingly, however, pride events, intended to celebrate the liberation of sexuality and challenge contemporary mores, are seen as appropriate venues – queer spaces – for women to be bare-breasted.

Fully nude marchers in Toronto's pride parade have been even more contentious. TNT Men caused controversy in the 1997 parade when the group's members marched in the nude. TNT member David Drascic put forward a liberationist view on the subject by asking, 'How can we claim to be proud of our sexuality, how can we celebrate our lives in all their complexity and wonder, and yet be ashamed of our bodies.'[132] Another TNT Men member expressed similar sentiments just before the 1998 parade. 'Anyone who finds my bare bum and dick offensive, please look away,' stated Peter Grey who had 'marched naked and proud' in previous years. Grey and others took the view that nudity should be acceptable in queer spaces. 'Pride Day seems the perfect venue to make a political statement about body acceptance and to call for social change.'[133]

But such views are, by no means, universal within lesbian, gay, bisexual, and transgendered communities. Sharp divisions have emerged, and vituperative discourse has been launched, between conservatives and assimilationists on one side and liberationists and sex radicals on the other. Among the many letters published in *Xtra!* about nudity during pride day, one appearing in 1998 is illustrative of the opposition that has been voiced. A gay man adamantly maintained that the pride march was not really the place for nudity. Such 'exhibitionism' is an indication of 'insecurity,' he wrote, which detracts from celebrating the community's fights over many years against injustice.[134] Another gay man expressed the view that marching in the nude and exhibiting SM behaviour had 'nothing to with being gay. It does not represent the stuggles that gay men and women endured to bring us to where we are today.' He asked that nudists wear clothes and sadomasochists 'leave your fetish at home.'[135] Toronto's Pride Day Committee angered many in the community when, in 1998, it publicly encouraged marchers to stay clothed and threatened to inform police if nudity was encountered. Later, some marchers were enraged over an incident resulting in the arrest of a nude woman, after police were summoned by pride committee marshalls. To make matters worse, when the marchers began chanting, 'Shame, shame' and 'Keep your laws off our bodies,' the marshalls turned their backs to them, giving the impression that they were protecting the police from the marchers.[136]

THIRTEEN

Identity, Community, and Visibility at the End of the Millennium

The lesbian and gay liberation imperatives of fostering positive identity, building community, and asserting visibility have not diminished, despite the great progress towards achieving legal equality made over the last thirty years. In fact, these imperatives were manifest in many ways at the end of the millennium, continuing the inexorable transformation that began in the late 1960s, flowing ever outward in two significant ways. First, they flowed from the largest urban centres to many smaller, geographically isolated and rural places. Secondly, the racial and ethnic homogeneity of historical lesbian, gay, and bisexual communities gradually evolved into multicultural and multiracial diversity, to include gays, lesbians, and bisexuals who are people of colour, Aboriginal peoples, and members of various ethnocultural communities. In the process, both old and new challenges had to be confronted, and the necessity of combatting homophobia and heterosexism in new contexts had to be addressed. Doing so meant something other than simply pursuing legal equality. It required for new generations of gays, lesbians, and bisexuals, just as it did for the first few brave liberation pioneers of three decades ago, asserting, publicly and unapologetically, pride in same-sex sexuality. It involved, as always, liberating that sexuality through coming out of the closet, and organizing queer people so that they have safe and welcoming places to congregate, and so that the larger heterosexual community takes notice. But it also meant acknowledging and addressing issues of racism and marginalization within queer communities, as well as challenging the now traditional notion of 'community' itself.

Struggling to be Visible outside the Big Cities

Many Canadian lesbians, gays, and bisexuals, at the beginning of the twenty-first century, still live in isolation and fear. The debates over queer space and what occurs within them take place in an entirely different world from the one which they actually inhabit and in which they hope to survive. In the small cities, towns, and villages, and in the rural or isolated areas of Canada, they continue to struggle, often alone, and with great vulnerability, against homophobia and heterosexism. They fight to develop or maintain positive self-images and identities, and strive valiantly to develop networks for survival in the face of great adversity. In fact, simply being open and honest about their sexual orientation can, and often does, result in confrontation or hostility, social exile, discriminatory treatment and, sometimes, acts of violence. In far too many places in Canada, even after thirty years of the lesbian and gay movement, the forces of homophobia and bigotry frequently threaten to overwhelm them. 'The religious right and Christian fundamentalists are still very strong,' commented Calgary gay activist Stephen Lock in 1997.[1]

The isolation, social ostracism, and hostility experienced by lesbians, gays, and bisexuals living in small communities can be severe. One recent example is a lesbian who moved to the Gulf Islands of British Columbia and encountered profound social isolation. She didn't know whether to feel safe or to whom she could come out as a lesbian as there were no visible gay or lesbian social networks. She eventually joined a small 'Women's Spirituality Evening' but met 'silence, stares, a gap in the discussion' each time she mentioned being lesbian; the other women didn't feel safe talking about it.[2] Hers is not an anomalous situation. A 1998 study by the Quebec Council on the Status of Women similarly reported the difficulties Quebec lesbians continue to face in coming out publicly. Of the women surveyed, only 40 per cent had told their heterosexual friends about their sexual orientation. Revealingly, only 11 per cent had come out of the closet in their workplaces.[3] Two other lesbians living in a Quebec town of two thousand people, who met over an Internet chat line, had rocks thrown at their house after it became known they were living together. The mother of one of the women, who lives only twenty minutes from the couple's home, had not spoken to her daughter since she came out.[4]

AIDS Saskatoon education coordinator Antonia Botting observed in a 1996 interview that right wing fundamentalism and an overwhelming sense of isolation characterize the lives of gays, lesbians, and bisexuals attempting to come out in central and northern Saskatchewan. The common lament was, 'There are no gay people here, which in some cases is true.' Gays and lesbians, Botting noted, 'get the hell out of town as quickly as possible.'[5] In the same article, a sixteen-year-old growing up in Peterborough, Ontario, recounted the physical attacks and verbal harassment she received after coming out. 'I would sit on the playground and have rocks thrown at my head. I bled. And I went and complained to the principal and he said that if I wasn't so openly bisexual there would not be this kind of problem and that it was my own fault and that I was provoking the kids to do it.'[6] A high school student in Bradford, Ontario, told the *Toronto Star* in 1999 that people known or suspected of being gay have been threatened, harassed, subjected to physical assaults, endured homophobic graffiti, and had their personal property vandalized.[7]

Paul Pasenan, active with Sudbury All Gay Alliance in the early 1990s, commented in a 1994 interview that Ontario's North generally did not offer a very safe environment for gays and lesbians: 'I can really see where our society as a whole has a long way to go, you know. I mean, the attitude is, if you're gay, get out of town. Go to Toronto where in some small little area of some big city you'll be accepted and can walk down the street and hold your head high. But not here.'[8] In Thunder Bay, gays and lesbians seeking escape to a larger community with a more established queer community, even for a short visit, are faced with travelling several hundred miles. And even in 1999, the city's only gay bar was an unmarked building with windows painted black. Finding out about the social scene required making contacts with other people, or approaching the AIDS Committee of Thunder Bay. For one young lesbian quoted in *Xtra!* the only option was moving elsewhere. 'You can't be out here. There's no place for gay teens to go and be themselves.'[9]

Similar difficulties face gays, lesbians, and bisexuals in the Canadian north. The remoteness of the communities, the difficulties of travelling in areas with no roads, the sparse populations spread over a vast geographic area, and the low level of urbanization present particular challenges. Living in the Yukon means 'being paranoid that someone will see me and my lover together,' commented a lesbian named Ann in a 1987 newspaper interview. 'We always have to be careful.' Another lesbian, identified as Barb in the same interview, added, 'It's like you live a deep dark secret that you can't tell anyone about so it feels like you are lying all the time.' Summing up the difficulties of life in the North, she lamented, 'Many other lesbians are closeted and many of us don't even acknowledge our sexuality to each other. It's difficult to talk and find support.' They accepted isolation, secrecy, and fear as part of their lifestyle because of the hostility towards gays and lesbians that existed in their communities.[10] A decade later, gays and lesbians in the North were still 'looking for opportunities to talk about their lives,' stated Zoe Raemer of Yellowknife, a founder of Out North. She commented in 1998 that the Northwest Territories has a population of only sixty thousand, and 'you could probably fit all the gays and lesbians in the penalty box at Maple Leaf Gardens.'[11]

As a result of these very different circumstances, the organizing exigencies in smaller and rural communities, even in the late 1990s, were quite different from those of the larger cities, and were reminiscent of what transpired in larger communities two decades earlier. There was still a need to break through loneliness and isolation, to establish safe meeting places, to build support services such as phone lines, to conduct education about homophobia and sexual orientation discrimination, and to begin to be more visible. Yet, the issues important to queers in smaller and rural communities rarely penetrate the consciousness of the mainstream lesbian and gay movement situated in the larger ones. As Gens Hellquist of Saskatoon, who was involved with rural outreach in Saskatchewan in the 1990s, has noted,

There is a perception that gay people live in the big cities and don't exist in the small towns of Saskatchewan or Ontario or PEI. I have been struck by the number of farmers out there who are gay, who are living fairly isolated lives and not much effort is made by the larger gay and lesbian community to reach out to these people. They are so hungry to have some contact, and for me it has been really rewarding to watch these people change and grow. They have joined the organization. Often they are fearful, often they are using aliases. Over a period of time when they meet other gay people and communicate with other gay men and start feeling better about themselves as a gay person, they start taking those steps to come out. Some of those people actually have become focal points in their small community because they have come out in varying degrees and some of them, a few, even have become involved in setting up groups in small cities.[12]

Michael Riordon has chronicled the experiences and aspirations of queer people who live in Canada's small and rural communities in his marvellous book, *Out Our Way*, published in 1996. He writes, 'When mainstream culture notices gay and lesbian folk, it tends to see us as urban. And our own media-makers have their hands full transmitting the stories of lesbian and gay downtowners. But more and more of us are choosing to live wherever it suits us. This is a free country, no? And as one gay man in northern Ontario said, "It's my goddam country, too."' But, as Riordon also observed, living in such places is not always welcoming: 'You'll find very few people of colour in this book, alas. By and large rural areas are about as welcoming to them as to homos, only we can hide better than they can.'[13]

It is illustrative of how little things had changed in large parts of the country if we look at the kinds of organizing done in smaller and rural communities over the period between 1985 and 1999. In stark contrast with pursuing human rights code amendments, winning spousal benefits, or fighting police harassment, queer organizing in such places largely meant establishing visibility and safe-space infrastructure for social and recreational activities. In Nanaimo, British Columbia, for example, the first community centre for gays and lesbians opened in 1995 after thirteen years of effort, aided by the presence of a growing and visible gay community that held weekly social events and monthly dances.[14] Similarly, on mainland BC, a significant event in the history of community organizing occurred in 1993 when the Okanagan Gay and Lesbian Organization held 'A Harvest of Rainbows' at a camp overlooking Lake Okanagan. It featured sports, recreation, and arts and crafts.[15]

In Alberta, gay, lesbian, and bisexual organizations were formed in Red Deer, Grande Prairie, Lethbridge, and Medicine Hat during the 1990s. One of them, Red Deer's Gay and Lesbian Association of Central Alberta, founded in 1991, had as its mission to 'organize, promote, and encourage a wide range of social activities that would bring together the gay and lesbian community of central Alberta.'[16] Along the same lines, Saskatoon's Gay and Lesbian Health Services began a rural outreach program in 1994 to help network gays and lesbians in areas outside Saskatoon and Regina, to assist them in developing support and social systems, and to educate professionals and agencies in such communities so that they were better informed about and equipped to assist gays and lesbians.[17] Similarly, groups providing safe social environments formed in places like Brandon, Manitoba, and in various smaller communities throughout Ontario. One of these was Gays, Lesbians, and Bisexuals of North Bay and Area, started in the mid-1990s, that has organized 'Building Bridges' conferences since 1997 to provide opportunities for networking, information exchange, and assistance for similar groups throughout northern Ontario. Another group, Timmins and Area Gays and Lesbians, thrived since starting up in the early 1990s at the initiative of Valerie McNab and Brian Calhoun. Timmins, until then, had virtually no meeting places other than people's homes. No identifiable bar or club for gays, lesbians, and bisexuals existed and small, discreet social networks were difficult to contact. Consequently, the group quickly established a phone line, enabling it to make contact with gays and lesbians throughout northern Ontario, and organized various social activities such as barbeques, brunches, parties, and dances.[18]

In Quebec, the first gay and lesbian organizations in Rouyn-Noranda, Joliette, and Trois-Rivières were launched only in the mid-1980s. One particularly successful group, Action Gaie Abitibi-Témiscamingue, since 1992 has offered alternatives to a disco or the private parties that were until then the only social options. Running dances that drew gays and lesbians from all over northern Quebec and northern Ontario, the group grew quickly, becoming the third largest gay organization in Quebec.[19] By the late 1990s, organizations had spread to a number of other Quebec communities, including Victoriaville, Baie-Comeau, Rimouski, and Rivière-du-Loup.[20] Across the border in New Brunswick, Bathurst and Edmonston also saw their first organizations emerge in the early 1990s. John Young, one of the founders of Bathurst's Gai.es Nor Gay (GNG), recalls the impetus was the closing of a bar in which dances had been held on weekends, one of the few places where gays and lesbians in the area could gather publicly. GNG began holding its own dances, that over the next few years attracted gays, lesbians, and bisexuals from a wide geographic area: Campbellton, Dalhousie, and other places on the North Shore; Tracadie and other communities on the South Shore.[21]

Elsewhere in Atlantic Canada, Geraldine Dawe and a gay man founded the first group in Sydney, Nova Scotia: the Island Gay, Lesbian and Bisexual Group, in February 1992. Functioning only for a few years, it held social events that attracted both women and men, put out a newsletter, and advertised its existence through a local cable TV station and postering. Many lonely and isolated gays and lesbians from smaller communities contacted the group.[22] St John's, Newfoundland, despite the sporadic organizing of the 1980s, did not see a new group until 1990, when Gays and Lesbians Together (GALT) emerged. GALT ran a phone line that functioned for two years, holding actions to protest gay bashing and organizing pride week in St John's.[23] Similarly, gays, lesbians, and bisexuals on Prince Edward Island had no organizations or services they could access until 1986, after the Lesbian Phone-Line formed.[24] For lesbians, organized activities included coffee houses, dances, and a coming-out group, although house parties and similar gatherings continued to be the main social outlets. Leith Chiu, a gay man in Charlottetown, indicated when interviewed in 1993 that the city had only a straight-owned bar frequented by local gays but otherwise parties and other social events were the main way gay men stayed in touch with each other.[25] It was not until the late 1990s that the Gay and Lesbian Coalition of PEI and its successor, the Abegweit Rainbow Collective, were formed.

The first community organizing in the North also took place only in the late 1980s and early 1990s. Helen Fallding and a small group of long-time Yukon lesbians and gay men began with barbecues and potlucks during 1988 but soon expanded to opening a post office box and advertising in the classifieds of local newspapers. From these efforts, a mailing list was built, growing to about '100 names of men and women (both native and non-native) from almost every tiny Yukon community.' By 1991, the Gay and Lesbian Alliance of the Yukon, based in Whitehorse, had become an incorporated organization, organizing periodic dances and other social events, producing an occasional newsletter, and operating a phone line.[26] In the Northwest Territories, Out North was launched in the late 1990s, holding regular dances and organizing the first gay pride events in Yellowknife in June 1997.[27]

Lesbian Organizing: Local Focus, Familiar Issues

Over the last fifteen years of the twentieth century, lesbians continued to organize in much the same way they always had, at the local level, in women's organizations, mixed gay and lesbian groups, or separate lesbian organizations. For the most part, the issues and challenges remained unchanged from earlier decades. Working with straight feminists remained problematic, and confronting homophobia and heterosexism continued as priorities. One of the worst climates for lesbians within feminist organizations existed in St John's in the late 1980s, according to Beth Lacey and Peggy Keats, two lesbians active in organizing within the women's community at the time. Lacey has recalled that 'being called lesbians ... was sort of the worst thing you could call somebody.'[28] The climate within the women's centre was so hostile that at one point, Lacey noted in an interview, heterosexual women complained that lesbians were taking over the organization.

Keats remembers bitterly that the straight women 'basically turned their backs on the lesbians who had worked like dogs to make sure this place [the abortion clinic] opened.' 'It was the dykes who kept the place open, it was the dykes who came down and slept here at night when, you know, there were threats of danger,' Keats added.[29] Nor was the homophobia in feminist groups limited to white, middle-class women. Regina's Sue Cook related, in a 1990 interview, the comment made by a Black feminist at a 1985 International Women's Day symposium that Black women's issues were being trivialized because lesbians were included in the symposium's discussions. Mirtha Sepuldeda, a lesbian of colour, also told of confronting another symposium speaker, a straight woman of colour who strenuously objected to the agenda's encompassing lesbian issues, and being told by that woman Sepuldeda was 'really defiling our race.'[30]

Regrettably, problems also persisted for lesbians working with gay men. Often, as in the past, confrontations arose over male sexual imagery, male privilege, or the failure of gay men to understand issues that were important to lesbians. A fascinatingly illustrative case was the shirtless incident at Rumours, the bar and dance club run by Halifax's Gay and Lesbian Alliance (GALA) in the early nineties. A policy of prohibiting men from dancing shirtless had simmered as an issue for years. The policy recognized that because women were not free in our society to be bare-breasted, gay men should not exercise a freedom denied to lesbians.[31] Three men ultimately challenged the policy by dancing shirtless, causing much acrimony, but also a change that permitted shirtlessness for men, but not women. GALA argued it could not risk the revocation of its liquor licence by permitting women to dance with bare breasts. Nevertheless, at this point some women also removed their tops at dances, while other women remained opposed to all shirtlessness. An organizational crisis erupted, which resulted in reverting to a ban on all shirtlessness. Outraged, six gay men flouted the policy, arguing that shirtlessness was a question of liberation, and that women also should be able to go shirtless at the dances. After being barred from Rumours, the men picketed it.[32] But some lesbians in GALA saw things much differently, feeling betrayed by men they considered friends and political allies. GALA member Lynn Murphy recalled in a 1993 interview, 'What we saw was that men and, in many cases the men that we had felt were the most attuned to women's issues in the community, were perfectly ready to claim for themselves a privilege, in spite of the fact that women would not be allowed to have that privilege.'[33]

For these and other reasons, including the fact that social options for lesbians, even in the largest cities, have remained severely limited, autonomous lesbian organizing proceeded in many communities. The focus in that context remained on some old familiar issues, as well as attempting to deal with organizing challenges that gay men largely did not face. Calgary's Kam K. Wong notes that 'Money is an issue. I think that's one of the major things women tell me is that, money, men do make a lot more money than women do. So many lesbians out there that do have children, that are single parents that, I guess, can't get a job or whatever, they don't have enough of an income ... And that is one of the major problems, you know, that lesbians can never get above, stay above water because we don't have the financial support.'[34] Carmen Paquette, a lesbian long active in Ottawa, cited another challenge for autonomous lesbian organizing when interviewed in 1990. Lesbians, she observed, continue 'to put either the mixed groups or the women's movement first, but it means that ... we never put ourselves first.'[35]

Still, groups specifically for lesbians continued to form in the latter years of the twentieth century. The emphasis, as in earlier times, was on social support, and cultural activities. Two noteworthy organizational successes occurred in Vancouver and Toronto. The first, the Vancouver Lesbian Centre, opened its doors in 1985, and functioned as Canada's only lesbian community centre for many years until, unable to sustain itself any longer, it folded in early 1999. During its illustrious lifetime, the centre offered a meeting place for a variety of lesbian groups, ran a phone line, and provided a number of other services.[36] Toronto lesbians wanting a meeting place as an alternative to the bars and clubs also organized for a separate women's space, eventually opening the Woman's Common in June 1988. The common quickly became a venue for concerts, art shows, dining and dancing, films, and meetings of women sharing common interests. Sadly, it never became economically viable and closed in 1994.[37] On the East Coast, a group of Fredericton lesbians began meeting in the early 1990s to discuss how to bring lesbians together in the community socially. Soon, Ann Marie Wallace, Sharon Myers, and other women began collecting donations to hold women's dances. This led to the formation of WOMYN in 1991, as New Brunswick's first exclusively lesbian organization, holding dances, barbecues, sporting events, and other social activities.[38] In Toronto, a pioneering group, Lesbian Youth Peer Support, was formed in January 1991. It fulfilled a need for young lesbians to meet, come out, and find support in a lesbian-only environment, and was, as well, more racially and culturally diverse than any other group that preceded it. During its existence into the mid-1990s, Lesbian Youth Peer Support was in fact the only group of its kind in the country, helping and supporting young lesbians (twenty-six years of age and younger) with coming out.[39]

Autonomous lesbian organizing also continued sporadically over this period in more political and public contexts. Since 1986, annual International Lesbian Week activities have been held in Vancouver and Ottawa, separate from both International Women's Day, and Lesbian and Gay Pride Day. Lesbian Avengers, a direct action group, formed in Guelph, Winnipeg, and Ottawa in 1994 and 1995. The Ottawa group organized a Dyke March, attended by about two dozen lesbians, as part of the 1995 International Lesbian Week. A Dyke March was also introduced into Toronto's Lesbian and Gay Pride events in 1996, held the day before the main parade. By 1998, the Dyke March had grown to attract about five thousand marchers and thousands of onlookers.

Disability and Race Issues in a Changing Community

As was chronicled in chapter 8, by the early 1980s the identifiable and organized queer communities of Canada were becoming increasingly diverse. They ceased to be so predominantly European and caucasian, as other gays, lesbians, and bisexuals on the margins began to assert a presence within them. These minority communities, largely ignored or dismissed by the broader gay and lesbian community, articulated issues and promoted agendas that were new in many ways, reflecting experiences and perspectives far different from the increasingly mainstream activist cadres, but which also echoed the rhetoric and strategies of the early lesbian and gay liberationists. They challenged the established institutions of the maturing community and the ever more narrow concerns of the activist groups. Issues of race, ability, and marginalization were asserted, and lack of awareness and underrepresentation in community institutions were exposed. Lesbians and gays with disabilities, queers of colour, and two-spirited people responded by forming or expanding organizations providing support for and services to their communities. Notions of identity and community that had acquired nearly unassailable orthodoxy were critically questioned. Similarly, class issues, including calls, in larger communities, to support antipoverty activists or protest police crackdowns against prostitutes, homeless people, and squeegee kids (young street people who earn money by washing the windows of cars when they stop at inter-

sections) were hotly contested. Sharp divisions, for example, characterized raucous public meetings after the police action on the Bijou in
Toronto. Older white gay men seemed concerned only about the infringement of their right to engage in consensual sex, while many
others wanted to broaden the advocacy by allying with others also
being harassed by the police.

While impressive progress had been made in the period between
1985 and the end of the century in respect of community development
and the pursuit of legislated equality rights, much less was achieved on
issues particularly of concern to lesbians, gays, and bisexuals with
disabilities. By the mid-1980s, groups organized by and for them had
not emerged in any significant numbers. The remarkable Toronto Rainbow Alliance of the Deaf, formed a decade earlier (see chapter 8),
continued to function. In addition, lesbians with disabilities became
visible and active within the DisAbled Women's Network (DAWN). As
Joanne Doucette noted in *Lesbians in Canada*, DAWN, a national organization, was one of the few places that disabled lesbians could gather.
The fact that disabled women also had difficulty finding employment
and maintaining economic stability, and the pervasiveness of stereotypical attitudes towards persons with a disability generally, made it
difficult for disabled lesbians to be visible or to find each other. DAWN
thus filled a number of needs, and provided a relatively safe environment.[40] Other recent organizing initiatives by gays, lesbians, and bisexuals with disabilities have been the Disabled Gay Men's Association
of BC, in Vancouver, and the Differently Abled Rainbow Club (DARC),
formed in Winnipeg in 1998. DARC, a social support group for gays,
lesbians, and bisexuals with disabilities, tellingly faced its first challenge attempting to find a wheelchair accessible location for holding
meetings that was available without having to pay a rental charge.[41]
Deplorably, all gay men, lesbians, and bisexuals with disabilities regularly confront the inaccessiblity of meeting places, especially in bars
and clubs, but also in the venues for ostensibly gay and lesbian 'community' events. Accessibility remains a critical issue not being significantly addressed.

One of the more successful attempts to create awareness of the issues
faced by disabled lesbians and bisexual women was organized in 1993,
when a Toronto art gallery hosted 'Poster Kids No More.' One of the
objectives of the show was to emphasize the fact that 'there is almost no
imagery depicting disabled women, let alone disabled dykes and bi-
women.' Shelley Tremain, the exhibit's coordinator, noted what little

imagery that exists is 'patronizing, asexual, with white women in wheel-chairs soliciting donations.'[42] Tremain, writing in *Quota Magazine* in 1993, questioned the claim that lesbians are building 'a progressive and diverse lesbian culture.' She noted that 'disabled lesbians remain invisible there too. In lesbian novels, theatre, film, and so on, dykes are (with few exceptions) depicted as non-disabled. Within non-disabled dyke culture, the experiences and perspectives of disabled lesbians are not represented, articulated, not even imagined.'[43]

Gay men with disabilities have similarly spoken out to create greater awareness of the obstacles they face. Matthew Pompilio, a gay man in Toronto, who attempted in the early 1990s to start a group for gays and lesbians with disabilities, addressed the challenges he faced in a 1993 interview. He had problems shopping and bar-hopping in the heart of the city's gay district; there were no ramps or elevators into most bars and businesses. Once inside, after having been carried upstairs, he was often asked to move to the back where his wheelchair would not be in anyone's way. Washrooms were usually at the end of a flight of stairs and were not accessible.[44] Jeff Peters, a gay man in Toronto with cere-bral palsy related in *Xtra!* his experiences in gay bars and the attitudes of many gay men. They assume he's drunk because he is unsteady on his feet and slurs his speech. While this does not prevent them from taking him home for sex, he added, 'The morning after, they find out I have a disability, and I kind of get the rub off.'[45]

Discrimination against disabled people within queer communities is compounded by the generally disadvantaged social and economic sta-tuses of people with disabilities as a whole; added to these difficulties is the need to fight against homophobia and the vulnerability of being out of the closet within communities of people with disabilities. In the broader Canadian community, people with disabilities all too often are institutionalized or placed in situations of dependency. Their rates of unemployment and receipt of social assistance far exceed that of the rest of the population. Many people with disabilities, even if employed, live at subsistence levels because they cannot obtain jobs thought by employers to be beyond their abilities. As Jean B., a Calgary activist, commented in a 1997 interview: 'I feel that there is a double closet, that you are a second-class citizen because you're disabled and you are a second-class citizen because you're gay and it will take a few more years for people to come to realize that you're first-class citizens no matter what.'[46]

Echoing these remarks, a study into the health and social service needs of Ontario's sexual minorities, published by the CLGRO in 1997, summarized the experiences related by people with disabilities who participated in a focus group, as follows: 'First, they feel alienated from lesbian, gay, or bisexual organizations. In addition, people with disabilities live in a world that sees them as sexless or just possibly heterosexual. Group participants felt that lesbian, gay, and bisexual people internalize this oppression, and find it difficult to be public about their orientation, even at an event like this [focus group]. Focus group members also pointed out that information about lesbian, gay, or bisexual events is often not circulated to or within inpatient facilities or residences and organizations for people with disabilities.' CLGRO's study, called *Systems Failure*, found, not surprisingly, that 'homophobic service providers, even if their technical service is of high quality, offer an environment of discomfort and stress.'[47]

Even those living independently experience vulnerability and pressure related to homophobia, or the fear of it, in respect of attendant care and other service-providers who visit their homes. Fear that a homophobic response will result from a provider seeing artwork, books, photographs, or other materials with lesbian, gay or bisexual themes, or becoming aware of a same-sex relationship, is genuine and well-founded.[48] Equally problematic is the homophobia displayed by providers of transportation services for people with disabilities. Pat Israel, a Toronto bisexual woman and long-time activist on both disability and sexual orientation issues, has helped publicize homophobic expressions by drivers for Wheel Trans in that city. In a 1999 *Xtra!* article she recalled being on board a Wheel Trans vehicle when one driver told another about 'telling off' the dispatcher for asking him to pick up a passenger at a gay bar. 'I said I wasn't going into that faggot bar to pick anyone up,' she remembered him saying.[49] With attitudes like that on the part of straight service providers, and the difficulties experienced feeling welcome within queer communities, the lives of gays, lesbians, and bisexuals with disabilities remain filled with oppression, discrimination, stress, and fear. Sadly, the lesbian and gay movement, until now, has largely failed to include them.

By the mid-1980s, lesbians and gays of colour also were beginning to speak out publicly, and to challenge what by then had become some of the institutions of the gay and lesbian communities. One of the first to do so was a Black gay activist, Doug Stewart, who observed in a May 1985 letter to *The Body Politic* that people of colour were excluded from a gay community, and a lesbian and gay liberation movement, meant only for white people. Racism among gay men, Stewart observed, 'forces gay men like me to prioritize my concerns.' Accordingly, 'Black gay activists define themselves first and foremost as Black and as gay second.'[50]

Stewart's letter was one of several that had appeared in *TBP* in the months following the paper's publication of a classified advertisement from a white gay man seeking a 'young, well built BM [Black Man] for houseboy.' A gay man of colour, a volunteer with *TBP*, had argued, upon receipt of the ad, that it was racist and should not be published. White members of the *TBP* collective that produced the paper argued it should be published, and it ran in the February 1985 issue. Angered by that action, the volunteer notified Zami, the Toronto group of West Indian lesbians and gay men, resulting in a meeting with *TBP* and representatives of Zami, Lesbians of Colour, and Gay Asians Toronto (GAT). A raging debate erupted, within the *TBP* collective and the wider community, over, as *TBP* noted, 'racism, the role of this magazine and the [sic] even the nature of gay liberation itself.'[51]

The meeting with *TBP* was a disaster. The collective members who felt the ad should have been published remained intransigent. The representatives of gays and lesbians of colour felt their concerns were not heard, and left feeling angry and betrayed by the paper that had become the voice of Canada's gay liberation movement. It was 'one of the most unpleasant meetings I have ever attended ... we were made to feel that our arguments were non-representative, our objections hysterical, and our feelings defensive,' lamented Alan Li of GAT in a subsequent letter to *TBP*. Li criticized the middle-class white gay men on *TBP*'s collective for putting sexual libertarianism and the defence of the 'inviolability of desire' at the centre of their politics, whereas 'women and third-world gays have added battles to fight because of the fact that we are at the other end of the power differential. To us, racism, sexism, and socio-economic as well as political oppression are equally important issues to be confronted.'[52]

Gays and lesbians of colour, and a small handful of white liberationists, condemned the majority of the collective members for abandoning liberation in favour of a sexual libertarianism that contributed to the oppression faced by queers of colour. 'To champion the cause of uninhibited desire without addressing the impact of racism and sexism in the sexual arena is to call for the entrenchment of white male privilege ... It also does not surprise me that by advocating sexual libertarianism as its main priority over community organizing, the paper maintains the colour, class and, up to recently, gender of the people who work there ... Non-white lesbians and gays are just not seen as totally gay. We are outsiders, our interests are appendices,' wrote Richard Fung in a letter to the collective. 'Why is the fulfillment of your desire more important than the struggle of my oppression?' asked a gay man named Lim. 'If the philosophy of the BP collective is sexual libertarianism at any cost, then please do not call yourself a gay liberation journal 'cos I'm part of the gay liberation, and when your liberation oppresses my life, it ain't no liberation.'[53] A few days after the meeting with the collective, community members attending a screening of Fung's film, *Orientations*, both white and people of colour, condemned the decision to run the advertisement.

Throughout the 1990s, lesbians and gays of colour continued to find that their interests, experiences, perspectives, and concerns were diminished or trivialized by the predominantly white community groups. al-Qamar Sangha, a founder of The Atish Network in Vancouver, launched in the early 1990s for lesbians, gays, and bisexuals who identify themselves with South Asia, Africa, and the Middle East, wrote in 1993 that there had been, on the part of mainstream lesbian and gay organizations, the 'denial of recognition, promotion and support of cultural diversity and ethnic identity, and racism and discrimination where the "ethnic" individual is marginalized, exoticized, and stereotyped to meet a definition.'[54] Sangha also articulated the sense of not belonging that is common to lesbians, gays, and bisexuals having different racial and cultural backgrounds than those of the vast majority:

A critical examination of these [North American gay rights] organizations reveals that while the mandate and purpose of such groups is to challenge global discrimination and inequality, the gay rights movement is centred in the European historical, cultural, religious, political, [and] social ideology which excluded ethnic minorities. These organizations while advocating universality are controlled and managed by Euro-North Americans. The claim to diversity is also contradictory when the overwhelming majority of the members are of European descent, and visible minority members who join are implicitly informed that their religion, language, culture and history, and immigration experience is secondary or unimportant.[55]

African lesbian feminist Adonica Huggins has noted that people of colour are often put in the position of having to choose what they should fight against: sexism, racism, or homophobia. 'And of course, people of colour are taking to task white lesbians, gays, and bisexuals for their notorious ability to denounce homophobia while practising racism,' she added.[56] Other gays and lesbians of colour have been similarly critical of community organizations claiming to fight against oppression and discrimination but which fail to act on racism within the community. Imtiaz Popat, following a gay bashing incident in Vancouver in 1994 in which the perpetrators of the violence were people of colour, observed in *Angles*, 'Racism has hit us in the face recently ... Somehow, the colour of the bashers became an issue. It gave free licence to use racist slurs in graffiti and conversations. Unfortunately, the community chose not to become as irate over the racism as they did over the bashing.'[57] Such incidents, Popat concluded, mean that, 'For queers of colour, there is no one organization that represents us. Many of us feel that we don't belong to the community.' In other cases, it has not been racism so much as a sense of being overwhelmed when attempting to access organizations that are predominantly white, as well as predominantly male, even when the groups profess to having an open door to all. As Kristyn Wong-Tam, active with the Lesbian Youth Peer Support group in Toronto, stated in 1991, 'Yes, but through those open doors, once we walk in, there are no women in those organizations. All I see is a sea of white, able-bodied middle class men and as an Asian lesbian ... it doesn't do anything for me and I don't feel safe.'[58]

Socially, gays and lesbians of colour also have encountered racism, stereotyping, and marginalization within the bars and other gathering places of the broader queer community. Nickolus Plowden, a Black gay man living in Ottawa, reported in *GO Info* in 1992 that some gay men did not want to speak to him because of his colour, while others 'tell me that they really like black guys because we're great in bed and we have big dicks.' Because of these experiences, Plowden felt isolated. 'I reached the point where I would go to the bar with my friends and I wouldn't cruise or approach anyone that I was interested in. The odds of meeting someone who would like me as a person first, regardless of my colour, seemed too great, and I was tired of being used.'[59] Dr Kirby Hsu, a gay Asian, exposed other elements of racism in queer communities, when writing in 1995 that 'I certainly feel discriminated against [in the gay community] because of my skin colour. I felt very ignored, didn't feel part of the community, didn't feel I was desirable because of my skin colour ... In the gay community, the discrimination comes from a lack of interest. They just ignore you. They don't want to take the time to talk to you because they presume you can't speak English. People were always so surprised that I can speak English without an accent.'[60] Natasha Singh reported in 1994 that, in a meeting in Toronto, lesbian and bisexual women of South Asian descent dismissed the notion of a gay and lesbian community that included them. 'Many women questioned the notion of "community" and some expressed cynicism about it,' she wrote. In an attempt to define what they meant by community, the women came up with '[A healthier community] entails creating more respectful and constructive ways of dealing with our differences. It involves asserting values that are different from the dominant and oppressive ones in place – values which support building connectedness, respect, and self-determination.'[61]

Similarly, Aboriginal two-spirited people often find urban centres foreign and unfriendly, even if they allow people to be more open about their sexuality. The notion of a capacious lesbian and gay community in which they are welcome and safe is difficult for them to imagine. Issues of culture and language create problems, as can racism and stereotyping from within the larger gay and lesbian communities. 'It's very hard for us to practise our culture within lesbian and gay organizations,' Susan Beaver, active with Two-Spirited Peoples of the First Nations in Toronto, has said.[62] A 1998 publication of Two-Spirited Peoples of the First Nations, *We Are Part of a Tradition*, written by two-spirited activist Gilbert Deschamps, articulated the problem of connecting with established gay and lesbian organizations: 'We are not likely to turn to many organizations that are supposedly responding to the needs of a community. Our issues of safety are much more sensitive. We know that if we walk into an organization that is the "lesbian and gay community" we may not be welcome because our traditions are too foreign and our skin is too brown.'[63] Even finding other two-spirited people can present challenges. Given the diversity of bands and nations, Aboriginal people may have very little in common, other than being called Indians and being poor. In addition, poverty, low self-esteem, and lack of education are common among First Nations people. There is a real need to do safe-sex education about AIDS and about addictions. Many two-spirited people get into drugs and prostitution, engaging in high-risk behaviours that can lead to HIV and AIDS. Evan Adams has spoken passionately about the need to reach Native gays and lesbians moving to urban centres, particularly youth, to alert and warn them that there are people who will exploit them or treat them in a racist way. He has emphasized that 'There are colour lines in the gay community. We cannot afford to be naive when we come into that community.'[64]

Liberating Queers of Colour, Queers from Cultural Minorities, and Two-Spirited Peoples

Coming out and creating safety and community for gays, lesbians, and bisexuals of colour and for two-spirited peoples has for them meant adopting liberation consciousness and analyses, modified to fit their particular circumstances, that, nonetheless, are reminiscent of the early days of lesbian and gay liberation. As was the case with the mainly white liberation activists of the early 1970s, pursuing these objectives has involved becoming visible as gays, lesbians, and bisexuals, positively asserting a same-sex orientation, and dealing with heteorsexism and homophobia. Their organizational missions and the materials they produced are rich and ring with the language of liberation, of fighting oppression and internalized homophobia, of consciousness-raising and a sense of community, and of engendering pride and assertiveness. But in contrast with the experiences of the earlier activists, lesbians, gays, and bisexuals of colour and two-spirited people have also necessarily had to combat racism, the effects of double or multiple oppressions, and, in many cases, the cultural impact of Christian evangelism and the vestiges of colonialism.

Within tightly knit communities of recent immigrants where the imperative of banding together to survive the racism of the dominant Canadian society is paramount, the risks arising from coming out as a gay, lesbian, or bisexual can be enormous. In many such communities, the preservation of cultural and religious beliefs takes on particular importance, and the consequences of social disapproval or ostracism are much more isolating and traumatic. Gays, lesbians, and bisexuals in such communities commonly feel anguish about the negative affect the disclosure of their sexual orientation will have on their parents and other family members within their neighbourhoods or communities. 'To some extent, my coming out put my family in the closet,' commented Rahim Chunara, a gay Muslim, recently.[65] For others, coming out as gays or lesbians means severing all ties. As Subira M'Walimu and Fatumar Omar noted in a 1993 article in *Quota Magazine*, 'It is not uncommon ... to renounce their faith in Islam and their Muslim identities because they believe, or are forced to believe, that being Muslim and homosexual are totally incompatible.'[66]

In fact, as the Muslim population of Canada has grown, queer Muslims in increasing numbers have come out of the closet publicly. That process has meant that issues faced for decades by gays and lesbians from Christian cultures have begun to be played out in much the same way within the Muslim communities. It has also produced a similar backlash of homophobia, with a number of public anti-gay pronouncements being made in recent years. Islamic clerics have publicly opposed the social acceptance of homosexuality and the extension of legislated rights to gays and lesbians. Some such clerics joined with Christian fundamentalists to oppose Parliament's adoption of Bill C-23 that recognized same-sex common law relationships. A prominent Islamic community leader in Toronto announced in 2000 his public support for the Canadian Alliance because, in his words, it fights to 'prohibit the lifestyle of gays and lesbians.'[67] The Toronto District Muslim Education Assembly, along with Christian family values advocates, waged a vigorous campaign throughout 1999 and 2000 to prevent the Toronto District School Board from including sexual orientation issues within a human rights and equity policy for Toronto schools.[68] A member of the Muslim Student Union at McMaster University in Hamilton wrote an editorial in the campus student paper in 1999 labelling homosexuality a 'sexual deviation.' He charged that 'This perverted act is a reversal of the natural order, a corruption of man's sexuality, and a crime against the rights of females. The same applies equally in the case of female homosexuality.'[69] A few years earlier, the head of an Islamic social services agency in Toronto had condemned homosexuality as 'deviant behaviour punishable by death' under Islamic law. He added, 'There are a lot of people in the homosexual community who are evil.'[70]

Despite such attitudes and obstacles, gays, lesbians, and bisexuals in Canada's Muslim communities, throughout the 1990s, organized and become more visible. Salaam, a Toronto group founded in 1992, was likely the first group specifically for gay and lesbian Muslims. Stressing that it was not a religious organization, Salaam stated it 'allows lesbians and gays with Muslim backgrounds a safe space and the opportunity to explore what being Muslim means to them – be it spiritual, cultural, political or social. It's also simply a place to find support.'[71] A subsequent group, Al-Fatiha, a faith-based group of lesbian, gay, bisexual, and transgendered Muslims, adopted a similar mission. The group's coordinator, Mohammed Khan, adopting a stance vividly reflective of lesbian and gay liberation activists of the 1970s, challenged the chair of an Islamic community group over his homophobia. His opinion piece appeared in *Xtra!* in 2000: 'gay and lesbian equality will change mainstream and Muslim cultural definitions of masculinity and femininity, we will redefine the family, broaden marriage and its embedded and restrictive gender roles, and challenge dominant views about sexual and reproductive choice. We will challenge old boundaries between the private and the public, as the public has always been defined in such a way as to exclude women and gay people.'[72]

Issues of identity, disclosure, and homophobia also affect Black gays, lesbians, and bisexuals, making organizing imperatives in those communities different in significant ways. Wesley Critchlow, an academic and activist, has made the point that Black men who have sex with other men often refuse to consider themselves to be homosexual, especially if they are married. Internalized homophobia also is a factor, with many feeling compelled to hide their sexual identities: 'People are still killing themselves, or getting married or trying to have kids in order to "cure" themselves,' added Critchlow. 'In the black community there is nothing to come out to. You come out to the white gay world.'[73] Coming out of the closet, and feeling comfortable with that, is still the main issue for Black men, Kwame Stephens noted in 1998. Doing so risks 'the comfort of family.'[74] Black lesbians face similar obstacles, as well as discrimination because of being Black women. Black lesbian activist Debbie Douglas commented in early 1999 that there is, in addition, a perception by other gays and lesbians that 'to be black is not to be gay,' and by straight Blacks that 'to be gay is not to be black. This makes those of us with both identities invisible within our community.'[75] And the experiences, cultures, and issues are different for Black people from Africa than those from the Caribbean. Many have cultural differences around sexuality, and discussions of it that complicates matters. A Toronto AIDS group, Africans United to Control AIDS, has stated in a leaflet: 'Among many African communities sex is something you only discuss with somebody your own age.'[76]

There is also homophobia within Black communities, as elsewhere, that must be confronted. A Toronto Rastafarian publication, not too long ago, carried an article declaring 'homosexualism' a 'depraved crime against humanity ... [that] is being promoted as an integral part of the plan of the wickeds to eliminate a significant percentage of the human population, and to reduce the human family to what they consider to be controllable proportions.'[77] Carol Allen, of Lesbians of Colour, when speaking about homophobia in Black communities at a meeting in 1988 observed, 'It is hard when those communities are the places we get our cultural reinforcement. It's where we get a sense of who we are as lesbians and gays of colour or as immigrants in this country and those are the communities that shut us out because of homophobia.'[78] As is the case for gays, lesbians, and bisexuals generally within the Canadian population, Black gays and lesbians who come out publicly can face harassment and threats. A Black gay man at York University related in a 1997 newspaper interview the hostility he experienced speaking as part of a panel discussion at a meeting of the Caribbean student's association. One man in the audience said he would kick his ass if he entered his neighbourhood.[79]

Confronting homophobia and heterosexism has also been an issue for groups organizing within Asian communities. Gay Asians Toronto, for example, mounted a concerted campaign in 1996 to counteract homophobia in Toronto's Chinese-language media. A newspaper had printed a diatribe that claimed: 'Because human beings feel a sense of shame and dirty feelings towards the phenomenon of "same sex copulation," it is unavoidable to have a phenomenon of hatred, contempt, and discrimination ... towards people afflicted with homosexuality.'[80] Such views were attributable in no small way to religious beliefs, noted GAT's Keith Wong: 'Many members of the Chinese media are under the control of Christian fundamentalist churches.'[81] A somewhat different problem faced Toronto's Alliance for South Asian AIDS Prevention when attempting to access South Asian communities to conduct AIDS education and provide information. Discussion of sex or sexuality in such communities was taboo, and AIDS/HIV was perceived as 'a white homosexual problem.'[82] Asian immigrants, in particular, face a number of challenges when contemplating coming out of the closet. Dwayne Pastrana of Central Toronto Youth Sevices has stated in that regard, 'Growing up as a gay Asian youth is very difficult, particularly if you were born, or grew up, outside Canada. Coming out is very difficult because the family is non-Westernized.' In addition, finding places to go to be with other gays and lesbians, where their concerns will be acknowledged, is problematic: 'Our concerns, as a minority, aren't being addressed.'[83]

Comparable challenges face Filipino gays and Filipina lesbians. Clarissa Lagartera, a young lesbian activist in Winnipeg, commented in a 1998 interview: 'there is the issue of being accepted within the Filipino community as a lesbian ... I'm not shunned by the community but I am alienated from it.'[84] The great difficulties presented with coming out in a relatively small cultural community were evidenced by a Toronto conference of Filipina lesbians held in 2000. The local Toronto participants, according to a news story in *Xtra!*, reported not being out to family and friends.[85] And, like other lesbians and gays of colour, queer people of Philippine origin must deal with racism within Canadian society, sometimes not knowing whether racism, homophobia, or both are the factors causing discrimination and marginalization. For Filipina lesbians, and other women of colour, gender and race issues add to the mix. Noted Lagartera, 'there is a whole array of issues ... never mind being queer, let's first talk about, you know, being coloured in a white society and the struggles within that. Now let's talk about being coloured and gay in this society ... issues of places of work ... issues of housing and safety ... being a visible minority ... it's sort of like, I mean, a triple whammy, even for myself, of being a lesbian of colour.'[86]

Increasingly throughout the late 1980s and the entire nineties, gays, lesbians, and bisexuals of colour formed organizations devoted to meeting their needs and assisting in their liberation, socially and sexually, battling homophobia and heterosexism in the process. In 1987, Khush, Gay South Asians, was formed as a 'group of South Asians of diasporic origin (South Asia, Africa, Indo-Caribbean ...) and diverse cultural/ religious backgrounds.'[87] Khush – the word is Urdu and means 'happy, pleased, good' – was founded by a group of men including Nelson Carvalho, Karim Ladak, Deep Khosla, and Chris Paul. Khush held regular meetings and social activities and published a newsletter, *Khush Khayal*, until the late 1990s.[88] Over the years, Khush attracted 'new immigrants, people who are just coming out and seasoned pros,' and engaged in public education and political advocacy issues as well as providing a range of social activities.[89] In 1988, Khush and Gay Asians Toronto jointly organized 'Unity Among Asians,' a groundbreaking first conference for Asian lesbians and gay men in North America. Khush also held 'Salaam Toronto!' in 1989 to celebrate diasporic gay and lesbian cultures and identities. That event was so successful that it led to the launching of an acclaimed annual cultural festival, Desh Pardesh, that from 1990 to 2000 showcased the art, culture, and politics of diasporic South Asians living in the West. It consistently had substantial gay, lesbian, and bisexual content, including workshops and forums, readings, dance, and theatre by gay and lesbian writers and performers.[90] Blazing still more new trails, Khush hosted 'Discovery '93,' the first international South Asian Gay Men's Conference, which men from all over the world attended.

A women's caucus existed in Khush until 1989, at which time it decided to become part of Asian Lesbians of Toronto (ALOT). The new group was launched when a significant number of Asian women came together at 'Unity Among Asians.' They had their own agenda dealing

with 'questions of identity, of empowerment, the question of our contradictions in history, of being Asian and lesbian and the links between
our oppression – sexism, heterosexism, racism, and classism.'[91] Inspired by organizations for Asian lesbians in the USA, a decision was
made to establish a similar group in Toronto, resulting in ALOT. Founded
in the fall of 1988, ALOT existed until sometime into the early 1990s.

In Vancouver, Gay Asians and the Long Yang Social Club formed in
the mid-1980s. Another group, Very Asian/Vari/Asian appeared in
early 1998, and a youth drop-in for gay Asians in Vancouver under the
age of twenty-five, called Asian GAB, also started up in that year.[92] The
first 'Lotus Roots: A Gathering for East and South-East Asian Lesbians,
Gays, and Bisexuals,' was held in Vancouver in 1996, committed to
'finding out who's out there, getting to know our differences, fighting
conservatism in our various communities, ending internalized racism
and homophobia, giving voice and having voice.'[93] Ottawa's Asians
and Friends was founded in the mid-1980s. In Montreal, Gais et
lesbiennes asiatiques de Montréal has held discussion groups, conducted activism, and put on other activities since the early 1990s.[94]

Following the demise of Zami (see chapter 8), a group specifically for
Black gays did not exist in Toronto until AYA was formed in 1993. It was
dedicated to 'providing support, education, advocacy, and consciousness raising around issues affecting [Black gay men],' and functioned
until 1998.[95] Other organizing efforts by Black gays and lesbians have
included Juka, the Nova Scotia Black Gay, Lesbian, and Bisexual Association, started in the late 1990s, and Black Sisters Supporting Black
Sisters, formed in Toronto in 1998.[96] Another group launched in 1998,
Blackness, Yes, helped broaden the diversity of Toronto's pride events,
through Blackorama – a tent featuring DJs and live music, including
African drummers. It was a response to the fact that black people felt
lost in the overwhelming whiteness of pride, and, as Blackness, Yes
member Junior Harrison stated, the fact that, 'there were spaces where
[Black] people did not feel comfortable.'[97]

Calgary's Of Colour, founded in 1992, was dedicated to addressing
'the issues of racism/homophobia/sexism in the Lesbian and Gay
population of Calgary; and the effects of these oppressions on people of
colour.'[98] Of Colour was also committed to 'resisting the internalization
of white, oppressive ideology in the way that we resist internalized
homophobia and heterosexism.' According to Michelle Wong, a member of the group, it was mostly 'Asian (Chinese) and South Asian with a
very small number of black people and no aboriginals.'[99] In 1997, a

group for Calgary lesbians, Dykes of Colour, began holding dances and other activities such as potlucks and parties.[100] Diversity, a group for gays and lesbians of colour, was started by a Filipino gay man in Winnipeg in 1994, but unfortunately did not last long.[101] Winnipeg's Lesbians of Colour also existed briefly around 1994. A new social support group, and a second Winnipeg group called Diversity, formed in 1998 for people who are 'queer and colored.'[102] Ottawa's Queer Women of Colour, which held its first meetings in 1998, was started, co-founder Angie Riley noted, because 'there are other women in the community who are alone and who face a lot of the same issues we have.' The group organized discussions, potlucks, and social outings, and described its mandate as being 'a social group that aims to provide a safe space for queer women of colour.'[103]

The increasing ethnocultural diversity of Toronto's gay, lesbian, and bisexual communities, beginning in the late 1980s, also resulted in the growth of groups for queers who are Greek, Italian, Portuguese, and Polish. Launched in the late 1980s was the first group for Latino gays in Toronto, known as ¡Hola![104] In Montreal, the Association des gais et lesbiennes latino-américains de Montréal started in the mid-1990s.[105] Latin American lesbians in Toronto formed their own group in 1993, called No Me Digas Que No Sabias. One of the founders, Marta Calderon, stated at the time: 'The lesbians wanted a more political group, not just a social club,' in order to fight against homophobia, sexism, racism, and other forms of oppression. Another concern she cited was the racism she encountered in lesbian bars. 'I see, hear, and feel it all the time,' she stated.[106]

The challenges and issues facing two-spirited peoples have been quite similar in some ways to those of gays, lesbians, and bisexuals of colour, but they have also differed significantly. Homophobia and heterosexism, both externally manifested and internalized, are factors which two-spirited people also have had to deal with, along with the language and cultural differences they encounter when leaving Aboriginal communities for the gay and lesbian communities of Canada's cities. They do so because of homophobia on the reservations, where they are generally fearful about openly expressing their sexuality. Sue Beaver of the Two-Spirited People of the First Nations has noted this about being a lesbian on the reserve in Ontario where she grew up: 'It's difficult for me to be open [on the reserve] ... You never know who'll accept or reject you. It's the type of place where everyone knows everybody else, and it was just too claustrophobic.'[107] According to

Albert McLeod of the Manitoba Aboriginal AIDS Task Force, those staying on reserves may be able to lead discreet lives if they have supportive families, but the situation depends entirely on family attitudes.[108] The publication, *We Are Part of a Tradition*, written by Gilbert Dechamps for Toronto-based Two-Spirited People of the First Nations, is blunter, noting that, as a two-spirited person, 'You grow up knowing that the reserve is no place for you.'[109]

Michael Riordon, in *Out Our Way*, his book about gays and lesbians in the small and rural communities of Canada, tells of the experiences related to him by Robert Michael, a resident of the Shubenacadie Micmac reserve in Nova Scotia, who was known in that community as a gay man. His father, when a twelve-year-old Michael disclosed that he was gay, beat him up. In 1992, Michael ran for the band council and was called 'faggot' and 'child molester'; rumours were spread that he had AIDS. His efforts to obtain a house on the reserve were unsuccessful, with some members of the band council saying that he should leave and move to the city. Lamentably, given this homophobic climate, Michael stated he knew about ten kids on the reserve who were gay.[110] Another gay man interviewed by Riordon, identified only as Rick, lived on a reserve on Bear Island in Lake Temagami. He stated it was during a period when he lived in Toronto that he was brought into contact for the first time with the concept of being two-spirited. Rick told of knowing only one other two-spirited person on the reserve, a closeted man with a drinking problem to whom he had never spoken. Rick also indicated he was unable to find some people with whom he could be comfortable talking about the fact that he is gay.[111]

Amidst this adverse climate, groups for First Nations gays, lesbians, and bisexuals emerged in the late 1980s and the early 1990s. An important component of that organizing was reclaiming their history, traditional beliefs, and spirituality. The first significant group for aboriginal gays and lesbians during this period was the Nichiwakan Native Gay and Lesbian Society in Winnipeg. Founded in 1986, it held various social events but, according to member Albert McLeod, it could not sustain itself. 'There needed to be a coming out process' in the group, he recalls. Unfortunately, the group slowly died in the early 1990s. One of its most notable achievements was organizing the third international gathering of native gays and lesbians a few miles outside Winnipeg in August 1990. Called 'Spirituality in the 90's,' it included Native sweats, workshops on traditional Native values, and the first gay and lesbian Native powwow. In 1998, the eleventh annual conference, hosted by the

330 BETWEEN QUEER AND THE MAINSTREAM

Manitoba Aboriginal AIDS Task Force, was also held in rural Manitoba. The majority of the one hundred attendees were from North America, but some came from as far away as South America and Australia. Important to the organizing of such events have been the need to meet in alcohol- and drug-free environments, out of recognition of the level of substance abuse in Aboriginal communities and the desire to reclaim native culture and languages.[112]

At the beginning of 1989, Art Zoccole and Billy Merasty held a meeting at which the Toronto-based Two-Spirited People of the First Nations (TPFN) was born. Zoccole recalls, 'there [were] a lot of Aboriginal people in the gay scene. We would see each other in a bar but we didn't talk to each other. We knew from the beginning there was a need [for a group].'[113] TPFN's goals include providing a place where Aboriginal gays and lesbians can meet, and reclaiming and honouring the sacred role of two-spirited people – members of some Aboriginal communities that were thought to maintain balance and harmony by housing within themselves both male and female spirits. The group fosters a positive image of two-spirited people, especially through traditional teachings. Over its lifetime, TPFN has provided counselling, produced information about and conducted education on AIDS and HIV, engaged in anti-homophobia work, and published a newsletter. It continues its work today.

In January 1993, the Aboriginal Circle of Two-Spirits was formed in Edmonton to help members understand their culture and language and to support one another in dealing with society's stereotypes. James Tsannie, a spokesperson for the group, said at the time of its founding that it would also 'bring about a better awareness of the Aboriginal existence as gays and lesbians in today's society.'[114] In Vancouver, the Two-Spirit Youth Group also formed to hold education sessions on alcohol and drug abuse, HIV, First Nations culture, and suicide prevention. And, for the last couple of years, the Alberta Gay, Lesbian, Bisexual, and Two-Spirited Rural Youth Outreach project has been operated by Planned Parenthood in Calgary.

As with the organizing among other lesbians, gays, and bisexuals of colour, two-spirited activists have taken a distinctly liberationist approach, rather than a narrow equality-seeking assimilationist one. Asserting a positive same-sex sexuality, building self-esteem, dealing with internalized homophobia, being out and visible as two-spirited people, creating a sense of community, and fighting against the homophobia and heterosexism of heterosexuals have been in the forefront of their battles. Working towards legislative change has necessarily been of secondary importance. They have melded lesbian and gay liberation consciousness with pride in being Aboriginal and, significantly, with the honour of being two-spirited. Gilbert Deschamps, in *We Are Part of a Tradition*, notes, 'It is well known that before the Europeans, most indigenous societies had names for homosexuals and far more than just identify us, these names reflected a recognition of the sacredness of two-spirited people. We were respected and vital parts of our societies.' Citing the influence of colonization and the imposition of Christianity, Deschamps then observes, 'We often grow up without a language to describe ourselves: Lesbian, gay or queer are used as curses and insults. With the influence of the Church and Europeans, two-spirited is a tradition pushed so far away, only a few remember it and even fewer honour it. You receive no support and you see no role models and you are left to find your own way. Maybe your life is threatened because people "know" or maybe it's just your sanity that is in danger.'[115] Then, using an analysis that any lesbian and gay liberationist of the 1970s would have readily understood – the gay is good message in a different context – *We Are Part of a Tradition* identifies a solution: 'We, as the two-spirited community, must heal. We must re-learn that to be two-spirited is an honour. We have grown up with the single message that lesbians and gay men are sick. We are in the process of rebuilding a positive self-image as a result of this past. And if, as in the larger First Nations community, two-spirited people suffer from suicide, substance abuse, and short life spans, then we must recognize this as symptom of a very different illness.'[116] Continuing that analysis, Deschamps declares:

> We did not choose our sexuality; our sexuality chose us. The Creator made us different and the Creator made us special for a reason. Our lives are radically different from 'straight' Native people. We understand that as Native people, we have been oppressed and do not enjoy Canada as one of the best places in the world to live. We also understand that heterosexual Native people enjoy more privilege in this society than we as two-spirits do. To be two-spirited is more than who you sleep with. We are community in and of ourselves. Our ways of talking, interacting with each other, ways of seeing the world and how we experience life are different from other First Nations people.[117]

For those seeking signs that lesbian and gay liberation remains alive, reading such inspiring and affirming language of liberation gives assurance that homophobia and heterosexism still are being militantly combatted. Indeed, many queers still urgently need the freedom that can be wrought by the revolutionary force of lesbian and gay liberation, in much the same way as did the ghettoized and oppressive lives of the mainly white, urban, and young queers of the early 1970s. Examining contemporary groups for lesbians and gays of colour and two-spirited peoples, and their ethoses and missions – something that rarely has been done to date – testifies to the fact that lesbian and gay liberation remains a potent and empowering force, even in these days of seemingly endless equality-seeking triumphalism. Those convinced that lesbian and gay liberation is dead, or at least is a spent force, have not taken the time to look around at what is happening outside the comfortable, white, middle-class existences populating the contented realm of assimilationism. The struggles of lesbians and gays of colour and two-spirited people to liberate themselves and their sexualities do not garner bold headlines or attract the massive public attention that now features prominently in campaigns to secure spousal benefits or the right to marry. The new struggles for liberation do not make demands on the politicians and the mainstream institutions in the way that equality-seeking advocacy does. But in the long run – just as the message that gay is good and the militant beseeching by gays, lesbians, and bisexuals to come out of the closet and wage war against homophobia and oppression revolutionized queer communities thirty years ago – organizing by queers of colour and Aboriginal gays, lesbians, and bisexuals will have a profound and long-lasting impact, changing forever the consciousness and lives of the members of those communities.

Queering the Arts

Encouraging signs of the existence and vibrancy of lesbian and gay liberation at the end of the twentieth century were also found in endeavours to assert queer presence and visibility within, and inject queer themes and sensibilities into, the arts. In fact, there has been over the last fifteen years an explosion of queer culture. Queer fiction and poetry, drama and art, film and video have thrived. More gay, lesbian, and bisexual authors, poets, artists, entertainers, and filmmakers have come out of the closet. Community-based companies and community-organized cultural events testify to the progress made under the banner of lesbian and gay liberation. Grass-roots cultural initiatives have provided venues and audiences, and in some cases, the foundations for a strong cultural infrastructure that otherwise would not have been built through mainstream organizations because of homophobia and heterosexism and their resultant censorship. A noteworthy example of a liberationist embarking on new frontiers has been Sky Gilbert. In 1985, he conceived of an annual festival in which drama dealing openly, and sometimes outrageously, with gay and lesbian characters and situations could be performed in a comfortable environment before gay and lesbian audiences. Thus was born 4-Play, which by 1990 had become part of a much larger Queer Culture festival in Toronto. Queer Culture featured drag performances, music, film and video, dance, visual arts, and parties. Gilbert also founded Buddies in Bad Times Theatre that, in the mid-1980s, opened its own small theatre after initially operating out of other venues, including, for a time, the 519 Church Street Community Centre. In 1994, assisted by funding from the City of Toronto, Buddies moved into the refurbished Alexander Street Theatre in downtown Toronto, establishing it as Canada's foremost gay and lesbian theatre.

Similarly motivated by the need to provide a forum for queer expression, Queer Press was founded in the late 1980s in Toronto. Since then, it has been dedicated to publishing works by gay, lesbian, and bisexual authors. One of its book was the pioneering anthology, *Rice: Exploration into Gay Asian Culture + Politics*, published in 1998. Another alternative publisher, Sister Vision: Black Women and Women of Color Press, founded in 1985 by Makeda Silvera and Stephanie Martin, has contributed enormously to the growth of queer culture and, in particular, to the promotion of works by lesbians of colour. Through Sister Vision, Silvera published *Piece of My Heart*, a 1991 anthology of writings by lesbians of colour and, in 1994, *Her Head a Village*, which, among other experiences, tells of the homophobia encountered by a Black lesbian couple. Sister Vision continued to break new ground in 1994 by publishing *The Very Inside: An Anthology of Writings by Asian and Pacific Islander Lesbian and Bisexual Women*, a rich anthology edited by Sharon Lim-Hing. Also fostering the production of more art, poetry, literature, and theatre for lesbians of colour, De Poonani Posse, a Toronto Black lesbian-focused collective, was formed in the early 1990s. The first national conference dedicated to queer writers was held in Vancouver in 1997. 'Write Out West: Canada's First Lesbian, Gay, Transgender, and Bisexual Writers' Conference,' featured as speakers or panelists such authors as Persimmon Blackbridge, Stan Persky, Rosamund Elwin, and Shani Mootoo.

Visual and performance art, film, and video have been equally crucial to the development of queer culture in Canadian cities. Since the mid-1980s, Vancouver's Kiss & Tell collective has produced photography, multimedia exhibits, performance art, and books. Consisting of Susan Stewart, Persimmon Blackbridge, and Lizard Jones, their works have featured lesbian and queer themes and have dealt with issues such as gender and marginality.[118] In Toronto, the Xtra Space Gallery was founded in 1989 to profile community-oriented art. Between 1990 and 1995, Gallery Without Walls carried out a mandate to 'promote, encourage, and facilitate the creation and exhibition of works or art by, about, for or of interest to the gay and lesbian community, regardless of content, context or source.'[119] To provide an opportunity for gay, lesbian, and bisexual film and videomakers to show their work and for members of the community to view them, annual film and video festivals have been established in several Canadian cities. The first international festival, *Inverted Image*, organized by *Xtra!* in November 1986, featured thirty-one films screened over a ten-day period. Its success prompted the founding of Inside Out lesbian and gay film and video festival, in 1991. In 1996, the Asian Heritage Month Festival was kicked off by a weekend that focused on the works of gay and lesbian artists, writers, and filmmakers. Elsewhere, Winnipeg began holding an annual gay and lesbian film festival in 1987. Ottawa's annual Lesbian and Gay Film and Video Festival commenced in 1992, as did the annual lesbian film festival in London. Vancouver launched the Lesbian Film Festival in 1988, which later became the annual Out on Screen festival.

As with other social and political endeavours by queer communities to assert visibility, celebrate their sexualities, and promote a distinctive culture, some of these initiatives generated furious backlash, outraged indignation, and homophobic hatred, often at the instigation of fundamentalist Christians aided by conservative politicians and media. This has been especially true concerning funding of queer culture through tax-supported programs, or the use of tax-supported venues for queer culture events. One such incident occurred in Saskatoon, when some city councillors voiced outrage over a showing of works by gay artist Evergon in the city-owned Mendel Art Gallery in 1990. The protest, spurred by a group called the Society of Christian Counselling Services, fortunately did not succeed in closing down the exhibition but generated a great deal of media coverage.[120] Provision of grants by the Canada Council to gay and lesbian arts groups, including Buddies In Bad Times, was described in early 1990 by the federal minister of national revenue as 'ridiculous' and an abuse of taxpayers' money.[121] In another incident, angry, right wing backlash fuelled by the *Alberta Report* magazine and the Canadian Taxpayers Foundation engulfed a gay and lesbian cultural festival held in the tax-funded Banff Centre in 1992. The particular foci of homophobic outrage were an exhibition of erotica and a performance by the Kiss & Tell Collective. The latter was denounced as 'a sacrilegious obscenity' by 'foul-mouthed, sex-obsessed lesbians.'[122] Seizing upon an SM seminar and one called 'The Female Ejaculation Pajama Party' held at Buddies in Bad Times, a *Toronto Sun* columnist, aided by a group called Concerned Citizens of Toronto, launched a campaign in 1993 to stop city funding for the theatre, and to reject an application for funding of the Inside Out film festival. A council committee, swayed by the campaign, recommended that the two groups not be funded, making them the only two out of 230 cultural groups that were not supported. In the end, a counter effort mounted by gay and lesbian activists and the arts community persuaded the city council to maintain funding for Buddies, but not for the film festival.[123]

In Calgary, the 1995 lesbian and gay film festival, The Fire I've Become, gained national publicity when religious fundamentalists criticized it as being 'a pornographic film orgy.' They were particularly upset that the festival received a $4,000 grant from the Canada Council and was taking place in a tax-funded civic facility. One evangelical minister was quoted in the press as saying, 'I'm not after the homos or the bi's, I'm after the fact they're showing porno movies in a tax-funded situation.'[124] Michelle Wong, a spokesperson for Of Colour, which organized the festival, retorted: 'We do put money into government coffers,' by paying taxes. Explaining the purpose of the festival, Wong added, 'It's bringing gay, lesbian, and bisexual issues into the public.' Unfortunately, in an example of how the desire for respectability on the part of some activists can excuse homophobia, a member of Calgary's Project Pride supported the outcry: 'They [the organizers] have put the gay and lesbian community back 20 years.'[125] Although all the films and videos shown were cleared by the Alberta Film Classification Board, members of the governing Conservative Party vowed to review provincial arts funding programs.

A comparable clamour erupted over Queer City Cinema 2000 in Regina, after conservative politicians and Christian activists protested government grants to the festival, which showed erotic films and featured a panel discussion on pornography. About twenty fundamentalist Christians picketed outside the festival's venue and the neoconservative Saskatchewan Party raised questions in the provincial legislature about 'a bunch of porn stars coming to Regina to promote porno movies sponsored by the Sask Arts Board, SaskFILM, and Sask Tel.' Festival organizer Gary Varro countered: 'Regina doesn't really have a festival that shows different types of queer expression. This festival provides an opportunity for queers in Regina and Saskatchewan to discuss issues of community attitude and allows viewers to see different images of being gay or lesbian.' However, an article in *Xtra!* reported that other members of the city's gay and lesbian community objected to the festival and the inclusion of a discussion on pornography.[126]

Liberating the Schools

Over the last decade or so, gay, lesbian, and bisexual groups across the country have also intensified their efforts to eradicate heterosexism and homophobia as all too powerful influencers in Canada's educational systems. It's a daunting challenge, as the schools, universities, and colleges of this country are often hostile and unsafe places for lesbians, gays, bisexuals, and transgendered people in the first place. The religious teachings of sin and immorality and the medical theories of sickness or deviation still dominate the portrayal of homosexuality in the education system at all levels – when it is discussed at all. One result is that openly lesbian, gay, or bisexual students face ostracism, harassment, and violence, and feel vulnerable and at risk. Resources on sexual orientation issues generally are not available to them. Even tolerant or enlightened teachers and counsellors seldom receive training in how to deal with gays, lesbians, bisexuals, or transgenderists who are their students, or with the harassment such students receive from their classmates. As Madiha Didi Khayatt has chronicled in *Lesbian Teachers: An Invisible Presence*, the belief that the role of schools is to shape obedient, conformist, and therefore heterosexual citizens is deeply entrenched and arduously supported by the state.[127] Not surprisingly, educational institutions generally have been unreceptive to suggestions they should play a positive and proactive role in promoting awareness and understanding of sexual orientation issues. In addition, attempting to use the system to counteract homophobia and heterosexism leads to charges of gays recruiting the young and impressionable, of proselytizing on behalf of an unacceptable or immoral lifestyle.

It challenges traditional notions about role models and mentoring. The rare attempts to address homosexuality as a topic in school curricula have been, for the most part, timid and tepid.[128]

Religious right and social conservative groups fiercely resist curricula changes or policy measures to positively address sexual orientation issues. They respond to such initiatives with outraged, noisy condemnations, using fear, stereotypes, religious teachings, and the dubious claims of certain psychiatrists to pressure school boards and administrators to preserve family values. They have organized strenuously against initiatives to remove discrimination or make the schools safer places for gays, lesbians, and bisexuals. They have savagely denounced the inclusion of positive, or even neutral, references to homosexuality in sex education or other curricula. They oppose educating teachers, administrators, and other students about homophobia and its effect on gay, lesbian, and bisexual students. Religious fundamentalists, or organizations dominated by them, have waged bitter battles to prevent AIDS education about safer sex practices and measures dealing with homophobic harassment and violence in schools.[129]

The Toronto Board of Education has long been the target of such groups because of its efforts over several years to develop policies and curricula dealing with sexual orientation. Religious zealots and other social conservatives organized massively in 1992, following the Toronto board's repeal of an anti-proselytization policy, adopted several years earlier. At the same time, it released a gay-positive curriculum guideline, developed with input from members of the gay, lesbian, and bisexual communities, for use in the schools, called Sexual Orientation: Homosexuality, Lesbianism, and Homophobia. Ken Campbell's Christian Freedom Party responded by running an advertisement in the *Globe and Mail* exhorting the citizenry to rise up in protest against 'the perversity of this gay/lesbian propaganda' being imposed on classrooms 'AGAINST THE WILL of the overwhelming majority of PARENTS.'[130] Hudson Hilsden, representing Canadians for Decency, Judy Anderson, national president of REAL Women, the Evangelical Fellowship of Canada, and Citizens United for Responsible Education (CURE) joined the protest. CURE was particularly active in mounting an emotionally intense, high-profile campaign that sought to frighten parents by asserting that the new policy would subject students to 'thought control ... hypnotic techniques ... [and] emotional control.' They accused the policy of being 'intolerant against 90 per cent of the population [heterosexuals].'[131] Fortunately, their efforts were not successful.

The Toronto board did not repeal its policy. Nonetheless, renewed religious organizing greeted the efforts of a new, amalgamated City of Toronto Board of Education in 1999–2000 to adopt a human rights and equity program that specifically addressed discrimination and harassment on the basis of sexual orientation. This time, many of the efforts to defeat the initiative were led by Muslims opposed to any sex education in the school system, as well as to any discussion of homosexuality. A spokesperson for The Toronto District Muslim Education Assembly commented, 'In my religion, [homosexuality] is not normal – at school the teacher says its normal, and this is not good for the kids.' Described by the school board's chair as 'fractious and intolerant,' members of the assembly would attempt to hijack board meetings and, she noted, 'Sometimes they would just scream.'[132]

CURE and like-minded groups remained active in several communities during the 1990s. A CURE group formed in 1994 by a school trustee and parents, organized to prevent a professional development workshop by the London Board of Education on lesbian and gay issues, and to impose a moratorium on sex education in the schools. Packing a meeting of the school board, they displayed anti-gay and religious placards. CURE, promoting abstinence and chastity as the basis for AIDS education in the schools, also publicly condemned the AIDS Committee of London for conducting 'values neutral' AIDS education in London schools. It was part of a systematic, North American–wide effort by evangelical Christian organizations. Clarence Crossman, the AIDS committee's education coordinator, noted that 'a lot of the resources and materials developed by the religious right in the United States is being utilized here in Canada.'[133] Another group, the Citizens' Research Institute, conducted initiatives in BC communities during 1993 to gain support for its 'Declaration of Family Rights.' Among its demands was forbidding a teacher from talking about homosexuality in a positive way to any student if the student's parent had signed a copy of the declaration.[134] Also active was the Family Coalition Party, which opposed inclusion, in 1997, of sexual orientation in the Coquitlam Board of Education's antidiscrimination policy, as well as changes in the curriculum that would have permitted the discussion of sexual orientation issues.[135] In Manitoba, a furore was generated in 1998 and 1999 over the plan of Winnipeg School Division No. 1 to introduce anti-homophobia programs. Local radio stations condemned the move, urging listeners to lodge protests with the school board. Social conservative groups organized massively against the policy, calling it a 'moral issue.'

Fortunately, the board held firm and the opposition eventually dissipated.[136] A group calling itself Parents' Choice Association (PCA) led a public campaign attacking a 1996 decision by the Calgary Board of Education to establish an Action Plan for Gay/Lesbian/Bisexual Youth and Staff Safety. PCA's chair, who purported to counsel 'recovering homosexuals,' accused the policy of teaching children that 'homosexuality is a healthy, acceptable lifestyle.'[137] Citing a common tactic of such groups, Stephen Lock, a long-time Calgary gay activist, wrote in *Xtra! West* that one group 'twisted a variety of research findings to suit their arguments, relied heavily on "research" done by Paul Cameron and his Washington DC-based Family Research Institute ... Unfortunately, as falsified and distorted as their arguments often were, they were presented in ostensibly reasonable, well researched, and objective fashion.'[138] Ultimately, despite the outcry, the board unanimously adopted the policy.

Book banning has also been a feature of recent Canadian history. In 1997, an advocacy group dominated by evangelical Christians succeeded in having the chief superintendent of the Calgary Public School Board ban from school libraries two books dealing with homosexuality, using arguments that they were 'really pro-gay.' Only one of the books was later reinstated, after a review committee determined that it had 'considerable literary and social value.'[139] In 1997, a group based in Milton, Ontario pressured the local school board to ban a book by award-winning American author Joyce Carol Oates. *Foxfire: Confessions of a Girl Gang* had been assigned as reading to a Grade 12 high school class. The action prompted a parent of one student to form a group that distributed 60,000 copies of a flyer condemning the book as 'nothing but a cheap imported sex manual from the United States, glorifying the homosexual behaviour of its lead character.' This resulted in the book being restricted to small groups of students whose parents received prior written notice of its 'controversial material.'[140]

Perhaps the most notorious incident of book banning in recent history occurred in Surrey, British Columbia, in 1997, when the school board prohibited two books in which children have same-sex parents, after religious right trustees had gained a majority of the seats on the board.[141] Advocates for gays and lesbians in British Columbia challenged the banning in the courts, and succeeded in obtaining a judgement that the action was contrary to the British Columbia School Act because it was based on the religious beliefs of board members and parents. The presiding judge ruled that school policies must be governed by strictly secular principles.[142] The board appealed, and, in September 2000, the BC Court of Appeal issued a decision that permitted both sides to claim victory, but left the broader issues unresolved. The appeal court struck down the lower court's overturning of the board's ban. Three justices unanimously found the books in question met the board's criteria for being included in school libraries, and thus could be made available for use in classrooms by teachers who withdrew them from the library. But the justices also rejected the argument that strictly secular principles should govern public education policies. Rather, they held that religious beliefs, along with other beliefs, can properly be used to make decisions about moral issues of education. A prudent teacher, they stated, would use professional judgment and consult with various parents, other teachers, and the principal before using sensitive materials in the classroom. Whether or not the issues raised in the Surrey case are destined ultimately for argument before the Supreme Court of Canada (a decision about further appealing the verdict had not been made at the time of publication), it is doubtful that litigation will prove to be the most effective strategy.

Despite the admitted progress being made by some boards of education in instituting policies to address homophobia and sexual orientation issues in schools, homophobic remarks and harassment, ostracism, vulnerability, and fear about coming out remain features of Canada's schools. A member of the Toronto School Board's Human Sexuality Program recently observed that 'That's so gay' is the current phrase used in the schoolyard to refer to anything considered silly or stupid. A few years ago, he found that 'fag' was one of the first words learned by students whose first languages were not English.[143] Such attitudes can lead to alienation and violence, or at very least, the fear of violence. A Toronto high school teacher, writing in an essay printed in the *Toronto Star* in 1997, related the experiences of a Grade 9 male, as communicated to him in a written assignment: 'Well, I dress as many people have said to me, very feminine, as if I were gay. So simply enough when people look at me they usually think I am just a gay guy ... I have been beaten up many times just because of the suspicion that I may be gay.'[144] Another article in the *Star* a few weeks later noted, 'The lack of a supportive school atmosphere drives some gay, lesbian, and bisexual teens to leave school.' To illustrate that point, it reported the experience of a high school student who dropped out because of constant harassment: 'The big thing was when someone wrote "fag" all over his locker,' commented a friend. 'He went to the school administration and they moved his locker, but they didn't erase the slurs on it, so he still had to walk by it everyday.'[145]

Clarissa Lagartera, remembering her days as an out-of-the-closet high school student during the early 1990s, highlighted in a 1998 interview some typical fears and concerns:

> Was I going to be beaten up? Was I going to be raped? ... Would my marks drop because my fear was, it wasn't even so much people beating me up, actually, it was, you know, my failing grades because then it was sort of a source of my parents' pride, high academics, and this and that. And so, I thought that teachers could possibly prejudice, you know, themselves because of my sexuality if for some reason they're homophobic there was absolutely no way that they would fairly, you know, mark any of my papers and essays. So that was the big thing. The other big thing was not necessarily to be beaten up, but just to be excluded from my athletics by my coaches and what not and whether I would be treated differently.[146]

She also recalled subtle forms of prejudice in the locker room with other members of the basketball team: 'The girls I was playing basketball with, that was really, because we had to change all in the same fitting room and it was an open fitting room, you know. I noticed automatically that three quarters of the room would move, you know, migrate to the other corner or they would find little nooks and crannies where they would be hidden from me as if they didn't want me to look at them.'[147] Equally troublesome was the fact that Lagartera's friends experienced more homophobia than she did. They had to deal with 'being lesbians by association' and were subjected to homophobic remarks about being seen in public with Lagartera.

It is not only students who suffer in this repressive atmosphere: teachers who do not have a heterosexual orientation are vulnerable in the face of homophobia and heterosexism. They fear that if their sexual orientation becomes known they may be fired or, short of that, will risk undermining their authority in the classroom by facing anti-gay remarks or taunts, possibly even threats of violence.[148] Often they have little or no prospect of receiving tangible support from school administrators, school boards, or other teachers. Teachers in the Catholic school systems are particularly vulnerable because of the role played by the church's teachings on homosexuality.[149] And for gay male teachers, there is the dreaded accusation of child molestation. 'There's a tremendous hunt on against pedophiles and homosexuals in the schools,' commented a Quebec teacher's union representative as recently as January 2000.[150]

Given these realities, it is no surprise that fighting homophobia and heterosexism in schools and the education system is quickly moving to the forefront of lesbian and gay organizing. All over the country, in places like Kingston, Ottawa, and Saskatoon, Safe School projects have been launched. Gay-Straight clubs, intended to combat homophobia and provide safe spaces for gay, lesbian, and bisexual students to come together with supportive straights, have cropped up in a number of cities. Other organizations like British Columbia's Gay and Lesbian Educators and the Rainbow Classroom in Ontario have also been formed to deal with homophobia and other issues for teachers, administrators, and students. Joining them in this battle are more established groups like Gay and Lesbian Health Services in Saskatoon and CLGRO. Significantly, as the Surrey case and other volatile skirmishes have indicated, confronting homophobia and heterosexism in the schools will not be won principally by citing equality arguments, or resorting to the Charter of Rights and Freedoms. The issues relate to values and morals, and to which voices are heard and which constituencies count most. The arguments enlisted on both sides are based in notions of indoctrination, socialization, gender identity, sexual morality, and role models. They raise troubling issues about the role of religion in what is allegedly a secular state. Engaging in battles to liberate gays, lesbians, and bisexuals, and their sexuality in the education system must necessarily involve enlisting the fundamental tenets of lesbian and gay liberation. They require sustained ideological warfare waged with resolute conviction in pursuit of clear and uncompromising lesbian and gay liberation objectives, foremost of which is that homosexuality is a natural and healthy sexual orientation. What are needed are liberation strategies based on asserting visibility and rejecting negative images and stereotypes; in the process, these strategies will educate the broader community and foster alliances with progressive heterosexuals who reject religious and heterosexist indoctrination as an objective of the public school system.

Homophobia and Heterosexism in Health and Social Services

The other emerging area of advocacy that draws more upon liberation analyses and strategies than upon equality-seeking advocacy is fighting to eradicate homophobia and heterosexism from health and social services. It is in such fields that the medical models and theories that we discussed in chapter 1, based on homosexuality's being seen as deviant, abnormal, or dysfunctional, are still prevalent. Accordingly, these perceptions impact in many adverse ways the lives of gays, lesbians, and bisexuals accessing services. As well, many health and social service agencies are run or funded by religious organizations. Appallingly, too many individuals are found among Canada's health care and social service professionals who put forward views that homosexuality is sinful, shameful, unnatural, or deviant. Others, while not necessarily holding such views, have failed to educate themselves about gay, lesbian, bisexual, and transgendered people. They know little if anything about the needs of this diverse community. It is no mere coincidence that, as they did at the advent of lesbian and gay liberation, health and social service issues remain an important element on the lesbian and gay liberation agenda at the beginning of a new century.

It is insightful to compare articles written in the early 1970s with some more recent proclamations to see just how little change has occurred in the provision of health and social services, and why liberation advocacy was renewed in the 1990s by taking up this issue. Radicalesbians Health Collective, in the early 1970s, published a document, *Lesbians and the Health Care System*, which proclaimed, 'The health system as it is now postulates superior-inferior relationships where the professional knows everything and the lesbian patient has no right to speak for herself.' Observing that 'the health system is geared to serving the heterosexual nuclear family,' the collective spelled out its agenda: 'We demand that health "professionals" stop destroying our lives by teaching that lesbianism is a sickness that should be cured or abolished. They perpetuate and give validity to a society where lesbians are forced to hide.' They then issued a call to action: 'HEALTHY LESBIAN MINDS IN HEALTHY LESBIAN BODIES!'[151] Equally radical in condemning conventional medical professionals, the Chicago Gay Liberation Front, in 'A Leaflet for the American Medical Association,' declared:

> The establishment school of psychiatry is based on the premise that people who are hurting should solve their problems by 'adjusting' to the situation. For the homosexual, this means becoming adept at straight-fronting, learning how to survive in a hostile world, how to settle for housing in the gay ghetto, how to be satisfied in a profession in which homosexuals are tolerated, and how to live with low self-esteem.

The adjustment school places the burden on each individual homosexual to learn to bear his torment. But the 'problem' of homosexuality is
never solved under this scheme; the anti-homosexualist attitude of society,
which is the cause of the homosexual's trouble, goes unchallenged. And
there's always another paying patient on the psychiatrist's couch.[152]

Over two decades later, CLGRO, in its *Systems Failure* report on the
experiences of sexual minorities in Ontario's health care and social
services systems, stated, in terms echoing the early liberationists:

Heterosexuals are clearly the targeted constituency of health care and
social services in Ontario. Others are mainly invisible. They are noticed
only when they assert themselves, or when their needs are so dramatic
that they cannot be overlooked (as in the case of gay men and AIDS).
Then, what is offered may be well intentioned, but is just as likely to be
inadequate or inappropriate.

At the very least, these services anticipate that, if people are not heterosexual, they will be heterosexual-like in both appearance and lifestyle. For
example, those whose relationships do not fall into the nuclear-family
model or members of such communities as leather, drag, or S/M are not
accepted. Individual service-providers are often aware of their existence,
but the services themselves are not prepared to receive them.[153]

The respondents to a survey conducted for the CLGRO project reported
psychiatrists and religious leaders as the most problematic of the most
commonly seen service providers, followed by psychologists, social
workers, and medical doctors.[154] Revealingly, the top five reasons cited
by respondents from across Ontario for accessing social services were
coming-out issues, self-esteem and self-confidence, loneliness and isolation, family problems related to sexual orientation, and sexual abuse
as a child.[155]

The ravages of homophobia and heterosexism on the lives of individual gays, lesbians, and bisexuals cannot be fully or adequately addressed by legislative changes achieved by equality-seeking advocacy
or by finding the nearest gay or lesbian bar. As Gens Hellquist, of
Saskatoon's Gay and Lesbian Health Services – one of the Canada's
leading gay activists in the field of health and social services – observed
in a 1997 interview:

In order for people to maintain a healthy life, they need to be able to develop a broad-based support system, not just a bar they can go to on a regular or semi-regular basis but, I mean, if you look at how the heterosexual world develops, they are able to access peer support, and build a supportive network in all kinds of places. Gays and lesbians, we don't. We often get herded into a bar somewhere or a club or we have one or two venues that only allows us to access that group. So I think what we are trying to do is develop a wide range of programs that allow people to develop a broader personal and peer support system that allows them to maintain their good health, and also to help them cope with all the shit we as queers have to live with in this society.[156]

The needs are certainly great and urgent. Tragically, homophobia and heterosexism lead many gays and lesbians to hate themselves or cause them to have low self-esteem. Suicide is the leading cause of death among gay and lesbian youth, who account for as many as 30 per cent of all successful suicide attempts. Negative reactions to their sexual orientation, either actual or anticipated, have been found to be a primary reason for this.[157] Various forms of mental illness have been found prevalent among lesbians and gays: severe depression, anxiety, paranoia, and extreme loneliness. In addition, bashing victims require medical treatment, and discrimination in employment or housing can cause stress and stress-related illnesses. Alcohol and drug dependency, often the result of attempting to live in a homophobic society, puts gays, lesbians, bisexuals, and transgendered people in contact with a host of social service and medical professionals.[158] Gay and Lesbian Health Services in Saskatoon reported, as part of a research project in 1996, that 'lesbians, gay men, and bisexuals experience a range of health and social problems that are significantly out of proportion with the rest of our society. Homophobia and heterosexism are major health and social issues in our society today, however, there are precious few programs developed to address the impact that homophobia and hate have on the health of lesbians, gay men, and bisexuals.'[159]

Yet, the experiences of gays, lesbians, and bisexuals when seeking access to health and social services are often negative or unpleasant. They face denial of services, or inappropriate services based on heterosexual biases or models, a blame-the-victim attitude, and responses that are judgmental, hostile, patronizing, or moralizing. Health and social service agencies, hospitals, and institutions refuse to recognize same-sex relationships, denying to those who are in them access to family services, visitation privileges, or same-sex partner decision-making rights. Relationship situations that would be treated with sensitivity, compassion, and dignity when heterosexual are often dealt with in just the opposite manner when they are same-sex. As CLGRO's *Systems Failure* reported, there is a nearly total absence of comprehensive, system-wide programs and strategies dealing with the health and social service needs of gays, lesbians, and bisexuals. Virtually no Ontario organizations were found to be proactively dealing with homophobia and heterosexism on the part of service providers. Governments have not made service equity for gays, lesbians, and bisexuals a priority. Few health care and social service providers have information specifically prepared for gay, lesbian, and bisexual clients, or know about or make contact with community groups in their locales. Similarly, professional associations that train and qualify health care and social service professionals have only the most minimal of policies (if any at all) about sexual orientation issues, and virtually no training programs to ensure services are provided for gays, lesbians, bisexuals, and transgendered people.[160] Gays, lesbians, and bisexuals working for health and social service agencies frequently live in fear of having their sexual orientation disclosed with detrimental effects for their careers.

The urgent need to address the abysmal state of health and social services for queer Canadians is fostering a new advocacy agenda that, by the early twenty-first century, showed signs of becoming a fully-fledged national movement. In addition to pioneering groups like GLHS and CLGRO, others across the country have begun conducting research and organizing around health care issues. In British Columbia, the Gay, Lesbian, Bisexual and Transgendered Population Health Advisory Committee was established by the Vancouver-Richmond health board in 1997 to liaise with members of the gay, lesbian, bisexual, and transgendered communities, to define health issues and to develop viable solutions. A conference identified as a top health priority the need to conduct public education to reduce homophobia.[161] Also in British Columbia, the Lesbian, Gay, Bisexual, and Transgendered Health Association launched its Health Care Access Project in 1998. It grew out of the Health Committee of the December 9th Coalition to identify the health issues and concerns for queer people in BC's lower mainland. The new group planned to develop a resource guide and to conduct focus groups, one-on-one interviews, and other outreach activities.[162] Similarly, a group formed in Ottawa in 1999 to explore and address a variety of health issues for queer communities. At the national level,

GLHS sponsored a national conference in the fall of 2001 that explored national strategies and cooperation.

'We Are Everywhere': Lesbian and Gay Pride

At the beginning of the twenty-first century, lesbians, gays, and bisexuals, as a distinct group or community, are gradually becoming tolerated by and within the mainstream – so long as they behave and espouse the prevailing heterosexual mores. Significantly, however, their sexuality, and their expressions or depictions of it, continue to be seen in much the same way as they have always been, as deviant or unnatural, as 'queer.' Great progress has been made in achieving legal equality and social tolerance (as distinct from acceptance of homosexuality as a natural and healthy alternative to heterosexuality). This is most immediately evidenced by the grudging extension by the state of legislated human rights protections in response to dogged activism by lesbians, gays, and bisexuals, and the beginning of legal recognition of same-sex relationships. Through such means, some of the most basic, day-to-day forms of discrimination are being addressed. The raising of these issues in the public realm has also helped immeasurably to challenge some of the pervasive homophobia and heterosexism, even if it has not eradicated them. Yet, gay, lesbian, and bisexual same-sex sexuality remains, at best, 'wrong' or in various ways inferior, unacceptable, or immoral – something not to be condoned or encouraged, and certainly not to be celebrated as a normal and natural alternative to heterosexuality. Depictions or descriptions of same-sex acts are censored and repressed. Inordinate concern is shown by the state and social institutions over the harmful affects thought to arise from having children or youth exposed to openly gay, lesbian, or bisexual people, and over youth being lured into the depraved and immoral homosexual lifestyle.

As for the lesbian and gay movement in the period from 1985 to 1999, we have seen that some aspects changed significantly, while others remained very much in the mode of two decades earlier. Two distinct tracks or ideologies emerged to vie for influence and dominance in this period. While equality rights campaigns thrived and succeeded, campaigns based on liberated sexuality and resistance to state repression remained an important, if more controversial and marginalized, element of gay and lesbian activism. But other dynamics also characterized the period. Lesbians continued to experience tremendous difficulties working with both gay men and straight women, and a national lesbian movement did not materialize. AIDS advocacy and the groups affected by AIDS/HIV were profoundly changed. Queer culture prospered and community building expanded. The increasing diversity of lesbian, gay, and bisexual communities led to the proliferation of groups specifically for people of colour, aboriginal peoples, Latin American gays and lesbians, and gays and lesbians from various other ethnocultural communities. And for gays, lesbians, and bisexuals in smaller urban centres and rural settings, very little was different in 1999 from what had been the case in earlier decades. They struggled to be visible, to escape from isolation and loneliness, to create safe spaces, and to live their lives without fear and harassment, in ways that remained distressingly unchanged. Accordingly, much remained on the movement's agenda, and many new battles lay up ahead.

As for the struggle between assimilationists and activists for dominance of the advocacy agenda, those looking for signs of whether or not lesbian and gay liberation continues to be a presence need look no further than the annual pride celebrations that flourished between 1985 and 1999. The notion of lesbian and gay pride, publicly and exuberantly celebrated, spread irreversibly beyond the biggest cities, embraced by gays, lesbians, bisexuals, and transgendered people in communities everywhere. Symbolizing lesbian and gay liberation through celebration of sexuality and queerness, these events exposed and confronted raw homophobia and pervasive heterosexism. The belief that one can have pride in a same-sex orientation that should be publicly proclaimed in festive fashion is still fiercely resisted. Accordingly, pride events have met with outrage from heterosexuals and, occasionally, produced acts of hostility by homophobes. Social conservatives have condemned them and mayors and city councils have refused to issue proclamations to recognize them.

Throughout the 1990s, pride events grew quite large in many cities, becoming distinctive cultural festivals. The largest, in Toronto, now attracts hundreds of thousands of participants and spectators. But many thousands also annually march in or watch Vancouver's Lesbian, Gay, and Bisexual Pride Day parade and turn out for Diverse/Cité in Montreal. Ottawa's event had grown to ten thousand participants by 1998. Pride Day parades and rallies in cities like Victoria, Calgary, Edmonton, Winnipeg, Windsor, London, and Halifax regularly attract anywhere from several hundred to a few thousand people. Wonderously, in the mid-to-late 1990s, lesbian and gay pride parade events were held for the first time in Kelowna, Nanaimo, Prince George, Kitchener-Waterloo, Kingston, Sudbury, Yellowknife, and Charlottetown. Sometimes, marching in a lesbian and gay pride parade took courage and perseverance. In Charlottetown, the first pride parade drew about one hundred participants who were confronted by onlookers hurling oranges and insults such as 'Go home you fuckin' perverts.'[163]

As much political as they are cultural events, lesbian and gay pride festivities have drawn the enmity of several mayors in cities across the country. Local politicians, along with or at the instigation of religious and social conservative militants, have rejected and denounced lesbian and gay pride. Successive Winnipeg mayors, for example, adamantly refused, from 1988 onwards, to issue pride day proclamations, despite repeated requests from the city's lesbian and gay communities. In 1990, Winnipeg mayor Bill Norrie was quoted publicly as saying gays should not 'go around parading their homosexuality.'[164] A vitriolic reaction greeted a decision by Regina's City Council to proclaim Lesbian and Gay Pride Weekend in June 1989. Councillors were inundated with accusations of promoting immoral and disease-ridden behaviour. Some received death threats.[165] Stung by the outpouring of hate, mayor Doug Archer refused to issue a proclamation in 1990, prompting a long ten-year period before another proclamation was issued and, even then, the issuance resulted from a ruling of the province's human rights commission that the refusal was discriminatory.[166] A similar uproar erupted in Ottawa following a proclamation issued by the city council in 1990. The fact that pride day was being held on Father's Day infuriated a segment of the heterosexual population, and, shaken by their protests, the council promptly rescinded the proclamation. Les McAfee of EGALE observed after these events, 'This whole thing is homophobic ... It's plain, utter, simple discrimination.'[167] Calgary's mayor Al Duerr was another who cravenly mollified a vociferous element within the straight community following a concerted anti-gay campaign in response to his 1991 proclamation for a lesbian and gay pride day. After about six hundred angry phone calls flooded his office, most of them from fundamentalist Christians, he recanted, vowing not to issue any other such proclamations in future.[168]

Other mayors have been even more belligerent. Toronto mayor Art Eggleton refused pride day proclamations every year from 1985 until leaving office in 1991, declaring at one point, 'I wouldn't declare a heterosexual day either.'[169] (The question of issuing a proclamation was finally resolved when Eggleton's successor, June Rowlands, issued one in 1992.) In Hamilton, mayor Robert Morrow was equally intransigent about issuing a proclamation, prompting that city's gay and lesbian community to file a complaint of discrimination with the Ontario Human Rights Commission. Predictably, a firestorm of criticism from the religious right, some media, and a variety of commentators followed a 1995 human rights board of inquiry finding that Morrow's refusal constituted sexual orientation discrimination. The commission was accused by a leading Christian fundamentalist crusader of becoming 'a front for the arrogant imposition on the majority of the agenda of special interest minorities.' A handful of supporters picketed outside city hall on the day Morrow finally issued the proclamation.[170] Religious views about homosexuality also featured prominently in the decision of London's mayor, Dianne Haskett, to refuse a proclamation. Like Morrow, she became the subject of a human rights complaint. A strong Christian, Haskett, as reported in Xtra!, acknowledged during testimony before a human rights tribunal that her position was motivated by her beliefs about homosexuality, namely, 'It's against God's will ... I don't believe it's the best way, the way that was intended. I know that people fall into it. I don't condemn them, but it's not the way God intended and I believe people should be set free from that.'[171] Haskett was deemed by the tribunal to have discriminated against the gay, lesbian, and bisexual communities and was ordered to issue a proclamation.[172]

Similarly, the mayors of Fredericton and Kelowna were found by human rights tribunals, in 1998 and 2000 respectively, to have discriminated when they rejected requests for pride day proclamations. Fredericton's mayor, Brad Woodside, claimed that, in doing so, he was representing the majority opinion in the city: 'It [a proclamation] does not represent, in my estimation, what the community is all about and what would be accepted by the community.'[173] Woodside was ordered to issue a proclamation and he did eventually, but grudgingly, comply. 'It's a travesty to order somebody to make a statement they do not believe,' he contended.[174] Kelowna's mayor, Walter Gray, made much the same argument when he agreed to issue a proclamation only if it said 'gay day' and omitted 'pride.' 'Don't ask me to say I'm proud of the event,' he told the press. Being forced to include 'pride,' he asserted, would infringe his right to freedom of expression.[175] Angered, the Okanagan Rainbow Coalition filed a human rights complaint. During the human rights hearing that ensued, Gray declared that he did not approve of homosexuality, and that he had changed the wording of the declaration so that it would be 'politically acceptable' to the citizens of his city. The tribunal chair, however, ruled that the mayor's decision was 'tantamount to a political insult,' and represented unlawful discrimination. Unrepentant, Gray responded to the ruling by announcing he would cease issuing any proclamations of any kind.[176]

Because of the importance to gays, lesbians, and bisexuals of expressing pride in their sexual orientation, and the bigoted reactions based on heterosexism and homophobia which are generated by that, pride day proclamations are likely to continue to be in the forefront of movement advocacy for many years yet. As barbara findlay, a lesbian activist in Vancouver has commented, 'The phrase [gay pride] is to the gay liberation movement what the phrase "black is beautiful" is to the American civil rights movement.' And, in reference to the Kelowna case, she added, 'To take away the word pride is to succeed in taking pride away from gays and lesbians and to imply that it is not pride, but shame that should be associated with them.'[177] It is sobering that, in the year 2000, the promotion of pride first conceived by liberationists in the late 1960s should still have had such resonance and militancy. The reality is that pride celebrations have impact because, in the words of Martha Shelley of the 1970s Gay Liberation Front – expressed so eloquently in the 'Gay is Good' manifesto – they are declarations of wanting 'something more than the tolerance you [liberal heterosexuals] never gave us.'[178] Pride is arguably the most visible and massive contemporary manifestation of the 1970s call to action: 'Out of the closets and into the streets! Gay liberation now!'

Lesbian and Gay Liberation
in the Twenty-First Century

It is clear, as this book documents, that lesbian and gay activism and organizing over the last three decades have achieved remarkable success, and have profoundly changed queer communities all across Canada. At the same time, homophobia and heterosexism remain pervasive and rampant. The historical notions of sin and criminality, and the more recent contentions of sickness and dysfunction, chronicled in Part One, continue to imbue contemporary attitudes and to motivate the actions of the Canadian state, police, media, and social institutions. Nonetheless, lesbian and gay liberation has left an indelible mark. The movement it began and continues to influence was, without doubt, one of the major social phenomena of the late twentieth century. Lesbian and gay liberation unleashed a momentum for change that, with varying degrees of strength and visibility, has managed to survive for over thirty years and remains potent within queer communities. More important, the advocacy agenda developed by liberationist activism in the early and mid-1970s has been doggedly pursued over the subsequent decades. Gays, lesbians, and bisexuals have become increasingly more visible, asserting their presence in Canadian society and resisting attempts from many fronts to drive them back into the closets and the fringes of society. They have built, and indeed are still building, diverse and viable communities using the analyses and organizational objectives pioneered three decades ago. Most significant is that such organizing is no longer restricted to the largest urban centres, and encompasses people of colour, two-spirited people, and people from diverse ethnic and cultural communities.

Remarkably, progress has been made despite the many divisions and controversies within queer communities over issues of gender and sexuality, of process and power, and between liberationists and assimilationists. It has been made by resisting the fierce and well-organized opposition of religious fundamentalists and other social conservatives, the reticence and duplicity of politicians, and, since the early 1980s, the advent of AIDS. Critically important has been the ability of advocates for gay and lesbian issues to adapt to and take full advantage of other changes, most notably the equality rights established by the Canadian Charter of Rights and Freedoms, to fight old battles in new ways. The result is that, at the beginning of the twenty-first century, sexual orientation discrimination in employment, housing, and services has been legally prohibited by all provinces and one territory, as well as by the federal government. Same-sex relationships are well on the way to being legally recognized in the same way as common law heterosexual relationships. These developments, in turn, have kindled a necessary debate over what the long-term objectives of the movement should be, and whether acceptance within the mainstream is desirable.

The attitudes and beliefs that create the social climate in Canada today are confused and contradictory. On the one hand, homosexuality is thought to be so abhorrent and abnormal that society must not condone it. On the other hand, it is so apparently attractive and seductive that stiff social sanctions must be imposed to protect people, especially the young, from being lured to it. Scientists and researchers persist in efforts – uniformly unsuccessful to date – to find the 'cause' of homosexuality, causing suspicion among gays and lesbians that the intent is also to find a 'cure.' During the 1990s, research focused on identifying genetic causes, most notably a 'gay gene,' which proved to be elusive. There was no corresponding research aimed at finding the cause of heterosexuality or a possible 'straight gene.'[1] Demonizing the homosexual, especially the gay male, as being, in effect, a child molester and paedophile remains a common feature of public discourse in efforts to whip up hysteria and hatred. Queer sexuality elicits homophobic outrage – especially the depiction or portrayal of it, or its too-public expression. Such actions invite the full force of state repression, through censorship, and targeted or disproportionate enforcement of laws. Same-sex sexuality continues to be met with swift social disapproval, evidenced by the pronouncements of a host of interests claiming it should remain a private or discreet matter and should be especially kept away from impressionable children and youth. When it comes to the acceptance of their sexuality, gays, lesbians, and bisexuals, at the dawn of a new century, remain in significant ways little more than the deviants, sinners, and misfits of old, albeit more politely tolerated. Coming out remains difficult for many. Issues of low self-esteem and feelings of guilt and self-loathing because of the acceptance of prevalent homophobia and heterosexism continue to take their toll on the lives of queer Canadians. Too many continue to experience violence and harassment, and live with fear of rejection.[2] The educational system is rife with homophobia and remains largely hostile to the presence and aspirations of gays, lesbians, and bisexuals. Heterosexism and homophobia saturate and impede the provision of health and social services.

Despite the notable progress made towards the establishment of equality rights for lesbians and gays in recent years, Canada is often a hostile place for openly gay, lesbian, or bisexual people. Even tolerance, when experienced, can be tainted with paternalism and the arrogance of heterosexual superiority. Positive acceptance of homosexuality as a natural and normal alternative equal in all respects to heterosexuality continues to be very much a minority view. Homosexuality is still largely condemned as morally wrong. For many, it is also gross, disgusting, and repulsive, a perversion or deviance that should be controlled if not cured. Opposition to homosexuality is frequently emotive and hostile. Sometimes these views are overtly and publicly expressed; more frequently, their expression is muted or subtle. The fraudulent, age-old distinction between being homosexual and doing homosexual acts is still prevalent. Tremendous pressure is exerted to be heterosexual. A vast chasm separates the right to be tolerated because of one's sexual orientation from the ability to express or promote positive, affirming images or depictions of same-sex sexuality. Individuals speaking too openly and freely about their sexual orientation or their relationships, or who display it publicly, are often accused of flaunting their lifestyle.

Like everyone else growing up in modern Canada, gays and lesbians continue to be socialized to believe that only heterosexual lifestyles and relationships are acceptable. Same-sex relationships are considered less meaningful, committed, or fulfilling. Gays, bisexuals, and lesbians are thought to be inappropriate parents. They are unacceptable as teachers, child care workers, youth counsellors, clerics, sports figures, and volunteers working with children.[3] The heterosexual majority, in fact, does not value gays, lesbians, and bisexuals as a group or as individual citizens. They are not envisaged as or encouraged to be leaders in politics, business, or other areas.[4] Even in the arts, music, and entertainment fields, where there is occasional acknowledgement of the contributions made by gays, lesbians, and bisexuals, individuals publicly disclosing a same-sex orientation or too overtly promoting queer themes or sensibilities nonetheless risk jeopardizing their careers. Movies and television programs dealing with gays and lesbians are still rare, and those dealing with them in anything other than the most sanitized and chaste manner are practically nonexistent. Television stations and networks alike generally view gay and lesbian themes with timidity or hostility. Out of the closet gays, lesbians, and bisexuals, even those who have visibility or prominence, or who have been outstandingly successful in their fields, are not in general the recipients of public acclaim.

Virtually no public education is being undertaken to promote even tolerance towards gays, lesbians, and bisexuals. Calls for fair and unbiased sex education curricula or accurate presentations in the media on all forms of human sexuality evoke hysterical and hate-tinged responses. The words 'dyke,' 'homo,' 'faggot,' and 'queer' are frequently uttered, whether menacingly or derisively, on the street and in shopping malls, schools, boardrooms, and theatres. Hearing 'fag' or 'dyke' in movies or music, either as a form of humour or as a way of putting down another character, is common, especially when the film or song is being marketed to the teen or young adult. Telling a derogatory joke about gays or lesbians in business and social situations remains acceptable. Violence against lesbians, gay men, bisexuals, and transgendered people is an everyday occurrence in Canadian society.

Undeniably, the lesbian and gay movement has many issues left to pursue. Heterosexism and homophobia have not been vanquished. Until they are, lesbian and gay liberation will not die. A host of battles remain to be fought, and victories won. In taking them up, gays, lesbians, bisexuals, and transgendered people can build on the social and legal progress, and the impressive community development, of the last three decades. But they must remain vigilant and active. The rights gained, the visibility achieved, and the progress made are not the gifts of a benevolent state, or of enlightened social institutions, freely and happily bestowed. They exist because militant community activists made demands and resolved to organize to achieve their realization. They did so publicly, in the streets and in other venues, using a variety of strategies, and maximizing the impact of their generally meagre resources.

There is also evidence that equality-seeking as a strategy for gays, lesbians, and bisexuals has nearly run its course. There are not many more laws that remain to be changed (Criminal Code sections being the notable exceptions). The future objectives of lobbyism are harder to discern: the options for legislative change are running out. The first track of the movement is facing a dead end, although that end may be years off yet. Even the prospect of successful Charter litigation seems more limited. Neoconservatives have successfully waged a war against what they call judicial activism, fulminating darkly that judges have transformed themselves into law-makers who usurp the role of elected politicians. Judicial decisions on gay and lesbian issues, especially the Supreme Court of Canada decisions in the *Vriend* and *M. v. H.* cases, have been particularly seized upon in that regard.[5] Perhaps there will yet be a decision of the high court that same-sex marriage should be legalized, but then again, perhaps not. To date, the courts have pulled up short of opening that door, carefully drawing a distinction they believe is justified between common law relationships and heterosexual marriage. And even if marriage rights are granted to gays, lesbians, and bisexuals, what then? It is hard to see any other equality issues on the horizon. Similarly, combating homophobia in the education system and in health and social services will require much more than an appeal to equality and fairness. They will involve challenges to dominant values, traditional morality, and entrenched heterosexism. A type of militant guerrilla warfare, waged against powerful conservative interests and a tenacious religious right, hold more prospect for success in the long term than meek or plaintive calls for equality, fairness, and tolerance.

As for the other issues on the movement's agenda – those that fall more clearly into the liberation mould – the courts would seem to be of little value. Significantly, the courts in general and the Supreme Court of Canada in particular have shown no real desire to break new ground on issues of sexuality, especially with regards to striking down outdated and oppressive laws against consensual sexual activity, and the depiction or representation of such sexuality. The decisions in the *Little Sister's* and *Sharpe* cases show the timidity of the high court and their comfort in deferring to the legislators on such matters. The outlook remains bleak that the Charter might be used to render ineffective the bawdy house, prostitution, pornography, and censorship laws.[6] The strategies deployed in campaigns to have these laws significantly reformed or overturned will need to take place in the public realm and not in the rarefied confines of the courts. Public education and militant agitation over a sustained period, similar to what put the amendment of the human rights codes onto the political radar screen, will be necessary.

But more fundamentally, assimilationism will not succeed because the vast bulk of gays, lesbians, bisexuals, and transgendered people can never truly be assimilated. We are here, we are queer, and we are delightfully sexual, and distinctly different. We are incorrigibly and happily deviant. We are sexual rule-breakers who embrace and celebrate diversity, flamboyance, and queerness of all kinds. Queer community standards and values are, thankfully, radically different than those of the bland but smug heterosexual masses. Let us exalt in these facts, notwithstanding the many dreary attempts by assimilationist advocacy to homogenize, sanitize, and legitimize, to make us 'respectable' so that the mainstream will tolerate us. As we enter a new century, it is becoming clearer that the issues and challenges that need to be and will be addressed require going back to the roots of lesbian and gay liberation for analyses and strategies. Coming out, being visible, throwing off the shackles of homophobia and heterosexism, and pursuing the liberation of sexuality in all of its diverse and thrilling forms will – as this book, I believe, conclusively demonstrates – continue apace. When devising the strategies of the twenty-first century, queer activists will do well to remember and learn from those liberationists who achieved so much in the last three decades of the twentieth. Activism and organizing since the late 1960s have left a proud legacy, and built a strong foundation. Because of the profound change wrought by small bands of defiant and courageous individuals in communities across Canada, queers can now more confidently proclaim that they are always moving forward – not in pursuit of monochromal assimilation – but towards their liberation, and they are never going back.

Notes

Abbreviations

A	*Angles*
CA	*CelebrAsian*
CX	*Capital Xtra!*
GM	*Globe and Mail*
GO	*GO Info*
NP	*National Post*
OutRights	OutRights, Second Pan-Canadian Conference on Lesbian and Gay Rights, Vancouver, BC, 1992
P	*Perceptions*
Q	*Quota*
qc	*qc magazine*
R	*Rites*
Sun	*Toronto Sun*
TBP	*The Body Politic*
TS	*Toronto Star*
X	*Xtra!*
X, XS	*Xtra! XS*
XW	*Xtra! West*

A name followed by a date refers to a taped interview (e.g., Jane Doe, 31 Oct. 1999).

Introduction: Coming to Terms

1 Didi Herman, *Rights of Passage: Struggles for Lesbian and Gay Legal Equality* (Toronto: University of Toronto Press, 1994), 49.

2 Miriam Smith, *Lesbian and Gay Rights in Canada: Social Movements and Equality-Seeking, 1971–1995* (Toronto: University of Toronto Press, 1999), 23.
3 David Rayside, *On the Fringe: Gays and Lesbians in Politics* (Ithaca: Cornell University Press, 1998), xiii.
4 Gary Kinsman, 'Lesbian and Gay Liberation and Socialism,' *New Socialist* 3 (June–July 1998), 9.
5 Wainwright Churchill, *Homosexual Behavior among Males* (New York: Hawthorn, 1967), 70–88.
6 K. Smith, 'Homophobia: A Tentative Personality Profile,' *Psychological Reports* 29 (1971), 1091–4.
7 Joseph H. Neisen, 'Heterosexism: Redefining Homophobia for the 1990s,' *Journal of Gay and Lesbian Psychotherapy* 1(3), (1990), 22.
8 George Weinberg, *Society and the Healthy Homosexual* (New York: St. Martin's Press, 1972), 1–20.
9 Gays of Ottawa, *Understanding Homophobia*, leaflet, 1975.
10 Brian Mossop and Ken Popert, 'Why Are Gay People Oppressed?' ca. 1978.
11 Ibid.
12 Chris Bearchell, 'Why I Am a Gay Liberationist: Thoughts on Sex, Freedom, the Family and the State,' *Resources for Feminist Research* 12 (March 1983): 60.
13 Katherine Arnup, 'Lesbian Theory,' *Resources for Feminist Research* 12 (March 1983): 54.
14 Audre Lorde, *Sister Outsider* (Freedom, CA: Crossing Press, 1996), 45.
15 Mariana Valverde, *Sex, Power, and Pleasure* (Toronto: Women's Press, 1985), 82–3.
16 Neisen, 'Heterosexism,' 25.

Chapter 1: The Roots of Oppression

1 Among the many sources that could be cited in respect of the religious roots of the taboo against homosexuality, one of the best is C.A. Tripp, *The Homosexual Matrix* (New York: American Library, 1976).
2 Kathleen A. Lahey, *Are We 'Persons' Yet? Law and Sexuality in Canada* (Toronto: University of Toronto Press, 1999), 108.
3 Ibid., 111.
4 An excellent account of the history of the anti-homosexual religious and criminal laws is found in H. Montgomery Hyde, *The Other Love* (London: Heinemann, 1970).

5 Louis Crompton, 'The Myth of Lesbian Impunity: Capital Laws from 1270 to 1791,' *Journal of Homosexuality* 6 (fall and winter 1980–1). Cited by Madiha Didi Khayatt, *Lesbian Teachers: An Invisible Presence* (Albany: State University of New York Press, 1992), 248.

6 Jeffrey Weeks, *Coming Out: Homosexual Politics in Britain, from the Nineteenth Century to the Present* (London: Quartet Books, 1977), 14.

7 Gary Kinsman, *The Regulation of Desire: Homo and Hetero Sexualities*, 2nd ed. (Montreal: Black Rose Books, 1996), 128–9.

8 Weeks, *Coming Out*, 106–7.

9 Kinsman, *The Regulation of Desire*, 183–7.

10 Ibid., 107–47.

11 Brenda Cossman and Shannon Bell, introduction to *Bad Attitude/s on Trial: Pornography, Feminism, and the Butler Decision* (Toronto: University of Toronto Press, 1997), 12–13.

12 Ibid., 15–16.

13 Ibid., 14.

14 Ibid., 15.

15 Kinsman, *The Regulation of Desire*, 61–2.

16 Khayatt, *Lesbian Teachers*, 15.

17 Mariana Valverde, *Sex, Power, and Pleasure* (Toronto: Women's Press, 1985), 80.

18 Kinsman, *The Regulation of Desire*, 183–7.

19 Gail Donaldson and Mark Kingwell, 'Who Gets to Decide Who's Normal?' *GM*, 18 May 1993, A23.

20 Paula J. Caplan, *They Say You're Crazy* (Jackson, MI: Addison-Wesley, 1995), 56.

21 D.J. West, *Homosexuality* (1955; reprint, Harmondsworth: Pelican Books, 1968), 110, 230–1.

22 Ibid., 232.

23 Ibid., 261.

24 J.L.E. [Jim Egan], 'Widespread Nature of Homosexuality Revealed in Kinsey Report on Male's Sexual Behaviour,' *Justice Weekly*, 6 March 1954, 13.

25 Ibid.

26 Jim Egan, articles in *Justice Weekly*, March and April 1954, reproduced in *Jim Egan: Canada's Pioneer Gay Activist* (Canadian Lesbian and Gay History Network, Publication No. 1, 1987).

27 Kinsman, *Regulation of Desire*, 171–81.

28 Dean Beeby, 'RCMP Was Ordered to Identify Gays,' *GM*, 25 April 1992, A5.

29 Kinsman, *Regulation of Desire*, 177–8.
30 For comprehensive analysis of the evolution of human rights law in Canada and its impact on sexual minorities, see Lahey, *Are We 'Persons' Yet?* 100–26
31 Edgar McInnis, *Canada: A Political and Social History*, 3rd ed. (Toronto: Holt, Rinehart and Winston, 1969), 358.
32 Bill Black, *Report on Human Rights in British Columbia*, December 1994, 6.
33 Glenn Wheeler, 'Charter "Black Book" Controversy Brewing.' *TBP*, Dec. 1982, 10.
34 John F. Conway, *The Canadian Family in Crisis*, 3rd ed. (Toronto: James Lorimer, 1997), 5.
35 Mariana Valverde, 'Gay Couples and Spousal Benefits' (Testimony on Behalf of Human Rights Commission) 1991 (Toronto, 1991).
36 Conway, *The Canadian Family in Crisis*, 15.
37 Albert McLeod, 8 Oct. 1998. Matthew Hayes, 'Native Communities Respond to AIDS.' *XS*, Sept. 1992, 9.
38 Harold Cardinal, *The Unjust Society: The Tragedy of Canada's Indians* (Edmonton: Hurtig, 1969), 83.
39 Albert McLeod, 10 Aug. 1998. Cardinal, *The Unjust Society*, 85–9.
40 Evan Adams, 12 Oct. 1992.
41 Derek Vance Steel, 'Native Gay Sexuality,' *P*, 8:1, 17 Jan. 1990, 18. Gilbert Deschamps, *We Are Part of a Tradition* (Toronto: 2-Spirited People of the First Nations, 1998), 10–23.
42 Two-Spirited Peoples of the First Nations. *2 Spirited People of the First Nations*, leaflet circa 1995.
43 Deschamps, *We Are Part of a Tradition*, 11, 22.
44 Arelyn Wiseman and Lynne Fernie, *Forbidden Love* (National Film Board, 1992).
45 Tamai Kobayashi, 'Asian Lesbian Experience,' *CA*: 16, 1988, 9.
46 Nickolus Plowden, 'A Gay Black Man's Perspective,' *GO*, Feb. 1992, 15.
47 Paulette Peirol, 'Minority Homosexuals Invisible to Their People,' *GM*, 21 May 1997, A1.
48 Celene Adams, 'Get Mad and Get Even,' *X*, 30 July 1998, 20. 'Conference Notes: Asian Lesbians and Gays vs. Families,' *CA*: 16, 1988, 23.
49 al-Qamar Sangha, 'Yari South Asian Lesbian and Gay Organizing,' *Outcomes*, from OutRights, 19.
50 'Conference Notes,' *CA*: 16, 1988, 16.
51 Bruce DeMara, 'The Persecution of the Gays,' *TS*, 8 Sept. 1992, B1.
52 Jim Egan, 11 Oct. 1992.
53 DeMara, 'The Persecution of the Gays.' The first of these *Toronto Telegram* articles appeared on 7 June 1963.

54 Doug Sanders, 'Our History Panel,' OutRights, 11 Oct. 1992.
55 DeMara, 'The Persecution of the Gays.' Kinsman, *The Regulation of Desire*, 252.
56 Dave Kehr, 'Popular Culture Accepts Gays but with Sinister Undertones,' *TS*, 29 April 1993, A17.
57 DeMara, 'The Persecution of the Gays.'
58 Ibid., Quoted from 'Degenerates Parade, Inspector Says. Blames Lack of Public Disgust for Growth of Homosexuality,' *GM*, 14 Nov. 1963.
59 Bruce DeMara, 'Woman Recalls '50s Harassment,' *TS*, 10 Aug. 1992.
60 Nik Sheehan, 'Stately Homo,' *X*, 26 Oct. 1990, 15.
61 John Grube, '"No More Shit": Toronto Gay Men and the Police,' La Ville en Rose Conference, Montreal, 15 Nov. 1992.
62 Charlie Hill, 26 May 1991.
63 Line Chamberland, 19 Dec. 1990.
64 Interview, *Forbidden Love*.
65 Kinsman, *The Regulation of Desire*, 264.
66 ASK, 'The Sentencing of Homosexual Offenders,' research paper, June 1967.
67 Jim Egan, 'Civil Liberties and the Homosexual,' *TS*, 23 Oct. 1963.
68 Doug Sanders, 13 Oct. 1992.
69 Ibid.
70 George Hislop, 28 Oct. 1993.
71 Diane McMahon, 3 June 1997.
72 'Uppity Women,' *TBP*, March–April 1974.
73 'Partial Win for Brunswick 4,' *TBP*, July–Aug. 1974.

Chapter 2: Decriminalization and Early Gay and Lesbian Organizing

1 Gary Kinsman, *The Regulation of Desire: Homo and Hetero Sexualities*, 2nd ed. (Montreal: Black Rose Books, 1996), 243.
2 Jeffrey Weeks, *Coming Out: Homosexual Politics in Britain, from the Nineteenth Century to the Present* (London: Quartet Books, 1977), 158–66. Kinsman, *The Regulation of Desire*, 214–24.
3 Kinsman, *Regulation of Desire*, 185, 196, 252.
4 Stephen Clarkson and Christina McCall, *Trudeau and Our Times*, vol. 1, *The Magnificent Obsession* (Toronto: McClelland and Stewart, 1991), 107–8.
5 Donald W. McLeod, *Lesbian and Gay Liberation in Canada: A Selected Annotated Chronology, 1964–1975* (Toronto: ECW Press/Homewood Books, 1996), 17, 19. Kinsman, *The Regulation of Desire*, 238–9.
6 McLeod, *Lesbian and Gay Liberation*, 20.
7 Ibid., 47.
8 Kinsman, *Regulation of Desire*, 253–4, 263.

9 Ibid., 252.

10 Ibid., 257–64.

11 Ibid., 267–73.

12 McLeod, *Lesbian and Gay Liberation*, 21, 23, 25, 37.

13 Sydney Sharpe and Don Braid, *Storming Babylon: Preston Manning and the Rise of the Reform Party* (Toronto: Key Porter Books, 1992), 76–7, 96–9.

14 Bob Wallace, 'Read This [Before You Vote]' *TBP*, July–Aug. 1972, 5.

15 Ibid.

16 'Just What Some Members of Parliament Said About Homosexuality,' *GM*, 19 April 1969, 7.

17 Wallace, 'Read This.'

18 'Just What Some Members of Parliament ...' *GM*, 19 April 1969.

19 Sharpe and Braid, *Storming Babylon*, 81–104. Murray Dobbin, *Preston Manning and the Reform Party* (Halifax: Formac, 1992), 22.

20 Mary Axten, 'Setting the Agenda,' Community Forum, 10 May 1988.

21 Doug Wilson, 'Rites Interview: Ninety-one Years Gay,' *R*, Oct. 1984.

22 Doug Wilson, 23 March 1991.

23 John Grube, *Natives and Settlers: An Ethnographic Note on Early Interaction of Older Homosexual Men with Younger Gay Liberationists* (Toronto: Hawthorne Press, 1991), 119–35. The reference to Crisp is to Quentin Crisp in *The Naked Civil Servant* (London: Jonathan Cape, 1968).

24 Ibid, 119–20.

25 John Grube, 'Queens and Flaming Virgins,' *R*, March 1986, 15. Marion Foster and Kent Murray, *A Not So Gay World* (Toronto: McClelland and Stewart, 1972). Gerald Hannon, 'Epitaph for the Parkside,' *TBP*, April 1980, 1. George Hislop, 28 Jan. 1993.

26 Jim Egan, 11 Oct. 1992. Jim Egan, *Challenging the Conspiracy of Silence*, ed. Donald W. McLeod (Toronto: Canadian Lesbian and Gay Archives and Homewood Books, 1998), 33–9, 79–94.

27 'Before Stonewall ... Vancouver Style,' *A*, July 1994, 18.

28 Maureen Irwin, 21 June 1997.

29 Line Chamberland, 19 Dec. 1990. Line Chamberland, 'Social class and integration in the lesbian sub-culture,' paper presented at the Learned Societies, 28 May 1990.

30 Elise Chenier, 'Cruising at the Continental: The Centre of Lesbian Life in Postwar Toronto,' *Q*, 1 Oct. 1994.

31 Interviews in *Forbidden Love*.

32 Burf Kay, 18 Dec. 1990. Mike Bazinet, 29 Feb. 1992. Lloyd Wagner, 17 Sept. 1993. Jim Schafer, 19 June 1997.

33 Harold B. Desmarais: 24 Aug. 1997.

34 'The Great Canadian One-Shot Queer Flick,' *TBP*, May 1982.

35 Bernard Courte: 22 Nov. 1990.

36 McLeod, *Lesbian and Gay Liberation*, 1.

37 Ibid., 40.

38 Ibid., 41, 47.

39 Jim Egan, 11 Oct. 1992. George Hislop, 28 Jan. 1993.

40 Charlie Hill, 26 May 1991.

41 Doug Sanders, 'Our Histories,' OutRights, 11 Oct. 1992.

42 Madiha Didi Khayatt, *Lesbian Teachers: An Invisible Presence* (Albany: State University of New York Press, 1992), 20–1.

43 Mary Meigs, 12 Dec. 1990.

44 Regina woman, 28 Aug. 1990.

45 Maureen Irwin, 21 June 1997.

46 'Sapho,' 'Women Shun Us! – Men Scoff at Us! Toronto Lesbian Tells All!' *Flash*, 20 Aug. 1951, 7.

47 Val Edwards, 'The Time, the Place, and the Person,' *TBP*, Nov. 1980, 23.

48 Jim Egan, 'More Tolerance Needed Toward Homos,' *True News Times*, 31 Dec. 1951. 'Parliamentary Legislative Committee Ignored this Letter from Homosexual Suggesting Changes in Criminal Code,' *Justice Weekly*, 19 April 1955. Egan, *Challenging the Conspiracy of Silence*, 41–59.

49 Jim Egan, 11 Oct. 1992.

50 Ibid.

51 Stuart Timmons, *The Trouble with Harry Hay* (Boston: Alyson Publications, 1990), 154.

52 Eric Marcus, *Making History: The Struggle for Gay and Lesbian Equal Rights, 1945–1990* (New York: Harper Perennial 1993), 70–5.

53 Joan Nestle, 'Butch/Fem and Sexual Courage,' *TBP*, Sept. 1981, 29.

54 Marcus, *Making History*, 77.

55 McLeod, *Lesbian and Gay Liberation in Canada*, 7.

56 ASK, *So You've Heard about ASK!* leaflet, circa 1967.

57 Doug Sanders, 13 Oct. 1992.

58 Charlie Hill, 26 May 1991.

59 UTHA, 'Constitution,' circa 1970.

60 George Hislop, 28 Jan. 1993.

61 CHAT: 'Articles of Incorporation' 1 June 1974; Minutes: 11 Dec. 1970, 4 Jan. 1971, 21 Jan. 1971, and 4 Feb. 1971. Robert MacDonald, 'Kookie LIP Grants Make the Mind Boggle: MP,' *Sun*, 2 March 1971.

Chapter 3: Lesbian and Gay Liberation

1 Donn Teal, *The Gay Militants: How Gay Liberation Began in America, 1969–1971* (New York: St Martin's Press, 1994), 29.

2 Ibid., 21.

3 Ibid. 34–5

4 Ibid., 35.

5 Martha Shelley, 'Gay Is Good,' in *Out of the Closets: Voices of Gay Liberation*, ed. Karla Jay and Allen Young (New York: Douglas Book Corporation, 1972), 31.

6 Ibid., 32.

7 Allen Young, 'Out of the Closets and into the Streets,' in Jay and Young, eds., *Out of the Closets*, 7.

8 Gay Liberation Front Women (New York City), 'Lesbians and the Ultimate Liberation of Women,' in Jay and Young, eds., *Out of the Closets*, 202–3.

9 Radicalesbians, 'The Woman-Identified Woman,' in Jay and Young, eds., *Out of the Closets*, 172.

10 Ibid., 173.

11 Ibid., 176.

12 Young, 'Out of the Closets and into the Streets,' in Jay and Young, eds. *Out of the Closets*, 28.

13 Carl Wittman, 'A Gay Manifesto,' in Jay and Young, eds., *Out of the Closets*, 330–42.

14 Ed Jackson and Stan Persky, eds., 'Victories and Defeats,' in *Flaunting It! A Decade of Gay Journalism from* The Body Politic (Vancouver: New Star Books, Toronto: Pink Triangle Press, 1982), 227. McLeod, *Lesbian and Gay Liberation in Canada*, 54.

15 Barry Adam, 25 Jan. 1998.

16 UTHA, *Gay Is Good*, leaflet, ca. 1970.

17 Toronto Gay Action, *What Is Gay Liberation?* leaflet, ca. 1971.

18 Teall, *The Gay Militants*, 110.

19 'A Program for Gay Liberation,' *TBP*, Nov.–Dec., 1971, 14.

20 Ibid.

21 Nancy Walker, 'Closet Door, Closet Door, You Ain't Got Me Anymore!' *TBP*, Nov.–Dec., 1971, 13.

22 GATE Toronto, *GATE: Gay Alliance Toward Equality*, leaflet, ca. 1974.

23 Brian Waite, 'A Strategy for Gay Liberation,' *TBP*, March–April, 1972, reprinted in Jackson and Persky, eds., *Flaunting It!*, 221.

24 Brian Waite, 14 Oct. 1992.

25 Denis LeBlanc, 26 May 1991.

26 McLeod, *Lesbian and Gay Liberation in Canada: A Selected Annotated Chronology 1964–1975* (Toronto: ECW Press/Homewood Books, 1996), 79, 82.

27 Ibid., 101, 134. CHAT, *A Brief Regarding the Ontario Human Rights Code, Submitted to the Members of the Legislative Assembly of Ontario*, 1972.

28 McLeod, *Lesbian and Gay Liberation in Canada*, 119, 137.

29 NGRC, 'Gay Liberation and Quebec,' *NGRC Forum* 2 (fall 1977).

30 'G.A.T.E. and the B.C. Elections Successful Campaign,' *TBP*, July–Aug., 1972, 7.

31 'Human Rights Code Still Ignores Gays,' *TBP*: March–April, 1974, 6.

32 'Vancouver Paper Turns Down Ad GATE Protests, Demands Justice,' 6, *TBP*, Nov.–Dec., 1974.

33 McLeod, *Lesbian and Gay Liberation in Canada*, 108.

34 Ibid., 132, 134, 154.

35 Ibid., 91.

36 Greg Bourgeois and Bob Wallace, 'A More Aggressive Stance,' *TBP* Sept.–Oct., 1973, 17.

37 'Manitoba Gays Demand Change,' *TBP*, Nov.–Dec. 1974, 6.

38 Michael Lynch, 'Bill Lewis: The Shy and Stubborn Activist,' *TBP*, Sept. 1977, 22.

39 McLeod, *Lesbian and Gay Liberation in Canada*, 78.

40 Ibid., 121–2.

41 'Halifax Gays Conduct Poll,' *TBP*, May–June, 1974.

42 Gays and Lesbians Together, 'Here to Stay! Lesbians and Gays in Newfoundland and Labrador Fighting for Our Rights,' brief to the Newfoundland House of Assembly, 1991.

43 'We Demand,' *TBP*, Nov.–Dec., 1971, 4–5.

44 McLeod, *Lesbian and Gay Liberation in Canada*, 105. NGEC, *Gay Rights Now*, leaflet, 1972.

45 'National Gay Election Coalition,' *TBP*, winter 1973, 5.

46 Letter, Doug (Gens) Hellquist, Zodiac Friendship Society & Saskatoon Gay Action to Jearld Moldenhauer, 5 Dec. 1972.

47 McLeod, *Lesbian and Gay Liberation in Canada*, 125–6.

48 *NGEC Newsletter*, no. 1, 1974. 'Guelph Group Pickets Trudeau,' *TBP* 14, 1974, 18.

49 Tom Warner: 'NGEC: Model for a National Movement,' *TBP*, Sept.–Oct., 1974; 'National Coalition Will Promote Civil Rights Fight.' *TBP*, Nov.–Dec., 1974, 8.

50 McLeod, *Lesbian and Gay Liberation in Canada*, 179.

51 'Government May End Ban on Immigrants,' *TBP*, Sept.–Oct. 1974. 'Andras Reaffirms Support for Immigration Law Change,' *TBP*, Nov.–Dec. 1974.

52 Becki L. Ross, *The House That Jill Built: Lesbian Nation in Formation* (Toronto: University of Toronto Press, 1995), 27. Andrea Weiss and Gretta Schiller, *Before Stonewall: The Making of a Gay and Lesbian Community* (Tallahassee: Naiad Press, 1988), 65.

53 Ross, *The House That Jill Built*, 24–5; Frances Wasserline, 'Our Histories Panel,' Out Rights, 11 Oct. 1992.

54 McLeod, *Lesbian and Gay Liberation in Canada*, 67–8.
55 Ibid., 89, 102, 105, 120.
56 Wasserline, 'Our Histories.'
57 Ibid., 171, 221. Alan V. Miller, 'Canadian Gay Archives Holdings of Lesbian Periodicals (Canadian),' in *Resources for Feminist Research*, 12 (March 1983), 85–6. Ross, *The House That Jill Built*, 28–9.
58 Marie Robertson, 29 April 1993.
59 Maureen Cullingham, 17 Dec. 1990.
60 Erin Shoemaker, 29 Aug. 1990.
61 Beatrice Baker, 'Confessions of a Lesbian Gay Liberationist,' *TBP*, Oct. 1979, 23.
62 Lynn Murphy, 26 July 1993.
63 Ross, *The House That Jill Built*, 34–5. Herb Spiers, 'CHAT Gets a Constitution,' *TBP*, Jan.–Feb., 1972, 14. Chris Fox, 'Why We Need Equal Representation,' *TBP*, Jan.–Feb., 1972, 15, 19.
64 Spiers, 'CHAT Gets a Constitution.'
65 Ross, *The House That Jill Built*, 35.
66 Ibid., 27–8
67 Ibid., 15–16.
68 Ibid., 28–9. Marie Robertson, 29 April 1993.
69 Diane McMahon, 3 June 1997. Also, historical research done by Maureen Irwin, notes given to me 21 June 1997.
70 Wasserline, 'Our Histories.'
71 McLeod, *Lesbian and Gay Liberation in Canada*, 128. Chris Vogel, 8 Oct. 1998.
72 Lesbian Organization of Toronto, 'Lesbian Organization of Toronto – A History,' ca. 1978.
73 Laura Yaros, '*Mouvements Des Lesbiennes au Québec* / Lesbians' Movements in Quebec,' a paper presented to the Sixth Inter-Actions Day, Montreal, 2 and 3 Oct. 1987.
74 Laura Yaros, 'Long Time Coming: Long Time Gone,' *Amazones d'Hier: Lesbiennes d'Aujourd'hui*, vol. 5, March 1988.
75 Jeanne, 'Lesbian Mother,' *TBP*, March–April 1974, 21.
76 McLeod, *Lesbian and Gay Liberation in Canada*, 90.
77 'Saskatoon Mother Loses Children,' *TBP*, Sept.–Oct. 1974. *Case v. Case* (1974), 18 R.F.L. (2d) 132 (Sask. Queen's Bench).
78 '1973's Gay Pride Week: A National Event ...,' *TBP*, Nov.–Dec., 1973.
79 Erv (Tom) Warner, 'Homo, Home on the Range,' *TBP*, spring 1973.
80 Evelyn Rogers, 27 Aug. 1990. McLeod, *Lesbian and Gay Liberation in Canada*, 90.
81 Ibid., 72–3.
82 Ibid., 115–16.

83 'Saskatoon Gay Centre Opens,' *TBP*, spring 1973.

84 Erin Shoemaker, 29 Aug. 1990.

85 McLeod, *Lesbian and Gay Liberation in Canada*, 78–9, 101.

86 Ibid., 64.

87 Ibid., 63.

88 Ibid., 116.

89 Ibid., 138. Ron Dayman, 'Little Rock, Ont?' *TBP*, March–April, 1974, 23.

90 Harold B. Desmarais, 24 Aug. 1997.

91 McLeod, *Lesbian and Gay Liberation in Canada*, 159.

92 Lloyd Wagner, 17 Sept. 1993.

93 McLeod, *Lesbian and Gay Liberation in Canada*, 147–8.

94 Ibid., 96, 147.

95 Ibid., 153.

96 Noella Richard, 31 July 1993.

97 Ibid.

98 McLeod, *Lesbian and Gay Liberation in Canada*, 167. John Cashin, 6 Aug. 1993.

99 Wittman, 'A Gay Manifesto,' in *Out of the Closets*, 339.

100 John Forbes, 'The Gay Ghetto,' *TBP*, Nov.–Dec., 1971, 17. Paul Pearce and David Newcome, 'The Gay Ghetto,' *TBP*, Jan.–Feb., 1972, 13.

101 George Hislop, 'The Alternative,' *TBP*, Jan.–Feb., 1972, 11.

102 McLeod, *Lesbian and Gay Liberation in Canada*, 55, 138.

103 Ibid., 235.

104 Ibid., 45, 51, 58, 95, 116–17, 167.

105 Christopher Richards, 'A Little Song, A Little Dance,' *X*, 26 March 1998.

106 Evan Adams, 14 Oct. 1992. Mitchell Raphael, 'Drag Racing,' *X*, 9 June 1995.

107 McLeod, *Lesbian and Gay Liberation in Canada*, 130.

108 Ibid., 115.

109 Ibid., 48, 115, 146.

110 Ibid., 114, 146.

111 Ibid., 125, 169.

112 Leif Harmsen, 'Fantastic Polaroids,' *Epicene*, Aug.–Sept. 1987, 34.

Chapter 4: Police Repression and Judicial Homophobia

1 Bruce MacDougall, *Queer Judgments: Homosexuality, Expression, and the Courts in Canada* (Toronto: University of Toronto Press, 2000), 11, 21.

2 Ibid., 87.

3 NGRC, *Gay Rights: A Program for Change*, leaflet, 1975. GATE Toronto, *GATE, Gay Alliance Toward Equality*, leaflet, ca. 1974.

4 CGRO, *Toward Equality: The Homosexual Minority in Ontario*, leaflet, 1975.
5 *K. v. K.* (1975), 23 R.F.L. 58 (Alta. Prov. Ct).
6 Paul Trollope, 'Court Cool on Custody,' *TBP*, Nov. 1977, 5.
7 *D. v. D.* (1978), 3 R.F.L. (2d) 327 (Ont. Co. Ct.). Bill Lewis, 'Gay Father Wins Custody,' *TBP*, April 1978, 14.
8 *B. v. B.* (1980), 28 O.R. (2d) 136 (Prov. Ct.). 'Lesbian Mother Wins Custody,' *TBP*, May 1980, 11.
9 *Bezaire v. Bezaire* (1980), 20 R.F.L. (2d) 358 (Ont. C.A.).
10 'Woman Gets Custody but Decision Anti-Gay,' *TBP*, March–April 1979, 11.
11 'Judge Says Gayness Is No Bar to Custody,' *TBP*, Nov. 1980.
12 Ibid.
13 *Droit de la Famille – 31* (1983), 34 R.F.L. (2d) 127.
14 Francie Wyland, 'Lesbian Mothers,' *Resources for Feminist Research*, 12 (March 1983), 41.
15 MacDougall. *Queer Judgments*, 178.
16 Thomas Moclair, 'The Homosexual Fad,' *Police News and Views*, Feb. 1979. Extract printed in 'Uproar over Bigoted Cop Mag Forces Apology from Policy Chief,' *TBP*, May 1979, 8.
17 Arnold Bruner, 'Out of the Closet: Study of Relations between the Homosexual Community and the Police,' 24 Sept. 1981, 99–108.
18 Ibid., 96.
19 Gerald Hannon, 'Anatomy of a Sex Scandal,' *TBP*, June 1976, 10.
20 Ibid.
21 Bruner, 'Out of the Closet,' 120.
22 'Catcalls Greet 18 Men at Court,' *The Packet*, 20 Sept. 1983, 1.
23 'Guilty Pleas Smother Real Questions,' *TBP*, July–Aug. 1984, 8.
24 Ken Popert, 'Hallowe'en: Pressure Gets Action,' *TBP*, Dec. 1977–Jan. 1978, 8.
25 Ross Irwin, 'Cops Meet with Gay Community, Say They'll Halt Hallowe'en Mob,' *TBP*, Nov. 1979.
26 Editorial, 'Cops, Co-operation, and Closetry,' *TBP*, Nov. 1978, 7.
27 Geoff Mains, 'A Lot Can Be Gained by Working Together,' *TBP*, Dec. 1979–Jan. 1980, 7.
28 Robert Cook, '350 Demand End to Police Harassment,' *TBP*, May 1977.
29 Ken Popert, 'Pacific Gays and Lesbians Rally to Combat Rising Street Violence,' *TBP*, Sept. 1970.
30 Glenn Wheeler, 'Liaison Committee Cop Goes Spring Cleaning,' *TBP*, May 1984.
31 'City Cracks Down,' *TBP*, July–Aug., 1975, 8.
32 Ed Jackson and Stan Persky, eds., *Flaunting It! A Decade of Gay Journalism from* The Body Politic (Vancouver: New Star Books; Toronto: Pink Triangle Press, 1982), 230–1.

33 NGRC, 'The Great Olympic Clean Up: A Chronology of Events,' 30 May 1976.
34 Ibid.
35 'Thousands Take to the Streets in Protest,' *TBP*, Dec. 1977–Jan. 1978.
36 Jim Bartley, 'Truxx Trial Date Reset,' *TBP*, Dec. 1982.
37 Robin Hardy, 'Montreal Police Storm Tavern in Repeat of Truxx Raid,' *TBP*, Nov. 1978.
38 Stuart Russell, 'Montreal Police Raid on Sauna David Sparks Largest Protest Since Truxx Raid,' *TBP*, June–July 1980.
39 Gary Kinsman, 'Montreal Police Raid Buds,' *R*, July–Aug., 1984.
40 'TBP Raided and Charged,' *TBP*, Feb. 1978.
41 'Support, Loud and Strong,' *TBP*, Feb. 1978.
42 'Barracks Defence Goes Full Steam Ahead,' *TBP*, March–April 1979.
43 'Homosexual Leaders Attack "Conspirators",' *Sun*, 13 Dec. 1978.
44 Robert Trow and Bill Lewis, 'Cops Raid Hot Tub Club, Private Homes on Eve of Opening of Ontario Legislature,' *TBP*, Nov. 1979.
45 'Judge Rules Man's Apartment Is Not a Common Bawdy House,' *TBP*, Dec. 1981.
46 Gerald Hannon, 'Rage! Taking It to the Streets,' *TBP*, March 1981, 11.
47 Ibid.
48 Jim Monk, 2 March 1998.
49 Ibid.
50 Christine Donald, 5 Jan. 1998.
51 Hannon, 'Rage!'
52 Ibid.
53 Jim Monk, 2 March 1998. Gary Kinsman, 27 July 1993.
54 Gerald Hannon, 'Exposing the Big Lie,' *TBP*, May 1981.
55 'Brent Hawkes: Hungry for Rights,' *TBP*, April 1981.
56 Gerald Hannon, 'Putting On the Pressure,' *TBP*, June 1981, 9.
57 Kevin Orr, 'Fifth Bath Busted in Daytime Police Raid,' *TBP*, July–Aug., 1981.
58 'Back to the Baths; Back to the Streets,' *TBP*, June 1983. Ed Jackson, 'The Back Door Raid,' *TBP* special supplement, May 1983.
59 Gerald Hannon, 'Edmonton: Bath Raids Move West,' *TBP*, July–Aug., 1981.
60 Michael Phair, 18 June 1997.
61 Ibid.
62 Hannon, 'Edmonton: Bath Raids Move West.' Gerald Hannon, 'Guilty Verdict in Pisces Trial Discouraging Sign for Found-Ins,' *TBP*, Sept. 1981. Gerald Hannon, 'More Guilty in Pisces Trials but Court Lowers Owners' Fines,' *TBP*, Oct. 1981.

63 Craig Patterson, 'Defending the Right to Read,' *TBP*, June 1982, 8.

64 Gary Kinsman, 27 July 1993.

65 Jim Monk, 2 March 1998.

66 Michael Phair, 18 June 1997.

67 John Blacklock and Paul Trollope, 'How a Steambath Becomes a Bawdy House,' *TBP*, Nov. 1977, 17.

68 'Truxx Owner Appeals Bawdy House Rap,' *TBP*, May 1980.

69 Roger Spalding, 'The 87 Per Cent Solution,' *TBP*, April 1983, 13.

70 Stuart Russell, 'Owner Found Guilty in Quebec Bath Case,' *TBP*, Sept. 1981, 11.

71 Bernard Courte, '46 Bud's Defendants Plead Not Guilty,' *R*, Nov. 1984.

72 Chris Bearchell, 'Making Gay Sex Dirty,' *TBP*, May 1981. Gerald Hannon, 'Judge Finds Group Sex Indecent: Two Found Guilty in Barracks Case,' *TBP*, July–Aug., 1981.

73 Robert Trow, 'Bawdy House Rap Sticks in Tub Trial,' *TBP*, Oct. 1980. Spalding, 'The 87 Per Cent Solution.'

74 'New Bath Trials Tally: Fresh Air, More Wins,' *TBP*, July–Aug., 1982.

75 Chris Bearchell, 'Legal Status of Found-ins in Doubt as Guilty Plea Ends Keepers' Case,' *TBP*, Dec. 1981. Lee Waldorf, 'Club/Barracks Conspiracy Charges Dropped,' *TBP*, Nov. 1984.

76 'On the Road with the Found-in Follies,' *TBP*, May 1982. Ken Popert, 'Last Bath Raid Case Ends in Plea Bargain,' *TBP*, March 1985.

77 Gerald Hannon, 'Found-ins Civil Liberties Fight Earns Conviction in Pisces Case,' *TBP*, Dec. 1981.

78 RT, 'High Court Overturns Third Found-in Verdict,' *TBP*, Dec. 1981. Gerald Hannon, 'Guilty Verdict in Pisces Trial Discouraging Sign for Found-ins,' *TBP*, Sept. 1981.

79 Craig Patterson, 'Still Not Guilty after All These Years,' *TBP*, Nov. 1983, 11.

80 Gerald Hannon, 'Sewell: Unleashing the Whirlwind,' *TBP*, Feb. 1979.

81 'The Judgment: *The Queen vs. Pink Triangle Press*,' selected passages from Judge Sydney Harris' verdict of 14 Feb. 1979, in *TBP*, March–April 1979, 10.

82 Roger Spalding, 'Double Victory over Double Jeopardy,' *TBP*, July–Aug. 1982. Craig Patterson, 'Facing Off against *Triple* Jeopardy,' *TBP*, Sept. 1982.

83 'Another TBP Trial, Another Not Guilty Verdict,' *TBP*, Dec. 1982. Craig Patterson, 'Defending the Right to Read,' 'Another TBP Trial, Another Guilty Verdict,' *TBP*, Dec. 1982.

84 Craig Patterson, 'Court Convicts in Glad Day Case,' *TBP*, April 1983, 7. 'Orr's Appeal Victory Overturns Precedent,' *TBP*, May 1984. 'Goodbye 1984,' *TBP*, Jan. 1985.

Chapter 5: Raging Debates, Elusive Consensus

1 GATE Toronto, *GATE*, leaflet, 1976.
2 Maurice Flood, 'Never Going Back,' editorial, *TBP*, spring 1973, 2.
3 Ken Popert, 'Third National Conference Launches Gay Rights Coalition,' *TBP*, Oct. 1975, 3.
4 Ibid.
5 Terry Phillips, 12 Oct. 1992.
6 Chris Bearchell, Rick Bébout, and Alex Wilson, 'Another Look,' in *Flaunting It! A Decade of Gay Journalism from* The Body Politic, ed. Ed Jackson and Stan Persky (Vancouver: New Star Books; Toronto: Pink Triangle Press, 1982), 173.
7 Ibid., 167–8.
8 Becki L. Ross, *The House That Jill Built: A Lesbian Nation in Formation* (Toronto: University of Toronto Press, 1995), 171.
9 Maureen Cullingham, 17 Dec. 1990.
10 Jane Rule, 'Teaching Sexuality,' *TBP*, June 1979, reprinted in *Flaunting It!*, 163–4.
11 Chris Bearchell, 'Lots of Talk: Not Much Action,' *TBP*, Sept. 1984, 7.
12 Jim Monk, 2 March 98.
13 Ibid.
14 Ron Dayman, 20 Dec. 1990.
15 Gillian Rodgerson, 'Gay Sex Book Taken Off Sale,' *TBP*, Nov. 1985.
16 Gerald Hannon, 'Censored,' *TBP*, April 1977, 1.
17 Ibid.
18 Andrea Dworkin, 'Pornography: The New Terrorism,' *TBP*, Aug. 1978, 12.
19 Thelma McCormack, 'Censorship, Access and the Politics of Porn,' *TBP*, July–Aug. 1983, 11.
20 Gerald Hannon, 'Pornography, Feminism and Children's Literature,' *TBP*, April 1978, 5.
21 Susan Cole and Eve Zaremba, 'Letter,' *TBP*, May 1978, 12.
22 McCormack, 'Censorship, Access and the Politics of Porn.'
23 'Resolution Wrap-up,' *TBP*, Aug. 1978, 5.
24 Mariana Valverde, 'Freedom, Violence, and Pornography,' *TBP*, March–April, 1979, 19.
25 Chris Bearchell, 'Why I Am a Gay Liberationist: Thoughts on Sex, Freedom, the Family and the State,' *Resources for Feminist Research* 12 (March 1983), 59. Chris Bearchell, 'Art, Trash and Titillation: A Consumer's Guide to Lezzy Smut,' *TBP*, May 1983, 33.
26 Andrew Hodges, 'Divided We Stand,' *TBP*, Feb. 1977, reprinted in *Flaunting It!*, 181.

27 Ken Popert, 'Public Sexuality and Social Space,' *TBP*, July–Aug. 1982, 29.

28 Chris Bearchell, 'Doing It!' *TBP*, Sept. 1982, 30–1.

29 Ross, *The House That Jill Built*, 118–19.

30 Name withheld, *Dialogue* (Canadian Lesbian and Gay Rights Coalition, 1980), 4.

31 Bearchell, 'Why I Am a Gay Liberationist: Thoughts On Sex, Freedom, the Family and the State.'

32 Bearchell, 'Lots of Talk: Not Much Action.'

33 Lee Waldorf, 'If It Feels Good – Suspect It,' *TBP*, Sept. 1984, 7.

Chapter 6: Backlash and Social Conservative Insurgency

1 Alan Crawford, *Thunder on the Right: The 'New Right' and the Politics of Resentment* (New York: Pantheon, 1980), 146–7.

2 Focus on the Family, advertisement, *GM*, 29 Aug. 1997, B20.

3 Jimmy Swaggert, 'Homosexuality: Its Cause and Its Cure,' *The Evangelist*, Canadian ed., May 1983, 7.

4 Crawford, *Thunder on the Right*, 144–64.

5 Ibid., 90, 152–3, 313–14.

6 REAL Women of Canada, 'A Voice for Women,' Position Paper, Mar. 1994, 1, 41, 43.

7 Michael Lynch, 'Press Accuses Gay Activists of Jaques Murder,' *TBP*, Oct. 1977, 5.

8 'Media Fosters Bigotry with Murder Coverage,' *TBP*, Sept. 1977.

9 Gary Kinsman, 27 July 1993.

10 Ibid. Also, Tom Warner's recollections as a speaker at the rally.

11 'Canada Hits Back,' *TBP*, May 1978.

12 Doug Wilson, 23 March 1991. 'Bryant Tries Again, Fourth Visit Planned,' *TBP*, Sept. 1978. Also, Tom Warner's recollections as a speaker at the London demonstration.

13 Letter reproduced in a CGRO advertisement in *TBP*, Feb. 1978, 5.

14 Robin Hardy, 'Judge Slams Gays in Jaques Verdict,' *TBP*, April 1978, 4.

15 Robin Hardy, 'Commission Head: Gay Rights "Non-issue,"' *TBP*, March 1978, 1.

16 Gerald Hannon, 'Sewell: Unleashing the Whirlwind,' *TBP*, Feb. 1979. John Sewell, 'Speech to the Gay Community,' 3 Jan. 1979, reproduced in Sewell provincial election pamphlet, June 1999. Gordon Montador, 'Media: Getting (Some of) the Picture,' *TBP*, Feb. 1979. Chris Bearchell and Ed Jackson, 'Window on Sewell,' *TBP*, Feb. 1980.

17 'The Love-in That Wasn't,' *TBP*, Feb. 1979.

18 Ed Jackson, 'Media Raise Fear of Undue Gay Power as Sewell Endorses Hislop Campaign,' *TBP*, Oct. 1980, 10.

19 Ibid.

20 'Eggleton: Artful Dodger,' *TBP*, Oct. 1980, 9.

21 Ed Jackson, 'The Hot Little Issue Gets Big,' *TBP*, Nov. 1980, 15. Also, recollections of Tom Warner, co-chair of the Hislop campaign.

22 'And On Your Right ...,' *TBP*, Dec. 1980–Jan. 1981, 11.

23 Ibid.

24 League Against Homosexuals, *Queers Do Not Produce: They Seduce!* leaflet, 1980.

25 Chris Bearchell, 'Far Right Active in Election,' *TBP*, April 1981, 15.

26 Kevin Orr, 'The Ken and Jerry Show,' *TBP*, Dec. 1982, 10.

Chapter 7: Fighting against the Odds, Facing New Crises

1 'What Green Paper Says (or Doesn't Say) about Gays,' *TBP*, Jan.–Feb. 1975. 'Gay Community Effects Concerted Effort to Protest Failures of Immigration Paper,' *TBP*, July–Aug. 1975.

2 Barbara Freeman, 'Private Goes Public,' *TBP*, July–Aug., 1977, 13. 'Forces Ignore Outcry, Expel Thornborrow,' *TBP*, July–Aug. 1977, 4.

3 Gerald Hannon, '... Deemed Necessary to Discriminate,' *TBP*, Sept. 1977, 19.

4 Pat Spencer, pseud., 'Discrimination by Decree,' *TBP*, April 1985, 9.

5 'Taking the Forces to Court,' *TBP*, March 1983, 30.

6 Ron Dayman, 'Coalition Will Urge MPs to Put Gays in Human Rights Act,' *TBP*, April 1976. David Garmaise, 'Support Grows on Sexual Orientation Issue,' *TBP*, May 1977.

7 Ed Jackson, 'Tory MP Stifles Public Hearings on Sexual Orientation,' *TBP*, June 1983, 11.

8 Lawrence Martin, 'Racing Chairman Confirms Steward Fired as Homosexual,' *GM*, 15 Feb. 1975.

9 Committee to Defend John Damien, press release, 21 March 1975.

10 John Wilson, 23 Feb. 1993. 5 May 1977 letter to John Damien from Paul R. Jewell, QC.

11 Ken Popert, 'Opponents Black Out Damien Case,' *TBP*, Aug. 1976. Michael Lynch, 'Defending Damien,' *TBP*, Oct. 1977.

12 Tom Warner, 'John Damien's Legacy,' *Epicene*, Aug.–Sept. 1987. Mary Gooderham, 'Legal Fight Will Survive Ex-Jockey Dismissed for Being Homosexual,' *GM*, 1 Jan. 1987.

13 Doug (Gens) Hellquist, 'Breakthrough in Prairie Gay Rights Case,' *TBP*, Feb. 1976, 3.

14 Doug (Gens) Hellquist, 'Court Halts Rights Inquiry, Wilson Will Appeal Decision,' *TBP*, April 1976.

15 Doug Wilson, 23 March 1991.

16 Robert Cook, 'Gays Win Protection under BC Rights Code,' *TBP*, April 1976, 1. 'Supreme Court to Hear First Gay Rights Case,' *TBP*, May 1978.

17 Paul Trollope, 'Supreme Court Dumps Gay Tide,' *TBP*, July 1979.

18 Stan Persky, 'Getting Out from Under,' *TBP*, Feb. 1987, 13.

19 Michael Brais, 'Fired Man Won't Say Uncle,' *TBP*, Aug. 1986.

20 Persky, 'Getting Out from Under.'

21 'Homosexuals Should Have Rights Protected, 52 per cent Say,' Gallup Poll, *TS*, 29 June 1977.

22 Erin Shoemaker, 29 Aug. 1990.

23 'Choquette Kills Gay Rights Amendment,' *TBP*, Oct. 1975.

24 Stuart Russell, 'Quebec to Review Human Rights Code,' *TBP*, April 1977. Stuart Russell, 'ADGQ Seeks Justice Meeting,' *TBP*, Nov. 1977.

25 Ron Dayman, 'Unity Marks First National Congress,' *TBP*, Dec. 1977–Jan. 1978.

26 Stuart Russell, 'Rights Commission Backs Gay Protection,' *TBP*, Dec. 1977–Jan. 1978.

27 Stuart Russell and Michael Lynch, 'Gay Rights: *Oui*,' *TBP*, Feb. 1978, 5.

28 'House Debates Gay Rights,' *TBP*, Aug. 1976.

29 CGRO, 'Vote for Gay Rights Vote against the Tories,' poster, 1977. Robert MacDonald, 'Ont. Gays Out to Nail Bill's "Terrible Tories,"' *Sun*, 22 May 1977.

30 Tom Warner, 'CGRO Sets Strategy for Code Change,' *TBP*, Oct. 1977. Claire Hoy, 'The Limp Wrist Lobby,' *Sun*, 2 Nov. 1977.

31 Norman Webster, 'Hot Topic Coolly Handled,' *GM*, 18 May 1978.

32 Paul Trollope, 'Handicapped Stay with Gays,' *TBP*, Dec. 1978–Jan. 1979. Coalition for Life Together, *What Happened to Life Together?* leaflet, 1979.

33 Stan Oziewicz, 'Bill on Discrimination against Disabled Avoids Issue of Gays,' *GM*, 23 Nov. 1979, 5.

34 Robert Trow, 'Outraged Handicapped Groups Force Withdrawal of "Rights" Bill,' *TBP*, Feb. 1980.

35 Chris Bearchell, 'Strange Bedfellows?' *TBP*, Feb. 1981.

36 Chris Bearchell, 'Sticking with the Tories until 1984,' *TBP*, May 1981.

37 Ed Jackson, 'Human Rights: Last Round at Queen's Park,' *TBP*, June 1981. Ed Jackson, 'Ontario Human Rights "Omission" CGRO at Code Review Hearings,' *TBP*, July–Aug. 1981, 13.

38 Tom Warner was in the legislature at the time as a media spokesperson for the three men.

39 Peter J. Stendhal, 'Damien's Visit Raises $1,000,' *TBP*, Feb. 1977.
40 Bill Field, 'Gays and Manitoba Nix to Schreyer,' *TBP*, Nov. 1977, 4.
41 Chris Vogel, 10 Aug. 1998.
42 John Moreau, 'Gay Rights Back on Manitoba's Agenda,' *TBP*, July–Aug., 1984.
43 'NDP Backs Down: No Rights in Sask,' *TBP*, June 1979.
44 Gerald Hannon, 'Sexual Orientation Not Recommended In Proposed Changes in Rights Act,' *TBP*, March 1980.
45 'Conference Creates Provincial Group,' *TBP*, June 1979.
46 Russ Congdon, 'Add Gay Protection Says Alberta Group,' *TBP*, Oct. 1979. Michael Totzke, 'Albertans Fighting for Amendment,' *TBP*, Dec. 1984.
47 Hannon, 'Sexual Orientation not Recommended in Proposed Changes in Rights Act,' Gerald Hannon, 'Gay Rights Dropped to Please Tories,' *TBP*, April 1980, 11.
48 'Groups Pressure AHRC,' *TBP*, April 1982. 'Albertans Fighting for Amendment,' *TBP*, Dec. 1984.
49 Richard Summerbell, 'Would BC Legislators Rather Protect Chimps?' *TBP*, June 1984, 9.
50 NGRC, 'Statement of Principles, Structure and Programme,' 29–30 June 1975; amended 4–6 Sept. 1976.
51 David Garmaise, 16 Dec. 1990.
52 Miriam Smith, *Lesbian and Gay Rights in Canada: Social Movements and Equality-Seeking, 1971–1995* (Toronto: University of Toronto Press, 1999), 57–66.
53 'Lesbians Call for Autonomy,' *TBP*, Oct. 1976.
54 Paul Trollope, 'High Spirits and Hard Work,' *TBP*, Sept. 1977. 'Conference Votes New Structure to Canadian Coalition,' *TBP*, Aug. 1978.
55 Gerald Hannon, 'Celebration '79: A Return to Basics the Strategy for Our Next Decade?' *TBP*, Aug. 1979, 8–9.
56 'Delegates Bury National Coalition, As Movement Ponders New Tactics,' *TBP*, Aug. 1980, 9.
57 Ken Popert, 'Third National Conference Launches Gay Rights Coalition,' *TBP*, Oct. 1975.
58 Robin Metcalfe, 'What Is NGRC?' position paper presented to the 6th Annual Conference for Lesbians and Gay Men, Halifax, 20 June–3 July, 1978.
59 Gay Community Centre of Saskatoon, letter to the Canadian Lesbian and Gay Rights Coalition, published in *Forum*, 4 (winter 1979).
60 'Delegates Bury National Coalition as Movement Ponders New Tactics,' *TBP*, Aug. 1980.

61 David Garmaise, 16 Dec. 1990.

62 John Duggan, 16 Dec. 1990.

63 'Delegates Bury National Coalition.' Doug Whitfield, 'The CALGM Programme,' *TBP*, Oct. 1980. 'CALGM Calls for Gay Rights in Constitution,' *TBP*, Feb. 1981.

64 Smith, *Lesbian and Gay Rights in Canada*, 66.

65 Paul Trollope, 'GATE Vancouver Passes into History,' *TBP*, Aug. 1980.

66 Roedy Green, 13 Oct. 1992.

67 'New Rights Group to Stress Activism,' *TBP*, July–Aug. 1982.

68 John Wilson, 23 Feb. 1993.

69 Bernard Courte, 22 Nov. 1990.

70 Chris Vogel, 10 Aug. 1998.

71 John Duggan, 16 Dec. 1990.

72 Lloyd Plunkett, 16 Dec. 1990.

73 Robin Metcalfe, 25 July 1993.

74 Michael Lynch, 'The End of the "Human Rights Decade,"' *TBP*, July 1979, 25.

75 Editorial, 'Don't Mourn – Reorganize,' *TBP*, Aug. 1980, 7.

76 Stan Persky, 'Rob Joyce.' *TBP*, June 1984, 17.

77 '"Gay" Cancer and Burning Flesh: The Media Didn't Investigate,' *TBP*, Sept. 1981. Robert Trow, 'AID Diseases Reported in Canada,' *TBP*, Sept. 1982.

78 'Officials Investigate Cases of "Gay Plague,"' *Kingston Whig-Standard*, 19 Aug. 1982.

79 Evert A. Lindquist and David M. Rayside, 'AIDS Policy in Canada: Community Activism, Federalism, and the New Politics of Disease,' unpublished paper, Department of Political Science, University of Toronto, Nov. 1990, 1.

80 Bill Lewis and Randy Coates, 'Moral Lessons: Fatal Cancer,' *TBP*, Oct. 1981.

81 Michael Lynch, 'Living with Kaposi's,' *TBP*, Nov. 1982, 36.

82 Ibid., 37.

83 Bill Lewis, 'The Real Gay Epidemic: Panic and Paranoia,' *TBP*, Nov. 1982.' Bryan Texeira, 'AIDS as Metaphor,' *TBP*, Sept. 1983. Ed Jackson, 'Not a Victim: A "Person with AIDS,"' *TBP*, Oct. 1983. Rick Bébout, 'Is There Safe Sex?' *TBP*, Dec. 1983.

84 Michael L. Callen, 'AIDS: Killing Ourselves,' letter, *TBP*, April 1983, 6.

85 Walter Bruno, 'AIDS: Killing Ourselves,' letter, *TBP*, April 1983, 6.

86 Daniel C. Willoughby, 'AIDS: Killing Ourselves,' letter, *TBP*, Jan.–Feb. 1983, 4.

87 Lewis, 'The Real Gay Epidemic: Panic and Paranoia.'

88 Ed Jackson, 'Grassroots Action: Governmental Vagueness,' *TBP*, Sept. 1983.
89 Ed Jackson, 'Nationwide AIDS Report: Checking Up on the Experts,' *TBP*, July–Aug. 1983. Jackson, 'Grassroots Action; Governmental Vagueness,' 15.
90 Jackson, 'Grassroots Action; Governmental Vagueness.'
91 Rick Bébout with Joan Anderson, 'ACT: Some History,' *ACT Newsletter*, summer 1997.
92 Jackson, 'Grassroots Action; Governmental Vagueness,' 15.
93 Jackson, 'Not a Victim: A "Person with AIDS,"' 29.
94 Smith, *Lesbian and Gay Rights in Canada*, 96.
95 Ed Jackson, 'Facing a Common Enemy,' *TBP*, July 1985.
96 Jackson, 'Grassroots Action; Governmental Vagueness.'

Chapter 8: Liberating Communities, Changing Consciousness

1 'Gairilla Week and Quebec Fete Attract 10,000 to Gay Celebrations,' *TBP*, Aug. 1980. 'La Fête nationale 1981 – Perspectives "Fêons gai-e-ment la Gai-e-lon-la,"' *Le Berdache*, May 1981.
2 Ted Millward, 'Uncertain Future Shadows Gay Centre,' *TBP*, Oct. 1985. Richard North and Chris Vogel, 10 Aug. 1998.
3 Robin Metcalfe, 'Gay Community Centre Opens,' *TBP*, July–Aug., 1977.
4 'Better Service Is the Key to Success,' *Outlooks*, June 1997, 9.
5 Harold B. Desmarais, 24 Aug. 1997.
6 Michael Wellwood, 'Out in the Kootenays,' *TBP*, Sept. 1983, 31.
7 Margie Cogill, 10 Aug. 1998.
8 Bruce May, 1 June 1997. Stephen Lock, 2 June 1997.
9 'Sask. Gay Coalition,' *TBP*, Feb. 1978. Doug Wilson, 23 March 1991.
10 'Georgian Bay Gays to Stay: Organizing in Small-Town Ontario,' *TBP*, May 1979.
11 Chris Bearchell, 'Gay from Toronto to Thunder Bay,' *TBP*, Sept. 1980. David Bellrose, 'Getting Started,' *Gay Organizer*, CGRO, 1982.
12 Lloyd Wagner, 17 Sept. 1993.
13 Steve Brown, 17 Sept. 1993.
14 Val Fournier, 'Courage and Caring in North Bay,' *TBP*, Nov. 1981.
15 Alain Bouchard, 18 Feb. 1992.
16 'Gay Group Locked Out,' *TBP*, Feb. 1979.
17 Louise Turcotte, 31 May 1993.
18 Phillip Fotheringham, 'Rural Outreach: "What? Gay People Here?"' *TBP*, April 1982, 11.

19 James Duplessis, 28 July 1993. Ron Totten, 29 July 1993. John Markidis, 25 July 1993.

20 Robin Metcalfe, 'The Great Moncton Picnic,' *Making Waves*, summer 1982.

21 Bob DeWitt, 'Moncton Debut,' letter, *TBP*, Oct. 1986. Gwyn Martin, 'Beginning to Live As We Choose,' *TBP*, Feb. 1986. Noella Richard, 31 July 1993.

22 Scot Morison, 'Rebel without a Pause,' *Saturday Night*, May 1992.

23 John Alan Lee, *Getting Sex: A New Approach: More Fun, Less Guilt* (Don Mills, ON: Musson Book Company, 1978).

24 'When Genderpush Comes to Shove,' *X*, 13 Oct. 1995.

25 Jackie Goodwin, 'Strong, Striking Works Lost in a Mass of Verbiage,' *TBP*, Jan.–Feb. 1983.

26 Donald W. McLeod, *Lesbian and Gay Liberation in Canada: A Selected Annotated Chronology 1964–1975* (Toronto: ECW Press/Homewood Books, 1996), 221. Sue Golding, 'Angry Young Women,' *TBP*, Dec. 1982.

27 Keith Maillard, 'Don't They Listen to the Words,' *TBP*, Nov. 1977.

28 Bernard Courte, 22 Nov. 1990. Michael Jarry, 'L'ADGQ en panne ... d'avenir?' *Sortie* 36 (March 1986).

29 Louise Turcotte, 31 May 1993.

30 'Rites: Dedicated to the Struggles and the Joys,' editorial collective letter in *R*, May 1984.

31 Lynn Murphy, 26 July 1993.

32 Louise Turcotte, 31 May 1993.

33 Liz Massiah, 17 June 1997.

34 Marie Robertson, 29 April 1993.

35 Barb MacIntosh, 16 Dec. 1990.

36 Marie Roberston, 'Notes from The Full-Hipped Polish Dyke: The Long and Winding Road to Lesbian Separatism,' *TBP*, June 1976, 16.

37 Jean Hillabold, 27 Aug. 1990.

38 Ibid.

39 Christine Donald, 'Outfront Lesbians: Not Silent, Not Mommy,' *TBP*, Sept. 1982, 33.

40 Louise Turcotte, 13 May 1993.

41 Nancy Tatham, 29 Sept. 1990.

42 Line Chamberland, 19 Dec. 1990.

43 Maureen Irwin, 21 June 1997.

44 Marie Robertson, 29 April 1993.

45 Lynn Murphy, 26 July 1993.

46 Jane Rule, 'Strange Bedfellows,' Letter, *TBP*, April 1982, 4–5.

47 Marie Robertson, 29 April 1993.

48 Boo Watson, 'Conference Urges Lesbian Autonomy,' *TBP*, Aug. 1976, 7.

49 Ibid.

50 Halifax lesbian, 9 Aug. 1993.

51 Becki L. Ross, *The House That Jill Built: A Lesbian Nation in Formation* (Toronto: University of Toronto Press, 1995), 48–51. Ross gives a comprehensive history of LOOT.

52 'Phone Line Plans Expansion,' *TBP*, Jan.–Feb., 1982. Christine Donald, 5 Jan. 1998.

53 Laura Yaros, 'Long Time Coming: Long Time Gone,' *Amazones d'Hier: Lesbiennes d'Aujourd'hui* 5:3, May 1988.

54 Laura Yaros, '*Mouvements des lesbiennes au Québec*,' 1987.

55 Louise Turcotte, 31 May 1993.

56 Line Chamberland, 19 Dec. 1990.

57 Marie Robertson, 29 April 1993.

58 Rose Stanton, 17 Dec. 1990.

59 Ibid.

60 Stephen Lock, 2 June 1997. Jean B., 3 June 1997. Kam K. Wong, 2 June 1997.

61 CB, Untitled, *TBP*, July–Aug., 1983. Jean B., 3 June 1997.

62 Diane McMahon, 3 June 1997. Also, historical research done by Maureen Irwin, notes given to me 21 June 1997.

63 Lorna Murray, 18 June 1997.

64 Beth Traynor, 27 Aug. 1990.

65 Sue Cook, 27 Aug. 1990.

66 Chris Bearchell, 'Lesbian Pride March Is a First for Canada,' *TBP*, June 1981.

67 Ross, *The House That Jill Built*, 218.

68 'Out of the Silent Closet,' *TBP*, Feb. 1980.

69 Jean B., 3 June 1997.

70 Roy Hallett, 29 Sept. 1990.

71 'Conference Explores Lesbian Autonomy,' *TBP*, Sept. 1976.

72 Ken Popert, 'Race, Moustaches and Sexual Prejudice,' *TBP*, June 1983, 34.

73 Tony Souza, Eng K. Ching, and Richard Fung, 'Racism and Action,' letters, *TBP*, Sept. 1983, 6–7.

74 Gay Asians Toronto, 'GAT: Reflections on Our 15th Birthday,' in *Celebrasian '95 – Generations Together*, Dec. 1995.

75 Gay Asians Toronto, *GAT Gay Asians Toronto*, undated leaflet.

76 Philip Solanki, 'Exploring a Double Identity,' *TBP*, Jan. 1985, 23. Sean Hosein, 'Orientations: A Video – Gay Asians Speak Out,' *R*, Dec. 1984–Jan. 1985.

77 'Gays of Colour Get Together for Parties and Politics,' *TBP*, Dec. 1984. Lesbians of Colour, *Lesbians of Colour*, leaflet, ca. 1984.

78 Evan Adams, 14 Oct. 1992.
79 Ken Popert, 'Gay Rights Now!' *TBP*, July–Aug., 1975, 16.
80 Ibid.

Chapter 9: Victory in the Human Rights Campaigns

 1 Gary Kinsman, *The Regulation of Desire: Homo and Hetero Sexualities*, 2nd ed. (Montreal: Black Rose Books, 1996), 375.
 2 Miriam Smith, *Lesbian and Gay Rights in Canada: Social Movements and Equality-Seeking, 1971–1995* (Toronto: University of Toronto Press, 1999), 101–6.
 3 For a detailed exposition of the impact of the Charter on lesbian and gay activism, see Smith, *Lesbian and Gay Rights in Canada*. Kathleen Lahey, *Are We 'Persons' Yet? Law and Sexuality in Canada* (Toronto: University of Toronto Press, 1999), and Bruce MacDougall, *Queer Judgments: Homosexuality, Expression and the Courts in Canada* (Toronto: University of Toronto Press, 2000), also provide extensive analysis of the evolution of the law in relation to sexual orientation since the advent of the Charter.
 4 Lahey, *Are We 'Persons' Yet?*, 5.
 5 Smith, *Lesbian and Gay Rights in Canada*, 109–10.
 6 Letter from Tom Warner (CGRO) to D. Martin Low, General Counsel, Human Rights Law Section, Department of Justice, 4 March 1985.
 7 Svend Robinson, letter to gay groups, 29 Nov. 1985.
 8 Government of Canada, *Equality for All*, Equality Rights Sub-Committee of the Standing Committee on Justice and Legal Affairs, 1985.
 9 Government of Canada, 'Minister of Justice Tables Progressive Measures for Equality and Social Justice,' news release, 4 March 1986.
10 Kinsman, *Regulation of Desire*, 359–60.
11 *Hansard*, House of Commons Debates, 20 Oct. 1986.
12 Ibid., 1 Dec. 1986, 1665.
13 Kim Campbell, *Time and Chance: The Political Memoirs of Canada's First Woman Prime Minister* (Toronto: Doubleday, 1996), 213. Tim Harper, 'Tories Give Up on Plans to Let Gays in Military,' *TS*, 25 Jan. 1992.
14 Campbell, *Time and Chance*, 213.
15 John C. Crosbie with Geoffrey Stevens, *No Holds Barred: My Life in Politics* (Toronto: McClelland and Steward Inc., 1997), 272.
16 Geoffrey York, 'Tory Politicians Form Family Compact,' *GM*, 3 June 1992, A4.
17 *Haig v. Canada*, 5 O.R. (3d) 245–8. *Haig v. Canada (Minister of Justice)* (1992) 94 D.L.R. (4th) 1 (Ont. C.A.), 24.

18 Geoffrey York, 'Ottawa Accepts Court Ruling on Gay Rights,' *GM*, 31 Oct. 1992.
19 The Honourable Paule Gauthier, PC, QC. 'In the Matter of a Complaint Under Section 42 of the Canadian Security Intelligence Service Act.' Security Intelligence Review Committee, 14 Aug. 1990, 5.
20 Stephen Bindman, 'Military's No-Gay Rule under Fire in Court,' *TS*, 27 Oct. 1992, A21. Geoffrey York, 'Gays in Military Live in Limbo,' *GM*, 6 Nov. 1991, A5.
21 David Vienneau and Jack Lacey, 'Ruling Seen as Precedent for Gays,' *TS*, 28 Oct. 1992. Eleanor Brown, 'Canadian Forces Surrender,' *X*, 30 Oct. 1992.
22 Bob Rae, *From Protest to Power: Personal Reflections on a Life in Politics* (Toronto: Penguin Canada, 1996), 250. David Rayside, 'Gay Rights and Family Values: The Passage of Bill 7 in Ontario,' *Studies in Political Economy* 26 (summer 1988), 109–47.
23 Andrew Lesk, 'Victory Near in Ontario,' *TBP*, June 1986.
24 Andrew Lesk, 'It's All in the Family,' *TBP*, Dec. 1986, 11.
25 Coalition for Family Values, letter from Hudson T. Hilsden, 4 Oct. 1986. *Hansard*, Official Report of Debates Legislative Assembly of Ontario, 25 Nov. 1986.
26 Cheryl Cornacchia, 'Planned Bill to Protect Gays Is in Trouble, Churchman Says,' *GM*, 3 Nov. 1986. Robert Sheppard, 'Ontario Liberals Consider Permitting Rare Free Vote on Homosexual Rights Bill,' *GM*, 5 Nov. 1986.
27 William Clark, 'Passage Urged of Homosexual Rights Bill,' *TS*, 21 Nov. 1986. Gary Kinsman, 'Ontario: Battling for Our Rights,' *R*, Dec. 1986–Jan. 1987. Andrew Lesk, 'Victory In Ontario!' *TBP*, Jan. 1987.
28 *Hansard*, Official Report of Debates, Legislative Assembly of Ontario, 27 Nov. 1986.
29 Ibid., 1 Dec. 1986.
30 Harold B. Desmarais, 24 Aug. 1997.
31 Helen Fallding, 12 Oct. 1992.
32 Ken Popert, 'Gay Rights in the Yukon,' *TBP*, Jan. 1986.
33 Ibid.
34 Helen Fallding, 12 Oct. 1992.
35 Ted Millward, 'Hungry for Rights,' *TBP*, May 1985. 'Fifty-Nine Days and Still Hungry,' *TBP*, June 1985.
36 Chris Bearchell, 'Manitoba Amends Rights Act,' *Epicene*, Aug.–Sept. 1987, 9. Margie Cogill, 10 Aug. 1998.
37 Bearchell, 'Manitoba Amends Rights Act.'
38 Ibid., Patrick Barnholden, 'Manitoba Finally Does It,' *R*, Sept. 1987.
39 Margie Cogill, 10 Oct. 1998.

40 Ibid.
41 Sharon Carstairs, *Not One of the Boys* (Toronto: Macmillan, 1993), 108.
42 Bill 45, *The Human Rights Code*, 2nd Session, 33rd Legislature, 36 Elizabeth II, 1987.
43 Bearchell, 'Manitoba Amends Rights Act.'
44 Robin Metcalfe, 'NS Gays and Lesbians Get Protection,' *X, XS* Nov. 1990, 3.
45 Lois Corbett, 'Nova Scotia to Ban Gay Cops,' *TBP*, Aug. 1986, 9.
46 Robin Metcalfe, 25 July 1993.
47 Gary Kinsman, 'The Long Fight for Legal Protection: Interview with Maureen Shebib,' *R*, Sept. 1989, 9.
48 Wilson Hodder, 22 Aug. 1993.
49 Kevin Elliott, 'Rights Battle Won,' *X, XS*, Sept. 1991.
50 Wilson Hodder, 22 Aug. 1993.
51 Fredericton Lesbians and Gays, Human Rights Committee, Minutes, 31 Oct. 1987. Committee for Human Rights Reform, Minutes, 23 Jan. 1988.
52 Francis Young, 29 July 1993.
53 Claude Olivier, 29 July 1993.
54 Shawn Symes, 'N.B. Rights Fight Continues,' *R*, April 1991, 7.
55 Claude Olivier, 29 July 1993.
56 New Brunswick Coalition for Human Rights Reform, 'Gay Rights Amendment Adopted in New Brunswick, Canada,' media release, 21 May 1992.
57 Neil Whaley, 'Biting the Hand that Leads,' *TBP*, Aug. 1985.
58 Richard Banner, 'The Rights Step,' *A*, July 1992.
59 PS, 'Regina Groups Hopeful about Rights Code Bid,' *TBP*, April 1985. 'No Rights in Sask.,' *P*, 7:6, 23 Aug. 1989, 8.
60 'Romanow Has Difficulty,' *P*, 8:8, 21 Dec. 1990.
61 'Morality Campaign Fails,' *P*, 9:7, 6 Nov. 1991, 9.
62 Ibid.
63 'Right against Rights,' *P*, 10:7, 28 Oct. 1992, 9.
64 'Saskatchewan Rights,' *P*, 11:5, 28 July 1993.
65 Ibid.
66 'Still Fighting,' *P*, 11:6, 15 Sept. 1993. 'Campaigning Tories Bash Gays,' *P*, 13:5, 26 July 1995.
67 Gays and Lesbians Together, *Here to Stay! Lesbians and Gays in Newfoundland and Labrador Fighting for Our Rights*, a brief to the Newfoundland House of Assembly, 1991.
68 Brenda Ponic, 6 Aug. 1993. Gary Kinsman, 27 July 1993. 'Gays and Lesbians Together (GALT) brief, 26 Aug. 1991.
69 Gary Kinsman, 'Making Homosexuality the Problem Once Again,' *New*

Maritimes, Jan.–Feb., 1993. Michael Harris, *Unholy Orders: Tragedy at Mount Cashel* (Toronto: Penguin, 1991).

70 Gary Kinsman, 27 July 1993.

71 Brenda Ponic, 8 July 1993. Transcript, 'Provincial Women's Lobby,' 9–11 May 1992, Gander, Newfoundland, 117.

72 'Newfoundland Protection,' *P*, 11:2, 10 March 1993. 'Human Rights on the Rock,' *X*, 8 Dec. 1995.

73 'Gay Life on the Rock,' *P*, 14:5, 24 July 1996, 21.

74 'Rights Code Passed,' *TS*, 10 Dec. 1997.

75 Lee Fleming, 2 Aug. 1993.

76 'PEI Rights?' *X*, 28 Aug. 1997.

77 Michael Totxke, 'Alberta PCs Hear Case for Rights Protection,' *TBP*, March 1985.

78 'Alberta Rights,' *P*, 7:4, 31 May 1989. Shawn R. Mooney, 'Not Families,' *P*, 7: 8, 23 Nov. 1989, 8. 'News Brief,' *R*, June 1990.

79 'Klein's PCs Hardly PC,' *GM*, 15 April 1993.

80 Delwin Vriend, 21 July 1997. Lynn Iding, 'Alta. Community to Aid Fired Gay Professor,' *R*, April 1991, 7.

81 Matthew Hays, 'Gay Man Challenges Alberta Government,' *X, XS*, July 1992.

82 'Commission Picketed,' *P*, 9:4, 12 June 1991, 17.

83 'A Big Step in Alberta,' *P*, 11:1, 27 Jan. 1993.

84 'Homosexuals Get Better Deal, Tory Claims,' *GM*, 4 Jan. 1993.

85 'Rights in Alberta?' *P*, 27 April 1994. Scott Feschuk, 'Alberta Tories in a Bind Over Gay-Rights Decision,' *GM*, 14 April 1994.

86 Jonathan Eaton, 'Top Court to Rule on Job Rights for Gays,' *GM*, 30 June 1997.

87 'Alberta Rights Laws Now Applies to Poor,' *GM*, 15 May 1996.

88 Brian Laghi, 'Gay Seeks Rights-Code Protections,' *GM*, 04 Dec. 1997. Janice Tibbetts, 'Alberta Defends Gay Rights Exclusion,' *TS*, 5 Nov. 1997.

89 *Vriend v. Alberta*, Supreme Court of Canada, 1 April 1998.

90 Brian Laghi, 'Charter Action Urged,' *GM*, 9 April 1998. Brian Laghi, 'Rage Finds Its Voice in Alberta,' *GM*, 11 April 1998.

91 Alanna Mitchell, 'Phone-in Talk Show Reflects Full Spectrum,' *GM*, 3 April 1998.

92 Brian Laghi, 'Alberta's Gay-Rights Fight Turns Ugly,' *GM*, 9 April 1998, A1. 'Dealing With the Sickos,' *X*, 23 April 1998.

93 Larry Johnsrude, 'Tory MLAs Feeling Heat to Override Court Ruling,' *Edmonton Journal*, 4 April 1998. Don Martin, 'Barrage of Phone Calls has Klein Starting to Waffle,' *Calgary Herald*, 17 April 1998. Brian Laghi, 'Alberta to Let Court Ruling on Gay Rights Stand.' *GM*, 10 April 1998.

94 Campbell, *Time and Chance*, 216–17.
95 Graham Fraser, 'Rights Protection Extended to Gays,' *GM*, 10 Dec. 1992, A4.
96 Graham Fraser, 'Bill Protects Gay and Lesbian Rights,' *GM*, 11 Dec. 1992. Jim Oldham, 'Ploys R Us,' *X*, 25 Dec. 1992. Stan Persky, 'Don't They Know When It's Time to Declare Victory?' *GM*, 21 Dec. 1992.
97 Geoffrey York, 'Human-Rights Bill Appears Doomed,' *GM*, 18 March 1993.
98 Marc A. Morrison, 'Grits Lobbied in Ottawa,' *X*, 10 Dec. 1993.
99 'Discrimination Against Gays to Be Forbidden By Law,' *GM*, 23 Dec. 1993.
100 Philip Hannan, 'Prime Minister's Fears Delay Changes,' *X*, 23 Dec. 1994.
101 Tu Thanh Ha, 'Dissident Liberals Fight Bills on Gays,' *GM*, 28 Sept. 1994, A1.
102 Tom Wappel, MP, 'Sexual Orientation,' *Issues to Consider*, 16 Nov. 1994. Edward Greenspon and Tu Thanh Ha, 'Dissident Liberals Balk Over Hate Bill,' *GM*, 27 Oct. 1994. Philip Hannan, 'Hate-crimes Bill Goes Through,' *X*, 23 June 1995.
103 REALWomen, *Laws Protecting Homosexuals or 'Sexual Orientation' Legislation: How It Will Affect Canadians*, leaflet, ca 1986.
104 Evangelical Fellowship of Canada, 'You Were Asking about Homosexuality.' Evangelical Fellowship of Canada, 'Urgent! Family Concerns Petition,' leaflet, ca 1993. Brian C. Stiller, executive director of the Evangelical Fellowship of Canada, 'Protect Family Values,' Jan. 1995, fund-raising letter and petition.
105 Anne McIlroy, 'Adoption Cited for No Vote on Gay Bill,' *GM*, 3 May 1996. Coalition of Concerned Canadians, 'Jean Chretien and Allan Rock vs. the Canadian Family,' advertisement, *GM*, 7 May 1996.
106 Sean Durkhan, 'Reform Takes Stock' *Sun*, 10 Oct. 1994. Sean Durkhan, 'Presto Pans Plans,' *Sun*, 7 Dec. 1994, 54.
107 Edison Stewart, 'Minister Waffles on Outlawing Homosexual Bias,' *TS*, 21 Feb. 1996. Anne McIlroy, 'Yalden Flunks Liberals on Gay Rights,' *GM*, 20 March 1996. David Vienneau, 'Chretien Vows Law Banning Discrimination against Gays,' *TS*, 21 March 1996.
108 Anne McIlroy, 'Liberals Introduce Gay-Rights Reform,' *GM*, 30 April 1996. David Vienneau, 'Gay Rights Free Vote Divisive: Liberals,' *TS*, 17 April 1996.
109 David Vienneau, 'Divisive Bill on Gay Rights Is Passed,' *TS*, 10 May 1996.
110 Didi Herman, *Rights of Passage: Struggles for Lesbian and Gay Legal Equality* (Toronto: University of Toronto Press, 1994), 49.
111 Smith, *Lesbian and Gay Rights in Canada*, 22.
112 *EGALE Equality for Gays and Lesbians Everywhere*, leaflet, early 1990s.

Chapter 10: Legal Recognition of Same-Sex Relationships

1 Sky Gilbert, 'A Dark Victory for Queer Culture,' *TS*, 16 Aug. 1997.
2 Christine Donald, 5 Jan. 1998.
3 Nikki Gershbain, 'Waiting at the Altar,' *X*, 22 May 1997, 37.
4 Kathleen A. Lahey, *Are We 'Persons' Yet? Law and Sexuality in Canada* (Toronto: University of Toronto Press, 1999), 272.
5 Carol Allen, 'Family Ties,' *Q*, June 1992, 6.
6 Krishna Rau, 'Whites Apply for Spousal Benefits,' *X*, 13 Aug. 1998, 11.
7 Gershbain, 'Waiting at the Altar.'
8 Kate Barker, 'Let's Call the Whole Thing Off,' *X*, 26 March 1998, 23.
9 Tom Warner, 'Story of a Same-Sex Spousal Rights Strategy,' *X*, 5 June 1997, 28.
10 Jeff Dodds, 'Queer Marriage: Our Most Pressing Issue?' *P*, 18:3, 19 April 2000, 6.
11 Barker, 'Let's Call the Whole Thing Off.'
12 Ibid.
13 Chris Vogel, 8 Oct. 1998.
14 'Gay Couple Battle to Be Wed,' *TS*, 2 Dec. 1992. 'Two Men Can't Be Married Court Says,' *TS*, 16 March 1993.
15 Sarah Binder, 'Homosexual Couple Seek to Be Legally Married,' *GM*, 15 Sept. 1998.
16 Krishna Rau, 'Crashing the Party,' *X*, 15 June 2000.
17 Jim Wilkes, 'Gay Nuptials Plan Popular,' *TS*, 6 Dec. 2000.
18 Ian Bailey, 'Court Lets B.C. Fight Ban on Same-Sex Marriages,' *NP*, 10 Jan. 2001.
19 John Wilson, 'On Our Own Terms?' *R*, Sept. 1989, 4.
20 CLGRO, *Happy Families: The Recognition of Same-Sex Spousal Relationships*, brief to members of the Ontario legislature, April 1992.
21 Ibid.
22 Minutes, CLGRO Working Group on Relationship Recognition, 16 Feb. 1991.
23 For more on the liberationist versus assimilationist perspectives on relationship recognition, see Mirian Smith, *Lesbian and Gay Rights in Canada: Social Movements and Equality-Seeking, 1971–1995* (Toronto: University of Toronto Press, 1999), 101–6.
24 Frances Lankin, chair, Management Board of Cabinet, 'Extension of Ontario Public Service Spousal Benefit Coverage to Same Sex Spouses,' Statement to the Legislature, 20 Dec. 1990.
25 Dayne Ogilvie, 'Getting in a Family Way,' *X*, 11 Jan. 1991, 1.
26 Bob Rae, *From Protest to Power: Personal Reflections on a Life in Politics* (Toronto: Penguin, 1996) 251.

27 David Rayside provides a detailed accounting and thorough analysis of the relationship recognition campaign in Ontario, in *On the Fringe: Gays and Lesbians and Politics* (Ithaca: Cornell University Press, 1998).

28 CLGRO, letter from Tom Warner to the planning and priorities committee of the NDP caucus, 13 April 1992.

29 Paula Todd, 'Gays Fight for Legal Reforms,' *TS*, 11 Aug. 1992, A13.

30 CLGRO, media statement, 01 Sept. 1992.

31 CLGRO, *Your Rights Are at Stake*, leaflet, Sept. 1992.

32 Tom Warner and C.M. Donald, 'Way to Go! CLGRO 1975–1995: A Short History,' 24.

33 CLGRO, letter from Nick Mulé 8 May 1993 and enclosure, 'An Act to Recognize Same-Sex Spousal Relationships.'

34 Bruce DeMara, 'Courts Pushing Same-Sex Rights Minister Says,' *TS*, 11 June 1993.

35 Doug Ewart, 'Fall 1993 and Spring 1994 Legislative Program,' memorandum, Director, Policy Development Division, Ministry of the Attorney General, to the Honourable Marion Boyd, Attorney General, 6 Dec. 1993.

36 Thomas Walkom, 'Gay Lobby, Attorney-General Can Push Rae Only So Far,' *TS*, 24 Feb. 1993.

37 Rae, *From Protest to Power*, 252.

38 CLGRO, Minutes, Steering Committee, 26–7 Sept. 1992.

39 Lyn McLeod, Leader of the Opposition, letter to the Honourable Bob Rae, 9 March 1993.

40 Bill 45, An Act to Amend the Human Rights Code with Respect to Sexual Orientation, 1993.

41 David M. Rayside, 'Inside the Fringe: Mobilizing for Same-Sex Benefits in Ontario,' a paper presented at the 2nd annual meeting of the Canadian Lesbian and Gay Studies Association, Montreal, 3–4 June 1995, 5. 'MPP Pushes Same-Sex Bill,' *Sun*, 9 June 1993. Bruce DeMara, 'Benefits Bill for Same-Sex Couples Criticized,' *TS*, 9 June 1993. 'Working Group Gearing Up for Relationship Recognition Campaign,' *CLGRO Newsletter*, Aug. 1993.

42 'Gays Stage Noisy Protest,' *Sun*, 22 Feb. 1994.

43 *Hansard*, Legislative Assembly of Ontario, 23 Nov. 1993, 'Petition Fights Gay Marriage Law,' *Liberal*, 5 Dec. 1993, 3.

44 Rayside, 'Inside the Fringe: Mobilizing for Same-Sex Benefits in Ontario,' 7.

45 Leslie Papp, 'Same-Sex Couples to Get New Rights,' *TS*, 1 March 1994. 'Same-Sex Pairs to Get All Rights,' *TS*, 25 March 1994.

46 Rae, *From Protest to Power*, 252. William Walker, 'NDP Delays Spousal Benefits Package for Gays,' *TS*, 27 April 1994.

47 Mark Zwolinski, 'Catholics Split on Same-Sex Benefits Letter,' *TS*, 30 May 1994.
48 Papp, 'Same-Sex Couples to Get New Rights.'
49 Linda Leatherdale, 'Open Your Wallets: Same-Sex Benefits Will Cost Untold Millions,' *Sun*, 1 March 1994, 39.
50 David Frum, '"Alternate" Taste Written into Law,' *Sun*, 5 March 1994, 11.
51 Smith, *Lesbian and Gay Rights in Canada*, 125–6.
52 Campaign for Equal Families, *Fact Sheet: Family*, leaflet, 1994.
53 Campaign for Equal Families, *The Campaign for Equal Families Asks You to Support Lesbian and Gay Families and Our Human Rights*, leaflet, 1994.
54 Eleanor Brown, 'Deciding Whether to Decide,' *X*, 19 July 1994.
55 Equality Rights Statute Law Amendment Act, 1994.
56 William Walker, 'Same-Sex Rights Bill Will Go to Free Vote,' *TS*, 11 May 1994, 1. Craig McInnes, 'Spousal Rights Bill Backlash Stings NDP,' *GM*, 24 April 1994, A4.
57 William Walker, 'Same-Sex Rights Bill Alive, for Now,' *TS*, 20 May 1994, 1.
58 Heather Bird, 'Making Amends,' *Sun*, 9 June 1994.
59 William Walker and Leslie Papp, 'NDP Alters Same-Sex Bill,' *TS*, 9 June 1994. 'Boyd Backs Off on Gay Spouses,' *GM*, 9 June 1994. Heather Bird and James Wallace, 'Retreat,' *Sun*, 9 June 1994.
60 'MPPs Crush Same-Sex Bill,' *TS*, 10 June 1994. 'Thousands Protest Vote,' *X*, *News Flash* 10 June 1994.
61 Readers seeking details of these cases are directed to two comprehensive sources: Lahey's *Are We 'Persons' Yet? Law and Sexuality in Canada* and MacDougall's, *Queer Judgments: Homosexuality, Expression and the Courts in Canada*.
62 Bruce MacDougall, *Queer Judgments: Homosexuality, Expression, and the Courts in Canada* (Toronto: University of Toronto Press, 2000), 49.
63 Ibid., 72.
64 'B.C. Now Allows Gays to Apply for Adoption,' *TS*, 17 Feb. 1995. Cindy Filipenko, 'BC Grits Slam Adoption,' *X*, 26 May 1995.
65 'B.C. Tables Same-Sex Legislation,' *GM*, 6 June 1997. 'Church Decries Gay Spouses,' *GM*, 24 June 1997, A4. Robert Matas, 'Religious Leaders Out to Scuttle B.C. Spousal Law,' *GM*, 11 July 97. Wendy Cox, 'B.C. Bill a Boon to Gay Couples,' *GM*, 16 July 97. Richard Banner, 'Queer Families Okay,' *A*, Aug. 1997. Craig McInnes, 'B.C. Passes Legislation Redefining Term "Spouse,"' *GM*, 23 July 97.
66 Robert Matas, 'B.C. Expands Same-Sex Rights,' *GM*, 23 June 1998.
67 Smith, *Lesbian and Gay Rights in Canada*, 113–14.
68 'The Rock Becomes Number 8,' *P*, 15:8, 3 Dec. 1997.
69 'Quebec Reforms on the Way?' *R*, Nov.–Dec. 1991.

70 Richard Mackie, 'Quebec Urged to Follow Ontario on Gay Benefits,' *GM*, 2 June 1994, A5.
71 'Rights in Quebec,' *P*, 24 April 1996. 'Spousal Rights in Quebec,' *X*, 14 March 1996.
72 'Conjoints de même sexe: on passe aux actes s.v.p.!' *RG* 190 (July 1998). Eleanor Brown, 'Spousal Rights Fight,' *X*, 2 July 98.
73 Lysiane Gagnon, 'Vive le Québec gai,' *GM*, 22 May 1999.
74 Réal Ménard, 'Quebec and Gay Rights: A Long Road toward Tolerance and Openness,' *Icon* 73 (Nov. 1996), 73–4.
75 Caroline Mallan, 'Tories Set to Move on Same-Sex Legislation,' *TS*, 25 Oct. 1999, A1.
76 Tom Warner, 'Bill 5: Ontario's "Same-Sex Partner" Law,' *Outwords*, CLGRO newsletter, Nov. 1999.
77 Mallan, 'Tories Set to Move on Same-Sex Legislation.' Richard Mackie, 'Ontario Bill Could Force Gay Politicians Out of Closet,' *GM*, 26 Oct. 1999. Ian Urquhart, 'Contentious Bill Voted into Law Quickly and Quietly,' *TS*, 28 Oct. 1999.
78 Brenda Cossman, 'Separate, but Equal,' *X*, 4 Nov. 1999, 11.
79 EGALE, 'Ontario Introduces Omnibus Legislation, Refuses to Extend Definition of "Spouse,"' press release, 25 Oct. 1999. EGALE, 'Ontario's "Separate But Unequal" Regime to Be Challenged in Supreme Court of Canada,' press release, 25 Nov. 1999.
80 Joanna Radbord, 'Tory Segregation,' 'Letters,' *X*, 2 Dec. 1999, 8.
81 Domestic Relations Amendment Act, 1999. Jill Mahoney, 'Gay-Rights Advocates in Alberta Vow to Contest Revised Spousal-Support Law,' *GM*, 16 Feb. 1999, A4.
82 Dean Bennett, 'Alberta Seeks Referendum before Using *Charter of Rights* Clause,' Canadian Press, 29 Nov. 1999.
83 Constitutional Referendum Amendment Act, 1999.
84 Kelly Toughill, 'Nova Scotia First Province to Bless Gay Partnerships,' *TS*, 4 June 2001. 'Nova Scotia Passes Same-sex Rights Bill,' *GM*, 2 June 2001.
85 'Manitoba to Study Adoptions by Gays,' *GM*, 20 June 2001. 'Adoption not Allowed,' *P*, 19:5, 1 Aug. 2001, 20.
86 'Equal Relationships,' *P*, 19:5, 1 Aug. 2001.
87 EGALE, 'History of EGALE,' *Info EGALE*, 01:01, Feb. 1988.
88 Brenda Cossman, 'No Sex Please,' *X*, 25 Feb. 1999, 11.
89 'Rock Knocks Same-Sex Bill,' *Sun*, 27 May 1994, 21.
90 David Gamble, 'Ottawa Looks at Extension of Benefits,' *TS*, 27 May 1994. Allan Thompson, 'Liberals Split on Benefit Plan for Gay Couples,' *TS*, 16 March 1996.

91 'Feds Vote Down Spousal Recognition,' *X*, 29 Sept. 1995. Shawn Dearn, 'Réal Ménard Loses Bid for Spousal Recognition Bill,' *CX*, 19 Feb. 1999.
92 Stephen Thorne, 'Liberals Face Strife for Same-Sex Part of Pension Bill,' *GM*, 24 May 1999. Tim Harper, 'Vote Shows Dissident Liberal MPs Getting Bolder,' *TS*, 27 May 1999. Tonda MacCharles, 'MPs Tie the Knot on Marriage,' *TS*, 9 June 1999.
93 Bruce DeMara, 'Gay Rights Suit Poses Challenge to 58 Federal Laws,' *TS*, 8 Jan. 1999, A11.
94 John Barber, 'Gay Pride Parade Gains Mainstream Acceptance,' *GM*, 26 June 1999, A6.
95 Daniel LeBlanc, 'Ottawa May Draft Same-Sex Omnibus Bill,' *GM*, 27 May 1999.
96 Valerie Lawton, 'Gays Hail Federal Rights for Same-Sex Partnerships,' *TS*, 4 Nov. 1999.
97 Valerie Lawton, 'Same-Sex Legislation Is Expected this Week,' *TS*, 8 Feb. 2000.
98 Brian Laghi, 'Gay-Rights Bill Stirring Up Liberal Caucus,' *GM*, 10 Feb. 2000. Brian Laghi, 'Ottawa Introduces Same-Sex Benefits,' *GM*, 12 Feb. 2000.
99 Valerie Lawton, 'Same-Sex Bill to Exclude Gay Marriage,' *TS*, 23 March 2000. 'Same-Sex Benefits Bill Sails Through,' *TS*, 12 April 2000.
100 Rob Hughes, 'Love Across Borders,' in *Outcomes 1993*, from OutRights, 1992.
101 Lesbian and Gay Immigration Task Force, *Taking the Next Step*, brief to the Minister of Manpower and Immigration, 1994.
102 'Building a Strong Foundation for the 21st Century,' Citizenship and Immigration Canada (Ottawa: Minister of Public Works and Government Services Canada: 1998), 21–6.
103 Barber, 'Gay Pride Parade Gains Mainstream Acceptance.'
104 Steven Maynard, 'Modernization or Liberation?' *CX*, 17 March 2000, 19.

Chapter 11: AIDS Radicalism, Queer Nation, and Identity Politics

1 'AIDS Update,' *TBP*, Jan. 1987.
2 John Edgar, 27 July 1990; Stephen Lock, 2 June 1997. Michael Phair, 18 June 1997. Mike Johnston, 29 Feb. 1992; Maurice Michaud, 26 July 93. AIDS New Brunswick, Minutes, Support Committee, 13 Jan. 89.
3 Ed Jackson, 'Facing a Common Enemy,' *TBP*, July 1985, 13.
4 John Edgar, 27 July 1990.
5 Roy Hallet, 29 Sept. 1990.

6 Maurice Michaud, 26 July 93.
7 Claude Olivier, 29 July 93.
8 Stephen Lock, 2 June 1997.
9 Michael Phair, 18 June 1997.
10 Jim Monk, 2 March 1998.
11 Kelly Toughill, 'Frank Talk in War on AIDS,' *TS*, 11 Jan. 89. Christina Blizzard, 'Time to Clean Up Their ACT,' *Sun*, 21 Jan. 93.
12 Jim Monk, 2 March 1999. Tom Gale, 18 June 1997.
13 Evert A. Lindquist and David M. Rayside, 'AIDS Policy in Canada: Community Activism, Federalism, and the New Politics of Disease' unpublished paper (University of Toronto, Department of Political Science, Nov. 1990), 21.
14 Ibid., 8.
15 Ibid., 34.
16 Wilson Hodder, 22 July 1993.
17 Gary Kinsman, 27 July 93.
18 Bernard Courte, 22 Nov. 1990.
19 Lindquist and Rayside, 'AIDS Policy in Canada,' 28.
20 Gary Kinsman, 27 June 1993.
21 Lindquist and Rayside, 'AIDS Policy in Canada,' 9.
22 Desmond Bill, 'AIDS Activist Issues Drug Plea in Video Made before He Died,' *TS*, 6 Jan. 93. Rachel Giese, 'Catastrophic Drug Plan Announced,' *X*, 9 Dec. 1994, 1.
23 Thomas Walkom, 'Whatever the Motive, NDP Improves Drug Coverage,' *TS*, 12 Jan. 94.
24 Giese, 'Catastrophic Drug Plan Announced.'
25 Kate Barker, 'Getting Their ACT Together,' *X*, 23 April 1998.
26 Tim Harpur, 'HIV's Rate of Spread Rising Again,' *TS*, 1 Oct. 1997. Jamey Heath, 'Emerging Epidemics,' *X*, 4 Nov. 1997. 'Statistics Show a Decline in Incidence and Deaths,' *GM*, 1 Dec. 1997.
27 Philip B. Berger, 'The Waning of AIDS Activism,' *GM*, 10 Aug. 1998, A13.
28 Barker, 'Getting Their ACT Together.' John Kennedy, 'AIDS Is Public Enemy Number One,' *X*, 5 Dec. 1996, 27.
29 Black Coalition for AIDS Prevention, *Black Coalition for AIDS Prevention*, leaflet, early 1990s.
30 Kennedy, 'AIDS Is Public Enemy Number One.'
31 'Life of GAAP,' *X*, 26 Nov. 1993, 17.
32 Glenn Sumi, 'Asian AIDS Group Seeks Executive Director,' *X*, 26 Nov. 1993, 17.
33 GAT, 'Message from the Sponsors,' Fifteenth anniversary CelebrAsian '95 program, 1995.

34 Pat Johnson, 'The Denver Principles,' Interviews, *XW*, 16 Nov. 1995.
35 Steven Pereira, 'ASAP – Ready to Roll – and Rock,' *Khush Khayal*, May 1992, 4.
36 Matthew Hays, 'Native Communities Respond to AIDS,' *X, XS*, Sept. 1992, 9.
37 Ibid.
38 'Aboriginal Awareness,' *CX*, 14 Nov. 1997.
39 Feather of Hope Society, *Feather of Hope*, leaflet, 1997.
40 Evan Adams, 14 Oct. 1992.
41 Tyrone Hewhook, 'Low Self Esteem and High-Risk Behaviour,' *X*, 9 Dec. 1994, 20.
42 Hays, 'Native Communities Respond to AIDS.'
43 Rick Hammond, 'Two-Spirited People,' *Sightlines*, April 1991, 16.
44 Evan Adams, 14 Oct. 1992. Patti Flather, 'Snapshots of Native Struggles with AIDS,' *R*, Feb. 1990.
45 Allan Berube and Jeffrey Escoffier, 'Queer/Nation,' *Out Look* 11 (winter 1991), 14.
46 Ibid.
47 Gary Kinsman, *The Regulation of Desire: Homo and Hetero Sexualities*, 2nd ed. (Montreal: Black Rose Books, 1996), 299–300.
48 Gillian Morton, 'Critical Mass or Critical Mess?' *X, XS*, Sept. 1992.
49 Barry D. Adam, *The Rise of a Gay and Lesbian Movement*, rev. ed. (New York: Twayne Publishers, 1995), 163–4.
50 Alexander S. Chee, 'A Queer Nationalism,' *Out Look* 11 (winter 1991).
51 David Collins, 'Fabulous Fighting Queers,' *X*, 11 Jan. 91, 5.
52 Steven Maynard, 'When Queer Is Not Enough,' *Fuse Magazine* 15 (fall 1991), 14.
53 Lori Lyons, 'On Queer Nation,' *X*, 26 June 1992, 15.
54 Yuki Hayashi, 'On Queer Nation,' *X*, 26 June 1992, 14.
55 Tonia Bryan, 'Black Lesbian Consciousness,' letter, *GO*, Feb. 1992, 13.
56 David Pepper, 'Queer Nation Comes to Ottawa,' *GO*, March 1991, 4.
57 Annamarie Jagose, *Queer Theory: An Introduction* (New York City: New York University Press, 1996), 77.
58 Tom Patterson, 'Year of the Queer!' *A*, April 1991, 11.
59 Jagose, *Queer Theory: An Introduction*, 92–3.
60 Allen Young, 'Out of the Closets and into the Streets,' in *Out of the Closets: Voices of Gay Liberation*, ed. Karla Jay and Allen Young (New York: Douglas Books, 1972), 28.
61 Bert Archer, 'Un-Gay: No Room for Ambiguity,' *fab* 94, 27 Aug. 1998, 26.
62 Ibid.
63 Bert Archer, *The End of Gay (and the Death of Heterosexuality)* (Toronto: Doubleday Canada, 1999), 15, 22–3.

Chapter 12: Queer Community Standards and Queer Spaces

1 Government of Canada, Special Committee on Pornography and Prostitution, *Pornography and Prostitution in Canada, Report of the Special Committee on Pornography and Prostitution: The Fraser Commission Report*, vols. 1 and 2, 1985. Ottawa: Ministry of Supplies and Services.

2 Ibid.

3 'Back in the Gutter Again,' *TBP*, Aug. 1984, 9. Lise Gotell, 'Shaping *Butler*: The New Politics of Anti-Pornography,' in *Bad Attitude/s on Trial: Pornography, Feminism, and the Butler Decision*, Brenda Cossman, Shannon Bell, Lise Gottell, and Becki L. Ross (Toronto: University of Toronto Press, 1997), 103–4.

4 John C. Crosbie with Geoffrey Stevens, *No Holds Barred: My Life in Politics* (Toronto: McClelland and Stewart, 1997), 274–6.

5 For detailed assessments of the impact of the *Butler* decision, see Janine Fuller and Stuart Blackley, *Bad Attitude/s on Trial: Pornography, Feminism, and the Butler Decision*, and *Restricted Entry: Censorship on Trial* (Vancouver: Press Gang Publishers, 1995).

6 *R. vs. Butler* [1992] 1 S.C.R. 452.

7 *Glad Day Bookshop Inc. v. Deputy Minister of National Revenue for Customs and Excise*, 14 July 1992 (unreported) (Ont. Ct. Gen. Div.). Fuller and Blackley, *Restricted Entry*, 44–5.

8 Catherine Douglas, 'Guilty Verdict Forces Glad Day to Censor,' *Q*, March 1993.

9 Val Ross, 'Glad Day Case Tests Community Standards,' *GM*, 17 Dec. 1992. For more on this case, see *Bad Attitude/s on Trial*.

10 Ibid.

11 'Lesbian Porn,' *Q*, May 1992, 5.

12 Chris Bearchell, 'In Harm's Way,' *X*, *XS*, Nov. 1992, 3.

13 Lynda Hurst, 'Coming Out,' *TS*, 26 June 1993, D4.

14 Susan G. Cole, *Pornography and the Sex Crisis* (Toronto: Second Story Press, 1989), 126–7.

15 Bet Cecill, 12 Oct. 1992.

16 Chris Bearchell and Denis LeBlanc, 'Contemporary Feminism and Gay Liberation Explored – Part Two,' *GO*, April 1991, 6.

17 Jean Hillabold, 'Erotica and the Feminist Sex Wars – Part One,' *P*, 17:7, 27 Oct. 1999, 8.

18 Jean Hillabold, 'Erotica and the Feminist Sex Wars – Part Two,' *P*, 17:8, 8 Dec. 1999, 7.

19 Jean Hillabold, 'Erotica and the Feminist Sex Wars – Part Three,' *P*, 18:1, 26 Jan. 2000, 7.

20 Tomiye Ishida, 'How Far Can We Honour Our Lusts?' *X*, 24 Oct. 1996, 24.
21 *Customs Act*, S.C. 1986, c 1; *Customs Tariff*, S.C. 1987, c 41.
22 Cossman, Bell, Gottell, and Ross, *Bad Attitude/s on Trial*, 33. Christopher Sunter, 'We Know It When We See It,' *TBP*, July 1985.
23 Memorandum D9-1-1: Interpretative Policy and Procedures for the Administration of Tariff Code 9956.
24 Jeffrey Moore, 'Why Is Customs Allowed to Censor?' *TS*, 16 Oct. 1990.
25 Alan Orr, 'Sex Is Okay – If It's Not Gay,' *TBP*, Sept. 1986.
26 Elaine Carey, 'Customs' Power to Ban Infuriates Book World,' *TS*, 25 Feb. 1989.
27 Nik Sheehan, 'Bureaucratic Buggery,' *X, XS*, 27 July 90, 13. H.J. Kirchoff, 'A Sad Chapter in "Homophobia,"' *GM*, 14 July 1990, C9.
28 Robert Hough, 'Degrading Customs,' *GM*, 12 Feb. 1994, D1.
29 Bruce MacDougall, *Queer Judgments: Homosexuality, Expression, and the Courts in Canada* (Toronto: University of Toronto Press, 2000), 56.
30 Fuller and Blackley, *Restricted Entry*, 57.
31 Hough, 'Degrading Customs.'
32 Val Ross and John O'Callaghan, 'Books and Magazines Detained by Customs,' *GM*, 12 May 1993.
33 Kirchoff, 'A Sad Chapter in "Homophobia."'
34 'Customs Targets Gay Book Distributor,' *X*, 28 May 1993, 13.
35 Fuller and Blackley, *Restricted Entry*, 8.
36 Deborah Wilson, 'Bookstore's Seizure Challenge Going Ahead,' *GM*, 17 Nov. 1992. Fuller and Blackley, *Restricted Entry*, 19, 117.
37 Fuller and Blackley, *Restricted Entry*, 184. The details of the specific legal arguments presented by Little Sister's and the Crown, and of the testimony of various expert witnesses, are comprehensively chronicled by Fuller and Blackley in *Restricted Entry*.
38 Judy Stoffman, 'Lesbian Bookstore Renews Fight with "Flawed" Customs,' *TS*, 23 Jan. 1996, B5.
39 Judy Stoffman, 'Bookstore Wins Customs Round,' *TS*, 2 April 1996.
40 Enzo Di Matteo, 'Customs Seize Gay Books,' *Now*, 30 April 1998, 15.
41 Frank Prendergast, 'Homo Harassment Continues,' *X*, 12 Feb. 1998.
42 Rob Ferraz, 'Canada Customs' Sleight of Hand,' *Now*, 26 Nov. 1998, 15.
43 Brenda Cossman, 'The Ghost of Butler,' *X*, 2 July 1998, 11.
44 Brenda Cossman, 'Return of the Loonies,' *X*, 30 Dec. 1999, 11.
45 Ibid.
46 *Little Sisters Book and Art Emporium v. Canada* (Minister of Justice), 2000 SCC 69. File No. 26858, 3, 5.
47 Brenda Cossman, 'Little Sister's Still Needs a Babysitter,' *X*, 28 Dec. 2000, 11.

48 Rory MacDonald, 'Customs Chokes on Meat Men,' *X*, 27 July 2000.
49 *Little Sisters Book and Art Emporium v. Canada.*
50 'It's Still a Bad Law,' editorial, *GM*, 11 March 1994, A24. 'Child Porn Law,' editorial, *GM*, 25 April 1995.
51 'Shoddy Justice in Race to the Polls,' editorial, *TS*, 17 June 1993, A22.
52 *Hansard*, Commons Debates, 15 June 1993.
53 Ibid.
54 CLGRO, 'CLGRO Backgrounder Bill 128, Paedophiles, etc.,' Sept. 93, 1–2.
55 Ibid.
56 Forum 128 and CLGRO, *Young People and Sex*, leaflet, Oct. 1993.
57 EGALE, *InfoEgale*, special election issue, 1993, 13.
58 Brenda Cossman, 'Judge Is Getting Death Threats,' *X*, 19 Feb. 1999, 17.
59 Kate Taylor, 'Child-Porn Law Used for the First Time,' *GM*, 22 Dec. 1993.
60 Thomas Claridge, 'Prosecutor Rates Langer Works in Breakdown for Court,' *GM*, 15 Oct. 1994.
61 Donn Downey, 'Art Works No Risk to Young,' *GM*, 25 April 1995. 'Langer Appeal Refused,' *X*, 17 Nov. 1995.
62 Jane Armstrong, 'Child-Porn Law Is Struck Down by B.C. Judge,' *GM*, 16 Jan. 99. Tom Yeung, 'Why Not Plead Guilty?' *X*, 19 Feb. 1999.
63 Jane Armstrong, 'Kiddie-Porn Law Headed to Top Court,' *GM*, 1 July 1999.
64 Janice Tibbetts, 'Ottawa Fights for Law on Child Porn,' *NP*, 7 Jan. 2000, A4.
65 Brenda Cossman, 'A Weak Squeak of Courage,' *X*, 8 Feb. 2001, 13.
66 *R. v. Sharpe*, 2001 SCC 2. File No. 27376, 2.
67 Gerald Hannon, 'The Kiddie-Porn Ring That Wasn't,' *GM*, 11 March 1995. 'Operation Scoop,' news release, 31 May 1994, London Police.
68 'Operation Scoop,' news release, 31 May 1994, London Police.
69 Joseph Couture, 'Cops Suffer Memory Lapse?' *X*, 15 Sept. 1995.
70 Enzo Di Matteo, 'Fantino Exposed,' *Now*, 12 Oct. 1995.
71 Joseph Couture, 'Sexual Abuse,' *X*, 14 Oct. 1994, 22.
72 HALO, *We Are under Attack: Get the Facts,'* leaflet, 1994.
73 Di Matteo, 'Fantino Exposed.' Joseph Couture, '"Victim" Signs Affidavit Stating He Was Never Sexually Assaulted,' *X*, 14 Oct. 1995.
74 Hannon, 'The Kiddie-Porn Ring That Wasn't.'
75 HALO and CLGRO, *On Guard: A Critique of Project Guardian*, Sept. 1996, 10.
76 Joseph Couture, 'Project Guardian's Tiny Error ...,' *X*, 28 March 1996. Hannon, 'The Kiddie-Porn Ring That Wasn't.'
77 *Criminal Code*, RSC 1985, S. 155.
78 Thomas Claridge, 'Anal Intercourse Provisions Ruled Rights Breach,' *GM*, 29 July 1992, A11.
79 Canadian AIDS Society and CLGRO, 'Factum of the Intervenors Cana-

dian AIDS Society and Coalition for Lesbian and Gay Rights in Ontario,' Ontario Court of Appeal, 1994, 13.

80 Tracey Taylor, 'Law Against Anal Sex by Under-18s Thrown Out,' *TS*, 26 May 1995, A2.

81 Eleanor Brown, 'Anal Sex Law Overturned,' *X*, 17 March 1995.

82 CLGRO, letter to the Honourable Anne McClellan, 4 May 1998. Anne McClellan, letter to CLGRO, 23 Feb. 1999.

83 Phillip Hannan, 'Common Understanding,' *CX*, 17 June 1994, 13.

84 Gigi Suhanic, 'On the Cutting Edge,' *CX*, 17 March 2000, 1.

85 Liz Massiah, 19 June 1997.

86 Imtiaz Popat, 'Policing Homophobia,' *A*, Jan. 1996, 1.

87 'Police Chief Marches,' *P*, 15:6, 10 Sept. 1997, 26.

88 'The Calgary Gay and Lesbian Community Police Liaison Committee Survey,' *qc*, March 1997.

89 'Cover Model,' *P*, 15:8, 3 Dec. 1997.

90 Carol MacPherson, 'Pink Police Blues,' *qc*, June 1997, 16–17.

91 Neil Smith, 'Montreal Police Attack,' *X*, 27 July 1990.

92 Ibid.

93 Neil Smith, 'Eight Gay Killings in Montreal,' *X*, *XS*, Jan. 1992.

94 Leif Harmsen, 'Montreal Activists Respond to Gay Killings,' *X*, *XS*, Feb. 1993. Hannan, 'Common Understanding.'

95 Ingrid Peritz, 'Coming Out of the Blue,' *GM*, 28 July 1999, D3.

96 Kathryn Payne, 'Conspiracy Flowers in Police Force,' *X*, 3 July 97, 11. Christie Blatchford, 'Story Rides Off in All Directions,' *Sun*, 20 May 1991; Michael Valpy, 'Here's a Smelly Smear Campaign,' *GM*, 23 May 1991, A8.

97 Joe Clark, 'Cops Out of the Closet,' *TS*, 4 May 1991, G1.

98 Bruce DeMara, 'Officer Finds Acceptance Comes Slowly,' *TS*, 10 Aug. 1992, A15.

99 Peritz, 'Coming Out of the Blue.'

100 Michelle Shephard, 'Ordeal Brought Out Best, Worst,' *TS*, 7 Sept. 1995.

101 Susan Eng, 'Cop Culture: For Us or Against Us?' *GM*, 27 Jan. 2000, A17.

102 Ibid.

103 Glenn Wheeler, 'Sex Raid Strikes Fear,' *Now*, 29 Feb. 1996. Rosie DiManno, 'Raid on Gay Troupe in "Salacious" Act Cited as Aggressive,' *TS*, 26 Feb. 1996.

104 Michael Grange, 'Raid on Toronto Gay Club Brings Fear,' *GM*, 12 March 1996, A7.

105 Colin Leslie, 'Cops Bust Gay Strip Bar,' *X*, 29 Feb. 1996, 11.

106 Vern Smith, 'Remington's Is Guilty,' *X*, 16 Dec. 1999.

107 Donovan Vincent, 'Gay Club's Manager Convicted,' *TS*, 14 Dec. 1999.

108 Vern Smith, 'Bijou Raids Keep Toronto Clean,' *X*, 1 July 99. Vern Smith, 'Porn Theatre's Shut Down,' *X*, 15 July 99.

109 Bruce DeMara, 'Drop Gay Club Charges, Community Groups Urge,' *TS*, 20 Aug. 1999. Phinjo Gombu, 'Crown Drops Charges Involving Gay Club,' *TS*, 9 Oct. 1999.

110 John Kennedy, 'On the Record,' interview with Kyle Rae, *fab*, 19 Aug. 1999, 18.

111 John Kennedy, 'Now *Those* Were Raids,' *fab*, 14 Oct. 1999, 19.

112 John Kennedy, 'Isn't It Time to Move On,' *fab*, 19 Aug. 1999, 11.

113 Rob Wilson, 'A Jewel of a Year,' *fab*, 23 Dec 2000, 21.

114 John Coulbourn, 'Equal or Special?' *Outlooks*, Nov. 1999, 14.

115 'Drop the Charges! Stop the Raids!' leaflet, 13 June 1999.

116 Vern Smith, 'Knock, Knock,' *X*, 2 Dec. 1999.

117 Vern Smith, 'Bottomless Bar Heads Less Bawdy,' *Eye*, 20 April 2000.

118 Paul Gallant, 'Toolbox Charged,' *X*, 2 Nov. 2000.

119 Stephanie Nolen and Colin Freeze, 'Bathhouse Raid Angers Lesbian Community,' *GM*, 16 Sept. 2000, A27. Eleanor Brown, 'Male Cops at Pussy Palace,' *X*, 21 Sept. 2000, 11. Allan Woods, 'Lesbian Bathhouse Organizers Charged,' *TS*, 27 Oct. 2000.

120 Vern Smith, 'Pussy Bites Back,' *Eye*, 28 Sept. 2000. Eleanor Brown, 'Under the Rug,' *X*, 2 Nov. 2000.

121 *fab* staff, 'Y2Gay,' *fab*, 7 Dec. 2000, 29.

122 Kerry Gillespie, 'Police Raid Abused Rights of Women,' *TS*, 1 Feb. 2002.

123 Rosie DiManno, 'Fantino's Critics Speak Only for Themselves,' *TS*, 19 Nov. 1999, A2. Urban Alliance on Race Relations and ten other groups, 'An Open Letter from Concerned Community Groups,' letter to the Toronto Police Services Board, 18 Nov. 1999.

124 Enzo Di Matteo, 'Fantino's Gay Ghetto Coup,' *Now*, 9 Dec. 1999, 26.

125 John Kennedy, 'Toronto's New Top Cop Speaks,' *fab*, 9–22 Dec. 1999, 12–13.

126 Jennifer Quinn, 'Fantino Criticizes "Rhetoric,"' *TS*, 19 Sept. 2000.

127 Gerald Hannon, 'Cruise Control,' *Now*, 11 Sept. 1997, 35.

128 Brenda Cossman, 'Crown Tries to Discredit Gay Activist,' *X*, 11 Sept. 1997, 20.

129 Ibid.

130 Nick Pron, 'Bar Owner Won't Have Record,' *TS*, 20 Jan. 2000.

131 Tomiye Ishida, 'Whose Morality?' *CX*, 17 Oct. 1997, 6.

132 Enzo Di Matteo, 'Keep Clothes On, Mel Says,' *Now*, 11 June 1998, 14.

133 Peter Grey, 'Nudie Patooties,' letter to *X*, 2 July 1998, 8.

134 Mike Hansen, 'Nude Is Rude,' letter to *X*, 21 May 1998, 8.

135 Christopher Raposo, 'Nudie Patooties,' letter to *X*, 2 July 1998, 8–9.

136 Duncan Hood, 'In the Buff,' *X*, 2 July 1998, 13.

Chapter 13: Identity, Community, and Visibility at the End of the Millennium

1 Stephen Lock, 2 June 1997
2 Anonymous, 'Country Living: As Brave As I Am Able to Be,' posting on internet web site of Rainbow BC Online, Sept. 1999.
3 'Lesbians Still Marginalized,' *TS*, 4 Aug. 1998.
4 Denise Belkissoon, 'The Only Lesbians in the Entire Town,' *X*, 10 Feb. 2000.
5 Heather Cameron, 'Gay Kids on the Farm,' *X*, 7 Nov. 1996, 13.
6 Ibid.
7 Alex Krueger, 'Small-Town Life Tough on Gay Teens,' *TS*, 29 June 1999.
8 Paul Pasenan, 24 Sept. 1994.
9 Julie Garro, 'Thunder Bay's Isolation,' *X*, 26 Aug. 1999, 14.
10 'Yukon Lesbians Speak Out,' *R*, May 1987, 17.
11 Bonnie Van Toen, 'North of 60,' *X*, 4 June 1998, 16.
12 Gens Hellquist, 23 Aug. 1990.
13 Michael Riordon, *Out Our Way: Gay and Lesbian Life in the Country* (Toronto: Between the Lines, 1996), xi.
14 Elizabeth Hargreaves, 'Cafe Activism,' *XW*, 16 Nov. 1995. Daniel Collins, 'Henderson Centre a First for Vancouver Island,' *XW*, 16 Nov. 1995.
15 'Harvest Rainbows in the Okanagan,' *A*, Oct. 1992.
16 'New Group in Alberta,' *P*, 9:2, 6 March 1991, 11.
17 'Out in Saskatchewan,' *P*, 12:6, 14 Sept. 1994.
18 Valerie McNab, 24 Sept. 1994.
19 Riordon, *Out Our Way*, 28–33.
20 'Calendrier,' *RG*, Oct. 1998.
21 John Young, 30 July 1993.
22 Geraldine Daw, 8 Aug. 1993.
23 Gary Kinsman, 27 July 1993.
24 Lee Fleming, 1 Aug. 1993.
25 Leith Chiu, 1 Aug. 1993.
26 Helen Fallding, 'Out in the Cold,' *Outcomes*, from OutRights, 1992. EGALE, candidate biography, Lynn K. Richards, Gay and Lesbian Alliance of the Yukon Territory, 1997.
27 'Canada's Pride Guide (Update),' *qc*, June 1997.
28 Beth Lacey, 6 Aug. 1993.
29 Peggy Keats, 6 Aug. 1993.
30 Sue Cook, 27 Aug. 1990. Mirtha Sepuldeda, 27 Aug. 1990.
31 Robin Metcalfe, 'Coming to Our Senses,' *Gaezette*, July–Aug., 1993.
32 John Markidis, 25 July 1993.

33 Lynn Murphy, 26 July 1993.

34 Kam K. Wong, 2 June 1997.

35 Carmen Paquette, 17 Dec. 1990.

36 Bet Cecill, 12 Oct. 1992.

37 'Common Closes after Six-Year Struggle,' *Q*, April 1994.

38 Ann Marie Wallace and Sharon Myers, 29 July 1993.

39 Kristyn Wong-Tam, presentation to 'Homophobia in Education' panel, Out in the Classroom CLGRO conference, 9 Nov. 1991.

40 Joanne Doucette, 'Redefining Difference: Disabled Lesbians Resist,' in *Lesbians in Canada*, ed. Sharon Dale Stone (Toronto: Between the Lines, 1990), 61–72.

41 'Differently Abled Rainbow Club,' *Swerve*, Aug. 1998.

42 Erin Gill, 'Disabled Dykes Fight Asexual Stereotype,' *Q*, Oct. 1993, 1.

43 Shelley Tremain, 'Coming Out as Disabled Dykes,' *Q*, Feb. 1993, 6.

44 Eleanor Brown, 'Up against the Stairs,' *X*, 29 Oct. 1993.

45 Eleanor Brown, 'Looking for Love,' *X*, 18 July 1996, 14.

46 Jean B, 3 June 1997.

47 CLGRO, *Systems Failure: A Report on the Experiences of Sexual Minorities in Ontario's Health-Care and Social-Services Systems*, final report, 1997, 90.

48 Ibid., 92.

49 Heather M. Ross, 'Bigot on Board,' *X*, 15 July 1999, 20.

50 Doug Stewart, 'letters,' *TBP*, May 1985, 5.

51 '31 Words,' The Collective, *TBP*, April 1985, 29.

52 Alan Li, 'Letters,' *TBP*, April 1985, 30.

53 Richard Fung and Lim, 'Letters,' *TBP*, April 1985, 30.

54 al-Qamar Sangha, 'Yari: South Asian Lesbian and Gay Mobilizing.' *Outcomes 1993*, from OutRights, 1992, 18.

55 Ibid.

56 Adonica Huggins, 'Gender, Race, Class and Sexuality,' *P*, 9:4, 12 June 1991, 7.

57 Imtiaz Popat, 'Racism and Queerdom,' Forum, *A*, July 1994, 7.

58 Kristyn Wong-Tam, 'Homophobia in Education,' a presentation to Out in the Classroom CLGRO conference, 9 Nov. 1991.

59 Nickolus Plowden, 'A Gay Black Man's Perspective,' *GO*, Feb. 1992, 15.

60 'Dr. Kirby Hsu,' *CA*: 20, 1995, 17–18.

61 Natasha Singh, 'Building a "Community,"' *X*, 18 March 1994, 19.

62 Rick Hammond, 'Two-Spirited People,' *Sightlines*, 03:15, April 1991, 17.

63 Gilbert Deschamps, 'We Are Part of a Tradition: A Guide on Two-Spirited People for First Nations Communities,' Two-Spirited Peoples of the First Nations, 14.

64 Evan Adams, 14 Oct. 1992.

65 Paulette Peirol, 'Minority Homosexuals Invisible to Their People,' *GM*, 21 May 1997, A12.
66 Subira M'Walimu and Fatumar Omar, 'Muslims-in-Exile,' *Q*, Nov. 1993, 1.
67 Mark MacKinnon, 'Manning's Image Dealt a Blow,' *TS*, 15 April 2000, A4.
68 Eleanor Brown, 'Morality Not Promiscuity,' *X*, 5 Oct. 2000.
69 Aidan Johnson, 'Stylin' on the Printed Page,' *X*, 17 June 1999, 33.
70 Zuhair Kashmeri, 'Islam's Hidden Homosexuals,' *Now*, 30 July 1992, 12.
71 M'Walimu and Omar, 'Muslims-in-Exile.'
72 Mohammed Khan, 'Memo To: Haroon Salamat Re: Islam and Gays,' *X*, 1 June 2000, 11.
73 Peirol, 'Minority Homosexuals Invisible to Their People.'
74 Krishna Rau, 'Whites Apply for Spousal Benefits,' *X*, 13 Aug. 1998, 11.
75 Heather M. Ross, 'Connecting the Dots,' *X*, 25 Feb. 1999, 19.
76 Africans United to Control AIDS, *Africans United to Control AIDS Myths, Attitudes, Values and Perceptions about Sexuality and HIV/AIDS in the African Community*, leaflet, mid-1990s.
77 'Rastafari Takes Stand on Homosexualism,' *Uprising*, July 1996, 1.
78 Carol Allen, Lesbians of Colour, Presentation to 'Setting the Agenda,' a CLGRO forum, 10 May 1988. Celeste Natale, 'Forum with Rights Commissioner,' *R*, June 1988.
79 Peirol, 'Minority Homosexuals Invisible to Their People.'
80 Marc A. Morrison, 'Rightwingers Control the Media?' *X*, 29 Aug. 1996, 13.
81 Ibid.
82 Steven Pereira, 'ASAP – Ready to Roll – and Rock,' *Khush Khayal*, May 1992, 4.
83 Kyla Wazana, 'Older White Guys and Asian Kids,' *X*, 24 Sept. 1998, 19.
84 Clarissa Lagartera, 9 Aug. 1998.
85 Irene Darra, 'Filipina Dykes Come Out, Quietly,' *X*, 27 June 2000.
86 Clarissa Lagartera, 9 Aug. 1998.
87 Khush, *Khush: Gay South Asians of Toronto*, leaflet, 1995.
88 '... on Khush,' *Khush Khayal*, 3:4 and 4:1, May 1992, 2.
89 Frank Prendergast, 'Dumping Politics in Favour of Fun?' *X*, 7 May 1998, 17.
90 Jessica M. Pegis, 'South Asian Artists at Home,' *X*, 28 April 1995.
91 Tamai Kobayashi, 'Asian Lesbian Experience,' *CA*: 16, 1988, 9.
92 'Gay Asians,' *A*, March 1998.
93 Chantel Phillips, 'Lotus Roots Gathering,' *A*, March 1996, 3.
94 'The Gay and Lesbian Guide,' *MTL Attitude*, 3:4, April 1995.
95 Andrew Zealley, 'Propaganda, Privilege and Power, Looking at the Black Gay Community from a White (ad)Vantage Point,' *Lexicon*, Jan. 1994, 7. Frank Prendergast, 'AYA Slowly Slips Away,' *X*, 21 May 1998.

96 'Groups and Services,' *Wayves*, July–Aug., 1997.
97 Krishna Rau, 'Adding to the Rainbow,' *X*, 17 June 1999, 11.
98 *Of Colour*, (Calgary), leaflet, ca 1997.
99 Michelle Wong, 3 June 1997.
100 Kam K. Wong, 2 June 1997.
101 Clarissa Lagartera, 9 Aug. 1998.
102 *The Alternative*, newsletter of the Winnipeg Gay and Lesbian Resource Centre, Aug. 1998, 2.
103 'Queer Women of Colour,' *CX*, 19 Feb. 1999, 9.
104 Jessica Pegis, 'A Growing Sense of Pride,' *X*, 9 July 1993, 23.
105 'The Gay and Lesbian Guide,' *MTL Attitude*, 3:4, April 1995.
106 Pegis, 'A Growing Sense of Pride.'
107 Rick Hammond, 'Two-Spirited People,' *Sightlines*, 03:15, April 1991, 17.
108 Albert McLeod, 10 Aug. 1998.
109 Deschamps, 'We Are Part of a Tradition,' 13.
110 Riordon, *Out Our Way*, 172–4.
111 Ibid., 194–8.
112 Albert McLeod, 10 Aug. 1998.
113 Tyrone Newhook, 'Low Self Esteem and High-Risk Behaviour,' *X*, 9 Dec. 1994, 20.
114 'Aboriginal Circle,' *P*, 11:3, 21 April 1993, 12.
115 Deschamps, 'We Are Part of a Tradition,' 13.
116 Ibid., 14.
117 Ibid., 14–15.
118 S.G. Lee, 'Susan Steward Clicks with Collaborators,' *A*, Nov. 1977.
119 Michael Ainslie, Michael Gallina, Guita Lamsechi, 'Michael Allen,' *X*, 20 June 1996, 87.
120 'Evergon Dispute,' *P*, 8:1, 17 Jan. 90.
121 Mark Michaud, 'Culture Minister Snubs Queer Culture,' *R*, Feb. 1990, 14.
122 David McIntosh, 'Sex-Obsessed Censors,' *X*, 16 April 1993, 17.
123 Eleanor Brown, 'Theatre Under Attack,' *X*, 16 April 1993. Royson James, 'Cultural Cash Cut for Gay Groups,' *TS*, 30 June 1993. Jane Coutts and H. J. Kirchoff, 'Grant Approval for Gay Theatre Group,' *GM*, 3 July 1993.
124 'Filmfest's Raunchy Fare Criticized on All Sides,' *GM*, 24 June 1995, C4.
125 'Film Festival Fuss,' *P*, 13:5, 26 July 1995, 10. 'Filmfest's Raunchy Fare Criticized on All Sides,' Abbe Edelson, 'Christians Picket "Porn" in Calgary,' *X*, 7 July 1995.
126 Gens Hellquist, 'Porn-Fest Raises Ire,' *X*, 18 May 2000, 18.
127 Madiha Didi Khayatt, *Lesbian Teachers: An Invisible Presence* (Albany: State University of New York Press, 1992), 145.

128 Stacy Stein, 'Reading, Writing, Respect for Gays,' *TS*, 18 Nov. 1997. Pat
     Johnson, 'New Sex Ed Curriculum Falls Short,' *XW*, 16 Nov. 1995.
129 Alanna Mitchell, 'School Trustees Create Storm over Gay Rights,' *GM*,
     7 March 1997, A2.
130 'Parent and Citizens Alert!' Advertisement, *GM*, 19 June 1992, A12.
131 'CURE the Queers,' *X*, 2 Oct. 1992, 7.
132 Nicholas Garrison, 'School Bullies,' *Now*, 17 Aug., 2000, 23.
133 Joseph Coutoure, 'London's Religious Moralists Flex Muscles,' *X*, 23 June
     1995, 35.
134 Hoddy Allen, 'The Fight for the Minds of Children,' *X*, 23 Oct. 1997.
135 'Gay Student Rights,' *P*, 15:2, 12 March 1997.
136 'Debate Rages On,' *P*, 17: 4, 2 June 1999, 14. 'Opposition Dying,' *P*, 17:8,
     8 Dec. 1999, 19.
137 Mitchell, 'School Trustees Create Storm over Gay Rights.'
138 Stephen Lock, 'Lessons from Calgary,' *XW*, 29 May 1997, 5.
139 'Gay-Friendly Book Reinstated,' *GM*, 7 Feb. 1998, A8.
140 Lawrence Hill, 'Parents' Smear Campaign Scores Some Disturbing Victo-
     ries,' *GM*, 11 Feb. 1997, E1.
141 Allan, 'The Fight for the Minds of Children' Robert Mata, 'B.C. Parents
     Council Crippled,' *GM*, 17 Feb. 1998.
142 'Surrey Board Appealing,' *P*, 17:2, 10 March 1999.
143 Virginia Galt, 'Hard Lessons in Gay Tolerance 101,' *GM*, 13 Jan. 1998, A1.
144 Brian Pastoor, 'Students' Views on Maintaining the "Look,"' *TS*, 25 Aug.
     1997, A13.
145 Stacey Stein, 'Reading, Writing, Respect for Gays,' *TS*, 18 Nov. 1997, B6.
146 Clarissa Lagartera, 9 Aug. 1998.
147 Ibid.
148 Madiha Didi Khayatt, 'Lesbian Teachers: Coping at School,' in *Lesbians in
     Canada*, ed. Sharon Dale Stone (Toronto: Between the Lines, 1990), 81–93.
     Khayatt, *Lesbian Teachers*, 173–226.
149 Duncan Hood, 'Teacher's "Sacred" Ceremony Scorned,' *X*, 23 Oct. 1997.
     Rosie DiManno, 'Gay Teacher's "Wedding" Costs Him Job,' *TS*, 6 Oct.
     1997.
150 Ingrid Peritz, 'J'accuse: A Teacher's Worst Nightmare,' *GM*, 29 Jan. 2000,
     A18.
151 Radicalesbians Health Collective, 'Lesbian and the Health Care System,
     in *Out of the Closets: Voices of Gay Liberation*, ed. Karla Jay and Allen Young
     (New York, Douglas Book Corp., 1972), 140.
152 Chicago Gay Liberation Front, 'A Leaflet for the American Medical
     Association,' in *Out of the Closets: Voices of Gay Liberation*, 145.

153 CLGRO, *Systems Failure*, xv.

154 Ibid., 22

155 Ibid., p, 20.

156 Gens Hellquist, 16 June 1997.

157 Prairie Research Associates, 'The Gay and Lesbian Youth Services Network Survey of Lesbian and Gay Youths and Professionals Who Work with Youth' (Winnipeg, 1989). Christopher Bagley and Pierre Tremblay, 'Suicidality Problems of Gay and Bisexual Males: Evidence from a Random Community Survey of 750 Men Aged 18 to 27,' Faculty of Social Work, University of Calgary, 16 Aug. 1996.

158 Gay and Lesbian Health Services, 'A Healthy Community with Dignity: A Project Proposal Submitted to Health Promotions Directorate, Health Services and Promotions Branch' (Saskatoon, 1991).

159 Gay and Lesbian Health Services, 'A Strategy towards Population Health and Wellness' (Saskatoon, July 1996), 1.

160 CLGRO, *Systems Failure*.

161 Don Elder, 'Homophobia: Danger to Health,' *A*, Oct. 1997.

162 'Care Access,' *A*, March 1998.

163 'Pride in the Maritimes,' *X*, 21 July 1995, 11.

164 Don Campbell, 'Mayor versus Gays,' *P*, 7:1, 18 Jan. 1989, 12. 'New Mayor Says No!' *P*, 10:8, 9 Dec. 1992. 'No Pink Triangle Day,' *P*, 28 Feb. 1990.

165 Gens Hellquist. 'We Got Suckered,' *P*, 7:5, 12 July 89.

166 Untitled, *P*, 8:6, 29 Aug. 1990. 'Proclamation Storm,' *P*, 9:7, 6 Nov. 1991. 'Gay Pride Sanctioned,' *GM*, 17 June 1999.

167 'Gay Pride Ruling Called Homophobic,' *TS*, 29 July 1990, A15.

168 'Proclamation Storm.'

169 Laurie Monsebraaten, 'Toronto Councillors Give Initial Approval for Gay Pride Day,' *TS*, 2 June 1989, A4. Paul Taylor, 'Pride Day for Gays Voted Down,' *GM*, 16 June 1989, A1.

170 Ken Peters, 'Morrow Wants Probe into Gay Pride Decision,' *Spectator*, 7 March 1995, A1. Jim Poling, 'Gay Day Ruling Reverberates,' *Spectator*, 11 March 1995. 'Hamilton Pickets,' *X*, 21 July 1995, 18.

171 Janet Money, 'London Mayor Explains,' *X*, 28 Aug. 1997, 22.

172 Mark Bellis, 'City Fined of Gay Pride Day,' *TS*, 10 Oct. 1997.

173 'Fredericton Mayor Refuses to Recognize Gays,' *TS*, 10 July 1998, A6.

174 Marina Jimenez and Charlie Gillis, 'Taking "Pride" Out of Gay Pride Day,' *NP*, 21 Dec. 1998, A3. 'Mayor Claims He Has Right to Stay Silent on Gay Issue,' *TS*, 11 July 1998, A13.

175 Jemenez and Gillis, 'Taking "Pride" Out of Gay Pride Day.'

176 Rod Mickleburgh, 'Mayor Discriminated against Gays, Tribunal Rules,' *GM*, 24 March 2000, A2.
177 Jimenez and Gillis, 'Taking the "Pride" Out of Gay Pride Day.'
178 Martha Shelley, 'Gay Is Good,' in *Out of the Closets*, 31.

Conclusion: Lesbian and Gay Liberation in the Twenty-First Century

1 David Gelman with Donna Foote, Todd Barrett and Mary Talbot, 'Born or Bred?' *Newsweek*, 24 Feb. 1992, 46–53. Chandler Burr, 'Homosexuality and Biology,' *Atlantic Monthly*, March 1993, 47–65. 'Progress Reported in Search for Gay Gene,' *GM*, 16 July 1993. Wallace Immen, 'Study Confirms Existence of Gay Gene in Men,' *GM*, 31 Oct. 1995. Jane Gadd, 'New Study Fails to Find So-called "Gay Gene,"' *GM*, 2 June 1998. Maggie Fox, 'Canadian Researchers Dispute Landmark Study on "Gay Gene,"' *NP*, 23 April 1999.
2 Timothy Appleby, 'In the Tolerant 1990s, Attacks on Gays Persist,' *GM*, 17 Oct. 1998. Lila Sarwick, 'Gay-Bashing Incidents on Rise in Toronto.' *GM*, 15 Oct. 1998. Jennifer Lewington, 'Hate Crimes Rise in Year's First Half,' *GM*, 12 Aug. 1999.
3 Sheila Morrison, 'The Fall and Rise of Betty Baxter,' *X*, *XS*, Feb. 1991. Allan Maki, 'Women's Hockey Is Not Ready for the World,' *GM*, 10 Feb. 1998. Kirk Bohls, Mark Wangrin with files from James Christie, 'Athletes Revel in Being One of the Guys, Not One of the Gays,' *GM*, 4 Aug. 1993.
4 Neil Herland, 'Behind the Ballot Box,' *X*, 17 Nov. 1995. Philip Hannan, 'REAL Women Attack Homo,' *X*, 7 July 1995. 'Winnipeg Elects Openly Gay Mayor,' *TS*, 29 Oct. 1998. Glen Murray, 11 July 1998.
5 Edward Greenspon, 'Reform Seeks Curbs on Judicial Activism,' *GM*, 9 June 1998. Campbell Clark, 'Supreme Court Must be Reined in, McGill Professor Says,' *NP*, 24 Nov. 1999
6 Brenda, Cossman, 'Little Sister's Still Needs a Babysitter,' *X*, 28 Dec. 2000. Brenda Cossman, 'A Weak Squeak of Courage,' *X*, 8 Feb. 2001.

Illustration Credits

Index

May 2/08